Praised Be Our Lords

Praised Be Our Lords

A political education
RÉGIS DEBRAY

Translated
by
John Howe

VERSO
London • New York

This book has been published with the aid of
the French Ministry of Culture – Centre national du livre

This edition published by Verso 2007
© Verso 2007
Translation © John Howe 2006
First published as *Loués soient nos seigneurs. Une education politique*
© Editions Gallimard 1996

1 3 5 7 9 10 8 6 4 2

Verso
UK: 6 Meard Street, London W1F 0EG
USA: 180 Varick Street, New York, NY 10014–4606
www.versobooks.com

Verso is the imprint of New Left Books

ISBN-13: 978–1–84467–139–7 (hbk)
ISBN-13: 978–1–84467–140–3 (pbk)

British Library Cataloguing in Publication Data
A catalogue record for this book is available from the British Library

Library of Congress Cataloging-in-Publication Data
A catalog record for this book is available from the Library of Congress

Typeset in Baskerville by Hewer Text UK Ltd, Edinburgh
Printed and bound in the UK by CPI Bath

Contents

Part One:
Los Comandantes

1

The Backdrop

*The drive for ascendancy, always and everywhere – Glory – The model B generation –
Hegemony, 1960 version –* El Quinto Regimiento *– Too much of a world revolution –
Myths of crystal, Utopias of smoke*

I loathe public life and politicians. This aversion has not saved me from
prolonged brushes with the species, but it has exempted me from run-of-the-
mill mandates, the ones accepted by the look-at-me types who jostle for places
on the platform. Even today I have barely got the better of this odious and
puerile superiority complex ('I'm worth *so* much more than all these demagogues, manipulators, killers, cynics, twisters, carpetbaggers, sleaze merchants,
etc., etc.'). What I most dreaded in the clamour of the forum was those workless
ephemera, those febrile short-lived entities, those ten weak-witted characters
whose faces, whose nervous tics, the timbre of whose voices, amplified daily by
radio and television (whose sole vocation this seems to be), obsess us for 30 years
until the tide of time erases them like faces drawn in the sand. I wonder now
whether I might not have mistaken my own deficiency for repugnance, sublimated physical weakness into strength of soul. Of the politician, who is not like
other higher primates, I possessed only the brain: a pretty small asset. I lacked
the essential: the digestive and dental apparatus (toasts, banquets, reopening
parties, lunches at the Lipp), the organs of phonation (meetings, in-depth
interviews, televised debates), the hormonal balance (calumnies, satirical broad-
casts, caricatures), the ability to disconnect with mechanized agility (cocktail
parties, barnstorming, walkabouts), without even mentioning the memory for
names, the footwork, the round-the-clock vigilance; all the innate qualities that a
year-round open season (required by representative government) imposes on the
carnivorous newcomer (soon to become prey himself). To this feeble native
equipment, add the remains of a childhood stammer, an incurable inconsistency
of outlook, a preference for diving over swimming, a taste for the frivolous and
gratuitous, a tendency to neurasthenia and the need for a lot of kip, and there
you have it: the classic portrait of a peaceable servant of the Muses, protected by
a small nature from the fury of that destructive democratic Mars (campaigns,
troops, confrontations, duels). Under universal suffrage, going into battle and
surviving means lending a sympathetic ear to old ladies, turning up at your

weekly committee meeting, going from door to door and floor to floor (there are votes at the top of the stairs), caring about dogshit, school canteens, retirement pensions, rubbish collection . . . and being bawled at in the street by loonies as a reward. In a word, it means clinging to the terrain, to the simple and brutish life of a constituency of fellow-citizens made of flesh and bone. To put it more clearly: loving people; and thus without hypocrisy loving yourself. I didn't have the strength: call me a misanthropist if you like. And since there is nothing worse than an ambition the body cannot support, from adolescence onward I sacrificed all possibility of a local position – President of the Republic, say, or of the United States of Europe – to aim for the universal empire . . . no, little slip there, what I mean is the empire of the Universal over people's minds. What would one of the Elect have made of an elective mandate? (One of the Elect: a pen-pusher awaited by his photo in the history manual on the cataclysms of 2095, contracted to a publisher still unborn, and who has not a minute to lose if he is to arrive on the page in time, slip his mugshot into its allotted place on the stated day).

Why then (you will ask), since I had little interest in anything but the lyre of Apollo, did I become a bandit? How did someone who, at 14, loved nothing so much as fine gilt-edged paper marked by the Greats, find himself a jailbird at 30 and a chamberlain at 40? The answer is that it is characteristic of passion to contradict vocation. By condition and volition, I seek truth: that is my mental tropism. My body itself wanted power. Over words? Too anodyne. Every sort of power: over beings, situations, ideas, and most of all over the powerful themselves. How could I resist the brute? Passion is worse than trickery, calculation, sales or career strategy. It is exquisite cruelty: play to a gambler, booze to an alcoholic. Fate can harbour certain blessings; mine has given me nothing but horrors. These I have cultivated. Pointless to resist: the *drive for ascendancy* rises from the bowels, a concupiscence as enslaving as any. Totally focused on her prey, Phaedra pales at the sight of Hippolytus and is helpless, but . . . Could I help it if, at 16, I blanched at the mere sight of Churchill's *Memoirs* in a bookshop window? If merely having seen, from a distance of a hundred metres, in the year of grace 1958, coming out of the Janson-de-Sailly lycée in the avenue Henri-Martin, the black DS19 carrying Charles de Gaulle (I didn't boast that I had seen his features, although I thought I glimpsed his heavy profile in the rear seat for a quarter of a second), with two motorcycle outriders and another car following, but no sirens, kept me awake for the whole of the next night? Excuse the vulgarity, but I was no longer aware of myself; or rather, I felt a miraculous elevation, an Ascension to the floor above. This meeting left its mark on my brow like a burn from a star, since it could not have been a coincidence. I was 17. This important incident went to my head.

You can hear the sniggers from here: 'bit full of himself', 'another blown mind', 'power, of course . . .'. What one says about oneself, I admit, is always fantasy, and nothing is more propitious to the ancient trail of vanity than the tears of the retired. In public affairs, the late lamented François-René noted long ago that 'everyone who has been a historic figure for more than twenty-four hours thinks he owes the world an account of his influence over the universe'. Well, I am going to prove the Vicomte wrong. A pox on melancholic vapourings and self-flagellatory fripperies. In matters of personal importance, literary affectation ought to lower its flag. Here I will opt for candour as carrying less risk, for – God knows – risk there certainly is. He knows about the double bind in which our repentant highnesses are trapped: self-regarding and lightweight if they blab, amnesiac and lightweight if they keep it buttoned. Common courtesy demands an account rendered at the end of the exercise; the culture of flux is an invitation to let things slide. Rush gaily ahead and they jeer at your recantations; go back over your bloodstains and you are wallowing in mea-culpa instead of politely arranging to be forgotten. And you will be melted down in the rancid butter of the locality: clammy graces, lordling's affectations. I have worshipped a bit at that altar in my time. But I am older now, and as weary as you are of brio and pirouettes.

This is bad for me but good for you. Examination of conscience is a murky game in which a scrupulous person loses every hand. I would rather have been alone in the dock. From behind my small story, alas – don't be misled, don't let my modesty fool you – the Other, with his big Axe, is going to let the tips of his ears show: the downfall of *sapiens sapiens* jostled by relations of force since the Stone Age. And I can hear in advance the snarling of my fellows, whom I am going to oblige once again, and therefore offend, by parading this mirror down the trail of my mistakes; for some may reluctantly recognize mistakes of their own. Antipathy before or antipathy after, there's no third way. Enemies, you know the way in advance because I didn't compete under your colours. Friends, who will do your best to like me, you will drop me because I'm blowing the gaff. Ours, theirs, yours . . . 'O unhappy creature who believe that I am not you'.

What is it that makes us get up one fine morning and renounce everything that has driven us until that moment? Quite a few million of us have slowed down, and would really like to 'understand what has happened to us'. They too, like your humble servant, will have to stretch the limits of decency to cope with the uneasy feeling that the 50-year-old has about his or her salad days: 'What sorcery induced me to live, suffer and rejoice for ideas (anxieties or hopes) that were not my own? How can my political consciousness have robbed me of my soul, pfft, gone just like that, never to return?' And my contemporaries, rendered lifeless by a big word – dead to their children and lovers, dead to acacias and the scent of lemon blossom, dead to the rustle of muslin and silk, dead even to themselves – would surely have gained by adopting a postmodern Boris Vian's profession of faith: 'All that is not colour, scent or melody is just childishness.' How comforting it would be to think that the evil hunchbacked fairy Carabosse, the thief of sensations who kills the poet and child in us, was crouched forgotten behind a hanging or an easel in the distant past! But we would just be lying to

ourselves again, like people who blacken 'the demonic face of power' and make
scapegoats of the ministers of the moment. Sitting in the front row, making an
impression, forming opinion, setting the tone, pulling the strings, being an
insider . . . are these privileges restricted to politicians? If only it were just a
matter of titles, cockades and baubles! Alas, the *libido dominandi* (as St Augustine
called it) is to be found in ourselves, at the stinking centre of a labyrinth far less
explored than the much newer Freudian one (cooing with family spirit and
somewhat schematic feeling), of which our littérateurs make so much. The little
sister only causes homicide; the big one, genocide. Including crimes of passion
and suicides, love causes at most a few hundred deaths a year; counting civil and
international wars, political passion kills hundreds of thousands in an average
year, and tens of millions during flare-ups. But although the 'dangerousness'
ratio is of the order of one to a thousand, the ratio in libraries is a thousand to
one. We know a thousand times more about the wellsprings of 'exclusive sexual
love' than about the sources of exclusive devotion to a cause or leader. And what
are we to say about the survivors? As I write these words there are on earth some
millions of ageing Swanns, whose Odettes in the East bore names like Stalin,
Mao or Tito, in the South Fidel Castro, Mobutu or Sankara and in the West
Mitterrand, Mrs Thatcher or Nixon. But no Proust deigns to pay them any
attention, as if the public domain were unworthy of the micro-surgeons of
sorrow. Establishments take too lofty a view of it, the yellow rags a view that is
too base. Forgive me, but – on the threshold of this continent darker than
sexuality – I cannot help flinching. Fearing the worst.

Responsible, but not guilty: don't expect whining or contrition from me. I was
neither taken in nor taken over. And my buddies paid the price while I lay low
accumulating rank. You won't see me beating my breast and saying mea culpa
over my successive lords, bewailing my lot as one *seduto e abbandonato*. I was big
enough to come to grief by myself. The profession of misleader is accessible to
anyone; all the faults were my own. I was neither taken over nor seduced; what
happened was that one part of me misled the other, the will to power prevailed
over the thirst for knowledge. Why not guilty, then? Because *Homo politicus* – not
our highest manifestation – is the biped without titles or decorations, you and
me, not that froth of eccentrics who 'do politics'. 'We are all German Jews',
aren't we? Yes; and we are all Gauleiters, caudillos and Medicis too. The face of
these much-decried figureheads is our own photofit in electoral-poster format,
freed from the grimaces and impostures that 'raw grandeur' imposes on us.
However sternly we feel we ought to judge the heads of clans, states or sects, we
do not really believe that these cannibals would be so successful if they did not
first make their victims salivate. Official leaderships are only the visible part of
the iceberg. Below the surface are their five billion accomplices – us – being
shoved about by luckier alter egos. But we would rather concentrate the blame
on governments and ideologies. When belief is at a low ebb, the 'past of an
illusion' – either communist or fascist – marvellously fulfils the role of screen-

memory. Criticism of our most recent *isms* absolves us from having to address the long future that still awaits illusion, the fruit of indestructible, recidivist hope. New enthusiasms every bit as crazed as the old ones will soon appear.

Being shut out of the humanities I have no access to the intricacies of the poetic ministry, but I do not imagine that at the age of 15, a time when I was murmuring to myself that I would 'be Chateaubriand or nothing', a young Victor Hugo would have wanted to be an errand-boy in a stationer's shop. When a budding musketeer of the same age has been telling himself every morning in the mirror that he will be 'a Companion of the Liberation or nothing', he is not going to be a deputy or senator. Even if it figures in the official almanac, the Order to which I retrospectively aspired is not very representative. A Russian aviator, a dilettante dauber, an opium-eating dandy were more likely to get into it than the president or first deputy. It had not escaped me that the real 'pros' of History are usually political amateurs. So to be sure of catching the capital H, I would be an amateur who didn't mess around, whose majestic detachment would take me to the winning post ahead of the young wolves trained in legal gerrymandering at the ENA. Outsider in charge of catastrophes is a full-time job. It suited my infirmities well enough for me to see it as a vocation, so I would follow Lenin's recommendation and become a 'professional revolutionary' in the field (to a bourgeois politician, the ultimate in amateurishness). On returning home ten years later I changed registers, but without losing my urge to *be alternative*. My ideal was to shift the globe without even glancing at the local elections. You could just as easily make a movie without crew or production facilities. I dreamed of a History without politics, something like cinema without a film industry. Short cuts like civil wars, cataclysms, invasions, are rare in modern life. While waiting for the right moment – Hannibal coming down the Alps, Alaric hurrying towards Rome or Hitler towards Paris – the candidate sidles along between stage and wings. I have been switching back and forth between goody-goody and prima donna since starting secondary school: top of the class, and chucking paper pellets from the back row. The smart-aleck teacher's pet is something else: see my plumage? Look at my hairy palms! Uncatchable. I thought to gain advantage by switching roles in this way. Wrongly, because one plus one is in between, neither one thing nor the other. Too realistic for an adventurer, too imaginative for an apparatchik, and there you are without a career, condemned to ardent waiting. Let no one quibble that I have never played a 'political role of the first rank' (or the second, or the eleventh for that matter). Ostensibly bound by the vow of obedience, governmental aides have their own grey forms of eminence and and an infinitely jollier type of celebrity.

The collapse of the Ottoman Empire rendered Lawrence of Arabia technically unemployed. Quite a few of us were similarly done down by the fall of the Third Reich. Even with large numbers of German tourists back in Paris, it took me some time to realize that the Order had shut down in 1946. So was it going to be 'nothing'? 'Come back to earth, young man, you're not T.E. Lawrence, or Romain Gary, or Jorge Semprun; nor are you going to be seen as a Jean-Pierre Vernant, or a François Jacob. You shouldn't confuse one period or character with another.' Easier said than done. Louis XIV's contemporaries had Henri II furniture. Who can ever claim to be contemporary with his own time? Without my rear-view mirror I might easily have become a faceless official. The little realists eternally twittering 'So look to the future!' are probably trying to discourage us in advance. To do is to redo or indeed to undo oneself. Anachronism motivates; those who walk in step are ciphers. The fact is that our predecessors in renunciation, emperors and civilians both, had witnessed stirring cruelties, while the ones we have seen since 1945 – anyway in Western Europe, until very recently – have been relatively colourless. Our thirty glorious years of growth left glory utterly routed.

Glory is less vulgar than celebrity; it is delayed-action renown, like a chrysanthemum bud planted by a prescient gardener at the foot of a freshly dug grave. In the playground of my lycée I imagined it – glory – as a prison yard at six in the morning, with an execution stake and a firing-squad commander treating me with honour before giving the order: 'Fire!' Then I would see the twelve rifles blossom all at once like the month of May, a posthumous triumphal crown. I am fairly sure that this pious image, this braggart's fantasy, was born of the conflation of two photographs: one, anonymous, from 1944 in France, the image of a maquisard, bareheaded, hands bound, smiling, facing a row of soldiers with their rifles in the aim; the other, signed Casasola, from 1917 in Mexico, showing the execution of Fortino Samano against an adobe wall with dark joins. A broad-brimmed felt hat down over one eye, cigar between his teeth, fists thrust into pockets, gallant and relaxed, one foot on the edge of the hole, the anarchist is directing a mocking rictus at his uniformed executioners, who are out of frame.

Fakery doesn't matter much provided the brand image is captured. Informed later scrutiny suggested that the smiling martyr was probably a young militia-man being executed for war crimes, as the Germans and Militia made captured maquisards kneel before shooting them; and it seems that Agustín Víctor Casasola, founder of the first photo agency in Mexico, was professional enough to get the famous Samano to pose *before* his execution. The glory of which I dreamed as a good pupil (a tinted rendering of Julien Sorel climbing cheerfully onto the scaffold . . . 'walking in the open air seemed to him a delicious sensation') actually fell to the collaborator Brasillach, shot by firing squad at Montrouge fort on 6 February 1945, and not to the resistance leader Jean Prévost with whom I would have identified much more willingly, summarily and anonymously shot at the side of a road on 1 August 1944. The wimpish Latinist was privileged to face death honourably; the intrepid hero was swatted with a random burst. *Todo pasa, pero al revés.* The activist's pose that the adolescent admires in the mirror is dispersed by action itself as by a burst of laughter. When it happened to me in reality – six rifles levelled at ten paces, wrists handcuffed – in a Bolivian barracks courtyard one April dawn in 1967, two days after my arrest, I did not recall my vainglorious image for a single second. There was no stake and no cigar; I was hirsute and staggering, with gluey eyelids and an intense desire to piss. I had been awakened by someone kicking my mattress, then shoved towards a patch of waste land by an NCO prodding me in the back with a firearm, followed by a handful of young Indian recruits looking as scared as I did (no one really knows how to behave on these occasions). I was clinging to sleep, seeking with eyes closed (although on my feet) to prolong a dream interrupted in the middle: a return to adolescence, a summer picnic beside a mountain torrent in the Pyrenees, with pretty women and friends. The previous night my interrogators had told me that I was to be put up against a wall, so I was apprehensive about something without really wanting to let myself know why. The sergeant lined his men up and they took aim at me for a good half-minute, but there was no *fuego!* and the NCO eventually walked away. On the way back to my cell, my mind still foggy, I tried to recall the details of the confused, too-rapid scene, in which my own part had been that of an extra caught short with his pants down. At the time, I had experienced that simulated execution as a gratuitous event, nothing to do with me, dream-like but neither nightmarish nor ecstatic. Life isn't 'tidied up', so why should death be?

Twenty years later, I was saved: my *folie des grandeurs* seemed to have turned out all right. Cinema, literature, banking, industry . . . Great Writer, Great Manager, Great Awareness, Great State Official, Grand Panjandrum of Communication, all of them far more sensible war aims than Great Helmsman of the Toiling Masses. One disadvantage of political (as opposed to literary) mythomania is that it is so dependent on the ambient weather. Just as works of art get bigger when the era shrinks, the cut of events themselves must conform to its reduced scale. Could I have made a bad choice? The period was boy-sized compared to others: la Pasionaria in besieged Madrid, the Moscow trials, the 18 June call to arms, Churchill in the Commons, Stalingrad, Buchenwald, Warsaw, Hiroshima. I was out of luck, obliged to travel the Sacred Way under a handicap that (despite some people's hopes) the war in Algeria and May '68 did not really remove: civil peace. Our elders, favoured by cataclysms, had the advantage. I belong to a grade B generation, condemned by a blank space in History to a pastiche of the one-off destinies that came before us, bagging all the first choices and leaving us the copies: sub-Blum, sub-de Gaulle, sub-Malraux, sub-Berna-nos, sub-Camus, sub-everyone. The generation that was in its twenties in 1930 or 1940 set the keys and themes for us; the one that followed, my own, plonks chords maladroitly down onto the score left by our elders. We are the clumsy managers of a portfolio of inaccessible classics that we have banalized and mythologized until – if I may compare the history-buff with the movie-buff – what we know about the great tragedies of the century is derived not from the original monochrome version or even the colour remake, but the summary on the poster for a once-a-week show in a small-town community hall. One politician after being questioned on a legal matter claims to have been 'followed like a Jew under the Occupation'; another spends three months in temporary detention and feels entitled to comment on 'the effectiveness of Nazi torture, imprisoning people in solitary confinement'. By 1968 the CRS had become the SS, a pile of three dustbins passed for a barricade and a farm in the Ardèche could be referred to as a 'red base' or a 'new Yunnan'. Every month the magazines deplore another 'Holocaust', our intellectuals go to cross the Ebro at Sarajevo over the weekend, and we complain about an education 'Munich' while awaiting 'Nuremberg trials' over contaminated blood. There is 'apartheid' in the suburbs and publicists denounce each other as 'collaborators' and 'apparatchiks', while the bolder ones 'join the resistance' by cancelling a recital in a district with a far-right council. Sculptors of ashes, nibblers of crumbs . . . The heroic and brutal dream had slipped away from under our noses, and it was thought almost meritorious to concoct one's own, out of peelings. Is it inherent in a 'child of the century' – any child, any century – to despise the ersatz in this way, when the sun of Austerlitz has already set and Little Napoleons are swarming everywhere? Perhaps it falls to every generation to conjure up this obscene impression of parody. Our own will certainly have done its best. Our young memorialists spice up normality with unofficial material, scandalous revelations, the file under the arm; cunning fellows who play the grand vizier to hawk their trivia. I prefer to be straightforward: I am not a leading contemporary or a great observer, and what I mean to set down here is the verbatim account of an endgame. When I arrived in my century the folding chairs were being packed up, the more interesting guests had nearly all gone, and the small fry were wolfing the tired remains of the canapés. So the things that I have done, heard and seen will occupy me less than the hare-brained ideas that induced me to go abroad and, on my return, to stand about watching a thousand notables biting each other in the leg over a hundred or so decent jobs. The fairy stories I told myself privately to spur myself on may well seem familiar to my colleagues in failure. They too are probably wondering: 'What was I going to do in that galley?' I hummed: 'Take me away in a caravel . . .', mistaking the one for the other, without looking twice to make sure (for in these matters, however redundant and oft-repeated, every time is the first time). This is the story of my caravels. If we hadn't had those little sails marked with the Latin cross and filled with wind, would we have boarded any galleys?

Perhaps my generation never saw the Buchenwald chimney belching smoke, or stormed the Hôtel de Ville at the age of 24. We were last on stage, but there's no need to feel sorry for us: we were just in time for the final curtain. Our swots had the good luck to see their first action on the last salient of Byzantine Caesaro-Papism, whose communist offshoot for a while almost managed to drag the industrial West back to the blessed and pastoral times of Joshua, Samuel and David. In biblical tradition, God's ministers on earth are of two sorts: princes and clerics. In old-time Judaea-Samaria the two had been combined, until Latin Christianity separated their domains, the tiara and the diadem. With the hammer and sickle, the exemplary couple reigned once more over our bibliophile heights. He who *knew most* about the things that had lain hidden since the beginning of the world was infallibly the one who wielded *most power* over his brethren (making them drool, making them dream: it's all one). Lenin, Stalin, Mao, Enver Hoxha and various lesser bloodletters have lent their faces to this mystic and scientific monarchy. All of them, in their salad days, started by lining up syllogisms on paper and criticizing in writing those of their neighbours: Mao the librarian, Lenin the publicist, Hoxha the teacher. Every one a man of letters, a product of the Book. The proletariat rewarded their prescience, Kremlin and Forbidden City alike falling into their laps like ripe fruit. In the West, thousands of acolytes took it as read: by starting on Latin and Greek at 10, moving on to historical materialism at 20 and dialectic at 25, a studious weakling could prepare himself for the job of king, with a reasonable chance of ending up as a Titan defending the walls. As the bastard offspring of Bandung and Karl Marx, Third-Worldist logorrhoea and Rhenish epigram, the atheist spokesman of a History still to be made – although spitting on army and Church both – I can say that by 1960 the mastery of souls and suburbs was already more than just a promise to me. I was a trainee official, living in and still studying: from the outside, a grey-faced usher in a grey gown. But the leader within was greedily eyeing the planet's red belt from between two quarto tomes. I didn't mind sharing: I would have colleagues in the Directorate, a mobile Executive Bureau, polyglot and rigorous. Student internationalists in the time of Brigitte Bardot, the Beatles and the first portable TV sets reversed the custom of seventeenth-century cardinals, by wearing their purple *under* their homespun robes (suedette or corduroy jacket). I was one of the more impatient members of this College of Cardinals in gestation, being far more interested in the outcome than in the practice, or the critical reading of Holy Scripture. None of us (let it be said in passing) dreamed of abusing, exploiting or manipulating anyone: the aim was to inspire, orient and guide 'the masses' by remote control, not to lead them directly in the manner of vulgar *Duces*. Which shows that these angry young sages, future commissars of the world's peoples, already saw themselves as people of government, seeking consent, shrinking from violence and despising dictators, like all responsible souls.

A proper understanding of this class photo calls for a little geohistory. Thirty years is just a sigh, I know; but the abyss between communism and our children is so wide that when asked about that period now I feel rather like a scribe in a Merovingian chancellery having to answer the amused queries of a PhD student from MIT: 'You lived in Chilpéric's reign, didn't you? What was it like under the last of the do-nothing kings?' Having no wish to retrace the complex genealogy of Clovis's descendants I would reply simply: 'The Frankish era, young man, was philosophic and fraternal.' Seen from Paris around 1960, the world of the East resembled a graduate school in which ten full professors, one for each 'socialist country', tried to outdo one another in rigour to spur on their student populations. Who would be first to pass the competitive examination for entry to communism the ultimate goal with no possible 'after' from the lower stage of state socialism: China? USSR? Albania? Cuba? Had not a billion new men been bred by those two systematic minds, Marx and Lenin? The grateful hierarchs raised giant statues to these recently deceased colleagues; red banners in the streets exalted the theory in letters of gold: 'Glory to Marxism-Leninism'. The life of the populations – unimportant trivia apart – boiled down to rivalry between schools, a hand-to-hand struggle between jealous *isms:* revisionism versus Maoism, Stalinism versus a nascent Eurocommunism, rational materialism versus bourgeois humanism. The chore of administration was left to subordinate utilitarian technologies: statistics, IT, physics and so on; today it is the other way round. We were emerging from a post-war period in which philosophy ruled the roost (anyway in the overheated greenhouses where humanities students were grown). Its predecessor in this role had been literature; its successor was to be the social sciences. The philosophy teacher's role went beyond that of 'awareness tutor' once fulfilled by the enlightened writer, and had acquired *in partibus* something of the Commander. This pre-eminence made the whole planet dependent on us distillers of quintessences; its future was being precipitated in our retorts. International current events, for those who knew how to read them, boiled down to a more or less patchy commentary on the articles in *La Pensée*, the theoretical organ of the PCF. The primacy of this central discipline was written into the constitutions of the proletarian regimes and their five-year plans. First among the compulsory subjects, philosophy was taught from primary school onwards, conditioning access to university and senior jobs; in Moscow, as in Tirana or Hanoi, institutes of Marxism-Leninism attached to the Central Committee were guarded much more closely than the French armed forces Operations Centre in the basement of the Ministry of Defence in boulevard Saint-Germain; the elite of the people was grouped in the Party, the vanguard of the proletariat, but the elite of the elite were explorers of the arcana of the Subject, matters opaque to the vulgar; and the thirty-seven volumes of Lenin's complete works, uniformly bound in almond green, lined the shelves of Mao Tse-Tung's office-library and our own garret bedrooms, like an arch of paper stretching from the Forbidden City to the Sorbonne, attesting to the unity of our destinies. Doubtless there was a good deal to be said on the rather domestic role of simple provider of services that had fallen to philosophy as the servant of the Party. Over there, the history of the leaderships and the history of ideas tended to get confused. So Theory needed to be replaced on its pedestal, its abandonment having produced the directionless opportunism in which state and party bureaucracies were foundering. An urgent task, but an internal matter; a family quarrel between initiates. Every society has its Jesuits. Thus in our territories the doctors of the proletariat would succeed the doctors of the bourgeois Republic (at one time the disciples of Comte, then those of Alain), evicting in the East the crocodiles of 'DiaMat'. The heart of the future was beating in our little persons which, for the time being, were camped virtuously (if provisionally) in a society of yokels not much enamoured of people of intellect, not even the ones on its side. If only our property developers had stretched a banner across the place de la Concorde saying 'Glory to immortal liberalism!' . . . If only our aediles had placed the slogan 'Glory to Tocqueville and Raymond Aron!' over the Arc de Triomphe, we could have argued. But meeting-ground and subject matter were both lacking. The only place where I have seen philosophy honoured properly in marble is northern Greece where, in the main square of Salonika and every village in Greek Macedonia, the standard municipal totem (in place of our war memorial) is the white bust of Aristotle, the country's favourite son.

At this point in universal history there existed a French peculiarity, bizarre by normal Western standards: the attribution of civic responsibilities to the literate, or to put it another way the politicization of the literary domain. 'The Republic of Professors', at the beginning of the century mocked or feared, along with what it implied, by people of classical and generalist background like Jaurès or the Council President Herriot, had for fifty years past been raising most of its dust in a Paris university establishment, the École normale supérieur, grouping under a residential system four or five classes of scientific and literary students. Anticipating the country at large, this microcosm after 1945 fell under the influence of the far left, an effect of the ascendancy of a handful of trailblazers. 'Scientific socialism' drew to its altars one scientific student for every five literary ones (an understandable imbalance). When I arrived there in 1960, the New Man's high priest was the former 'prince tala' (foremost among those-who-go-to-mass) at the Lyon khâgne,[1] Louis Althusser. Had he really been converted? 'I've taken to Marxism', he was to say later, 'because of its Catholicism: I have found the same sense of the Universal in communism. But as a Catholic I never knew what I was doing in Church, whereas the Party needs me for the concrete task of liberating people.' Cultivating anonymity and avoiding journalists, that recluse, soon to become a media celebrity, allowed a few seminarians in need of a Father Prior to gather around him. Not out of proselytism but politeness: he was a gentle man, who protected himself as best he could against external tumults, shrinking from the violence that, in his writings, he accepted all the more willingly because his character recoiled from it. The tutorial group he ran met every week in the 'salle des Actes' (aptly named, for to us the words uttered there possessed the value of actions) or the 'salle Cavaillès' (named after the mathematical philosopher shot by the Germans). Among the events held there was the famous strategic seminar of 1964–65 entitled *Reading Capital*, meant to change the course of the entire world – both the capitalist half and the revisionist half – in short order. As ill-luck would have it the world discovered retrospectively, in the aftermath of May '68, that its fate had been decided at the top behind closed doors by a clique of hermeneuts. I will pass over concepts and questions of copyright to cut straight to the essence of the subject: the method of management. The keystone was the school of theoretical training. These were springing up everywhere on the fringes of universities and youth organizations. With duplicated monthly reports and brochures. Whoever had the correct position would accede eventually – after an indeterminate period, but as the result of an inevitable process – to the leadership. Why? Because his or her theoretical views would inevitably be recognized as corrective and directive by the driving forces of the class struggle, in keeping with the axiom stated by Lenin: 'Marxism is all-powerful because it is true.' From truth to power, from 'working group' to general secretariat, was a straight road. The decisive thing was the upstream 'intellectual hegemony'. To transform it into leadership pure and simple, and project oneself physically into headquarters, there were two possible approaches in tactical terms. One was to use the 'oppositionist' method and inflect the line from within. This would mean taking over the Union of Communist Students, getting into the Central Committee by entrism and working on the existing leaders individually. The other was to cause a split and turn the machine from outside, the 'mass agitation' method. This would lead others, fraternal enemies of the official activists, to agitate at factory gates, form grass-roots Vietnam committees, start new Marxist-Leninist unions. Althusser dreamed of combining the advantages of revisionism and Maoism, leaving his rue d'Ulm circle of disciples free to choose and never condemning them.

I mention this novitiate only to memorialize it. It ran off me like water off a duck's back. I applauded these school gymnastics from afar, convinced that I would never be part of the Sorbonne network: too foggy and uncertain for my taste. The procedure failed in my opinion for lack of sacredness, of *secrecy*. Open (as they were) to dunces, our low masses lacked inner recesses and hierarchy. Despite the esoteric arguments and the quality of the participants, they did not seem to me to be restricted enough to be truly decisive: I expect thick layers of silence to separate the top from the bottom (noisy individuals are never dangerous). Our dry analytic efforts also suffered from a lack of femininity and moisture, the only trustworthy leavenings of sedition; too little that was attractive: colour, melody, image. Then again, unlike my schoolfellows, I did not see History by procurement as being especially meaningful: by leaving too much empty space between the terrain and the books, they multiplied (I thought) the intermediate links, and the risks. To act via the mediation of theories meant subjecting the execution of our directives in black and white to the unreliable interpretation of basic texts by naive individuals. The 'top leadership' had done its best to train 'mass leaders' – a second-level echelon in touch with popular thought, adept at organizing the natives and making public speeches – but lacunae and misunderstandings were still going to arise between the written directive and the crowd movements. Out in the wilderness, our bulls and briefs were certainly going to fall into unskilled hands, perhaps even irreverent ones (local communist leaders, the secular arm at the time, often being far from pious). Power growing from the muzzle of a concept, I feared, would merely be yet another two-speed History: head and limbs, prayer-book and rifle. The people I really envied were ones who had mixed ink, blood and grime in real time. From his perch on a vast stack of in-folio, our Master manned the turnstile to the future by teaching rules of grammar, without paying much attention to what would actually be said. The Marxist Althusser was resolutely ignorant of economics; the scientist of working science; and the revolutionary of current revolutions (which he carefully avoided witnessing at first hand). There remained the essence: Louis. A brilliant, intuitive and affectionate goodness. The fag-end hanging from his lip, his half-asleep voice greeting you: 'Alors, mon grand?' as he opened the door, eyes unfocused, his weary corpulence and frayed tweed. His penetrating silences, his suicidal humour. Among intellectuals you will seldom come across a better-filled or more alert head. That neurotic, full of tact, who was later to slide into psychosis and strangle the wife he venerated, had real insight into the heart: but only other people's hearts, alas, which (as a good pedagogue) he held in greater honour than his own. My mentor killed himself and his wife in 1980. The era had already been hijacked by Solzhenitsyn, *nouveaux philosophes* and boat people. A lot of candidates for the philosophic leadership of the world found themselves viscerally incapable of accepting the loss of intellectual hegemony. In 1979 one of my Marxist friends jumped off a high building, another into the Seine. The less badly damaged retreated into depression, silence or the Talmud. Struggles for influence are a lot more serious than people think.

'Marxism drives you mad,' one vengeful unfrocked individual concluded at the time. It could also turn a young acolyte into a wanderer, a freelance and truant, searching for a father capable of taking things in hand. When the homeland is too celestial there may be nothing to eat. In Paris, the abstract family of orphans I had joined offered me no one to cherish except ghostly great-uncles (Thorez, Mao, Ho Chi Minh), when what I really needed was flesh-and-blood brothers. Leaving one's country in search of brotherhood – something more than a collection of 'dear comrades and friends' – is a timeless need, and not over-particular in choosing a banner.

> *Con el Quinto, Quinto, Quinto*
> *Con el Quinto Regimiento*
> *Tengo que marchar al frente*
> *Porque quiero entrar en fuego*
>
> *Con Lister y con Galán*
> *El Campesino y Modesto*
> *Con el comandante Carlos*
> *No hay miliciano con miedo*

Con los cuatro batallones
Que están Madrid defendiendo
Va toda la flor de España
La flor más roja del pueblo . . .

Without the shadow of a doubt, religious music has made more converts than theology. As God enters us through our wounds, devotion enters us through our shivers of delight, and *To Die in Madrid* is still capable of raising goosebumps. That summer of 1961 I felt it vividly, before the famous documentary, a few weeks after the Bay of Pigs in the streets of Havana, where a number of former Spanish republicans had gathered, including the famous Lister and El Campesino. I was galvanized just by seeing them on a platform, from afar. With Ania Francos, who knew all those family tunes, François Maspero, the son of a resistance member who died during deportation, Rogelio Crúz Ver, a Guatemalan soldier and former head of security under Arbenz whose room in the Hotel Rosita del Hornedo I was sharing (Che had brought him into the Ministry of Industry), and a few Spanish 'reds' from Moscow, we walked in a group along the Malecón embankment, a seafront smelling of fish and petrol, on the way to a *concentración de masas* in Revolution Square. In the late morning the hot breeze became sticky and the asphalt started melting; and to spur themselves on, between arcades and bougainvilleas, my comrades, in their shorts and shirt-sleeves, started singing songs from the 1930s. I have never forgotten that one; even more than *La Jeune Garde*, or *Bandiera Rossa* in Italian, it sounds like a rallying cry, an audible flag, echoing long after the soldiers who followed it have vanished, fists aloft, over the horizon. Joining in with this ambulant choir, I started to feel part of an endless chain of cheerful self-sacrificers whose penultimate link, before our own maquis, had been the International Brigades. A garland of tragic joys circling the world across the years. The identity of sounds and colours between 'anti-fascist' Latin Europe and 'anti-imperialist' Latin America, the physical presence of surviving brothers and sons, attested that the Spanish Civil War and and the French Resistance were still alive in Cuba. Even more than my chubby, perspiring Guatemalan room-mate's accounts of the overthrow in 1954 of Arbenz's progressive regime by the CIA and its mercenaries, those red hymns made me feel the lyrical bond of the time. Poor songs of worship without the splendour or abysses of Christian chorale, but doing the same thing for new converts: an amazed appropriation of the holy mysteries, starting with the one that, to my green young faith, seemed to rule all the others in that new Church of ever-busy silence: the invincibility of the vanquished. Retracing the thread of my attachments, I still bump into that vocal dilation of the body, that fusional *vox ecclesiae*, those liturgies that rise from the gut, from our mass graves, to submerge the old self-centredness like baptismal waters. I had arrived a quasi-atheist catechumen, something like – if I may risk an extravagance – the young Claudel, before he burst into tears on first hearing the notes of the *Magnificat* one December evening at Notre-Dame de Paris. Only after four more years of internal struggle could he accept his conversion fully, kneel at the altar and receive the body of Christ. And that, reverentially speaking, is about the length of time it took me as a man on the threshold, at the edge of the mystery, to domesticate the commotion by overlaying it with our Marxist-Leninist Meccano set. Four years later I returned to my tropical crypt, ready at last to take communion.

I came from an individualist country populated by sceptical or mocking solitaries. Those singsongs had an air of slightly Boy-Scout absurdity, a touch of Youth Workshop, even of Nuremberg-style high mass. As a child I had been a choirboy; puberty had spoiled my singing voice, and on losing sight of God at 15 I had broken with psalmodists and collective readings. Far-left militants had a lot of meetings, in cafés, at cell meetings, in people's lodgings; but at these meetings, discursive or didactic, the *Internationale* was only ever heard at the end, when people were leaving. Whether through prudery or modesty, that counterculture had neither death-knell nor psalms. Just a single rather juiceless entry ritual: 'showing your card'. In those rationalist pastures untouched by the hot-blooded orality of southern peoples, where it was held that theory must precede and underpin practice, the written word was supposed to act directly on the mind without passing through the body: analytically, distributively, without liturgical integration of the neophyte. Left politics in France at the time resembled a theatre of text, not of scenic possession (and still less of song). It was in Venezuela in 1963, in the Falcón guerrilla campaign, that I first became aware of the true scale of my hymnodic deficiency. One night round the camp fire the guerrillas started to sing local folk songs to each other; when it was my turn Douglas Bravo reduced me to blushing silence by requesting a few songs from France, preferably from the workers' movement. *Alouette, gentille alouette*, although un-connected with the workers' movement, saved my bacon; I followed up with a pretty pathetic *Chant des partisans* and ended with the first verse of the *Marseillaise*. I was ashamed not so much of not knowing the rest by heart as of having to get myself out of trouble by resorting to this eminently 'bourgeois' piece (albeit martial and with a fairly bloodthirsty text, excessively so indeed for today's sensibility). With his vast repertoire and stentorian voice, Bernard Kouchner – a leading light among us communist students – would have performed a hundred times better. I often congratulated him on his ear and memory, not realizing that it was really a matter of heart and legs; that men of action are creatures of rhythm and cadence. Christian liturgists sometimes talk of 'action' through song. Song brings people closer to God, and they sing as they pray: with their bodies.

Could an 'ideological commitment' be kick-started with a few vaguely luminous soundwaves? They were shapeless and insubstantial, but sufficient. Of course decency required those shimmering castles in Spain to be clothed in something suitably rigid and drab. Back in France, instead of songs or paintings, what I made was starchy three-point interventions in study groups, in the hope of putting those nervous shocks into handy portable form for the benefit of people who had not experienced them. Bowing to decorum like a good logician of thrills, I was exporting emotion into dialectic: a lie in itself. By transforming effervescence into speculation – something the Cuban leadership was doing on its own account at the time, via the Muscovite vulgate – I was distorting (*traduttore traditore*) a patriotic adventure, rooted solely in mobilization of the landless with the slogan 'Patria o Muerte', into an episode of international class struggle. The Parisian version was dressed in an excess of learned finery, when it would have been more sensible, I believe, to leave the famous 'Cuban party' to its raw naivety, its unexportable tropicalism. That would have been more helpful in keeping its feet on the ground, or getting them back there.

Under that red and black halo, *the* revolution, the militant cobbled together his own motley palimpsest of coloured prints, like one of those collages of photos over mantelpieces or on kitchen walls. My own internal patchwork, which I took care to keep hidden, included calotypes of barricades in Paris from June 1848 and Buddhist priests in flames in the streets of Saigon in 1961, alongside icons of Blanqui, Lenin, Rosa Luxemburg, Bolívar, Victor Serge, Zapata, Beloyannis, Jean Moulin and Ho Chi Minh. Ill-assorted emblems taped together with a standard idiom, playing the same federating role as Church Latin in the mosaic of mediaeval fiefdoms, or classical Arabic – the 'language of truth' – in Islam today. In effect, 'Marxism-Leninism' had the privilege of being spoken from Hanoi to Caracas by way of Rome and Brazzaville, unifying a multilingual diaspora of believers in the illusion of a shared destiny. I continued to practise this dead language long after I had lost the faith, at least partly to explain the need for losing it. Our lexicons are signs of belonging, and sometimes calls for help; a vocabulary is chosen not to express certain things better, but better to preserve certain companionships that still arouse nostalgia. We thus risk sacrificing understanding of our universe, which needs the best and latest tools of comprehension, to the hallucinated proximity of our friends, or people who have become strangers but whom we refuse to drop, despite disagreements. I spoke 'Marxian' for twenty-odd years, eventually using that language of the head to satisfy a heart unwilling to divorce *militants*, a spectral community that survives in today's France only through the obstinacy of a few balding, jargonizing Blimps of progressivism. The joke is that this obsolescent Sanskrit, in a context thoroughly emancipated from its 1900 academic sources, deprived the celebrant of any real resonance, particularly in the minds of the neophytes for whose benefit he was using that vocabulary in that way: the lexical excesses hastening the end of the endangered species he hoped to revive by embracing its patois.

Like a varnish or lacquer, but without the flavour of veal jelly, this singularly bloodless medium masked the heterogeneity of the recycled materials used for purposes of edification. Once uprooted from their native soil, fragments of

History borrowed from established national traditions become wobbly or misleading. And that is how we end by growing an artificial plant – *the* Revolution – from natural roots. Majestic but evanescent, the planetary-Platonic Idea (fruit of a strictly speculative inversion between a qualificative and a substantive) still floated above its locally disappointing epiphanies – Algeria, Vietnam, Cuba, Guinea and so on – like a worldwide effort of imagination. Christianity had been another such, and on a smaller scale any country still is, while God grants it life. For a nation is in essence a collection of sounds and images linking individuals who do not know each other personally. The world revolution bit off more than it could chew, at least in the long term (what counts in these matters). *Cubanidad*, Frenchness, *italianità* all have long lives ahead of them. But their *isms* have bad surface crazing: cheap varnish.

Although all philosopher by training, I have never been much interested in *Utopias*. If by this word we understand, like Georges Sorel, a more or less arbitrary intellectual construction from the brain of an individual, and by *myth* the expression of an instinctive, collective and affective force, then revolution has a lot more to do with the second than the first. Strangely, it seemed to emerge from a more dynamic and colourful but less definable background than communism, and it seemed almost more attractive than communism's promise of a better society; as if there were no need to believe in a classless society to go looking for the biggest and finest of brawls. I was led to this retributive disorder more consistently by masters of image than masters of thought, whose only contribution was help in moulding the grain of the projections into concepts. Cinema, photography and novels forged the certainties that I justified to measure by reading the theoreticians, and my combative years owe more to Joris Ivens and Chris Marker, those documentarists of lyrical illusion, than to Bachelard, Canguilhem or Althusser himself, as if the first were continuously repairing the epic continuity that the 'epistemological break' taught by these philosophers was tearing apart. To tell the truth, fiction really carried more weight than documentaries; and – discreetly, without really admitting it – I identified much more strongly with Gary Cooper in *For Whom the Bell Tolls* and Gian Maria Volonte in *Il terrorista* than with those edifying figurines Lenin, Mao, Rosa Luxemburg and Maurice Thorez. The vision of Eisenstein and Dovchenko seemed to me pompous and monumental. Those old-time giants may have been making the fabulous early beginnings scintillate on screen, but they did not really succeed in conveying their true flavour to me. Secret or hopeless wars, heroes in disguise behind enemy lines or wandering through an unknown occupied town, murmured despairs without witnesses, moved me far more than the pompous grandeur of epic set-piece moments: crowds climbing the staircase of the Winter Palace or pouring down the Odessa Steps. The charms of celluloid may have staled with the advancing years, but the boredom that fills me at the sight of 'plans for society' on paper is as intense as ever.

The feminine gender aiding in the transfer, my mythic drive later, as if downhill, redirected itself from *la* révolution to *la* France. For myth is woman, and the Egeria on the barricade – *La liberté guidant le peuple* – could serve as a half-way mark between the two poles of our rallying imagination, the two figures of the modern democratic idea: national and international. The move took place in the form of a graduated and in a sense retrograde transition from, if you want to mock, la Pasionaria to Joan of Arc, via the Gaullian fairy-story princess, the Egeria/canteen-woman of 1830, Casque d'Or and Louise Michel. The same words serve in fact for both allegories: '. . . *A strong woman with powerful breasts / With raucous voice and hard charms / And with fire in her irises . . .*' Marx's proletariat is a narrowly masculine concept, Delacroix's people a carnal image which, like a woman's body, incarnates both haven and ocean, mooring and departure . . . One of my happiest memories is of taking Joan Baez to sing for Dolores Ibarruri, on holiday in the South of France, one summer day in 1975, on a terrace outside Mougins overlooking the Mediterranean. One was a 30-year-old pacifist and the other an octogenarian communist, but those two magnificent ladies seemed to share the same intensity, and hit it off wonderfully; to see them side by side – separated by language, general ideas and half a century – singing *La flor más roja del pueblo* in a duet was the best possible example of reconciliation between red and green. As the sun was setting America and Spain, embodied in what was most singular about each, moral idealism and chivalrous heroism, gave a face that evening – such a rare surprise at home! – to the radiant and motley France of which I still sometimes dream.

I am not unaware of the dangers to which one is exposed by vulnerability to mythologies. Party, army, Church . . . carnivorous flowers that lie in wait for the greenhorn with a taste for Epinal prints. Such communities – all ritual, insignia and emphasis – have stores of legend to lure orphans famished for marvels. I may have been rationalist despite everything, managed to keep my head and avoid the trap, but I am afraid this had nothing to do with my wishes. Although 'youth' is feminine in French and 'people' masculine, fascist mythology is aggressively macho, while left-wing myths have a very feminine, less dangerous gentleness. And a tiresome realism compels me, willy-nilly, to seek the precise or trivial detail that instantly punctures the scenography of success. The national colour-print of the storming of the Bastille still moves me more viscerally than the capture of Moncada barracks by Fidel Castro in 1953, but a bad angel keeps whispering in my ear that the people of Paris liberated a total of seven people that day: four perjurers, two lunatics and a compulsive gambler imprisoned for debt.

Even in the days when Theory dressed our convictions up as theorems and our assumptions as predictions, I could never have marched to the canon of rational reason; I needed a melodic base, something to make my nose twitch. This may not be the worst way to advance into the unknown. 'Misery laden with

an idea', said Victor Hugo, 'is the most redoubtable of revolutionary engines.'
Perhaps. But an idea without scent, a correct line without tune or film or picture,
is like a regiment without a flag or a brain without a heart: pure ectoplasm.

May 1st, strikes, marches, meetings, funerals, commemorations and reburial
of ashes (like Jean Moulin's in the Panthéon, Malraux the bard chanting in front
of his Charlemagne, that khaki standing-stone battered by the North wind): in
1965 everything came to the solitary at once, company and certainties together.
Forming a group, experiencing joy: it was all one. The gregarious and the
hormonal, twin levers of incorporation, were not much valued by the thinkers of
militancy. In our freethinkers' cloister at rue d'Ulm, where we took a lofty view
of things, the more Marxist individuals saw the folklore of the 'socialist countries'
(the Gaullist ceremonials at home meriting neither attention nor comment) – the
mass eroticism of banners, chants, uniforms and giant portraits – as mere
decorative mummeries, residues of an infantile disorder that would soon be
gone: the 'cult of personality'. Churchy leftovers, simple stage-props hiding the
hard centre: class struggle, dictatorship of the proletariat, planning. Unlike those
scholars made naive by excessive study, some of us had perceived that the
intrusion of scientism into the old religions of salvation was not a break with the
former basis of human belief, and that in a sense this was no bad thing. An
activist's reflex (I concede) that would have been rejected by most of our
theoreticians, who – however committed they were – judged things not in their
dynamic but by static division of matter. The vital spirit escaped them, along
with the body and the aesthetic. The Sorbonne believed strongly in the
precedence of Idea over matter, and of Reason over instinct. Poets, those
creatures of heart and cadence, from Garcia Lorca to Nazim Hikmet, make
better combatants than men of ideas, even those classified as left-wing; think of
the Spanish civil war, in which even the philosopher Miguel de Unamuno could
die like a poet. And of the French Resistance, where poets did far more to save
the honour of letters than essayists or novelists. Perhaps those who approach the
moral through the physical are better formed for idolatry, more apt for the
generous gift of the self, the unstinting expenditure of energy. Professionally
speaking, the psychosis of love is a strength in artists and a weakness in
academics. It isn't that 'intellectuals' do not fall in love like everyone else;
but they are much given to compartmentalizing. Of those who embraced the
cause of the Soviet Union, for example, how many did not have a Russian muse
(from d'Astier to Vernant, via Aragon)? A 'regime in keeping with their ideas',
they used to say, meaning the women in their lives. A militancy of the head –
André Gide's, say – doesn't reach the vital parts. That is why the reasoner is
unreasonable to mock 'philosophers who wander off into smoky abstractions'.
There was nothing smoky about my abstractions, and nothing abstract about my
smoke. In the abstract, everything was clear-cut and sharp-edged. Imperialism?
'The final stage of State monopoly capitalism . . .' Four-square definitions that
have since gone up in smoke, while the songs of the Fifth Regiment are still in

place. That hammered remorselessly at my skull, until in the space of a few decades smoke and crystal changed positions. No doubt I had located them wrongly in the first place, by attributing enduring significance to fragile logical constructions. What I took to be a complementary poetry was actually our prose, our bedrock. I can understand how teachers are driven by their work to put the cart before the horse: reasons are easier to teach than feelings. You can give a lesson in ethics or political economy but not in love-at-first-sight, or dreaming, or anger. 'Things that can be taught are not worth learning,' the Taoist precept runs. Our amours, and the movies, must have done far more for the cause than training schools for cadres ever did.

This narrative begins at the end of 1965. Being born into History twenty-five years after being born biologically, I am absolved from having to expand on the foetus I had been previously. That is the date I was *initiated*, inserted into my gunmen's Gotha, from the other side of the iconostasis separating the faithful from the executioners and martyrs. Ceasing at last to be a commentator on things that had already happened – the bitter lot of the profane – I was finally admitted to the knowledge of matters under preparation, aptly called 'the secrets of the Gods'. Solely on the basis of a very prosaic text – 'Le castrisme ou la Longue Marche de l'Amérique latine' – published in French a few months earlier in Jean-Paul Sartre's magazine, Fidel Castro, a serving demigod, had me summoned to his presence. In a telegram forwarded by his ambassador in France, he invited me as his personal guest to the Tricontinental Conference, due to open in Havana during the New Year break.

Until that December evening when, as an icy north wind howled through the empty streets of Nancy, the hotel porter brought that slip of blue paper to the chilly room where I was preparing my next day's lesson on the four figures of syllogism in formal logic, the closest I had been was the second balcony, devouring the leaders with my eyes, drinking in their words, swallowing the programme and pondering every silence. A year and a half in Latin America from 1963 to 1964, on foot, by mule, by lorry and train, in prison. Six months in Cuba, in 1961, in the audience, looking on but not admitted to the High Altar. This time I had my pass: a blue note fluttering down from the flies. In that conspiratorial Odeon where freedom of the corridors was equivalent to membership, the 'royal box' was not situated, as in an Italian theatre, facing the stage on the centreline of the pit, in the middle of the audience. The best view was from backstage, out of public view, behind the scenery, somewhere between the service catwalks and the property lockers. It was for that mysterious omega point that I was heading, if a moth can be said to 'head for' a light bulb.

2

Enrolment

1965 – Impossibility of political memoirs – Dangers of air transport – Unexpected luxuries – El entrenamiento – The exclusive fraternity of secrecy – 'War communism': a tautology – between Victor Serge and Richard Sorge – Plea of defence – Progressive retro – We were not what you think

The telegraphic *deus ex machina* interrupted a thrilling sequence of events: municipal elections in March, senatorials in September and in December, presidentials.

Such was the history of France in the year 1965. Futile ephemera. Remember the forgettable.

Socialists and communists signed a popular front pact in the Seine department. To a journalist's query: 'How are you feeling?', de Gaulle replied: 'Not too bad, but don't worry. I won't fail to die.' Gaston Defferre carried Marseille and launched the project of a 'Democratic and Socialist Federation'. *L'Humanité* denounced a slide to the right. The Permanent Council of Bishops reprimanded the weekly *Témoignage chrétien* for publishing an article entitled 'Christians and Marxists talk about God'. François Mitterrand called on the French to 'join the fight for a new hope', adding that to counter 'the regime of personal power . . . we need a revived citizens' Republic'. The 'Italians' and the 'Chinese' were ousted from all the important posts in the Union of Communist Students. The national council of the PSU expressed unenthusiastic support for F. Mitterrand. At about twelve-thirty on 29 October, in front of the Brasserie Lipp in boulevard Saint-Germain, two men carrying police identity cards invited Mehdi Ben Barka, leader of the Moroccan opposition and one of the leaders of the Third World, to get into a car. On 4 November de Gaulle appeared on television to announce his candidature: 'Let the candid and massive support of the citizens commit me to remaining in office; then the future of the new Republic will be decisively settled.' It was the first televised campaign. Pierre Viansson-Ponté observed in *Le Monde* that '. . . the actors need to ham it up to get across the footlights. Meetings and rallies are gatherings of the converted; now they have to reach the undecided and the hesitant.' On 3 December, in the first round, De Gaulle failed to get the majority he needed for an outright win. He changed his style and decided to make use of his airtime after all. On the 19th he was re-elected with 54.5 per cent of the votes cast.

Futile trumperies indeed, but what did it matter to me? For it was elsewhere – no longer in the West – that *it was all happening*. My compatriots were mere benighted Zulus, shaking their ballot-boxes like fetishes, unaware that serious things were going on behind their backs. Encirclement from the South, that was the important thing. This time would be the good one. And it was well overdue: 1917, Lenin and Trotsky, capsized; 1945, second chance missed, Stalinism and Iron Curtain. Dialectically, the third stroke should be the decider. How far would American escalation go in Vietnam, 'centre of the worldwide struggle between revolution and counterrevolution'? As far as *Apocalypse Now*. Our time was the time of revolution, capitalism was encircled, capitulationists wouldn't change anything. The proletarian nations of the Third World had taken up the torch from the exhausted or bribed hands of the Western proletariat. A planetary Dien Bien Phu was being prepared in the distance: the bourgeoisie surrounded, tens of millions of cycle-rickshaws hidden in the forest, bringing artillery into range. 'We're expecting war,' Chou En-lai declared when passing through Algiers. 'We're convinced the US is going to bomb China, and whatever sacrifices we have to make, we remain convinced that American imperialism will be crushed, just as you have crushed French imperialism.'

There wasn't going to be anything festive about the last waltz. If wounded, the atomic-toothed tiger could still draw blood. Five hundred thousand communists had been killed in Indonesia amid a collusive silence. The first GIs, a growing flood of them, were landing in South Vietnam for the dress rehearsal; Johnson said there were going to be a lot more. An American expeditionary corps also occupied Santo Domingo in April, to crush a spontaneous popular uprising in support of Francisco Camaño. De Gaulle was the only Western leader to condemn the American aggression, but what can a capitalist country do against the logic of capitalism, or a national bourgeoisie against the world bourgeoisie? Malcolm X, back from Mecca, was murdered by the white establishment (and not on the orders of Elijah Mohammed, his Dauphin Louis Farrakhan and the leaders of the Nation of Islam). In the middle of Harlem, on 21 February . . . another heavy blow. But I was sure the Black Muslims wouldn't panic (they had announced the end of the world for 1975). Moreover Cassius Clay had beaten Liston in Louisville, Kentucky, an Uncle Tom yielding the ring to a politically conscious black.

When Ben Barka was murdered on the outskirts of Paris he had recently (in Cairo, in September) presided, as head of the Preparatory Committee of the Tricontinental, over the last meeting to finalise the details. The 'triple A' – officially a conference of 'solidarity between the peoples of Africa, Asia and Latin America' – was the heir of Bandung, which in 1955 had sanctioned the end of the colonial empires and ushered a billion Chinese into History. In 1965, progress away from the Afro-Asianness of the early days led to the eruption of

Latin America onto centre stage, via the Cuban revolution. Ben Barka explained to a sceptic while visiting Prague: 'The Tricontinental will be a historic event through its very composition, because both currents of the world revolution will be there: the one that originated with the October Revolution, and the revolutionary current of national liberation.' Expected in Havana were the USSR, China, Indonesia, India, Japan, the NLF of South Vietnam, the UAR, Guinea, Algeria, Ghana, Tanzania, the ANC from South Africa, the National Liberation Movement of Mexico, the Chilian FRAP, the Guatemalan FAR (*Fuerzas Armadas Rebeldes*), the Venezuelan FLN. The Committee, which managed to make the official representatives of communist and neutralist countries coexist with the delegates of revolutionary organizations, called for 'the constitution of national committees to form the kernel of an anti-imperialist popular front in each country'. The schism in the socialist camp nearly aborted the whole thing (neither China nor the USSR would risk leaving the Third World to the other). Ben Barka's procedural shrewdness found a way out of the impasse: he had the idea of a committee within the committee, a sort of castling manoeuvre that replaced Cuba with Venezuela to disarm the Chinese delegation, which saw Cuba as a key Soviet asset. So it was the troika of Vietnam, the Venezuelan FLN and Algeria that launched the appeal entitled 'We, the peoples of the world' from Cairo. Ben Barka wrote that planetary convocation by himself on the corner of a table, and had it signed at dawn by three grumpy, yawning delegates, one of them my Venezuelan buddy Oswaldo.

The time for 1955-style 'positive neutralism' had gone and the time for frontal attack had arrived. Nasser was unifying the Arab world and Ben Bella had made Algiers a rear base for promising exiles, a home from home for the young Nelson Mandela (ANC), Abu Jihad (Palestine), Marcelino dos Santos (FRELIMO) and a few dozen others. In February, Che had dropped in on the Afro-Asian seminar to address a public challenge to the Soviet Union: if the word communism has any meaning (he said in effect), the haves should share what they have; so the socialist camp should finance revolution in the Third World. Pan-Africanism was marking time in Nkrumah's Ghana, but African unity had made progress. The Maghreb was going to be unified by the contagion of socialism, the feudal monarch Hassan II would soon be shot out like a champagne cork. 'Africa is Europe's Latin America,' Ben Barka noted; Che thought it readier for the decisive leap than his own continent. In Congo-Kinshasa, where Belgian paratroops had just retaken Stanleyville, the puppet Tshombe was under threat from a new Revolutionary Executive Council led by Gaston Soumialot. There was talk of a character called Mobutu. In July, Che landed in Tanzania with 136 Cuban officers, five of them white. Amilcar Cabral, leading the PAIGC, had liberated half of Guinea-Bissau; Agostinho Neto and the MPLA were looking strong in Angola; Mozambique too was taking up arms. In Guatemala the 13 November Revolutionary Movement (MR 13) had opened a *foco* in the Sierra de la Minas; the Venezuelan FLN already had three fully operational, and Luken Petkoff was training a hundred men in Cuba: a landing with fifteen Cuban officers was planned for early 1966. In Peru, a military communiqué on 24 October announced the death of Luis de la Puente Uceda, head of the MIR (Movement of the Revolutionary Left). He was replaced immediately by Hector Béjar. In Bolivia César Lora, general secretary of the Trotskyist POR, was killed in the Siglo XX mine; armed miners' militias mobilized in response and occupied the radio station. In Brazil, Francisco Juliaõ was organizing sugar-cane workers in the *Noreste*. In Paris, *Partisans*, a bi-monthly review (éditions Maspero, La Joie de Lire, 40 rue Saint-Séverin, 5th, ODÉ 68– 02, 3.90F) had reached its eighteenth issue. It published texts by Maxime Robinson, Adolfo Gilly, Pierre Vidal-Naquet, Paulo Baran (*What is an Intellectual?*), Vô Nguyên Giap, Bertolt Brecht, Frantz Fanon and Gérard Chaliand. Fortunately Maspero was there to render the PCF its due, if it could still claim to be a revolutionary force. And there were film-makers to see and make people see: *Before the Revolution* by Bernardo Bertolucci, Marco Bellocchio's *Fists in the Pockets*, *Pierrot le Fou* by Jean-Luc Godard.

The order of the day for the assemblies in which two-thirds of humanity would live could suffer no ambiguity, despite certain tactical difficulties. The deep-rooted Chinese chauvinism had to be neutralized by preventing it from splitting the live forces everywhere, and the revisionists' arsenal put to proper use, all without yielding to the sirens of peaceful coexistence. The USSR had no time for anything but the race to the moon, which it had started with Gagarin and still had every chance of winning. It was asleep, snoring, but it still produced what was needed for fighting. After all his sufferings, the mujik was at last allowed to catch his breath and eat his goulash in peace. But as that overweight rearguard feared real conflict, its hand would need to be forced without provoking an open break.

At Ijevsk, deep in the Urals, a 'poet in steel', comrade Mikhaïl Kalashnikov, was working for those left out of détente by making the world's best infantry weapon, the AK47. This bargain-priced jewel merits a few compliments. With its thirty-round magazine, short barrel, resistance to water and dust and practical simplicity, it outclassed the American AR15 and M16, which were needlessly complex, jammed easily and overheated. Dainty 17-year-old Vietnamese girls could jump up between card games and use it to concentrate lethal fire on F-14 fighter-bombers stuffed with electronics. Our sling was getting more accurate. Goliath's days were numbered.

The mopping up would take ten or twenty years. After that, by about the year 2000, we would be supervising the education of the new generations. Socialism triumphant would allow obsolete man to keep a few theme parks, future museums of capitalist ethnology: Switzerland, Holland, Monaco, Paraguay. Deserving Young Pioneers would be sent to these Bantustans of lucre on study visits to get an idea of prehistory, and to toss a few peanuts to the petty speculator scratching and gesticulating in his cage. And in the toughest redoubt of all, the United States, the blacks were about to rise *en masse* behind the Black Muslims and join the Latinos coming up from the Rio Grande, trapping Wall Street in a pincer movement. The outlook had never been better.

Clear as a rock pool. I was more than willing to share the Apocalypse with volunteers from my own country. But they still needed to open their eyes: not at all easy. The blindness of friends on the other side, whom I benevolently reminded to make appropriate arrangements, was a great burden to me. I still remember a meeting that year in Paris with a fellow-historian, Michel B., *cacique*[2] of his intake, who had arrived at rue d'Ulm a year earlier and with whom I sat on the school disciplinary council as a student representative. That piercingly ironic individual, deeply resistant to common sense, who wore a tie and made no effort to hide strong ambition, told me on the corner outside a café in rue Soufflot that he had decided to enter the 'École nationale d'administration'. He then told me what that strange appendage was for: to manufacture senior civil servants, prefects and ministers. This brought me down to earth with a bump. I had imagined my elder to be a Rastignac, a Rubempré attached to the positive; now I discovered a fool who mistook the shadow for the substance. Serving a bourgeois government, when proletarian cadres were going to take over tomorrow at dawn . . . the credulity! Quite apart from the fact that the literate give orders to technicians, not the other way round, the stay-at-homes vegetating in rue Saint-Guillaume seemed to me like land officials of the Roman Empire, applying for the lucrative Pompeii-Herculaneum region . . . in 79 BC. Vainly, I reminded the heedless fellow of the existence of Vietcong girl soldiers, Sputniks, new intercontinental rockets, T-34s and MiG-19s, without forgetting the science of History, whose reward and response these things were. But although mandated by the arsenals of justice, I failed to convince my friend: he thought me capricious for going to the tropics where the decisive games were starting, I thought him a dreamer for staying in France, where nothing was happening any more. I felt sorry for that visionary – an excellent man despite everything – who not long afterwards found his way onto President Pompidou's staff at the Elysée. I myself was holding out for reliable values, tangible and durable: the red star.

A lot of us wanted to divorce the *here* and espouse the *elsewhere*. So I saw nothing of the Swinging Sixties, either convulsed or prettily pop. The Chats Sauvages and the Chaussettes Noires passed me by, I shamefacedly confess, as had the June 'night of madness' two years earlier, when an announcement on the Europe No. 1 programme 'Salut les copains' jammed 150,000 young people into the place de la Nation to hear the 'boisterous prophet of the new age': Johnny Hallyday. For me the Beatles were eclipsed by Brel and Ferré. What I liked was bebop. The twist didn't seem serious; nor did yeah-yeah, rock'n'roll, teenagers, age-groups, the star system, Elvis Presley, the 45-rpm single industry or mass communications. Nor did the launch of the first French satellite from the

Sahara. Eurovision was a bourgois diversion, an idiot-trap, an American gadget. I never noticed self-service cafeterias, hamburgers or hot dogs because the Maheu and the Capoulade, the two old bistros at the junction of rue Soufflot and boulevard Saint-Michel, were stuck face to face for all eternity. No one mentioned gays, conviviality, software or video. Only much later did I learn the important things had happened in my country that year: Courrèges had declared war on short skirts; Sylvie and Johnny had been conjoined in legal matrimony; Madras cotton was in. I saw, without really noticing them, men with long hair and women in trousers; Bob Dylan's first tour, pop art and the Rolling Stones left me pretty cold. I did not notice the debate on contraception, in a country of abortions where 'taking the pill' was as unusual as smoking hash or grass; I did not know that Mick Jagger had an androgynous look or that Jean Shrimpton, the most beautiful girl in the world, was sweet, simple and sexy. I did not understand the Copernican revolution that was Vatican II. I did not read Jacques Borel's *L'Adoration* (*The Bond*, winner of the prix Goncourt), preferring Perec's *Les Choses* (*Things*, winner of the prix Renaudot), at least partly because Perec wrote in *Partisans* and had rented me his Paris flat while he was away sociologizing in Sfax. I retained nothing of the Roland Barthes–Raymond Picard duel, 'new criticism or new imposture'. I did not go through the Mont Blanc tunnel. I did not see Averty's *Le Père Ubu* on television or, in the cinema, Louis Malle's *Viva Maria*, Buñuel's *Simon of the Desert* or Milos Forman's *Loves of a Blonde*. I didn't see *La 317e section* (*Section 317*) by Schoendorffer (old Indo-China hand, suspect). Or *Doctor Zhivago* on the big screen (Hollywood, suspect). Or the Dubuffet and Nicolas de Staël retrospectives. In the shadow of Matisse there was no place for Warhol (who held his first exhibition in Paris): geniuses and champions are either French or do not exist. I could see strong gleams in the South, replacing the ones that had faded in the East. Two hundred million communists had their eyes turned to Peking or Moscow; five hundred million Catholics had theirs fixed on Rome; mine were focused on Algiers.

Colonel Houari Boumedienne had overthrown Ben Bella but my friend Oswaldo, a former sociology teacher at Caracas University, was keeping up the good work. After signing the appeal to the peoples of the world in Cairo on behalf of all Venezuela (alone, like a great man), he moved into the Villa Susini with FLN colleagues (the Venezuelan FLN, not the Algerian one). They started an import-export company, 'L'Huile Jujura'. Cuba had given Algeria 10,000 tonnes of sugar to be re-exported to People's China, in exchange for 120 tonnes of American weapons, acquired during the Korean war, for use by Venezuelan guerrillas, who for obvious reasons could not use Kalashnikovs. Oswaldo's team had the job of repackaging this quite cumbersome weaponry in small lots inside barrels of olive oil for shipping to Venezuela (excellent for the weapons but a difficult packaging exercise). A Sartreian who much preferred philosophic jargon to the welder's torch, he would buy *Les Temps modernes* in an Algiers bookshop to take his mind off things, and in the January number came across the article Claude Lanzmann had published under the title 'Le castrisme ou la Longue Marche de l'Amérique Latine'[3]. Just at that moment Che arrived in Algiers, and invited Oswaldo to the Cuban embassy where he was staying (Papito Serguera was Ambassador). The invitation was made partly with an eye to the future (for Che might go to Venezuela one day), but also to get Oswaldo to translate his proposed address to the Afro-Asian seminar into French. The two men played chess in the garden, discussing the bright prospects in store and (bizarrely) Egypt and its pyramids. Oswaldo confessed to having felt vertigo while climbing the Great Pyramid of Cheops, and Che scolded him as if he had been a child: '*Children* get vertigo, a revolutionary *never* gets vertigo.' Oswaldo agreed, but to change the subject produced the copy of *Les Temps modernes* that happened to be in his pocket. Che, who could read French, nationalized it on the spot. This small accident determined the course of my life, or the image that a few survivors will have of it (just one image each, for space reasons). I have still hardly recovered from it thirty years later.

Oswaldo performed the decisive or fateful act by handing over a few printed pages. Che took that copy back to Cuba and passed it on, translated, to Fidel Castro (who did not read French) a few weeks later, just before leaving for the Congo. The piece made Castro think of sending for its author (a *Fidelista* unknown to the battalion, who nevertheless seemed to have a sound grasp of the difficulties of urban and the advantages of rural guerrilla warfare). I accepted Fidel's invitation, and soon afterwards he sent me to do groundwork for Che's arrival in Bolivia. It was as a former companion of Guevara that Salvador Allende greeted me when I came out of prison in 1971. It was as the bearer of a message from Allende to Mitterrand that I first met the latter, near Pau, in 1972. And it was as a putative expert on the Third World that the newly elected president took me on at the Elysée in 1981. The entire sequence starting with an insignificant act.

So the trigger of the derailment, who introduced me to the Princes, the first link in the chain, was Oswaldo B. (who two years earlier, in a Caracas garden, had also introduced me to Elisabeth B., the mother of my daughter). My far-off pal was the sponsor of both life and death, a proper – if involuntary – confusion of powers. He had no idea what he was unleashing when he lent *Les Temps modernes* to a passing Argentinian (*never* lend books), and I had no idea what I was getting into when I went to the Tricontinental (*never* leave your bedroom). The first snag is the one that matters.

Around 1940, people horrified by the very idea were being bagged by History as they bolted from the cover of a phoney war. I can bear witness to an inverse phenomenon: one sighing for storm and tempest, caught in a flat calm and whistling for History to put wind in his sails.

While some traces of our galleys remain in the archives, the wake of our caravels has vanished, leaving only the twisted smiles of the disembarked. Their brief and magnificent voyages are not *certified*. How do we do justice to fairy stories that have ended prematurely, without yielding to the temptation to jeer? That is why political memory is less trustworthy than other kinds (and why we know less about certainties than clouds). Our militancies unravel into nebulosity, as if the mobilizing ideas for which we have striven so hard just evaporated into thin air. At the time, embarkation for Cythera seemed too obvious to need an explanation; twenty years later, it seems too extravagant to have one. The return to the introversion and solitude of private life sets two strangers glaring at each other like china dogs: the deluded one from before and the disillusioned one from after. It is a moment when the *ex* accuses himself of not keeping a safe distance from yesterday's events (but if we had done that, we would never have done anything). He should really blame official ephemera, those half-lies that only refer to events that befall, that fall rather, dropped from the clouds. Should not the clouds be restored to their place of honour? But perhaps we retain no more memory of collective enthusiasms than of physical suffering. We remember the treatment, the hospital ward, the doctor's face, the flagons of serum, the colour of the walls, even the names of the medicines; but not the fiery nephritic colic that necessitated all this deployment of skill and apparatus. In the same way we can re-read speeches, tracts, programmes and other verbosities, stuff we used to believe in (or even wrote ourselves), and be completely unable to find the silent bedrock of self-evident truth that once gave these texts their credibility; and whose disappearance over the horizon turns these black-and-white conviction pieces into ghostly icebergs, between dream and nightmare.

Recalling the Resistance, one veteran compared the fading of a 'high point' to a jazz jam session, an evening of sublime improvisation that has players and audience levitating at the time, but being unrecorded vanishes for ever. Although the miraculous sax solo was only played once, there are many registers that the curious can use afterwards to look up the event: almanacs, newspapers, books, photos, decrees, author's discourse . . . but these historians' instruments are of no use to us in bringing our transports back to life, reviving our 'snows of yesteryear'. However exhaustive the documentation, the caravel itself will be missing from the printout; and without it, such records – partly because of their very exactitude – will look like forgeries concocted to slander us.

The *possible* (what moves, *mobilizes* one generation after another) suffers from a disqualifying defect: it never goes 'in the can'. There is no video or audio device to capture fear or hope; there are no boxes of these things in store. Historians' history records content, but not states of mind; written professions of faith, but not floating vacillations, flights into shame, fear of ridicule or looking mad; political programmes, but not the electricity in the air. 'Former combatants' know all about this last-minute disappearance of the essential, for it transforms them instantly – when they try to recount their mini-Verduns, their personal Omaha Beaches or Gulags – into mumbling dotards opaque even to themselves. A revolutionary is first and foremost – even more than *homo politicus* in normal times – a watcher, a dreamer lying in ambush. Without mechanical means of preservation or storage, the flavour of imminence is as impossible to remember as a scent; yet only that feeling of anxiety could justify (like documentary proof) our past motivations. It is with that watcher that we try to keep faith, and by the yardstick of his expectations that we later measure the extent of our failures. But without those vanished frenzies our actions seem crazy even to us.

The feeling of strangeness produced by material evidence of our past might be imputed to imperfect recall, to the impalpability of a 'climate', to the archipelago of memories (an individual's peak period meaning nothing to his neighbour who was in the doldrums at the time), to the three-card trick of collective credos (transmuting what everyone believes in one decade into what everyone finds incredible in the next); even to time itself, which cools all ardours. But all these well-known causes count for little beside the most magical of all, the elusive character of that mysterious yet utterly commonplace time: the past future.

Accustomed as inhabitants of the videosphere to the 'instant totality' of electronic pleasure, we no longer tolerate waiting as well as we should. Live broadcasting techniques and televisual channel-hopping have given to the ardent patiences of yesteryear the antiquated, over-fastidious feel of an improving nineteenth-century novel. We are no longer in tune with the way we were in the days of books, of long projects and militant collectives. As if banned from our own memories. Every period is defined more by what it anticipates than what it accomplishes, none more so than the one that expects revolution tomorrow. So that absolutely any diaspora of former believers communes in its thoughts not on the basis of the defeats it suffered, but of the plans it pursued at such length which, over time, have slipped into the limbo of a shared bittersweet regret that give the diaspora its family cohesion. If you amputate a generation of militants, those prosaic Lawrences, from their Arab dream they immediately become the scatterbrained dupes of comic insanities. Hence our discomfort when faced with monochrome photos, the old documentary films we watch with amazement or vexation and that seem to us, when we see in them our friends, our street, even our own profiles, as laughable as hasty forgeries; because when we were living that present, the image was just the remains of a snippet scribbled at the bottom of the page, a memo to the self for the period after the operation under way. An unimportant reminder, a sequence of errors to be deleted from the Advent to come, that all-enveloping imminence that made it easy to bear or even ignore pratfalls, doomed passing fancies, sour notes during the solos. Gaff burgled, huge ink-splash on new mac, skiing holiday ruined by the wrong weather, all small miseries that cause great annoyance when you are living your life in the present, but seem insignificant to the optimist eagerly awaiting the Apocalypse: that great misfortune that will make us all happy tomorrow.

Happiness in 1965 was *politically* defined, hung on a battle of ideas rather inadequately expressed in the the insipid term *choice of society*. I am sure I never believed, even at the peak of that optimism, that 'everything is political', or that the whole of a man can be expressed in class or ideological terms. But the keys to private life which by their very nature fall outside these considerations – things like amorous sentiment, artistic taste, curiosity about the unknown – had to be shelved, set aside until later, until after the emergency. You might say that the ego was no less detestable to the 1960s millenarian in exclusive thrall to History than to the 1660s Jansenists in thrall to the Eternal. No individual war aims allowed. The expected catastrophe rendered people fairly indifferent to 'personal matters'. 'What are you going to do later, darling?' An idiot question. Later, there was going to be the revolution. All right: and after that? Black hole. What role was I going to play in it? Unspecified, but prominent of course. And might there, *afterwards*, still be theatre, with posters, divas, walk-ons and the rest? Obviously not. We would enter the arena firing rifles, trampling career strategies underfoot and banishing the worries of representation: on the eve of a planetary earthquake, the best of strategies. For I took it for granted – an assumption due as much to my inexperience of warfare as to my conviction of immortality – that the imminent conflagration would spare me (the advantage of cosmic slaughter over minor bloodbaths is that it is much easier to escape). Survival went without saying: nothing could hurt me. Marching towards his celestial Jerusalem, passing among men, the newly baptized man of the twentieth century, like his first-century predecessor, was in this world without being of it. His role was to carry the baton, to pass it from the martyrs of yesterday to those of tomorrow, as if the real baton-carriers were not the martyrs themselves. It is only after the only baptism that really counts – the baptism of fire – that one makes this very obvious discovery, through the threat of death in the first person (the one that is never mentioned by strategists or doctrinaires).

You don't cross three centuries in eight hours with impunity. To a heavier-than-air creature an aircraft is a paradox, and between Europe and South America, an imprudence. The old propeller-driven Britannias used by *Cubana de Aviación* in those days for the flight from Prague to Havana used to stop at Gander, in Newfoundland, Canada, sometimes for as long as two days if an engine had to be repaired and a spare part awaited. These valuable breakdowns were not long enough to provide the psychosomatic *glissando*, the gradual adaptation of the senses, that had previously been supplied by sea travel. In the days when travel was more than just transport the ethnologist, immigrant or tourist sailing over the ocean towards the West Indies had the time to take the air, to readjust his sight, hearing and sense of smell at every port of call. Flying has confiscated gannets and black-backed gulls, phosphorescence in the night, the dance of dolphins and flying fish along the bow wave, land breezes laden with pepper and sugar, violet dawns 'exalted as a multitude of doves', ports from which rowing boats emerge amid clamorous shouts laden with unknown fruits. Being deprived of the picturesque in this way is of far less importance than the abrupt time shift that occurs. Helped by the anonymity of airports, air travel dissimulates the change of century that accompanies movement between continents behind misleading superficial sensations, like the astonishing humidity experienced on the tarmac at the moment of arrival. In the case of the so-called New World, fascination with the wide open spaces somehow occludes the change of secular mentality zone being experienced at the same time (these zones should be mapped globally one day like the twenty-four time zones). The lie of air travel, the international con trick that misrepresents advances in navigation as cultural rapprochement (when, in reality, mental distances are widening as the physical ones narrow), was complicated in the case of that Paris-Prague-Havana journey by Marxist-Leninist *trompe-l'oeil*, a ribbon of words and images sewn together with red thread. That glittering carpet of icons and slogans that extended from Asia to America, via Europe and Africa (but without, it is true, taking in the North or South Pacific), bridging some of the geological faults that separated the different hinterlands from one another. Institutions set up from above were like detachable parts, hastily cobbled onto a subsoil of centuries of ingrained, slowly evolved habit. Sovietization resembled hasty plastic surgery, grafting the same allogenous implant into six different organisms, all more or less resistant, without taking any account of their immune systems. Even less is known about this mysterious defence system in societies than in individuals, the propensity to safeguard *the integrity of the self* that for lack of a better name we call 'the spirit of a people' or the 'national character'. Might not ideology be the passion of people who don't want to know about *immunology*?

In the Caribbean, the symbols of membership of the 'peace camp' – displayed all the more ostentatiously when they were still a novelty – had modified the vocabulary, but not the colonial past with its ingrained reflexes and habits. The sympathetic outsider imagined he had his finger on the pulse of world youth, but was really dealing with a pioneering fringe of conquering chivalry somewhere on the temporal frontiers of Christianity. The Lenin, Mao and Giap that I had in my luggage were the wrong psalters; to guide me in this old captaincy-general of the Spanish Empire I ought to have packed the *Book of Amadis* and Olivier de la Marche's *Le Chevalier délibéré* (*The Thoughtful Knight*), the bedside reading of Charles Quint. For lack of antecedents, the short-term visitor was liable to mistake a flashback for a leap forward and mediaeval knights for pioneering models of New Man. You can sing the *Internationale* lustily while wallowing in the past. Why should History be chronological, when our own lives so seldom are?

Havana still had the air of a small piece of North America stuck on the side of a Creole country (itself a small piece of black Africa lodged in Hispanic territory). A flat town laid out round a bay, a chessboard of ochre or sulphur-yellow *cuadras* from which projected, in vaguely seaside fashion, a number of sub-skyscraper structures (the Hilton and Riviera hotels, the Focsa building), with nearby, in *vieja Habana*, the whitish dome of a Capitol building modelled on the one in

Washington. Its potholed pavements, peeling arcades and crumbling rococo plasterwork had become noticeably more moth-eaten since 1961, when I still used to see on the Malecón (that *promenade des Anglais* in pink and blue distemper stained by salt and spray) itinerant sellers of pineapple and orange *batidos*, barrowloads of avocados, mangoes and paw-paws, and shoeshine boys (the sale of tombola and lottery tickets having already been banned). *Viva el internacio nalismo proletario, Aquí no se rinde nadie, ¡Comandante en Jefe, ordene! Hasta la victoria siempre*: along walls, everywhere in the streets, inscriptions in bright colours had eclipsed the Palmolive and Chesterfield ads of the American era. Battered, multi-coloured Buicks and Chryslers, their pitted chrome trim tied on with string, still lurched about the streets. Its growth stopped short by the revolution, as if tired out before being finished, the town's new anti-American varnish allowed reminders of hot dogs and Coca-Cola to show through: a sort of horizontal Broadway with tropical humidity instead of neon signs. There was still baroque in the stucco colonnades and the faded pink porticoes of the old houses, but nothing left to evoke colonial times, other than a lifeless cathedral, a few cobbled streets and a picture-postcard fort, with cannons and castellations, overlooking the waves like an abandoned movie set. In their 1940s Hollywood kitsch, the hotel-casinos put up by Meyer Lansky and Lucky Luciano, the Riviera and Capri, where Benny Moré and Rita Montaner were still breathing out languorous mambos and obsolete boleros, as well as the few nightclubs and restaurants that had managed to stay afloat – Tropicana or '1830' – seemed to expect Humphrey Bogart and Lauren Bacall – anyway certainly not a would-be Philip II – to climb out of a bulletproof Oldsmobile. It is in the New World that the Old one ambushes us most effectively. Added to that stretching out of the days, that stopping of clocks, building work and urban life that is somehow brought about by the communist ideal in every part of the world, the shop-soiled feel of the place could confuse the pilgrim. Amid that retro décor he might easily imagine that he had stepped back twenty years in the twentieth century, when really, in his high-level contacts, he was going to have to navigate without maps or compass somewhere between the Siècle d'Or and the Enlightenment. And very slowly: *cosas de palacio van despacio,* as they used to say in Madrid in the days of the Escorial. The most trivial act – a phone call, a meal in a restaurant, the purchase of a packet of cigarettes – took ten times as long as in a 'normal' country.

The internationalist languor common to hot countries and 'forward bastions of socialism' – often the same places – was aggravated in this case by a generalized maladjustment of clocks caused by 'Caudillist arrhythmia'. In decision-making circles, since even the most trivial initiative depended on an express order from the *Jefe*, all watches were synchronized, if that is the word, with his wholly unpredictable movements; so the *Jefe*'s legendary unpunctua- lities, amplified by those of his intermediaries, shunted their way down the chain of activists, an elite more expectant than active. Every international leader, every conspirator worthy of note who visited Havana in those years, was subjected to a game without rules during the agonizing wait for the Interview. The VIP of world revolution had to complete three stages. The first began at the airport, where a minder dressed in olive drab would murmur in a low voice: 'Fidel *wants* to see you', thus projecting him immediately into a select circle well above and entirely separate from the average pilgrim; but he would also be enjoined to stay where he could be located at a moment's notice, to be cautious in his associations and prepare for the miracle. The second stage, which would usually start the day before his planned departure (in extreme cases extending the visit to twice its intended length), began with: 'Fidel's *going* to see you'. This meant immediate and permanent immobilization in the hotel or *Casa de seguridad*, cancellation of all other meetings and the beginning of a long, indefinite period of nervous tension. A few days or weeks later, when the tension had become absolutely unbearable, the third stage would begin with the whirlwind arrival of someone of high rank, often Manuel Piñeiro (head of the secret services) in person, announcing in a triumphant tone: 'Fidel's *coming*' . . . In fact, just as the future tense of the previous announcement signified hope rather than probability, so the present in this one indicated not actuality but imminence. This acme of expectation could still last anything from thirty minutes to three days; the whole three-act routine could drag on for several months.

Under the coconut and banana trees everything looked like something else. Ragged hidalgos dressed as guerrillas, at the head of an army of peasants deemed to be proletarians; an old-style caudillo posing as a vanguard leader; 'anti-imperialist' rulers saturated with imperial culture, familiar with the American Way of Life, fond of baseball, ice-cream and comic strips (none more obsessed with America or, in his heart of hearts, Americanophile than Fidel Castro); Godless men preaching crusade; puritans scornful of any economic calculation buried in manuals of political economy; children of Bolívar training themselves to swear only by Marx, who loathed Bolívar (like his contemporary Chateaubriand, and for the same reasons). Will raised into a fetish, impatience in argument amid tropical indolence, in which every important matter is put off until the next day (*mañana compañero*); the cult of the martial in the fluid saunter of the crowds, the tramp of boots punctuating the shuffle of down-at-heel shoes, forage caps on some heads, curlers on others; bare-chested Cromwells against a background of rumba and *relajo* (Fidel and Che, neither of whom danced, had as little taste for Afro-Cuban rhythms as for *criollo* wit and humour); the five Stalinist laws of dialectic overlaying *santería*, the local voodoo; sacred necklaces of the Yoruba god Shango hung across icons of Che in wooden huts whose lintels bore the words: *Fidel, ésta es tu casa.*

Latin (as opposed to Anglo-Saxon) America is rightly proud of its mulatto side. The salutary syncretism of races is accompanied by a less ostentatious but more original syncretism of times, heavy with vertigo, risk and peculiarities. In revolutionary Cuba these intermixings sometimes reached heights of tragi-comedy equally bewildering to the 'imperialist' enemy and the 'new left' friend. Both were being treated to a real-life preview of a Spanish version of *Les Visiteurs*, a comedy film in which survivors of the battle of Agincourt are magically transported to the present, cross busy motorways in their armour and manage, by understanding nothing, to evade the pitfalls of a hostile century. These casting errors, endearing and exasperating, in the end became a stratagem for dealing with an enemy too Nordic and rational to grasp the rules of such a baroque game. They go a long way towards explaining the historical and geographical improbability of forty years of feudal Marxism-Leninism in what might have become at the beginning of the twentieth century, and might still become early in the twenty-first, the fifty-somethingth star on the US flag.

A nation's strength lies more in finance and trade than military exploits, and the country's interests must come before the service of God: these rather dispiriting views became current in European courts at the time of the Renaissance. But they had not yet reached Cuban shores; in that timeless isle the *comandantes* had embraced the sacred mission of saving humanity, while purging their own people of its slimier rejects (*gusano*, as exiles or would-be exiles were called, means 'earthworm'). Given the symbolic affinities between crusade and revolution, the imaginary overprinting of long-haired Rebels galloping in their *cañaverales* with the *Libertadores* – also horsemen – of the *Independancia* (Martí here taking over from Bolívar), a mediaevalist would have recognized immediately that the 'bearded cayman' of the Antilles, despite more advanced material development than its neighbours, was a pre-capitalist entity swamped in the supernatural, like a ritual-numbed society under the ancien régime. A supernatural rooted in chivalrous romance, the Abakua sect and the latifundist levels of the economy, but inhibited by harsh economic constraints and the spiritual mediocrity of Soviet-influenced Marxism. A supernatural without heaven, without resurrection of the body or any of the vast panoply of the Christian marvellous, without monasteries, cathedrals or tombs; countered, moreover, by the implacable Darwinism of bureaucratic selection (communist elimination of all but the very lowest in character and intelligence being more ruthless than the world average); a mystique therefore condemned in advance to accelerated entropy. But a supernatural whose first surge enabled this people to rise above itself (like the French in 1792 and the Russians in 1917). These mental habits, all the more mobilizing for being archaic, aided by intelligent handling of radio and television, plus an unparalleled instinct for power, made it possible for a clan of inventive machos grouped in the '26 July Movement' – soon renamed the 'socialist vanguard' – to construct, under cover of dialectical materialism, a State both militarized and spiritualist. Apart from free healthcare and education – very substantial gifts – the revolution heaped its flock with immaterial gratifications, force-feeding it indeed quite soon to the limits of physical starvation: military parades, solemn funerals, oratorical exorcisms, one congress after another, emphatic celebrations of founding events and anniversaries, 1 January, 1 May and 26 July, honorific rewards to workers (presentation of flags, diplomas, medals, etc.), regenerative pilgrimages to the Moncada barracks on the Pico Turquino (nearly 6,000 feet up at the highest point of the Sierra Maestra), cults of the two major saints, José Martí and Che, ritual invocation of the spirits of the martyrs and the exhibition of relics (to the point of repatriating Che's severed and mummified hands after his death). Just as a capitalist society (in Karl Marx's phrase) presents itself as 'an immense accumulation of goods', so the 'socialist' societies used to make up the shortfall in goods and services with an immense accumulation of ceremonies, and the poorest of them did it most thoroughly.

Having left the upper deck of Progress for the coal bunker, I found myself upgraded to first class, not far from the captain's cabin: in a double suite on the top floor of the ex-Hilton, rebaptized *Habana Libre*. Wanting to be a sacrificial victim doesn't make you one; in those days the organized populist wishing to descend had to start by climbing (a sort of inversion of the well-heeled graduate's season as a barman in London or a chauffeur in California before coming home to join the family business). The fact is that in the time of communism, going to the people did not mean embracing poverty. Not always, or not straight away. The hero's adolescence has its ups and downs, and changes of latitude favour jumps in social status. In the United States, the promised land, I had travelled the highways and wandered the Harlem streets without a penny to my name. Setting out two years later to join the wretched of the earth in Venezuela, a country I imagined to be wretchedly poor, I landed in surroundings of immense wealth. Hidden behind walls in the towns of Europe, money flaunted itself openly here in a dream-like country club nestling among the shanty-towns called *ranchos* that ringed the overflowing bowl of Caracas. There, although surrounded by city on all sides, one might have been on the plantation in *Gone with the Wind*, with lawns, black servants and white verandahs. A great gentleman with communist sympathies, a newspaper owner and good novelist, had generously invited me to stay in his *quinta* (villa) where with my own eyes I saw two pen drawings by Picasso in a lavatory, an original Rodin head of Balzac beside the swimming pool, Calders on the lawn, pictures by Léger and Max Ernst in every room. In that place at that time a great family thought it quite natural to have four American cars in the garage, five or six indoor servants and champagne at lunch. It is in poor countries that wealth makes least effort to hide itself, without necessarily being synonymous with reaction. Post-war communist-leaning high society, an informal International astride culture and politics, had a comfortable but insecure way of life. A leading figure like Neruda or Asturias could be under house arrest one day and an ambassador the next, or move overnight from the central prison to a *quinta* overlooking the Pacific. Tropical paradoxes were nothing new to me, but this grand way of life in the middle of a 'forward bastion' produced a certain feeling of imbalance. One got used to it, though.

The council of the planet's impoverished wallowed in luxury, and the whole spectrum of Third World cadres was living in a provisional style greatly above its means. The hotel the revolutionary government had chosen to lodge its guests, with plenary sessions and commissions held in the ground-floor lounges, was a palace. Badly dressed and out of place, the 'cadres' trailed about the gold and marble lobby looking gauche, like North African youths who had wandered into the Plaza Athénée by mistake. A newly appointed secondary school teacher has not usually acquired the habits (although it doesn't take long) of calling room service in the morning to order pancakes with maple syrup, drinking daiquiris and Cuba libres in the evening and having to choose between three restaurants – Polynesian, Italian and *criollo* – at mealtimes. Those of us with official *huésped* (guest) cards could just sign for everything, and everything was free, without extra costs or even a bill to look at. I was 24 years old: a car and driver were at my disposal day and night along with a sort of aide-de-camp, a balcony, a private lift and a white telephone (but no international calls, for reasons of political caution and technical collapse): it was like being in the movies. Most of the delegates headed back to their jungles or hideouts a few days after the conference, but we stayed put until our transfer a few months later to a modest anonymous house in the Miramar quarter, away from the centre and prying eyes.

Although the famine of the 'special period' was still in the future, I can imagine what feelings this account may arouse in today's suffering Cubans; even then, with their ration cards (the *libreta*), they were having to tighten their belts. Despite the ambient destitution, we did not seem to be resented. A tradition of hospitality, festive habits, strong popular consensus (among those not trying to emigrate) and the impossibility of public criticism combined to make people tolerate our standard of living; in a capitalist country, they would have complained bitterly if unproductive foreign guests were seen living the life of Riley at their expense. The French state (for example) gives its official guests, heads of government or ministers on what are called working visits, three days at the Crillon hotel, no more, and without extras. In 1983 I had to go down on my knees to get the protocol department to pick up a modest telphone bill that Maurice Bishop, the young premier of Grenada, was materially incapable of paying (the same thing happened to another young revolutionary, Thomas Sankara, president of Burkina Faso, also murdered by a rival): the officials were terrified of setting the dreaded *precedent* that haunts the dreams of the Quai d'Orsay. Stinginess, routine, fusty habit and ignorance of mass poverty make the very rich French state tight-fisted, economical, far from hospitable to foreigners. The poor Caribbean state by contrast was generous to a fault. 'Revolutionary tourism' by intellectuals and high-profile travellers from Europe, the object of much jeering, was the visible but unrepresentative face of a larger migration, more discreet and more intimately collusive. For many years the Cuban revolution sheltered tens of thousands of anonymous militants and refugees from America and Africa without charging them a penny. Today sexual tourism thrives where believers were once welcomed and given asylum. It seems to me that the apartheid of ideas was less scandalous than that of the dollar. Ideology is easier to share and less bumptious: no prostitutes or brothels, minimal black market, tipping seen as an insult, no obsequiousness in the hotel staff (Security-connected, and as much watched as watching). The fact that these causes of waste must have contributed to the general impoverishment, that the costs of so-called 'international solidarity' have always been written into 'totalitarian' budgets, in no way detracts from the gratitude that I still feel. Calculated generosity no doubt, but the real thing too, with improbable extra benefits, owing as much to a hospitable temperament as to internationalist ideology. Why insist on one or the other, since both were involved?

It is difficult not to cherish people's liberation personally, when it starts by liberating you from all truck with cheque books, customs declarations and electricity bills! I paid no attention to the details at the time: it would have seemed idle to discriminate between the different sorts of well-being: physical, from developing some muscle in the gym; moral, from free adherence to historical necessity; and economic, from living rather caddishly at the princess's expense. The slight embarrassment of the first few weeks I tried to rationalize, attributing the unexpected opulence to some special genius of the place, hiding the privilege behind the foreignness: a gift of the 'marvellous real' as Alejo Carpentier calls it. *Le Siècle des lumières*, my teenage bible, gave its readers a foretaste of these sensual splendours. Between the Cuban's novel and this belated confirmation there had been a brush with unvarnished reality: eighteen months of vagabondage, between 1963 and 1964, covering Latin America from top to toe, had vaccinated me against Eldorados. I travelled with my Venezuelan girlfriend, a person of like mind, and we made enough local contacts to escape the vice of exoticism: remembering landscapes rather than faces and dissolving the human beings into the local colour. The tourist dissociates geography from history. I always tended to graze on the opposite slope, making notes not of flora and landscapes but of chronograms, organigrams, diagrams and various other mementoes of friends and far-left movements. In early 1966 the relief of being rid of schoolboys, of freezing furnished rooms in Nancy, of the tunnels at Châtelet metro station, gave a special savour to that communism of milk and honey – not just correct, but almost free too – where money no longer counted. The surrealist Matta, extra lucid like his friend Breton, had told me before my departure of the dismay he felt after a visit to East Berlin: 'In that funereal, treeless Nice,' he said in Paris, 'even the young people live like the elderly, with mortal Sundays, as if already in a retirement home.' Not just because of the wall and the barbed wire, but from invincible boredom. He could only see one way to avoid this grey future: the Party down there should write into its statutes that: 'The duty of every young communist is to capture a whale off Greenland and tow it to Ceylon.' There are more sharks than whales in the Gulf of Mexico. To make up for this, a state itself dependent on aid lavished surreal daily expenses on us. Fresh mango and guava juice for breakfast; guacamole at cocktail time to accompany the daiquiris; a sublimely beautiful brown lift-girl; breeze stirring the palms beside warm swimming pools. The workers would soon have free access to these treats; the politico-military vanguard was just tasting them first, nothing strange about that. Is not revolution the Sunday of life, during its early hours? While awaiting the low-key Mondays Fidel had been promising ever since my arrival, I found it easy to disregard the tourist brochure in which I had been parked.

A provisionally exempt 'reservist' determined to desert rather than be sent to Algeria, I had managed to avoid my 'military obligations' in France. They caught up with me in Cuba, wearing a different uniform. My generation knew war only through books: Sun Tzu, Clausewitz, Giap, Mao, selected quotations from Lenin. I had certainly unburdened myself in writing, like every officer-cadet of the proletariat, of my 'strategic' analysis of this and that. These flourishes cost nothing after all, why deprive oneself of them? *Dulce bellum inexpertis* . . . war is quite pretty to the scribbler. During my improvised tribulations in earlier years, my baptism of fire had been limited to one or two loud bangs in a Caracas *rancho* and a mine in Bolivia; my prison experience to a few days' incarceration in Peru ('Chemical engineer and terrorist of Czech origin', one local paper reported the next day); and my experience of secret organization to a few indiscretions on the internal squabbles of this or that movement. At 25, it was high time for me to get down to things in earnest, especially as the test of affiliation, in the cohorts of believers, distinguished the good stuff from the small beer.

After clerical ordination in France, dubbing in an order of nobility on the battlefield. With Don Quixote judging, you must shine with the lance and the sword, not with words. The rite of passage called *el entrenamiento* had been mentioned by Fidel from our first meetings as an unavoidable formality whose necessity went without saying. The training course in clandestine warfare had the double function of certificate of qualification and entry sacrament. I accepted with enthusiasm, without the slightest doubt or hesitation. I was even impatient, so keen was I to catch up with my comrades. I had had enough 'strategy' and was thirsting for tactics. I was not 'recruited', nor did I 'commit' myself. I went to the source, to the kitchens, to the place where things were being decided, wanting not so much to believe as to act, eager above all to *belong*. That is why, a month after my arrival, I changed from swimming trunks into an olive-green uniform and left the grand-hotel poolside for the open air in the mountains, with forced marches, hallucinatory thirst, black beans and sardines. What a relief! A pair of combat boots restored the morale wonderfully in five seconds flat. An hour a day of karate training restored the true and proper values. Throughout 1966 I attended my classes happily, with but a single aim: to avoid demobilization.

They took place at an open-air military academy, where physical exercise recalled Loyola's spiritual exercises in devout excess, but which otherwise had the comforting routine of a boarding school: timetables, no work on Sunday, textbooks for the different subjects and squared-paper exercise books for notes. There was *self-defence*, an assemblage of martial arts; anti-personnel *target practice* with rifle and pistol, stripping and assembly of weapons; *assassination and sabotage*; *communication* (cipher grids, radio transmission, morse); *explosives; surveillance and counter-surveillance* (clandestine methods for urban use); and lastly, *tactics*. Everyone had their favourite disciplines. A poor cook and hopeless at maths, I got bad marks in *explosives:* there were too many complicated recipes for the calculation of charges, with a lot of coefficients and variables (the calculator must have simplified things a lot since then); too many salts, powders, barbarically named combustibles. Those sessions reminded me of fourth-form 'Nat. Sciences' at school, or 'Practical Chem.', with test tubes and laboratory scales. Potassium chlorate, ammonium nitrate, fulminate of mercury, lead acid . . . a nightmare in which even slightly incorrect mixtures could give unpredictable or useless results. Is culture what remains after one has forgotten everything? After all the effort I devoted to this discipline, I remember the almond smell of C3 plastic, soft and heady as marzipan; the idea – reassuring or worrying, I am not sure which – that a bomb can be made out of absolutely anything (toys, combs, sawdust); and a few formulae graven like Alexandrines: 'Nitrates of potassium are water soluble'; 'No pyrotechnics with liquid explosive'; 'Amatolites and chloratites are more powerful than amonalites and dynamonites'. I was rounding off my humanities with new subjects just as worthless as the old ones; but when you have spent your adolescence spelling out Latin conjugations (little used in today's world), it seems just as sensible to spend six months learning how to kill your neighbour properly (or yourself for that matter, if it is permissible to discriminate between these operations). Except that one dead language is forgotten as easily as another; the adult needs to be recycled periodically.

I made up for this weakness in target practice, the idler's favourite discipline. Our armouries were a fabulous Aladdin's cave for weapon freaks. I doubt that any country in the world had such well-stocked, well-oiled and readily accessible weapon stores. From revolver to bazooka and mortar, via carbine, grenade and light machine gun, pretty well all the small arms manufactured since the beginning of the century were at our disposal, with ample stocks of ammunition. We could blast away to our heart's content with Chinese, Soviet, European and American weapons. It was staggering. Whole days spent comparing the .45 Thomson with curved handgrips (as used in *Scarface* but also by Camilo Cienfuegos) with the Czech Skorpion 7.65mm (as used by Smersh in *Dr No*), the old Springfield or Garand 30.06 from the Second World War with the modern Belgian FAL or American AR15, the classic bazooka with the Chinese RPG2, left us with bruised shoulders and blistered fingers in the evening, but also with a certain internal lightness of heart, as if all the firepower were nourishing other powers within us. Through all the time I was trekking about the province of Pinar del Río being trained for active service, the Paris Academy believed me to be a philosophy lecturer at the University of Havana; but a small blip in the National Education indices seemed a cheap price for the skills I was acquiring.

Once or twice a month, at nightfall, Fidel would take a few privileged individuals to Punto Cero. This polygon was situated not far from the central *autopista*, about 30 kilometres east of the capital, so well hidden by the surrounding hills that holidaymakers taking the highway to the beach at Varadero would not even suspect that they were passing a 'centre of international subversion' known all over the world (to intelligence services), through which, in the 1960s and 1970s, there passed thousands of aspiring guerrillas from all countries (including a lot of future ministers, senators and presidents fully, although – or rather because – belatedly, legalist). A few hundred metres inland from the picture-postcard palm-fringed shore, one entered a very different world. A few bare hillocks under a white-hot sky, the arid dunes separated by dry *ríos* choked with thorn, cactus and clumps of leafless palm. The centre of the encampment consisted of wooden huts where the classes took place: explosives, weapons, sabotage, transmissions, *chequeo* and *contra-chequeo* in urban situations. The authorities would clear the area when the commander-in-chief came late at night to discuss some point of doctrine with the associates of the moment: Major Piñeiro, head of Security and Intelligence, nicknamed Red-Beard, evasive and teasing; Vallejo, Castro's personal doctor, phlegmatic, with a long white beard; Jesús Montané, stout and silent; and Papito Sergüera, former ambassador in Algiers, the young and mercurial court jester. Attached to this nucleus would be one or two Latin Americans, usually the heads of contingents undergoing training and – in the guise of interested bystander, something between mascot and makeweight – *Debraï, el Francés*. Because I took part in the exercises of several national guerrilla groups – Dominican, Venezuelan, Guatemalan – I found myself to some extent freed from the norms of *compartimentación* (combatants from different places, sometimes different organizations of the same nationality or even different factions of the same organization, were supposed never to meet). I was thus able to meet many different groups training in different corners of the island, each awaiting its own D-day landing or infiltration on one of an endlessly rescheduled string of provisional dates. The group from Santo Domingo, which came for three months, had to wait four years before going back home, most of its members having by then drifted away in despair.

Punto Cero was where the Commander-in-Chief came to experiment with the famous *manguera*, 'the sprinkler'. It was the craze of the moment, a new type of ambush using tracer bullets and carefully timed and angled bursts: the tracer enabled the aim to be adjusted constantly by sight, combining precision with weight of fire. Fidel had had a system of winches and cables set up on a sloping bit of road (guerrillas attack vehicles from the side) to tow a high-sided GMC truck laden with dummy enemy paratroopers slowly up the incline. From a nearby hilltop we would spray this distant but acquiescent target with our folding-stock AKs when the order was given. The point of the game was that there would only be three men firing. As I had eventually learned the procedure and was not a bad shot, the *Comandante* used to include me in the trio of recumbent shooters, with himself, concentrated and didactic, in the central position. The aim would be to convince some Latin American commander – that day 'Ricardo', head of the Guerrilla Army of the Poor (EGP) in Guatemala (still active) – that it was up to him alone to get things moving. An attack of this type enabled a force in a static self-defence posture to take the offensive. Such was the rule of the *foco* drawn from experience in the Sierra Maestra, and which these modern infantry weapons made even easier and more effective. You had to be frivolous or wimpish not to take advantage of such a happy windfall.

'Today with the AK47, three men have the same firepower as a company at the beginning of the century. Unbelievable, don't you think?'

'So? What does it mean, *Comandante*?' one of us would ask obligingly, so that Fidel, doubted, could finish his demonstration.

'You dreaming or what? What it means is that three men can start a war! The inventors of these *fierros* – these tools – had no idea what the effects were going to be,' our champion would resume between bursts, while soldiers were dragging the riddled truck back to its starting point.

Jovial protests on all sides. 'You're exaggerating, *Comandante*!'

'You really think so?'

'Too good to be true!' Everyone knew what to say. Fidel would look at the second hand on his Rolex.

'In nine seconds everyone in the truck was out of action (I tried it again yesterday with my *muchachos*). Duration of a burst on full automatic: two to three seconds. Changing magazine: four seconds. Three plus four plus three, you can work it out for yourselves. First burst of thirty rounds, following the direction of travel – very important that, I insist on it, otherwise you waste half your bullets, aim at the bed, traverse forward onto the cab, then as soon as the driver's been hit go back to the bed.' He would level his AK at the truck and empty his magazine. 'At the end of those three seconds, and simultaneously, the other two open fire. The simultaneity is crucial. You, Régis, on the truck bed, full automatic; and you, Ricardo, semi-automatic, picking off anyone who manages to jump out. That last weapon stays on single-shot and covers the other two if necessary as they advance towards the truck, or what's left of it. In ten seconds you've knocked ten of them out. Right?'

Once this point was established we would move on to combinations of ambushes: the first one against the forward vanguard, which would lead to the whole column withdrawing, then a second ambush, on the way back and preferably close to the unit's base. That is the best place, when a demoralized unit is close to its barracks and relaxes its vigilance. 'You attack at night on such and such a road, two or three times. Then the enemy stops moving about at night. All right: you attack him in the daytime, when he's on foot. So then he puts his men in trucks. Fine: the *manguera*. He puts armour on the vehicles. All right: blow them up with mines. When your surprise no longer surprises, you invent another one: always take the initiative.'

These pleasures kept us entranced for long hours among dotted cascades of silvery tracer, horizontal fireworks. *Puntería* competitions, tournaments punctuated by cheers and curses which Fidel, lord of everything, felt honour bound to win. The craze that year was night shooting: weapon at the hip, both eyes open, using the luminous line of tracer to correct the aim while firing. Problem: the muzzle-flashes located the shooter. Solution: fire short bursts, keep moving. Rule: keep weapon cocked at all times, so that the click-click of the mechanism will not reveal your presence in the dark. Fragmentation grenades are more useful at night than in daylight for breaking out of an encirclement; the combatant is difficult to locate, and does not have to hit a specific target. One day, through carelessness, I discharged my weapon unintentionally, just missing the Commander-in-Chief's head. Accidental regicide . . . in the heat of action, he was not too severe with me.

It went without saying that we, the good guys, always held the high ground, and the bad guys were always at the bottoms of gorges; that they would always be uncertain while we, firm of tread and sharp of eye, with full bellies and well-stocked minds, would have all the ammunition we needed, reliable intelligence, all access routes under our control and the *guajiros* – local peasants – converted to the cause. These conditions, naturally all present since we were waging the people's war, were never questioned (anyway so long as our exercises took place in friendly, well-protected mountains).

In the Falcón during the summer of 1963, the Venezuelan guerrilla war had introduced me to a different jungle, very inhospitable in comparison with the relatively pleasant, well-ventilated forests of an island without dangerous or poisonous animals. The thirty or so guerrillas I had met there, in company with two picture men, my friends Peter Kassowitz and Christian Hirou, had to devote so much time and energy to the chores of physical survival – water, hunting, transporting food, maintaining weapons, remaining vigilant day and night – that those disease-ridden unfortunates had too little strength left even to think of fighting anyone. Worst of all, the Venezuelan army took good care not to enter that remote zone, devoid of population and economic activity, and instead simply encircled it, waiting to scoop up the game when weakness and starvation forced it to emerge from the forest. Duly reprimanded by Fidel and the veterans of the Sierra Maestra, however, I was too ready to forget these counter-indications, which they attributed to erroneous strategy and deficient leadership: not thought through, badly done. No one seemed to have noticed that the Cuban Sierra Maestra is really almost bucolic . . . a sort of

Bernardin de Saint-Pierre Arcadia freshened by breezes, where water can always be found, where there are no *cascabeles*, poisonous snakes and spiders or *goros* (clusters of maggots that grow under the skin until they burst out of your arm or buttock and fly away), populated to just the right extent, well stocked with banana and palm trees, and above all easily accessible from the second city Santiago de Cuba. The *Comandante*'s war games were a very imperfect introduction to the forests of the mainland: a viscous, barely translucent aquarium, a resistant and rubbery ether through which the guerillero had to hack a tunnel with his machete, feet cut to ribbons and bleeding, 30 kilos on his back, skinny on fewer than a thousand calories a day, rest constantly interrupted by sentry duty on the camp perimeter, sleeping in a damp hammock under a dripping nylon tarpaulin. Add dysentery, a broken ankle, a bullet in the shoulder or thigh, festering sores, no penicillin, malaria and the absence of a rear base to fall back on, and you have a fair idea of the absolute distress of the guerrillero depending on his own resources.

This preparation – similar, I imagine, to many others – was elevated by a penumbra that made it vastly superior to the course of instruction on its own. The extra prestige had something to do with the dimension of the goal – world revolution – and also with the *confidentiality* of the places and the activities. The classical and mechanical military business was here associated with what Honoré de Balzac would have called high police matters.

What would become of revolutionary warfare without disguised enemies to unmask and without agents to infiltrate? The Rebels had a talent for these cruel games imposed by circumstances, and the organization's communist culture did not curb their talent in this respect. War culture in peacetime is espionage and intelligence. The Soviet world excelled at these things. Apart from the *coman-dantes*, those privileged bearers of surnames, all my *compañeros* had first names only, and false ones at that; they had no addresses, offices or telephone numbers. Nor did they have recognizable ranks or uniforms, for in town they wore civilian clothes in any case. They were attached for administrative purposes not to *Minfar* (the armed forces) but *Minint* (the Interior Ministry). They were 'Piñeiro's men': answerable to the head of the America department and coordinator of external clandestine operations, members of the *Frente Liberación* (for in feudal circles people are not attached to a department, they belong to someone). This hermetic freemasonry, which from the inside felt like a bunch of jolly fellows, informal and relaxed (but which a Sovietologist would have stupidly seen as my 'handlers'), trained me on the job in the culture of secrecy as a constituent dimension of revolutionary societies (much as advertising is in bourgeois ones). As a general rule, secretiveness was a way of living and ruling in the Eastern bureaucratic countries, which had no official Civil Service lists (often even no telephone directories), where road maps were classified as 'confidential defence material' and all foreign newspaper correspondents regarded as thinly disguised spies. In that Southern island the old habits had acquired the force of an existential passion, full of freshness and invention.

In our democracies, espionage is held to be a necessary if rather despicable evil, and entrusted to parallel or subsidiary departments in which career prospects are far from glittering; over there it was still the grandee's profession it had been in the 19th century (and in the view of Admiral Canaris, chief of German military intelligence during the Second World War). A priesthood magnified by propaganda and entrusted to the elite of the elite. Master spies in Cuba enjoyed a high degree of social visibility. Ulbricht in East Germany did not show himself in the company of Marcus Wolf, but Fidel paraded Red-Beard about with him everywhere. There was a tacit precedence in the security services: the routine functions of counter-espionage, civically necessary though they were, had a less prestigious aura than external intelligence and action, both reserved for the first circle (as if in France the DGSE held center-stage rather than the DST, or in the US the CIA was thought more above suspicion than the FBI). Blockaded on the starting line and forced onto the defensive, the revolution takes its revenge outside, running the blockade with clandestine exports. Whether counter-offensive or *fuite en avant*, salvation would come through taking the enemy in the rear, multiplying the seeds of revolution in his continental hinterlands. Tiresome and monotonous though this sector of activity is (much waiting, little action), the services we regard as parallel, but which in Cuba were then central, combined every possible advantage: a paranoia that was not just legitimate but approved and functional, the excitement of danger, the Jansenist pleasure of anonymity, the immunity conferred by oral culture (no written orders and an absolute minimum of records), and the exclusivity of a caste little inclined by nature, East or West, to succumb to democratic temptations.

In a religion centred on mysteries, the real hierarchies are for initiates only. From the Commander-in-Chief (whose private domain covered the US and Latin America) down to the most lowly security officer masquerading as a commercial attaché in some remote embassy, by way of the tight-lipped praetorians of the *escolta*, their eyes shining with pride at belonging to the impenetrable and much-envied Areopagus of those who, for eight hours a day or one day in three, could feast their eyes on the Supreme Being and even, sometimes, know where he was going to be in an hour's time. Membership of the concentric circles of the conspiracy, a completely different matter from our offhand 'corridors of power' and knowing what is 'behind the scenery', divided the dignitaries, the greater or lesser importance of their visible level measuring each individual's share of power. The withholding of information thus structured each level of man's dominion over man, imprisoning political life (if it can be called that) in a vicious circle that seemed from the top to be virtue itself (anyone thinking it vicious being 'counter-revolutionary'): since being at the top meant knowing what was going on, how could those who, being at the bottom, knew nothing (the official channels of information informing no one of anything) hold to account those who knew everything? How could an alternation of power be proposed, since it would mean either revealing the secrets held by the chiefs, thus betraying the country, or groping blindly in the dark, thus betraying it in another way? For the rest, to inform is to share, in other words to cut oneself off: Fidel compartmentalized on a large scale and in detail. And thousands of small Fidels repeated the game on every step of the ladder, dissimulation on orders from above reproducing the pyramid in every civil ministry, production centre, regiment, institute, writer's union, neighbourhood and individual life.

The word *nomenklatura* was not yet in use; we used the term *el aparato* as a generic term for members of the intermingled State, Party and Security apparatuses. It was to the last of these that I was connected, along with several hunded Latin Americans all on the point of departure. For was I not, as Piñeiro told me one day with a glint of irony in the depths of his eye, a 'strategic cadre of the revolution'? Someone else to protect, to watch, wear out and look after. These gymnastics in various combinations informed the parallel lives led by the former and future combatants scattered through the four corners of the town.

Even after leaving the hotel for various *casas operativas* I did not have to do my own shopping, let alone queue for anything. House workers – soldiers in mufti – discreetly attended to these needs, and the 'personnel security' department of the Interior Ministry twice a week sent a van and uniformed crew to deliver the necessary supplies in big kraft-paper sacks. We did not even have to go to the shop reserved for diplomats. The refrigerator filled up all by itself. If we fell ill we went to a clinic, the equivalent of the Val-de-Grâce[4] in France, but not open to allcomers. Even a masochistic reading of the daily paper *Granma* was unnecessary: every evening I received a duplicated bulletin entitled *Panorama Mundial*, a few stapled pages of articles from the American press and international news agencies. And when one visited a member of the Politburo or a comandante in good standing, what joy it was to get one's teeth into the real stuff, the raw wads of AFP, UPI and AP telexes reserved for the top level (of course in Europe absolutely anyone working for the government reads such material every day).

Gradually, I was infected by the prevailing neuroses, suspicion disorder and interpretation mania. Embraced by both extremes, left and right, the police vision of the world is a powerful hallucinogen that gives its addicts the blessings of coherence and the meticulous joys of verification: the paranoiac's two great advantages over ordinary mortals. It didn't matter much that one had got the general picture 'all wrong', if each detail seemed to confirm its overall soundness. Pierre Goldman, on returning to France from Venezuela, was to botch his detoxification cure for lack of time. My own took a good ten years. Habituation to police counter-surveillance hallucinates an agent in every insignificant passerby, sticks a double meaning into the most anodyne enquiry and reads 'disinformation' by 'media assets' into inside-page filler items. The dosage goes up bit by bit to avoid withdrawal symptoms. Seen from Havana, two out of three sociologists and eight out of ten journalists anywhere in Latin America, from whatever country, were either camouflaged enemies or false friends (Soviet for example). Not counting diplomatic personnel, international officials and businessmen passing through the island, all (rather reassuringly) agents by definition. Foreign authors guilty of writing critical books or articles on the revolution were immediately disqualified with an embarrassing secret that rendered their venom harmless, since such pathetic gents could only put out infamies. As a general rule, every dissident was 'a CIA agent' just as Achilles was fleet-footed and Athena had grey eyes. The epithet alone sufficed for the official press and official circles. As for the more exacting 'organs', when a new suspect entered their optical field the only point that merited discussion was the identity of the foreign security service for which the newcomer worked; presently a decision would arrive from on high, as peremptory as it was unexplained; uncheckable, like all rumours, it immediately allayed anxieties. Once the man of mystery had been labelled (CIA, Intelligence Service, SDECE, etc.) he ceased to be of interest; everything was in order, of course the imperialist hydra was many-headed; who's next? It went without saying that we were the delegates of Good on earth, but what I find astonishing today is our vision of the forces of Evil as a centralized, monolithic organization endowed with implacable coherence in every corner of the globe. Imperialism was a cynical planetary conspiracy striving day and night to manipulate, intoxicate, infiltrate and corrupt the weaker and more naive of the Just. When twenty years later (particularly as secretary of the South Pacific Council, where nuclear matters were of central importance) I had some dealings in France with those services known as 'special' to deflect generalization, I discovered a state of mind every bit as sincere and justified (spiders' webs, nests of vipers, Bulgarian umbrellas) on the 'good side', but the other way round, with misdeeds becoming exploits and traitors heroes. Communism was profiled in Parisian remarks and service notes as something repulsive lurking in the shadows, sneaking forward everywhere with moles and tentacles to manipulate, intoxicate, etc., etc. Even in France, a quick skim through the memoirs of the watchers of the Christian West's ramparts will convince you that the best distributed thing in the world is not common sense but paranoia, cutting across regimes and credos. Reciprocal satanization between East and West has kept hundreds of thousands of officials in work for forty years. Every service, on both sides of the Iron Curtain, and with the same pathetic indignation, supplied the sceptic with material proofs of the other side's infamy. Each had a museum of diabolically ingenious horrors from the other side: sophisticated listening devices, booby traps, fragments of spy planes, microfilms, miniature transmitters, plus a hundred documented cases of unmasked moles, shameless acts of blackmail, turned double and triple agents, and so on. In 1966, an hour's conversation with Manuel Piñeiro was enough to convince me that Evil was tirelessly on the prowl; exactly the same thing happened in the opposite direction in 1986 with the head of the DGSE. Doubtless they were both right. There is nothing so like a KGB as a CIA, and vice versa. Their common professional deformity is a despairing rationalism, paradoxically reminiscent of primitive thought in its intractable coherence and insistence that everything is a sign of something else. For adepts of the Great Game nothing is fortuitous, and there is no free will. Man is anything but the subject of his acts; an agent or acted upon, manipulator or manipulated, player or played, but never himself, stupidly and simply. Master spies have in common with magicians and sorcerers their ignorance of chance, which governs small things, and necessity, which governs great ones. A happy ignorance, which prevents them from recognizing the ultimate uselessness of their over-meticulous scaffoldings and throwing in the towel.

Individually and as a group, the *compañeros del aparato* seemed rather less like 'specialized idiots' than their Western equivalents, when I got to know them later. Strangely, the more fanatical individuals are not the ones you would expect. Our own military might have envied their political culture, their joviality and their freedom of tone. Trained on the job in the struggle against Batista, those super-sharp, motivated Latinos bore, I imagine, a closer resemblance to our Resistance agents than the career officers to whom the French Republic obstinately insists on entrusting responsibilities of that sort (preferring no doubt a narrow but predictable approach to more penetrating but less disciplined and 'secure' civilian intelligences). The Cubans were curious about the 'other side', read John Le Carré and Gilles Perrault, took an interest in their opposite numbers. They seemed less exposed to vanity. Doubtless these temptations are reduced in a 'closed society', while these days our own shadow warriors publish their memoirs and become celebrities as soon as they are sacked. The videosphere feeds and encourages indiscretion and exhibitionism, even in the people who should be least liable to these things. Socially, however, the Western way of going about it offers an infinitely superior collective solution. It relegates these neurotic efforts to the margins, but compensates for them, in full, with a superabundance of works of fiction. In this way our societies vaccinate themselves against a demonology as dreary as it is unproductive, and prevent the occultist passion from getting out of hand. Films, TV series and novels about spies and spying purge us ironically, along well-tried lines of aesthetic catharsis, of our paranoid and fabulating impulses; while in 'socialist countries' these drives were encouraged, officialized and taught to every citizen as a patriotic duty. It shows republican wisdom to relegate us to the margins, in remote places and during what are rightly called periods of 'emergency'. Venerable and Roman wisdom, for even in a city as gifted for war as Rome, the temple of Mars was situated outside the sacred enclosure of the Eternal City so that it would not be defiled, and the *imperium militiae* ended when the Consul returned from his campaign.

Like sexual obsession and cinema attendance, interest in intelligence matters diminishes with age. I was too exhausted, on my return to France, to turn the mania on its head, like those former communists who replaced the imperialist hydra with the totalitarian octopus. That obsessional figure, the Stalinist neo-liberal, was by then playing a dynamic role in journalism and on the political fringes. Somewhat half-heartedly, I chose to change my coat rather than turning it. A president of the republic who was once interior minister can ask the parallel agencies to do him the odd small favour where internal matters are concerned. But with external affairs (the only interesting ones to my amateur eyes), the rather depressing material in those black boxes is simply the product of sound administrative practice, and gets only wavering attention from decision-makers; any scum or froth from abroad is recycled into concocted novels or heavily edited scandal. Even Malraux succumbs to this rule in *Les Chênes qu'on abat*, when talking about Guevara during an imaginary conversation with de Gaulle.

'He was in the maquis with his Russo-Argentinian mistress, a Russian agent, who was said to have betrayed him?'

'But it wasn't true.'

'But it wasn't true. She had been urging him constantly to organize saboteurs in the mines, and to favour them over the villages which were more or less saturated by the American services. But he had his memories of Cuba, his Maoist illusions . . . thanks to that woman, and only because of her, the Russian services managed to protect him for a few months. Then she took five bullets in the belly during an engagement in the bush, she died, and he was given up eleven days later.'

This is almost all wrong. Tania was certainly not Che's mistress (he was quite happy to do without); she was not Russian but East German, born in Argentina. An interpreter in Cuba, she was recruited there and posted to La Paz as a 'sleeper' agent; she would not have gone anywhere near the tin mines; she was killed forty days before Che, with Joaquim's rearguard, in an ambush while crossing a river; Che no longer had any Maoist illusions since his visit to Peking, where he had been shown through a sheet of glass a living Buddha named Mao; James Bond and Felix Leiter would have found it difficult to pass unnoticed in the remote hamlets of Valle Grande, populated by frightened illiterate Guaranis who could hardly speak Spanish; and it is diffiult to see how the Russian services, whose most pressing concerns did not include the Indians of the Chaco, would have been able to protect someone whom the local communist leadership and their own political authorities in Moscow rather wanted to torpedo. But never mind: it all helps 'fill out the picture'. The only virtue required of the teller: firm resolve in ignoring maps and dates. Cavalier behaviour permitted in a virtuoso of bluff able, like the super-lucid Malraux, to reconstitute the real through the imaginary (even if in this case his myth-making brilliance gets a bit off track). The more mainstream bullshit that fills the kiosks and bookshops has swamped our capacity for astonishment.

The Cuban case was notably preferable to the European ones in its lack of hypocrisy. Cuba practised its military values decently and directly, without needing a Ministry of Truth blazoned with the words 'War is Peace' like the one in George Orwell's *1984*. That warlike socialism curled its lip at Peace Movement soppiness, 'sincere democrats and people of goodwill', Muscovite *mir i droujba* (peace and friendship) lullabies, youth hostel posters of handsome boys and girls trekking round the globe with red scarves and knapsacks. By putting the professionals of violence in the front rank that proto-communism, not yet labelled, had proudly and naively assumed the role of midwife of History. Our consumer societies play war down. Societies of force, however weak they actually are, played it up. Without becoming aware of its limitations. French-style Jacobinism peaks during mass uprisings and when the country is under threat, but it can outlive these events in less alarming forms (educational *battles*, a Plan called '*burning* obligation', an *energetic* reform of credit policy, etc.). Pacifist though its presentation – or rather disguise always was, the red star has become steadily more peaceful. Belligerence used to be consubstantial with it, the term 'war communism' almost a tautology: it was born out of war (international and civil, one after the other), perpetuated it, suffered from it and revelled in it. Partisan struggle or total war, conventional contest or insurrection, deep down that system did not know how to do anything else: not even fascism did it as well. Almost everywhere, except in Afghanistan, communism won the war and lost the peace; won the war of tanks and spies, lost the one of blue jeans, consumer electronics, rock, movies and stars. Its history even inside Europe speaks for – or against – its origins: born out of the entrails of the First World War, wilted between the wars, glittered once again at Stalingrad and in various *maquis*, became bloated in the aftermath of the Second World War, died of peace. In our collective memory, the International Brigades efface the Moscow trials and the heroism of the Red Army the Ribbentrop-Molotov pact, just as in France Fabien and l'Affiche rouge erased the desertions and compromises of 1940. In the French militant's imagination Tillon and Môquet absolve Thorez and Marchais, the maquis makes up for apparatchiks. The best militants came into the French and Italian parties during the Resistance and left them afterwards. Mauthausen and Buchenwald tipped some former democratic deportees, like Pierre Daix, into Stalinism; many other passive resistants or prisoners, like Althusser back from the Stalag, subsequently rejoined the Party because they felt its members knew something that so many others seemed to have unlearned: how to face death. Respect for the communist individual (which did not necessarily exclude a reasoned hostility to the system itself) faded gradually as memories of the world war hardened into scar tissue. So did our retrospective consideration for 'the great Soviet people'. In a Paris cinema in 1995, the audience of twenty-somethings let out a guffaw during the final scene of Spielberg's *Schindler's List* (in which a Red Army officer on a horse is greeted as a saviour by imprisoned Jews). My neighbours thought it a director's gag, to lower the tension. In 1945 French youngsters would have found the scene's allusive discretion suspect. Perhaps one day a balanced middle view will prevail in dispassionate minds.

In his war diary Ernst Jünger, after watching Céline besiege the German Embassy in Paris for permits and safe conducts in the spring of 1944, observed that it is 'curious to see how very deeply creatures capable of coolly demanding the heads of millions of human beings care about their own filthy little lives'. The barons and dukes of 'Patria o Muerte' weren't like that. They required themselves to practise what they preached. Counting majors (*comandantes*), captains and lieutenants (the only three commissioned ranks in the early days of the rebel army), nearly five hundred officers who believed in total war perished discreetly on 'international missions', the first in Santo Domingo in 1959. Then in Nicaragua, Venezuela, Grenada, Argentina, Bolivia, Chile and Guatemala. Only the Colombian guerrillas resisted this invasive fraternity by closing their ranks (especially their upper ranks) to all Cuban interference. In Africa on the other hand, after Guevara's disastrous escapade in the Congo, Cuba used conventionally equipped regular units. Up to a hundred and fifty thousand Cubans were sent to Angola in successive contingents, whether they liked it or not: they were officially described as 'volunteers', but anyone attempting to refuse was severely sanctioned.

In the 1960s Cubans *were* volunteers, so much so that they did not bother to use the word, and competed to be sent into countries where nothing – and usually nobody – really required their presence. Now the gift of the self has slipped from Marx to Allah, from Hanoi and Havana to Teheran and Algiers. We use the word 'fanaticism' to designate an unthinking devotion, causing the individual to risk his own and other lives for reasons other than the usual ones (defence of national frontiers and vital interests) without a view to profit (as with mercenaries or 'dogs of war'). What then is the difference between believers in 'Patria o Muerte' and 'God's madmen'? Their bearing, in the first place: pursuit of rum and girls; banter and joviality. That made a very marked contrast with the emaciated and pallid Afghans I was able to meet twenty years later on the Pakistan frontier, rigid medieval figures then wearing the glittering apparel of 'freedom fighters' in which the unanimous West – media, secret services and French intelligentsia in particular – had decided to drape those valiant obscurantists. The contrast between their states of mind is just as great. Those detached agnostics, Christians despite themselves, believed themselves to be unbelievers. The martyr who gives his life for Allah or Christ profits on the deal: he goes from purgatory to paradise. The suicide-bomber's death at the hands of the Infidel will hasten his felicity by delivering his soul from a calamitous body. But what about a secular Jihad? What possible interest can a materialist have in the Void? A gallant hero headed for legend – like Guevara – can hope to stay alive in the heart of a people, the only sort of eternal life that an unbeliever can dream of. But what about the clandestine combatant who lands on a remote beach with false papers in an undeclared war? I am thinking in particular of Tito Briónes (with whom I was trained), first head of special forces, killed on a Venezuelan beach in 1967. Or Demetrio Escalona, who accompanied Camaño to Santo Domingo in 1972. No posthumous reward for him: his government will disown him to avoid retaliation, and the local resistance (even if it knows who he is) will do the same, out of pride and organizational rivalry. Feudal death without the metaphysics of feudalism: only a very specific historical culture could understand that enigma.

It was a piece of good luck for Fidel Castro's regime that the American 'embargo', against which it nevertheless protested (and rightly so), came from outside to replace the more or less overt war of the 'years of lead'. Imperial imbecility thus enabled it, after the end of the Cold War, to stave off the peaceful coexistence and free trade which it would not have been able to survive. The state of siege was and remained to the very end the oxygen that kept it alive.

So what had I come to *do*, several light-years from my own patch?

Do? The question is too orthodox. It pushes away and reflects a less admissible worry: like *whom*? Which predecessor would I most like to resemble? No political treatise can help us answer these more pertinent and less frivolous questions, for each answer is a novel that no one else can write for us. Or rather it is engraved in us willy-nilly, from snippets some of which are unlooked-for, diverse anecdotes, film clips drifting across the retina. A deeply buried collage that, even if we managed the impossible and completed it, would still be meaningless to everyone else and arrive too late. When we did manage to finish the job, to recompose without false modesty our favoured type of ego, all became clear: we were not going to be the person we had dreamed of being. We were going to be much less, completely different or even the opposite. The metamorphosing insect that is a young man with a plan differs from caterpillars in that he almost never attains his adult butterfly form, what entomologists call the *imago*. Not that I had a particularly elevated image of myself: I magnified my comrades, our tasks and the era. Perhaps it is part of the human condition, the need to imagine great avenues before risking a few short steps.

If being great means 'espousing a great cause', average-sized people usually need some kind of boost. You had to get a bit worked up to believe that a handful of clowns with Kalashnikovs were going to 'make revolution'. But everyone *did* believe it, friends and enemies both. The spectre that had deserted Europe and was now running down the Andes befogged perceptions enough to prevent our manpower and equipment, supposedly capable of 'liberating' a continent, being accurately gauged. Anywhere else the project would have looked like presumption, but Latino history does not follow the usual norms; in those parts a handful of intrepid madmen can overturn the table. In Mexico in 1956 Fidel was planning to land in Cuba with 300 men; at the end of the year he arrived there with eighty-two; after a week there were twelve left standing, only seven with weapons. The first attack on a garrison was carried out by thirty guerrillas. After sixteen months there were 140 rebels. Eight hundred landed on the island at the end of 1958, and the rebel army that entered Havana numbered fewer than 3,000 men (1,500 recruited in the last month).

It was the usual microscopic military scale of the *Libertadores*. A lawyer had seized a country of 7,000,000 inhabitants with a force of company strength; the cavalryman Bolivar had taken a continent of 30,000,000 with a regiment. So was everything 'on the mysterious borders of the Western world' just a matter of will and tactics? Not everything, but a lot. From the *Conquista* to the new Zapatistas, this disproportion (between small causes and great effects) has been a constant in the West Indies. With 600 men and sixteen horses, Cortés smashed not just an empire but a whole civilization; with 180 men and thirty-seven horses, Pizarro broke the Inca pyramid by decapitating it; and Bolívar, with a handful of Englishmen and ragamuffins from the banks of the Orinoco, destroyed the oldest colonial empire in the world. Speed and mystique make up the deficiency in social and material resources. All the way from 1520 to 1960, this chaotic history displays the same sort of imbalance between the *de facto* subject and the subject by right of social upheaval; between the 'vanguard' and the 'masses'; between small cause and great effect. It would not be unreasonable to call Macondo politics *the art of the impossible*. In the long term, a lot of these countries give the impression that they advance in jerks, impulsive voluntarist leaps interspersed with long periods of somnolence; a handful of gifted children is enough to shake them out of this torpor from time to time (as recently in Mexico).

I had no intention of applying myself to catechesis, or taking up the pen as a weapon (like a good intellectual). I had no urge to convince: I was quite content to vanquish. It never occurred to me to teach in Party schools, to ponder the articles in *Granma* – the local *Pravda* – or sing the praises of the Leader. I dreamed of being a *franc-tireur* of the shadows, ink and blood, machine gun in one hand and typewriter in the other. I saw myself as one of the *missi dominici* of the Centre, an envoy of Central HQ vaulting from maquis to maquis and capital to capital. An 'Eye of Havana', along the same lines as the 'Eyes of Moscow' in Paris, Madrid and Berlin between the wars (the Swiss citizen Humbert-Droz, the Czech Fried, the Italian Togliatti). Agents gain from being foreign to the countries where they operate: their gaze is more objective, their relationships more impartial. I thus identified with the pre-war 'professional revolutionary', an outmoded idealized type more in keeping with *Mitteleuropa* than the Caribbean sea. That nomadic irregular, doomed to self-denial, switching between Underwood and 9mm automatic, had none of the panache, the tempestuous, strutting style that makes an 'insurgent' or 'rebel' remind us of a theatrical Hernani (although the Andes and the Sierra Madre make much more suggestive backdrops than Brussels and Berlin). The truth is that the introverts of the graphosphere, not raised in the restless channel-zapping videospheres, identified more willingly with personalities from the past, expanded by exegeses and the thesaurus, than with contemporary figures, devoid of biography and of very unstable repute.

Whom did I want to resemble, exactly? A sort of cross between Serge and Sorge. The first a printer's proofreader, the second a journalist. I saw myself in Havana at the Second Congress of the Communist International, welcoming as the author of *What Every Revolutionary Should Know About Repression* the American John Reed, the Frenchmen Alfred Rosmer and Raymond Lefebvre, the Dutchman Sneevliet, the Indian Roy (founder of the Mexican Communist Party) and the Hungarian Béla Kun. I privately renamed the Habana Libre hotel the Hotel Lux. I superimposed the stucco pillars and gilded panelling of the Taurida Palace on the plain pilasters of the Chaplin Theatre in Havana where the closing session of the Tricontinental was held. Bukharin, Zinoviev and Radek were on the platform, in olive-green uniforms, speaking Spanish; but the floor spoke five or six languages, and I zigzagged about there, a benevolent polyglot. I had been born in Brussels in 1890 to Russian parents; I had been imprisoned in the Santé for complicity with Bonnot's gang; soon I would be going not to Berlin but Caracas, as underground correspondent of a new *Inprekor*, monthly bulletin of the Bolshevik International. This time – an improvement – I would escape the GPU, and Romain Rolland would not have to twist Stalin's arm to get me freed, just after the international Congress for the Defence of Culture (Paris, 1935). Victor, the Russo-Belgian writer and member of the left opposition, died in Mexico in 1947, quietly; Richard, the German organizer of the Soviet network in Shanghai and Tokyo, had already been hanged by the Japanese in 1944, gloriously. My dream-pastiche combined high Trotskyist morality with *Reader's Digest* glamour ('Spy of the Century'). An ideal compromise formula, because an agent in wartime, unlike the permanent station chief of peaceful periods, is protected fom the facile disillusion of the moralist by the detailed and demanding activities of clandestinity. I would thus retain dual membership of the European Republic of Letters and the Secret Agents' International, agent librarian in charge of armoury liaison. Something between courier and officer, a sort of insubstantial and immortal elf. Despite the labels that set them against each other like dog and cat, the 'professional revolutionary' (black stare, hairy virility, petrol bombs under his coat, perpetual wandering) and the 'man of letters' (velvety gaze, feminine hands, dressing gown, sedentary gentleness) have patrolled the same zones of the mind, even the same parts of town: Lenin in Zurich in 1916 lived next door to the Cabaret Voltaire, the cradle of Dada, where he chatted one day with Tristan Tzara. Not far away lived James Joyce and Romain Rolland. 'Man of letters' is what Lenin wrote in the profession box on his application form for the 1919 Bolshevik Party Congress. He played chess with Gorki, as Trotsky used to converse as an equal with Diego Rivera or André Breton. Revolutionary and littérateur, angora poodle and pit-bull, two animals from the same urban fauna, the same condominium, both soon to find themselves without a billet (the cathode ray tube and the devaluation of politics making two has-beens at a stroke).

The clerical irregular belonged to a disciplined and hierarchized Order, and lived as the recluse whose spectacles, thinness and absent-minded air he often had. When he met Victor Serge in 1941 on the cargo ship taking them both from Marseilles to America, Lévi-Strauss found him 'an old maid with principles'. The old inmate of prisons in France, Spain and Russia, the ex-anarchist who had rallied to Lenin in 1917, the intractable opponent of Stalin hunted by police of every shade – red, brown and tricolour – projected the asexual image of a Buddhist monk. Our habit of envisaging the revolutionary as a wonderful marginal character living in a grand manner, half Sergio Leone and half André Malraux, ignores the fact that for a whole century social subversion was pivoted on devotees of order, obsessional and scrupulous. Keen to pass unnoticed, protective of their anonymity, devoting body and soul to the future. I do not know whether this psycho-historical type was driven, as one Nietzschean asserted, by resentment and hatred of life. Having met a number of examples from different tendencies and nationalities (Trotskyist, anarchist and communist), my impression is that this monastic pilgrim, rigid and rigorous, the absolute opposite of the 'figurehead', scorned braggarts and extremists and preferred a studious semi-darkness, even a measure of prudery, to the disorder of an egocentric and dionysiac bohemianism.

What gives this revolutionary counter-society such a superannuated outline is the confusion that the videosphere has introduced into our minds between the modern firebrand's taste for being seen and the culture of mystery that then surrounded subversive activities. In the period after October 1917 there were as few cinemas as there were dark glasses. Apart from Chaplin and Emil Jannings, silent cinema produced no stars; actors were to be seen only at the opera and the theatre, elite spectacles. Between the exuberant, provocative post-1968 agitator of the Jerry Rubin or Eldridge Cleaver type and those methodical monomaniacs, thirsty for learning and incapable of self-advertisement, who served as the anonymous armature of Stalinism and Trotskyism (those brother enemies), the gap is as great as between the Red Cross of 1930 and the 'charity business' of 1980 (the star of 'international terrorism' under this comparison having the same relationship to the old 'agent of Moscow' as the champion of humanitarian action to a Swiss stretcher-bearer). The same chronological and moral gap separates the cult of the Book from the cult of the Image, and movable lead type from the electronic press. My rather unsmart prototypes, those transnational 'cadres' who fell by the wayside, murdered by Stalin for the most part, hardly went to the cinema, I imagine, or anyway not enough. Those over-disiplined solitaries managed to leave names in the records but no faces: the Borodins, Ignace Reiss, Pianitsky, Willy Münzenberg, Koltsov, Hans Beimler, the head of the Thaelman battalion in Spain, Artur London, and so many others unknown to the general public, whom I had come across here and there in memoirs or footnotes. I consoled myself for their evanescence, those grey stars of red legend, by promising them a long and triumphant posterity.

'The more they talk about me the better,' the left-terrorist superstar 'Carlos' is said to have remarked one day. 'It makes me seem more dangerous.' Whether or not the remark was really made, that sort of swank would have been seen as vulgar in our circle, where a certain incognito-snobbery prevailed. Joining the Revolution meant taking vows of obscurity, poverty and obedience (not chastity). The most admired among us were the ones who were least talked about, or who had the most unappealing air. With his genius for publicity Fidel concentrated all the floodlights on himself, wiping out to his own profit any passing desire to figure that might be present among his supporters. Or could each of the majors have understood that evil might befall him if he looked like treading on the heels of the *Líder Máximo*? The first circle liked to lurk behind shutters and spot spotlights. But only the elite of the elite had access to the *ne plus ultra* of disfigurement by Ramiro Valdes's team of technical specialists, attached to the Ministry of the Interior. One of these, Che, when he finished his training in the hacienda he had been lent, returned to Havana to say goodbye to his children, utterly unrecognizable, and was told by his small daughter Aleidita that she would forgive him for the impertinence of taking her on his knee 'because he had an Argentinian accent like her Daddy'. The New Man was not identifiable by mugshot. The gentlemen of the anterooms did not seek to shine by making a stir but by the stealth of a *perinde ac cadaver*. With his official resignation and secret departure for Tanzania in March 1965, had not Che, *deus absconditus*, ensured his pre-eminence purely and simply by becoming invisible?

Fortunately, the personality cult around Fidel supplied everyone with narcissistic reassurances. This is characteristic of entourages which to differing extents have the art of sharing the chief's body, reflected as it is by 'doubles' and ventriloquists. Even at some distance from the hall of mirrors at Court, the 'men in the shadows' benefit from a reflection of a reflection that confers a sort of celebrity by procurement (whether in the Caribbean around a *Jefe* or in France around a president). The believer loves the chief as he loves himself, as we devour him with our eyes. We expect this long-distance ingestion to lead us into adopting his tone of voice, grafting onto our own bodies his gestures, his wrinkles, his way of going about things. I have witnessed the mimetic mastication of the same flesh by a thousand mouths, a thousand avid stares engendering (in Paris as well as Havana), in a miracle of loving cannibalism, hundreds of *comandantes* (and later, presidents), minor echoes of the original, surrounding him in concentric circles like the ranks of angels, all with similar faces, that surround the figure of the Father in some Flemish altarpiece. In the same way, more dangerously, from top to bottom of a Nazi Germany transformed into an entourage-population, were born millions of little *Führers*. Power, an optically (not sexually) transmitted disease, thus gives rise to imitative epidemics propagated from a central source, the Beloved.

Discretion, exhibitionism, it's all a question of surroundings. Just as the same personal temperament can be used by two different societies or one society at two different times to fulfil opposing functions – spiritual rumination or general insurrection – the same sort of conduct can have opposite meanings depending on the environment in which an interest is taken in glory. This chameleon has seen other environments. To speak plainly: this . . . specimen effaced himself when he was over there, but back here he's aiming the spotlights. A matter of ecosystem: in underground warfare, obscurity was the sign of power; in the society of spectacle, an individual's power is gauged by his social visibility. And when he declares, this . . . animal, that he feels more at home in one slot than the other, that he's better suited to ivory towers than the back of beyond, it should be borne in mind that some kinds of ambition take more pleasure in devotion than in demagogy. I urge you, ladies and gentlemen of the jury, not to be swayed by the slanted presentations of the accused . . .

To representatives of the 'politico-military vanguard', the pitfalls of ubiquitous *amour-propre* are backed by specifically sociological suspicions. Any chronicler of 'intellectual socialism' will have discerned here a case – one among many – of foxy greed in the general style of 'celestial bureaucrat-to-be'. Disenchanted charges, a well-known theory:

The socialist movement, sheltering behind the formal invocation of the proletariat, represents the material interests of a distinct social category of the working class, the intelligentsia, *which appeared in the nineteenth century with the democratization of education systems. The slogan 'power to the workers' in reality concealed the ferocious appetite for dominance of a stratum of 'declassés' (frustrated, dissatisfied, embittered), to whom the traditional order did not offer the sort of opportunities they aspired to. This individual is a typical upstart 'proletarianoid intellectual', yet another anti-bourgeois bourgeois, a failure given over to Bovaryism, using the anti-colonial uprising as a stepping-stone in a non-career juicier, in fact, than a run-of-the-mill careerism. For is it not the case that what remains of immaterial supremacy in a material world has devolved on the knight of the Just Cause? On the professional revolutionary 'armed with the scientific theory of History', who went abroad to give the toiling classes the consciousness they lacked? On a future State parasite, roosting for life on a more or less faked past as a combatant? This is the hothead who says he's ready to sacrifice himself for a better world. Don't believe a word of it: he wants to make himself feel better and avoid having to learn an honest trade. Don't go confusing love of the poor with an eldest son's self-hatred. The worst sort of egotism masquerades as altruism . . .*

These sarcasms would be completely out of place in the grip of *force majeure*, when foreign occupation, the abdication of a republic transformed into a 'French state', had encroached on the existential by coming and laying hands on you in your own house. No one would accuse those who joined the European Resistance in 1941 of anything like that: they were members because the situation was beyond urgency. But what motivates a foreign volunteer not driven by disaster, and who does not want to work solo, independently of hierarchy and framework? Because the awful thing is that I longed to be an organized, disciplined militant, not an adventurer, a free electron exploiting others to get drunk on himself. Colonel Lawrence, that superior being and peerless writer, was beyond my means; I had fallen back on a Latino-Kominternian remake more manageable in scale. But what were my real relations with the massacred of Latin America? With these plans to land in remote places, for stakes which could only be imaginary to an outsider? The sour and mildewy odour of poverty did not cling to my skin. A few weeks in a tin mine near Oruro in Bolivia, *Germinal*-style; a few chats with the peons in Ecuadorian banana plantations; contacts with one or two Chilean trade unionists in Santiago. On the whole I had had dealings only with 'cadres': permanent officials or grass-roots leaders.

The prosecution can produce another piece of evidence for the 'people's cause versus need to seem interesting' file: our official credo. We thought ourselves a bit too Leninist to make real Marxists. To be obsessed with politics is to forsake society. The revolution, without people. The state, without life: the common vice of the Jacobin. To this passive quality should be added an exaggerated sense of organization. The organizational diagram is the courtesy of command; like saying 'coordinate' for 'subordinate'. The optimum was to organize others, thus preventing them from organizing you first. Communist culture had turned this immemorial art into a second nature. 'Proletarian internationalism' meant subordinating the part to the whole, itself represented by a centre, Moscow as it happened, which had the sole right to specify what 'the permanent and general interests of the movement' were. Peking had rebelled, and from 1958 staked its own clear claim to universal doctrinal authority.

It was a long way, the accused did not speak Chinese, and Mao was more inaccessible than the Buddha. By a stroke of luck, however, he got another chance thanks to Ben Barka and his Cairo friends. Alienated by the extremist and excessively ethnocentric views of the Middle Kingdom, the Third World in 1965 had located its Rome in Havana by moving the headquarters of its representative institutions there. No matter: the accused discarded two of the five continents. The Tricontinental had not really come to grips with the African movements, seen as too chaotic, or the Asian ones, given the Chinese overlord jealously watching over its fields. So be it: Latin America alone would have to do, one misery, twenty-five countries. Deciding that that would be the epicentre, our armchair Bismarck associated himself with its 'Command Centre', Havana, believing that this would catapult him into the heart of things. Thus, to the hallucinatory satisfaction of making History instead of writing about it after the event, was added the presumption that give wings to the timorous: at centre stage, against a backdrop of very real miseries, happy with the worst provided he was given a part in the film . . .

For the time being, I had been tried out by being taught how to fire six linked packs of plastic with a single detonator to destroy a bridge in a hurry. I might not really ever have to use this skill, but acquiring it was more entertaining in any case than spelling out the table of Kantian categories to the final year of the lycée Jeanne-d'Arc in Nancy. Better to learn something new than run down your stocks. Quite apart from the benefits of continuous education, had I not in the final analysis made a sound *calculation*?

A matter of intent? No, of *fait accompli*, the proof being that I came back from it. No one can call you in for questioning when you are dead at the bottom of a ravine. Having saved my bacon, along with my name and career, I should have expected François de la Rochefoucauld (1630–80), author of the *Maxims*, to point a morose index finger at me. What could I say to that prosecutor of my sleepless nights? Of all possible tirades, this is the one I would risk:

> *Dear Duke, you reduce the whole world to the Court because your party, the Fronde, lost. Out of resentment. Under your razor, 'amour-propre', all our actions are worth the same and none is worthless. I can see quite clearly what lies behind your poisonous nihilism: you want to devalue human nature on its own in order to enthrone grace and lead those disheartened by Versailles back to the altar. But three centuries have passed, and God has his absences. Today we have to make do with the only available forces: our own. We may be apes, I agree; but do not conclude from that, dear courtier colleague, that we all play the same tune, and it sounds wrong. Mine does, perhaps. But I have heard enough cavatinas that make a man weep with happiness to know that apes are not devoid of intelligence. All right: all our virtues are 'disguised vices'. All except one: courage, which cannot be counterfeited. You who first took up arms at 16, you had plenty. I have less, but I have with my own eyes seen men of valour in action: in Venezuela, in Bolivia, in Cuba and even in France. Enough to know that a political education is not a moral treatise but a play without a text, improvised to fit against an opening backdrop, in which every walk-on character deserves a specific maxim to himself; and that a moralist from the* Grand Siècle, *or a Cioran from our own century, should leave his door ajar for the unexpected sincerities that will prove the rule and impose if not respect, then a measure of uncertainty. An 'all self-interested' that makes a desert around itself in advance seems to me a system of explanation as coarse and limited as the 'all on the take' you hear in the pub. Demagogy and old France both: a bit much, admit it.*

I don the toga to put people off the scent, but at one time I could be candid and naively unselfish. There was nothing calculated about my adhesion and I did not expect any positive benefits; I paid little heed to consequences and made no effort to balance advantages and drawbacks. Only desire was involved; the unconscious plays tricks, but does not calculate. Was it the best way for a tyro secondary-school teacher to accede to a university chair twenty years later, or for an aspiring writer to start the climb towards the upper slopes of Parnassus? Apparently not, judging by the results. So you are going to have to explain to me, my dear demystifiers, why it was possible to set off with such cheerful optimism on such a wrong road. What was desirable enough about the mirage of proletarian insurrections springing up like mushrooms from the Rio Grande to Tierra del Fuego to make me forget my egotistical I'm-all-right-Jack vices. If you have no answer neither have I, just another small Diogenes rummaging in his dark corners lantern in hand: 'I am seeking a man', who got lost.

As for my 'movie': don't make me laugh. The camera doesn't love Victor Serges, or Richard Sorges either for that matter. Even if Anthony Quinn and Alec Guinness would have been no more miscast as Stalin and Trotsky than they were as Feisal and a Bedouin, CinemaScope prefers golden dunes to red suburbs. Give or take the odd camel or keffiyeh, Serge's tribulations are just as important as those of Lawrence, his elder by two years; but what scriptwriter has been inspired by them? The rich, who lend only to the rich, gave plenty to the late author of The Seven Pillars of Wisdom, who managed when alive to promote a flattering image of himself (and defended, perhaps unknowingly, the cause of the Hollywood Majors), but nothing to the revolutionary hero of anti-Stalinism. In image terms, a derrick is worth more than a Bolshevik every time.

It occurs to me that during an exploratory visit to Bolivia a few months before Che's arrival there, between two inspection trips to possible zones of action, while reading Victor Serge's *L'Affaire Toulaïev* in French, I laid the book aside in a small guest-house in Santa Cruz to go and see *Lawrence of Arabia*, showing at one of the town's cinemas. In the audience were all ranks from the local garrison. A few weeks later, a Uruguayan engineer wearing big tortoiseshell glasses, who had arrived in the country under the name of Alfredo Mena, passed through Santa Cruz in a jeep on his way to the Argentine frontier. Balding, with a dental prosthesis, thickened eyebrows and special shoes with hollow heels to make him look shorter, beardless and without his beret, Che looked more like a greying, pot-bellied middle manager than the male lead in a movie. He told me later that he had passed the Eden cinema, where the film was still showing, but had not taken the time to buy a ticket. It was like a new version of Plato's Cave, the Bolivian Bedouins gazing so fascinatedly at Peter O'Toole on the big screen that they failed to notice their own flesh-and-blood Lawrence as he faded, unnoticed and unknown, into their forests.

Today I came across this page from an old travel notebook, written on the cargo ship taking me back to France from Rio de Janeiro at the end of 1964:

War – Deficiency of information, dismantling of organizations, American preponderance. Imperialist political apparatus *centralized*. Counter-apparatus to be set up, informative, not executive.

    I. *Bulletin* 'International Correspondence'.

    II. *Anti-imperialist base* (consultative/executive voice). Aim: *unify* movements. Free discussion. Anthology of experiences. Reports. Tactical evaluations > watchwords.

III. *File index*, documentation centre. Archives.
   – men
   – movements
   – reports > keep secret docs in *safe place*.
IV. *Informants*. 2 sorts.
     1. Permanent officer correspondents
     2. Approved travellers. Conditions:
        – knowledge of continent
        – Leninist principles
        – tactical neutrality

Create effective, non-formulaic continental awareness: problems of each national organization are the problems of all.

No negative polemic: *discussion*.

Final *form* of CI = Information Bureau

+ primary *content* of CI = organize conquest of power.

Analogous historical situation.

CI: Communist International, founded in 1919, dissolved in 1943 (*International Correspondence* was its liaison bulletin in the 1920s). An unsurpassable model, it seemed to me at the time. Comparing always, sooner or later, means pontificating. That particular comparison made me bigger, rendered the task itself more valorizing (it would do the opposite nowadays). It was not very sensible, but it was fortifying (much more useful for purposes of action). Intellectually, drawing an *analogy* between Latin America in the 1960s and the whole West in the 1920s was hardly serious ('*Compañeros* ! Let's carry on where Lenin left off, let's rebuild the Comintern in Latin America: the historical setting is the same!'). Quite apart from the economic and social parameters, Latin America – a geographical term devoid of political or cultural meaning, since there are several Americas and their Latinness is superficial – never knew the butchery of 1914–18, the main provider of vocations between the wars. Apart from Chile there were no old parliamentary democracies there. A century and a half of political independence (with the exception of Cuba, where it dates from 1898) and the absence of visible, military foreign occupation invalidated comparisons with the 'colonial question', as it existed from India to Turkestan and China to the Middle East at the time of the Baku Congress in 1920. Such rational considerations based on examination of the facts would not only have discouraged me more than a little (notably by eliminating the comparative advantage I derived from a moderate familiarity with the archives of the 'workers' movement') but, more importantly, would have broken a fine tradition of which the subversive, in the days of the graphosphere, used to be the bearer and up to a point the champion. Historical novelty aroused instinctive repugnance, and could be interpreted in only two ways: as a false novelty resulting from a hasty and superficial reading of the events, or as a deliberate manoeuvre by the enemy to divert the weaker brethren from the true path. I had too strong a sense of tradition to improvise. The commonplace conservative individual becomes a reactionary; only a radical conservative can be a revolutionary. In a denatured society, he must always go *back* to the sources. In the early 1960s, my golden age was 1917 Petrograd; five years later I had changed it for the 1956 Sierra Maestra; a sort of advance, although really any date seemed good to me provided it was in the past. The job of translator-interpreter of current events that falls to the militant, the cadre, in this context boiled down to matching a sacred past with a profane present. We will turn out to have been great plagiarists, despite ourselves. Doubtless that is what lost this generation of revolutionaries, like so many others before it. Lost it in terms of results. But without wanting to imitate our elders in everything, could we have found the energy, the strength, to try to get it all started again?

Lukács defined a revolutionary intellectual as 'one who looks at the world from the viewpoint of *totality*'. Without contradicting him, we may think *anteriority* would seem more exact. For everyone, the present is a transaction between an expectation and a crowd of reminiscences. In a militant, both expectation and memory are so strong that there is not much room left for the present moment. Backward-looking sensibilities, saturnine temperaments, are the most inclined to try restarting the world. Whatever the action-images of battle or general strike that inspire it, the mentality of a 'refounder' – for *re*foundation is the most recurrent fantasy of political vanguards – coexists a lot more harmoniously with a base of melancholy than people think.

A long chain of graphomane bookworms, cutting across continents and generations like a mountaineer's rope across the abyss, formed a *lineage* – our lineage – and everyone had the feeling, in his own corner, that he ought to *maintain it*. Why 'betray' the class into which you are born? Primarily to keep faith with your schoolbooks. A good pupil is more exposed than others to the 'virus of dreaming that infects one with action'. This measles was caught through reading. It was no accident that in Paris our gathering-place was a bookshop called 'The Joy of Reading'; although Maspero had not chosen the name, it was a good and appropriate one. For a French schoolboy, the relay race started with Gracchus Babeuf and Buonarroti; then the baton passed to the *Carbonari* of La Rochelle, the workers of June 1848, the communards of Père-Lachaise, the Berlin Spartakists, the heroes of the Shanghai and Canton communes, Spain's *Quinto Regimiento* and International Brigades, *l'Affiche rouge* and the Vercors maquis. All those blissfully unhappy volunteers, those clusters of semi-damned suspended between heaven and earth, could one just abandon them at the roadside, in sight of the pass? Deem that they had died for nothing? Become the weak link that allowed those Sisyphean theories, our ball and chain, to founder in ridicule? That feeling of indebtedness to the long-dead forerunners we adopt, like self-appointed god-children, as our sponsors or tutors, was enough to push a rebellious young bourgeois off the beaten path of his social class.

The joy of seeing has replaced the joy of reading, which so often prevented us from seeing and hearing real beings of flesh and blood (every medium has its defects, none is perfect). Fate in the guise of the cathode-ray tube has cut into the dynastic sense of obligation to distant predecessors. The subversive ideal and passion will survive only as long as the sacralization of the book, the main vector of the genealogical germ, with the literary intelligentsia as the centre of infection and the literate working class as the receptive environment (the state of our mediological knowledge makes possible this parallel with the spread of infectious diseases – a germ, a vector, an environment – which is more than an association of ideas, and not a value judgement at all). The Western TV viewer, target of live images, is rendered instantly guilty, starving people from Kurdistan to Rwanda pointing out of the small screen at his well-fed form. The long Promethean history of the people and professions of the book is being effaced by new crazes without ancestry or issue. The sprout, the little squit who dreamed of becoming the equal of the heroes of old used to be shackled to libraries, archives, the tabulated traces of victims, as well as the multitude of small publishings, bookshops, small-circulation reviews and duplicated bulletins which in all countries propagates the memory and works of past heresiarchs – libertarians, Blanquists, anarcho-syndicalists, Trotskyists – along with orthodox members of the movement. With the technological shift from paper to the screen, with readers becoming voyeurs and grandfather's stacks of bumf mouldering unread, the shame the putative heir feels – shame is the first revolutionary sentiment – at seeming unworthy of his former martyrs relaxes into remotely-controlled impulses: less blinkered, more compassionate, but essentially concerned with shifting the backdrops. In following the intrusive eye of the camera instead of the restless page-turning finger, it seems that we have deserted history for geography.

Even though it has haunted the political far left for two hundred years, the *backward-looking innovator* is a figure of literary extraction, of which the romantic writer offers a good prototype: that monarchist troublemaker of the industrial societies wanted to return to the Middle Ages by vaulting the Enlightenment and set Lancelot of the Lake against Voltaire. Our own forerunners include examples of retrograde regeneration. Saint-Just draped himself in Brutus's toga; Lenin danced in the snow-covered courtyard of the Kremlin on the hundredth day of the October Revolution, because it had lasted as long as the Paris Commune; the insurgent workers of Berlin, in the winter of 1918, called themselves Spartakus; Trotsky stigmatized Stalinism as a 'Thermidor', before himself being depicted as a Bonaparte by Stalinists who still saw their leader as a Peter the Great, having not yet recognized him as a new Ivan the Terrible. *Bis repetita placent*: the slogan of the pioneers, who try to prevent History from repeating itself, but in the process cannot prevent the present from invading the archetype.

In practice nostalgia, or the intellectual clouding of the past, while providing reasons for going there, deprives the plagiarist of the means of doing so. Like the

French Staff in 1939 preparing for the Second World War with the methods and weapons of the First, we were organizing the next revolution with the tools of the previous one. The continental International we were planning (which had an ephemeral existence not long afterwards under the title OLAS or Latin American Solidarity Organization) was represented in my imagination by a pyramid of correspondence, reports and liaison bulletins on airmail flimsy, with radio and aircraft making a secondary, external contribution at best. This apparently rational construction had about it much of the feel of Jules Vallès's *Cri du peuple*, even perhaps of the Saint-Simonians' recto–verso catechisms. From this side the Comintern we were copying technology and mystiques from the nineteenth century, like the underground leaflet as organizational mainstay . . . A more or less contemporary cobbling together of the telegraph, the republican 'banquets' at Belleville under Louis-Philippe and the 'communist republicans, with moustaches, beards and long hair' who so alarmed Chateaubriand when he visited the moderate Armand Carrel in Saint-Pélagie prison.

The thorough and serious side of the revolutionary can do him more harm than good. I had sorted the Spanish war into files: manpower, chronology, chains of command; made detailed studies of the battles of Teruel and the Ebro, and recruitment into the International Brigades; collected all the resolutions passed at the first six congresses of the International, between 1919 and 1928. In the months before travelling, I believe I read and annotated everything available in French on the workers' uprisings in Bavaria (1918) and Hamburg (1923), Béla Kun's Hungarian Commune (1919), the Shanghai and Canton Communes (1927 and 1928 respectively) and the Austrian *Schutzbund* (1934). Crossed with Caribbean creativity, the Chartist compulsion for the capitulary gave birth to a rather retro vanguardist. It is an error to think that 'advanced ideas' can somehow launder outmoded tools, as if the end could update the means. If a political project has the age of its instruments rather than its objectives, ours dated in the final analysis from about 1848. Through its limited implantation in the indigenous population, its neglect of the 'real levels of awareness' and the student or urban origin of its recruits, *foquism* (the doctrine of the centre of guerrilla activity) or *Guevarism* – Bolívar revisited by Blanqui (1805–31), with Lenin on the wrapper – had some chance of achieving in practice the very thing we were accused of, to our great indignation, by Chinese diplomats in Havana: drifting into 'banditism', the formation of armed bands cut off from the people. Auguste Blanqui . . . Different continents, different centuries: but surely the same bitterness, the same repressive harshness, the same obsession with policing on 'both sides of the barricade'. Aside from the details of armed struggle – guerrilla warfare, not rioting; forest, not cobbles – we occupied a similar space to some of the activist minorities of utopian socialism. In ideology we were somewhere between Robespierre and Lenin; in typography, somewhere between Monotype and Linotype; and in faith, somewhere between coalminer and Roman dicastery.

We were cut off from the peasantry by definition. People of the Book are town mice, and it was arrogant (and ignorant) to claim connection with a rurality of which, being pure products of urban culture, we knew absolutely nothing. A historian of the long term would perhaps see the contemporary revolutionary movement, Third-Worldism included, as a more than usually convulsive episode in the town-dwellers' slow seizure of control over the peasants, in written culture's predominance over oral culture: a ruse of capitalist modernization, you might say.

Submachine gun, cipher pads, invisible ink, notebook, chemical detonators, subversive leaflets: to us these accoutrements seemed unsurpassable. Our 1960s still belonged to the graphosphere: a time when people still made war with small arms and poems. When London parachuted slim volumes of Éluard into Nazi-occupied France along with the Sten guns. On the eve of the Internet, we children of Gutenberg were trying to ease the confinement of a cosmonauts' world using a *Carbonaro*'s forceps, all oblivious of the computers and networks that were soon to get our powder hopelessly damp.

In 1961 I had spent two months working on a Cuban literacy campaign in the mountains of *Oriente*, a sort of military-flavoured education that the revolution was giving the peasants in the Sierra Maestra. This chance experience seems to me not without significance. It speaks volumes on the faith that I – and the period in general – had in the alphabet, accompanied by a total unawareness of the potential social reach of images, from comic strips to the (resolutely despised and ignored) television. The regenerative virtues of the printed word still inspired me with the superstitious faith of a contemporary of Michelet or Barbès: elitist mystique, sure to become popularized thanks to the small format, easier to conceal and distribute. As a propagator I had maintained the same pedagogic drive, bartering a class of forty pupils in France for a graduation class of two hundred million. *Educare* means: to bring out one's troops. Have not *educator* and *duce* the same Latin root? There is nothing shameful about this. The desire to guide one's fellows – anchored in the heart of every mortal and a precondition for any enduring collective life – cannot just ignore objective changes in the technical means of transmission. Today's Islamists, with their audio cassettes, laptops and e-mail, are a whole era, and I don't just mean thirty years, ahead of the Guevarists of that time. It does not escape me that satellites and fibre optics have opened an abyss between our paper-based mentality and today's virtual communities, as wide as the one between Paleolithic hunter-gatherers and Neolithic herder-agriculturalists, wider in any case than the one between the copyists of 1450 and the printers of 1550. In the company of youngsters brought up on video games and CD-Rom, I still feel like a saurian lost among mammals after a Darwinian detour.

Time flattens all relief, silts up the fissures, transforms us into ants seen from far above, busy but insignificant. On top of everything else there arrives the vulture of memories. Day has broken; the historian gazes from his window, fresh and ready for anything, and is appalled to see, far below and a long way behind, these agitated little creatures going the wrong way, manifestly off course. If he is kind-hearted, the Michelet of failed attacks will do his best to understand the absurd creatures from the inside. If he lays pity aside for cold scrutiny, the examiner of lost illusions will award poor marks to a straggling troop of lunatics. This detached spectator will observe the beginnings in hindsight, via the dénouement. How will he find the time, let alone the much-decried but essential gift of empathy, to understand that those he judges so briskly rose while it was still dark and set out in an uncertain pre-dawn half-light? The historian does not know – does not want to know – that nothing resembles the uncertain demi-tint of dawn as closely as a dusk, as the nuptial song of a blue whale mimics the squeaking of rusty door-hinges. Did we, then, mistake the Indian summer of a Utopia for a spring? Yes, and it is *still* vexing (for a self-styled anti-conformist) to replay the classic scene of the fellow-traveller covering up new tyrannies in the name of liberation. Nevertheless I have not been able to bring myself to accept the telescopic historiographer's view of an 'army of dead revolutionaries': there are too many real memories.

History, of course, is not memory but its critique (otherwise memorialists could stand in for historians). The professional is there to discern the flaws in the evidence and dismantle the lies of memory. But one cannot help wondering whether the famous *distance* inherent in long focus might not be just as suffused with naivety as the actors' daily immersion in their motivating mists; and whether, given the scholar's retrospective illusions and the militant's prospective ones, any lies at all will be exposed. Although reversals that occurred over centuries during the first-phase history of the Apocalypse must now be measured in decades, the error of omission lies in judging the intended goal by what is achieved in practice. What would people think of a historian of Christianity who saw the first communities in Antioch and Ephesus, in the time of St Paul, as identical with the Church Triumphant under Constantine or the state religion under Theodosius?

It seems to me that, at this turn of the century, three distortions resulting from distance disfigure perceptions of revolutionary commitment at that time: the *totalitarian* prejudice, the idea that it was the Soviet Union that breathed awareness and life into our projects; the *terrorist* prejudice, confusing 'wars of liberation' with the campaigns of blind violence to which we have now become accustomed; and the *romanticism* prejudice, reducing what for many people was a strategic calculation to the 'call of the wild'. 'Régis Debray is a bloodthirsty adventurer', summarized a survey of my deeds and attitudes widely circulated in both Americas by a Miami, Florida, news agency in June 1967. Whatever the accuracy of this judgement, I am obliged to point out that I was not at that time pro-Soviet or a planter of bombs, still less a philanthropist. No one can reasonably accuse me of having wanted the good of humanity.

*   *   *

A totalitarian ending? The Gulag perspective? The sad thing about heresies is the way unjust time eventually reintegrates them with the orthodoxy they most passionately rejected; a few decades is all it takes for the black sheep to return, in people's minds, to the detested fold. As a 14,000-foot peak gradually disappears behind its buttresses as the mountaineer descends, the general indifference to distinctions now seen as obscure or Byzantine, and the replacement of things by their signs, seem overwhelmingly absurd to those of us who have returned to the plains, all dissidents from the same faith. To toss the 'new left' of the 1960s into the totalitarian stewpot (or indeed the Trotskyist left of the 1920s into the Stalinist cauldron) is to Disneyize the relics of the ancients. In our Guevarist circles we regarded with equal loathing the trigger-happy officialdom in Budapest and the Parisian 'social-traitor' willing to excuse racist police brutality and emergency powers. I admit that loathing bodes ill, for it ages one. You don't invent the future with good feelings; with negative ones you are sure to get there, but backwards: *post mortem*, we will all have the exact age of what we most execrated.

In *Guerrilla Warfare* (1959), Guevara had summarized the three lessons to be drawn from Cuba as follows: '1) Popular forces can win a war against the regular army; 2) It is not always necessary to wait until *all the right conditions* are present to make revolution: the insurrectional centre can create them; 3) In underdeveloped America, the main terrain of the struggle should be the countryside.' The first and third points seemed harmless enough, but the second led to ten years of close-quarters knife-fighting with the communists of the region and the various apparatuses of the Soviet world. The quarrel over 'conditions' (preliminary, concomitant, consecutive, partial, total) became in Latin America itself, to everyone including veterans, as evocative as – to us atheists – disputes like 'Filioque' in the tenth century (Does the Holy Ghost proceed from the Father *and* the Son or *through* the Son?) and those over predestination and grace in the sixteenth, which nevertheless split the West, and with it Christian power, in two. Only a scholiast of the history of political ideas could still unravel the ferocious subtleties of the 'foquist' schism. But his explanations will not help anyone to retrace the course of our beliefs.

Those parties, states and apparatuses horrified us far too much not to leave traces; on our ideas, certainly; on our behaviour, a little. Seen from the far bank the amalgam, sentimentally iniquitous on the protagonists' level, will more or less confirm the truth of the macroscopic view. Communists? One day, perhaps, we will appear to have been of that family in our aims, but differing in our choice of ways and means. The third-worldists had bid farewell to the proletariat – and Europe at the same time – but had not abandoned the central idea of a 'messiah class': the peasantries of 'colonial and semi-colonial' countries. The change of actors did not alter the metaphysics of the role, especially as (like all good fundamentalists) we preached a return to the sources as a means of reviving inspiration. It was a period of lay 'revivalism'. The upstream re-evaluation of Marx texts by European scholastics, to unmask distortions, was applied to Trotsky, Lenin, Rosa Luxemburg, Kropotkin, etc., by those more inclined to direct action. This position of proofreader, scratching away at the palimpsest layer by layer, turned us into internal anti-communists: purists, just a tad pedantic, who arrogantly maintained (like Sartre at the same time) that the external, openly liberal anti-communist was just a 'running dog'. My keenness to research the heroic years of internationalism, before the ex-guests of the Lux hotel in Moscow were shot in the back of the neck, resulted from the archaeologist's posture appropriate to all cases of religious dispute in an established religion. Like the reformers against the Simoniacal papacy, or today's integralists versus official Islam. There was a good communism buried under the bad one: all that was needed was to erase the last few decades, and the apocryphal version would disappear by itself. The thought that the bad communism was the real one did not lead to the idea that the good one was imaginary, but that the real one had gone wrong, through diversion, laxity or an error of 'reading' (like the lamentable confusion, denounced by the Althusserians, between the young idealist Marx and the mature structuralist). In a word: the new extreme left, an antiquated version of the old one, overshadowed its elder *in retro*. Labour, Sweden, even Togliatti were of no real interest; we stepped over the fathers' generation to reach the ancestors, our longing for Renaissance accompanied by an instinctive distrust of the faded prophets of the native soil, Jaurès in the lead, who seemed colourless and unattractive figures beside Guevara, Fanon and Giap. Reinventing the revolution meant inventorizing its lost protocols as exhaustively as possible, rifling the archives. The parties were a bit tired, but never mind: heroes were going to do the hard graft. They were very resolute, but still lacked the distilled wisdom of Chartists familiar with the convoluted records of the 'workers' movement'. It was up to us to bring them up to date and into the light. *Hay que echar a andar a las masas*, they used to repeat in Havana, adding the methodological footnote: *las condiciones previas para alzarse es la decisión de alzarse, y pa'el carajo* ('The preliminary conditions for insurrection are the decision to revolt, and fuck all else'). Although morally persuasive, this rustic discourse on method seemed to me insufficiently Cartesian to convince that town mouse the urban Marxist, a suspicious reasoner and cold-blooded animal who could hardly be expected to come and make warming contact with parataxical and syncopated tropical orality. It seemed to me that argumentation and deductive reasoning would be needed to impose any of it on the red priesthood scattered across the world (tepid hearts, twisted minds). Although I now see it as a bad grafting of ideas onto passion and doctrine onto conjuncture, my pamphlet *Révolution dans la révolution* was the fruit of this typographical scruple. The Cuban state circulated it, the air of the time gave it wings. Originally printed in Spanish in January 1967 by Cuba's state publisher *Editorial nacional*, in a run of 300,000, with a daily reading on Radio-Habana, it was distributed discreetly in all Spanish-

speaking countries (except Spain) and eventually, in translation, in lands far
removed from our cultural matrix.

Missolonghi? Romantic adventurer? In the way I used them, my partisan years
were no more Byronic and no less materialist than my years in the establishment.
I have always had my feet on the ground, and adapted my footing to changing
terrain. It was not out of 'romanticism' that people of my sort pitched their tents
at the extremes; it was to reach the extremes of the reality principle. I would
never have dreamed of espousing the cause of marginalized people who were
not aiming for the centre. Just as I was not a leftist in France after my return, so
over there we believed not in purifying violence but useful violence. By
deliberately attacking the 'weakest link'. Guerrilla war? A power discourse.
Déclassé individuals are not all alike. When a rich young Nicaraguan left with
weapons and baggage to join banana and maize cultivators (although the
mountains he went to were not unpopulated), he was moved by very different
motives from the bourgeois leftist or Simone Weil replica who volunteered for
factory work in the wake of May '68. The Central American believed he was
applying leverage to the most useful point in a system of forces. Perhaps the
Sierra was not the wellspring of power he imagined, but the point is that the
rebel was aiming directly at state power, by a short cut, rather than bearing
witness before God, History or Morality. Guerrilla war was the weapon of the
weak, yes, but used in an attempt to become the strong. There was nothing
intrinsically unachievable in this project, which had succeeded elsewhere. Dien
Bien Phu, followed by 'small wars' in China, Vietnam and Algeria, had
substantively modified the map of the planet, something not achieved by the
atomic bomb or the Third Reich's armoured divisions. Do we need to recall that
guerrilla warfare had ended the colonial empires, along with European hegemony over the world, or that Afghan *maquisards*, in their fashion, started the fall
of a colossus? That since the Paris Commune the only real uprisings of
contemporary history, from China to Mexico, have been conducted by peasants
and not workers? Was it so mad to say: old Europe is no longer the epicentre and
beacon of humanity?

I did not, it is true, attack the great Soviet rear by name. But how do you
accommodate to reality without compromising? Only great minds succeed in
making the grand slam; I have never managed it. Anyone who wants to *do*, and
not just be or seem, must *make do*, a *terzo incómodo*. Guevara himself, who can
hardly be accused of excessive realism, would without undue shame reach
compromise arrangements with existing bureaucracies, starting with 'the Caribbean tentacle of the international communist system'. He gave up his
ministerial post and Cuban nationality, but did not break with the Cuban
state or its chief. What could he have *done* in the Congo and Bolivia without the
officers and men, the weapons, training bases, radio, supplies, dollars and false
passports made available to him by a socialism already in the process of

disintegration? Would he even have been able to reach his 'combat post' in Africa or America? Did he not succeed in getting out of the Congo alive, with his men, following a tacit exchange of civilities between Havana and Washington (the latter perhaps unaware of his presence there, as he was of this pact). And what might have become of that little outpost of 'revolutionary romanticism' itself, without missiles and economic aid from the great rear base on the other side of the world, the Soviet Union? Thus from place to place led the chain of solidarities, the cascade of dependences that had to be accepted to achieve the desired breakthrough. Carving out in the South a 'third way' between East and West would mean depending on one camp against the other; and 'real socialism' contained only the sort of reality socialism could afford. The adjective, unappealing though it was, seemed more important to us Third-Worldists than the noun; but 'there was no choice' (that infallible political clincher). Would anyone really have dreamed of seeking Washington's help to fight United Fruit, or the Pentagon's to bring down the armies of Pentagon-trained torturers run out of Panama by South America Strategic Command?

In dealing with the bureaucratic (it was not done to say 'totalitarian') realities, playing the ostrich was possible for activists. This was done by distinguishing between the Revolution (untouchable) and the regime (subject to criticism). In that fortified camp, entered by passing under a scarlet banner at José-Martí airport that read: *Territorio libre de America*, the revolutionary masked the Cuban; but when it was time to assess 'derailments', the Cuban came to our rescue and let us off 'rethinking the revolution'. Was an enlightened *guerrillero* turning into a meddlesome *caudillo*? *Granma*, the sole newspaper, spouted slogans that would make you weep. The *Seguridad* had started roughing up, here and there, the odd poet, homosexual, dancer, intellectual or other *blandengue* (generic local term for 'sissy'). The housewife had to queue for six hours for her weekly ration of two eggs, because of the *libreta*. The trouble was (I used to reply) that a tropical island being subjected to a state of siege was cramped setting for a great idea: there were infrastructural deficiencies, a shortage of appropriate mentalities. Nor should these blips – regrettable of course – be allowed to obscure the fact of partition. Let us aspire, comrades, to a comprehensive point of view. The struggle is worldwide, and without the existence of the 'socialist camp' to back us, there can be no viable balance of forces with 'imperialism'. A pity, of course, that everyday life was so sour (and looked so alluring on the other side, in the Empire). They would just have to suffer patiently, those Cubans, Czechs and Poles: we would do better next time. Our kingdom was not for today. This attitude – 'hold on, we're getting there' – was nothing to be proud of. People didn't wait for us, and they were right. Godot never showed up and the future took the flak. It only took me a decade to replace the expectation of conflagration in the South with the expectation of 'socialism in freedom' in Europe (like the bridegroom of an *Arabian Nights* princess unable to consummate and falling back on a more approachable if less distinguished lady-in-waiting: social democracy); I imagine that by now, after fifty years or more, the hostages of those fossilized regimes must be quite tired of kicking their heels in front of empty shelves.

While visiting Prague in 1963 to see two Latino comrades – Roque Dalton from Salvador and Barreto, a Venezuelan – exiled there to represent their party on the review *Peace and Socialism* (latest avatar of the Cominform), I had already glimpsed, as if through a keyhole, that Eastern greyness without personality or transcendence. We used to joke about it as a kitsch and benign form of out-of-dateness. Compared to the sufferings of Bogotá street children, *favela* gangs and exterminated Guatemalan Indians, of the thousands of cadres tortured or murdered every year in that country alone, the East European purgatory seemed depressing rather than inhumane, somewhere between a bad moment to be endured and a regrettable minor accident that would soon be forgotten. From a North–South perspective, the East–West conflict looked like a noisy squabble in the rich people's camp. This may have been dismissive of the plight of simple people in 'kidnapped Europe', where Milan Kundera was working in silence, but East Europe looked less unlivable than the America of *ranchos* and *favelas* where you needed luck to reach 30 alive. In any case, our idea was not to embellish an established (therefore inevitably betrayed) revolution, but to make others occur ('one, two, three, several Vietnams'). The imminent mushrooming of new revolutions would soon allow our intolerant strongholds to relax. By building bridges of fraternity between continents, by spreading across the entire planet, the revolutionary wave would engender societies that were more viable because less insecure.

The *terrorist* label, finally. It is a fact that I passed through the same training centres in Cuba as the young 'Carlos', some time later. His subsequent career was more brilliant than mine, doubtless because he had more gifts, greater application and motivation, and because he was a few years younger. 'Terrorism' was not a technique used by our insurgent groups (which thus differed from the Irgun and Stern groups in the Israeli war of liberation), for a number of reasons of which the first was that television had no importance. The videosphere did not start until 1968, along with the first action by the world far left that one might call 'terrorist': the hijacking of aircraft belonging to El Al by George Habash's PFLP. This type of operation is not a pursuit of guerrilla warfare by other means, but a publicity-seeking substitute for its absence, to compensate for the inability of an organization with a weak popular base to make a decent showing on the battlefield. A combat which is locally impossible can thus be transplanted into spectacular ubiquity through the TV screen. The Guevarist vanguards of that time – in this respect very unlike the postmodern Zapatistas – were too grossly lacking in media sense and public relations awareness even to think of hijacking a plane or using the electronic media. Where that sort of thing was concerned they were a bit straitlaced. The *lucha armada* had its own rules of etiquette. Rob a bank to get money to buy weapons: fine. Deliberately kill civilians in the street: certainly not. 'Execute' a traitor or torturer: yes. Coldly liquidate a prisoner: never. Any captured wounded enemy was to be treated in the same way as a guerrilla. Car bombs, bombs in cafés or underground stations, extracting concessions by threatening to kill hostages, were not just unthinkable to my friends: the mere suggestion of anything like that would have led to the immediate expulsion, if not summary execution, of the degenerate who had made it. The 'professional revolutionary' – an expression that now sounds as grotesque as 'revolt administrator' – was to the terrorist of today what a parish priest is to a guru of the Solar Temple. The only connection is that one pair has 'violence' in common and the other 'the supernatural'. I can best define what distinguished revolutionary violence from repressive violence by pointing out that at that time the torture of a prisoner was unthinkable among adepts of revolution, and routine among adepts of repression. Anyone reflecting on this detail will see that it defines a very important difference.

3

Monarch and Crusader

Revolution: on the proper use of a word – Fidel, pointillist colossus – Moravia and Mussolini – A war king – Divine vertigo – Time, the great demolisher – Che, a man in a hurry – Posthumous misunderstandings – Sublimation of a suicide – Watchword: convert rout into victory

If one had only *listened* to it, that word that starts like *reverie* and ends like *destruction*. In French it resembles an advertising banner: in a single breath, an assault on the heavens and a fall from grace. But to hear the word properly, we would have needed the browsing sensibility of a poet. What I do remember is that the Spanish language gave a different reverberation to the name of that infernal machine, destroyer in the twentieth century of the dreams of the nineteenth. On the lips of the *comandantes* the word *Revolución* became a lyrical reservoir of different enchantment, new music. The guttural, growling *r* climbing from the gullet like a fat rumble of thunder, softening at the end into an earnest, baby-blue *ción*, the terror of the first syllable and the caress of the last, in the the local accent, perfectly reversing the phases of the process itself. After the bloodshed, silky brown girls in open-necked blue shirts with militia berets over one eye would open their arms to the survivors. In real life though it is usually the other way round: first caresses, then firing squad.

For fifty years adversaries and adherents in Europe have loved, hated, feared, suspected – in a word, been obsessed with – the *Party*. It haunted the Americas in a less circumscribed, more physical way, but one just as fatally embodied. A romanticism not so much of organization as of *fuite en avant*. To understand why tens, why hundreds of thousands of people managed to find it a sufficient – indeed *exalting* – motive for living and dying, it would not be useful to trace the history of the word in the manner of a sober semanticist. A cosmic unsaid transcended its literal meaning, crushing it under a burning charge brought up from the most silent levels of the collective soul. Ever since it came down from heaven to earth, complete with initial capital letter and definite article, in France around 1790, *revolution* has designated, literally, 'replacement of the class holding power, radical change to the state'. In underlying fashion it also came to represent an immemorial myth: the renewal of the world, Plato's *metabolè*, Cicero's *mutatio rerum*, St Augustine's *conversio*. That unstated meaning has lost most of its credibility in a few decades, so grey and faded has the word become under a mixture of disappointment and inflation. English, American, Atlantic, October, palace, keyhole and velvet, *revolution* has been doused in too many sauces: green, sexual, fashion, technological, scientific, quiet. It only recovers its dark mask in the rantings of a great counter-revolutionary like Solzhenitsyn, when he is doing something like exhorting the Vendéens to fly the fleur-de-lys and the white flag. While inaugurating in 1993 a memorial to victims of the Terror, at Lucs-sur-Boulogne, not far from Puy-du-Fou, the prophet gave it back a sort of flamboyant absoluteness, but an absoluteness of Evil. *Opus Dei* recovered its lost youth as *Opus Diaboli*, 'the unfurling of the horde' took on an epic, Victor Hugo dimension. 'Revolutions', cried the great Russian of the day to the plaudits of France's Whites, 'destroy the organic character of Society, ruin the natural course of life, annihilate the best elements of the population.' Arguments unchanged since Joseph de Maistre. *Revolution* now arouses among us, not just in the lineage of its victims but that of its authors and beneficiaries too, the same repulsive images as *revolt* or *jacquerie* in eighteenth-century drawing rooms (pale châtelaines sodomized by leering yokels). That kind of cannibalistic epileptic seizure was exactly what the long view of revolution, which tried to be universal, rational, far-seeing and scrupulous, was meant to draw the deprived away from. And here we are at a new chapter in the great book of changes, with the word coming to mean what it did in the first place, more than two hundred years ago: a complete rotation of a moveable object about its axis. Back to the starting point. The trajectory comes round on itself, a donkey-kick from astronomy to the bloodless lioness of politics. Two centuries, millions of corpses, one complete rotation: for nothing.

When a government rules for a great length of time, as in Mexico under the Institutional Revolutionary Party (PRI), and later in Cuba, its transformation into an effigy does have a few advantages. One is that failings and problem areas can be concealed behind an initial momentum that has faded away in reality but is still perpetuated verbally. People do not say: 'the government requires . . .' or 'the state has decided . . .', but 'the Revolution wants you to . . .' or 'the Revolution thinks that . . .'. This permutation of the real subject and the ideal subject of decisions, apart from conferring on a de facto dictatorship a legitimacy that absolves it from ordinary laws (as words like *Motherland* or *Nation* do for 'bourgeois' regimes), enables the stagnant to appear dynamic by repainting an established order in the colours of insurrection. The rebel-turned-official can then use this spell to blend three ingredients not normally seen as compatible: the evangelical precept, universal history and the defence of sectional interests. The corporatism of the leading circle dovetails with the messianism of the led to ensure that maintenance of the privileges acquired by a nouveau-riche class is taken to heart by the poor (this works, at least for a while). Outside the country, where its prestige is untarnished by everyday reality at home, the emblem guarantees a genuinely mythical packaging: in all the poor quarters of the hemisphere, from Caracas to Harlem, Fidel Castro, revered as half Prometheus and half David, carried all hearts with him. At the fiftieth anniversary of the United Nations in 1995 he was still by far the most applauded leader in the General Assembly: sacred monster, main attraction, champion of the down-trodden, his mere silhouette could still electrify the Third World. Latin America venerates him as a decorative resistance hero, North America as an original troublemaker. In Cuba, as always and everywhere, the tapping of the people's energies through the classic hydro-political dam benefited from the decline in initial demand. But to this nth 'bureaucratic freeze' *revolución* for a while gave the charm of a spring thaw. Government and opposition rolled into one, Fidel retained for his supporters – the vast majority – the anarchist prestige of a rebel. Could the humanist Zorro of 1958 have imagined that this medieval entelechy would soon have but a single head (his own)? A single body – his own – and a single purpose? Surely not. The use of the word as a shield, as an institutional carapace, has the virtue that it transforms a diversion of hope into a moral requisition.

The ideal protective bronze of *revolución* switches the autocrat into an *allocrat*, in his own wholly sincere view. His ego is the revolution, the people, to which he (a humble clerk) has given everything. When using the first person Fidel does not say *yo* but *nosotros*, like a Bourbon; the royal *we* (so to speak) combining egotistical majesty and altruistic self-effacement, attesting that since it is the masses that make History, their Commander is just a temporary incarnation of the First Principle, existing solely as their delegate. But also that anyone questioning the actions of Providence is playing the game of counter-revolution, of the CIA, of Miami. 'Where God is concerned, we are always in the wrong,' Kierkegaard said. And where the *Jefe* is concerned, so are revolutionaries, for to doubt his *ukases* is to insult their mother herself – the revolution – their father, and in consequence morality, honour and human dignity. Intelligent militants could take ten or even twenty years to arrive at an objective view of the *Comandante*'s sacred word. A painful divorce that could lead beyond disillusion to suicide, and nearly always to the loss of meaning from the person's life. Nothing unusual there. It is a universal phenomenon, that unhappiness of political consciousness (not the one in books: the vital, suffering, incarnate one) exposed to disavowal in deed. The Fidelista, Mitterrandist or Chiraquian (to stay in trivial or familiar channels) or, if you prefer it heavy, the Stalinist, Mussolinian or Pétainist, have in common that they instinctively view the vicissitudes of the moment through the person and the eyes of the Leader. This does not give them rose-tinted spectacles, much as they may need them. They are often the first and best informed on the shady areas, errors, faults, disasters and scandals affecting what sceptics prudently call 'the present regime' (communist, liberal, fascist, socialist, national, etc.). But they think that such problems, undeniable today, will have a solution tomorrow called Fidel, François, Philippe, Valéry or Jacques: indeed it is this thought, summary and generally ill-considered, that defines them as Fidelistas, Mitterrandists, Pétainists, Giscardians or Chiraquians. The discovery – hesitant, reluctant, confused – that the problem lies in the supposed solution causes the sky to fall. It forces the affiliated person into a painful revolution of outlook: the naive lover of paintings, used to looking through the picture as if through a window-frame at the represented landscape, starts to look at the actual workmanship: the impasto, the texture of the canvas, the system of brushstrokes. In a state of society that, unlike democracy, does not tolerate dissenting beliefs or alternative views of the world, the obedient adherent is reduced to catatonia by a double bind, like a mouse in his cage trapped between two electrodes: to continue serving the original principles of the Revolution, he will have to 'betray' the historic leader who incarnated those principles in deed; if he continues loyally to serve the leader (and with him the entire system for shoring up and maintaining his personal hold on power), he will have to 'betray' the spirit of the Revolution, or his idea of it, thus betraying himself. In Cuba this objective difficulty would be solved haphazardly by such means as alcoholism, clinical depression and suicide, depending on individual temperament.

Use of the key word is free, and very varied (to each his own corruptions of meaning, his own bad faith). For many, of whom I was one, it was more a motive for getting started than anything else. It incited me to do my packing, in much the same way as an obvious escape route when what matters most is to tear yourself away from stagnating surroundings, rather than pursue some specific goal. The aiming point enables the impatient one to place himself a couple of paces ahead of where he is, and to not be what he is at the same time: the essence of Bovaryism. I was not a happy revolutionary, for that reason, but I was happy inside myself to be like that, a sedentary person drawn by the luminous appeal of an escapade, like someone out of his tent before dawn and already striding the road, all possibilities open before him. As a horizon, its first merit is that it is unreachable, retreating as you advance and thus keeping you moving. To it I owe the prolongation well beyond adolescence of the intoxicating taste for departures, like a ship fresh out of dry dock whose hull is still shuddering nervously long after being launched. And no one in the world communicated it to me better, that trembling happiness of the refit, than Fidel: a suspense-movie character each of whose appearances, striding impatiently up and down the room like a wild beast in a cage, his index tapping you on the chest to emphasize a point, his arm falling across your shoulder for a murmured confidence, seemed to me like a *curtain up*. As he orchestrated that Promethean collective drama before your eyes, open-heartedly, he had the art, when briskly raising a subject, of involving you as one of the principal actors, indispensable to the proper course of things, someone on whom the ruler was going to be able to depend at last. An enrolment on the spot that left the person stupefied with gratitude and burdened with responsibility, mobilized to unprecedented heights for fear of not being 'up to it'.

*   *   *

Was it his singular ability to radiate energy, the metamorphosis of a large fit man into a titan, some magic in the air of the time or bedazzlement by the sunny nimbus of the word in which he was swathed: *revolución*? Contemporaries of Pol Pot and the 'Castrist shipwreck', the Canadian, French and Spanish tourists arriving in a ghost town to be briskly fleeced between leprous façades by troupes of prostitutes, cannot begin to imagine the warm halo of purple and gold that then surrounded one of History's Chosen: a man immortalized by a photo taken at the moment of his arrival in Havana with a dove perched on his shoulder, like the Holy Ghost sitting on Gregory the Great's shoulder in a medieval icon. I saw much more in him than himself alone, as if his person were an opening onto a landscape rich in nitrogen, a trembling completeness that made me breathe deeply. I have never found since the sensation of airiness, of openness to the future, that characterized those consultations fed with secret intelligence from all directions, whose focus zigzagged between Vietnam and Tanzania, Buenos Aires and Peking, Algiers and Baghdad. It was like being a cyclist and changing up several gears, as it were from provincial to planetary, to a ratio for which my mental calves had not been prepared by the cultural retort I came from. It has not been much noticed that natives of very small countries or city-states (as today Singapore or Hong Kong, in the past Amsterdam or Venice) are more inclined to think and feel as citizens of the world than nationals of vast continental territories more suitable for enclosure who, finding plenty of space at home, do not have the same need to unlock the horizon. The bigger a country is and the more it turns its back on the sea – ports are beneficial – the more enclosed are its people's lives. Islanders radiate. Has it been sufficiently noted that the best strategists often come from remote places like Corsica or Réunion, or countries surrounded by water like Britain or Japan? An avid autodidact's culture, cobbled together but pretty extensive, made Fidel vibrate in response to every shock on the planet. He had his whole island in his head, every nook and cranny; mentally sniffed out North America; instinctively understood South America (except for Brazil, a universe apart); and for his own Antipodes – the European countries – made do with journalistic approximations. Our chats – perhaps not the perfect word, for it implies a French-style sharing of the initiative that his *hidalgo*'s courtesy might have tolerated but that the inequality of ranks and his own character, once the preliminaries were over, rendered pointless – unconsciously followed Buckingham Palace etiquette, whether on a basketball court or a mountain path, without any formal rule or instruction: no thematic initiative allowed. *Never* change the subject broached by the Sovereign, relaunch it without departing from it. This seems to be a universal rule that tacitly regulates our exchanges with the powerful. They talk to us about what they want, not what we want, and we often end by wanting what they want.

That artist of the oral did not elude general questions artfully (I soon stopped asking them, as much for fear of ridicule as *lèse-majesté*). *El Caballo* (as he was nicknamed by the people) returned by instinct to his stable: his Sierra Maestra, his heroes Martí, Cespedes, Maceo, his own conspiracies. He was following his own nature and our folly. For paranoia is not the exclusive possession of the Madman-in-Chief: it was and still is that of a whole environment – Stalinist yesterday, Islamist today, Christ the King the day before yesterday – but in the concentrated state, carried to the highest pitch of infantile efficiency by the siege mentality. A madness that affected only the head would not echo and re-echo in every recess of the threatened social body, in the awareness of each of the believers standing guard against the villains outside. To this glow of heat, like Archimedes with the besieged city of Syracuse, the great orator holds out a parabolic sound-reflector that raises the ambient fervour to incandescence. Surely it is this exchange of civilities that creates the 'charismatic chief' and devalues the autonomous powers of the 'leader'.

His Micromégas side would have charmed Voltaire, whose story of that name was inspired by the court and person of Frederick II: I quickly learned to share his mania for details (no challenge to an obsessive). A scrupulous megalomaniac, expansive and secretive, naive and foxy, Fidel gave detailed attention to the anthill of the day, a small improvised court which he would kick to pieces and abandon without warning at the first change of mood or line. Like a ruthless horseman, he rode his entourages at top speed, indefatigably. Men of power are perforce versatile in friendship; they have no time for people who can no longer serve them. This utilitarian attitude to personal relations is more marked in all-of-a-piece 'totalitarians' than in 'liberals', who like to show their faces in town as well as at court and may keep a soft spot for useless old friends without obvious value. But the Cuban tempered the functional ingratitude of his job with a doubling of solicitude, excelling in that allegedly commonplace manoeuvre (which nevertheless, as far as one can tell, was not used by Stalin or Mao any more than Franco or Mussolini): the kindly brush-off. The boot, with love. He flabbergasted me, soon after my arrival, with the detailed care he took over my 'cover': first he arranged for me to be a jury member for the *Casa de las Américas* (awarding literary prizes); then he got me a medical certificate to explain my disappearance to the principal of my lycée, via the French embassy; finally, after exhausting these subterfuges, he invented another: a pseudo-appointment as a lecturer at the University of Havana, which I only visited on one occasion in a year and a half, to meet the staff of the review *Pensamiento Crítico* (that group of philosophers, avid for novelty and critically rigorous, among whom I had real friends, was dissolved after 1968 for 'ideological diversionism').

In a high shrill voice – surprising to newcomers expecting a tribune's baritone – a minor theme that slowly gained volume like an oboe after the overture, he questioned me carefully at the beginning of each meeting: on the progress of these cloak-and-dagger operations, the needs of my companion Elisabeth, the quality of some claret a guest had given him, the effectiveness of the hotel air-conditioning, the chauffeur's driving, the relative bitterness of Cuban coffee and Italian espresso . . . Having always believed in the Latin adage *De minimis non curat praetor*, I discovered as follows that, as Cardinal de Retz warned, 'there are no small steps in great affairs': six months after my arrival (as Che returned briefly to Cuba from Prague, but without my knowledge) he came to the hotel to pick me up in his car and show me things an estate agent would have thought a waste of time: the advantages and disadvantages of the apartment into which the security services proposed to move my partner and me, the neighbourhood, supplies, exposure of the terrace, the service entrance and garage. And to ask what I thought of it. I didn't give a damn (for the apartment, not him). Fidel, I can swear, was infinitely delicate, with a human warmth and considerateness that I have never found in any of his peers.

What one gained in breadth of view from associating with the *barbudos* one lost, of course, in nuance and complexity. Any strong involvement in a combat arouses in the militant, who is a soldier (*miles*), that curious mixture of arterial dilation and cerebral contraction. By simplifying existence, the culture of war also simplifies thought; there is a loss of subtlety but a gain in time; those idle and commonplace zones between gossip and reflection, banter and exegesis, in which 'politicized' people wallow in peacetime, disappear from the conversation. In close committee I never heard the comandantes 'talking politics', in the sense of shop or in-gossip, as our pro politicians do among themselves. Not even – like our over-cerebral news pundits – in the game-playing sense, as if it were snooker or chess. The professional *intrigues* all the time, the revolutionary *conspires*. The difference lies in the size of the stakes, and in a certain indifference to the 'human cost', the cost to individuals reduced to their potential for action. Disdaining all psychology, the *comandantes* jumped from an ethic without nuances to a technique without fluidity. 'Morality', with Fidel, consisted of the immediate attribution to anyone whose name came up of one of the innumerable Spanish synonyms for 'honour' (*honra, decoro, vergüenza, entereza, nobleza*, etc.) or its opposite (*blandenguería, claudicación, deslealtad, derrotismo*, etc.). Valiance or cowardice. A straight alternative: people had it or they didn't. Black or white. There was no purgatory. An individual could rise or fall (usually fall) in the blink of an eye, cast down from the heaven of heroes to the hell of *pendejos*, weaklings and wimps, depending on how he had lived up to the *Jefe*'s political expectations. Technique always concerned some detail of execution: what percentage of bombs dropped from aircraft fails to explode, thirty or fifty? What is the range of a carbine with telescopic sights, 400 metres or 750? Should we choose the new FAL 7.62mm rifle or the old Garand 30/06, and why? Should a marching column carry a Chinese bazooka, lightweight but only useful up to 150 metres, or a 60mm mortar weighing five times as much, with a range of 2 kilometres? Any of these debates could easily take a couple of hours, and morality and technique together a whole night.

Between these two extremes, no space remained for what a European would have called 'basic political questions' (on which the operational details that so absorbed the *Comandante*, and us with him, should theoretically have depended):

what sort of power exactly is to be 'seized', and what is to be done with it? Is 'imperialism' a dragon with a human face, a Lernaean hydra, or are there several decision-making centres, several poles of interest in the United States? Is it really useful to talk about 'neocolonial societies' in Latin America without discriminating between them, understanding the nuances? *El Caballo* saw these as quibbles and pedantries of interest only to 'little ideological popes'. If anyone quoted some authority or other he would get impatient. 'No point looking in Marx or Lenin for how to make a detonator out of a flashlight or a mortar out of the breech of a shotgun. You Europeans have theory coming out of your ears, but war isn't a theoretical matter.' He was perfectly right. I was far keener to get into his game. Since that time in all circumstances I have favoured people whose first move is to look at things and not consult books.

Although the portmanteau term *totalitarian* is used by publicists as a place to hide embarrassing corpses the word itself, which remains valid in the arts domain (where all is related, from Moscow to Berlin), would apply better to a boss's psychology than to a régime. That would make a totalitarian a man of action for whom his action was everything, nothing else having any importance: a man of destiny with no outside interests, totally identified with his role. Thus understood, the *totalitarian personality* cuts across the ages and surfaces in all sorts of historical bailiwicks, from Church to police and everything in between. A background of generalized hostilities will give it the best chance of prospering. War demands completely open-ended investment from the participant, the furnace of prolonged action making it impossible to take a long view or exercise mental restraint. At such extremes of intensity the distinction between the public man and the private one no longer applies. Mitterrand never had a serious war to wage, and there were two Mitterrands; but there was only one Fidel and only one Che. Educated by and for peace, democratic leaders can divide their time and engage in private activities, without allowing themselves to be wholly defined by their function; charismatic leaders have no shadowy areas because no one makes war half-heartedly. Our presidents make a point of appearing above or beside their thrones. In Paris, they cannot meet a writer without making the point that they too are of the fraternity and that, were it not for all their duties, they too would be churning out novels, essays and confessions. In other countries a president can be a failed Protestant minister, a businessman or a western actor who never really made it. In France he is a Flaubert *manqué*, victim of a shunting error. Unknowingly suffused with ancestral attitudes, with the aristocrat's statutory mistrust of clerics, the *comandantes* scorn such fripperies; they stare at intellectuals as at animals in a zoo; they themselves have no alibi, no second string. No game, no labyrinth: one holder of power, in a straight line. The democrat knows he is transitory. He lives at several tempos. He existed before his mandate and he will exist after it; his post is not his person. The totalitarian by contrast is a linear character, monomaniac, monochrome and metronomic. Power is not his job but his life; he gives himself to it completely, body and soul, without hope of a well-deserved retirement far from affairs: that would be an unthinkable abstinence. A man elected by the people leaves the Élysée at eight in the evening and moves on to *other things*: dinner in town, friends, family. To one elected by Providence these tender labyrinths are unknown. To Castro, who said he was wedded to the revolution (and who would see acting the husband, son, lover or father as dereliction of duty), playing basketball, sleeping with a woman or cooking spaghetti were simply amusements to restore his strength, pauses on the road without breaking the journey. Can anyone imagine him gardening and playing cards in a Mexican *finca*, a king in carpet slippers ending his days gently in gilded exile?

'Astonishing! A real Mussolini!' A beaming Moravia breathed these words into my ear without apparent irony. We were standing on the guests' platform in Revolution Square in 1966, listening to Fidel addressing a million Cubans, whom he had held spellbound for a good hour. 'You're taking the piss,' I replied. The remark seemed to me in pretty poor taste: if he had to mention an Italian, couldn't it be Garibaldi? 'No, no,' he said, unabashed, 'believe me, you weren't even born, but it was exactly like this.' His smile was foxy but delighted. (Alberto Moravia, who later became a friend, was anti-fascist to the core and remained pro-Cuban and 'Fidelista' for the rest of his life).

In distant hindsight I can see the lateral sagacity of a remark which, at the time, struck me as annoyingly sarcastic. Indeed I believe that in making it Moravia had found, paradoxically, the key to the seductive spell that an oral and declamatory island cast over our progressive minds. Scientific socialism, that cold medium in permanent subjection to its bookish origins, was singularly lacking in bombast, body, intonation. Communism, the last avatar of the religions of the Book, had grown up into a paper monster, pernickety and scholarly, resistant to improvisation. Its language was a *written* one, and Party orators *read* their speeches in neutral, monotonous tones. Astonishingly, old Soviet newsreels show Stalin at the worst moment of the Great Patriotic War, in a Moscow besieged by the Wehrmacht, calling on his compatriots for a great effort to save the country in a flat monotone, his face impassive, his nose close to the duplicated text he is reading into the microphone, like a branch secretary mumbling out a report on recent activities. In that heavy and grey world, where emotion was hardly shown, the sudden appearance of a Latin theatricality, a rhetoric of gesture and voice, would have had the effect, and not just the oratory, of 'a revolution within the revolution'. The change from the administrative delivery to which we had become accustomed – especially in Europe where the public ear had lost its familiarity with the grandiloquence appropriate to great circumstances, and where the TV talkshow had not yet privatized eloquence down to a murmur – was a youthfully refreshing discovery, a tonic return to the wellsprings of the rhetorical *actio* in ancient Rome. And it restored a great deal of vital vigour to the liturgy, fascist in style up to a point, but without Mussolini's ludicrous huffing and puffing, his 'peplum' side. Television, pursuing the 'fireside chat' development launched by radio in the 1950s, has now rendered these gesticulations retrospectively comic, the absurdity here serving as the external sign of the technological break between paragraph and soundbite.

In the process, though, the Caribbean island inverted the sexual symbolism underlying the secular role of Reason in History. To the heirs of the Enlightenment the written word was masculine, the mass of people feminine. The task of the Leninist cadre (and others too) was to deposit the seed of the written word in the lap of the supposedly literate masses, a scientific insemination that would produce nine months (or years, or decades) later a legitimate offspring: the Revolution. The population of peasants and workers, pregnant with his works (complete if possible), would give birth painfully but reliably when the time came. The fascists moved the rationalist baseline, by shifting their infantile omnipotence fantasies to the spoken word and restoring life-giving force and violence to orality and images, while feminizing writing. Fascist intellectuals, as well as leaders, aspired to be machos of the live spoken word. In *Je suis partout* and as late as 1943, Brasillach was still accusing democracy of having 'deprived the nation of images to the advantage of the dry written word'. Moravia had summarized the paradox with a witty observation that was also *true*: at a mass meeting in Havana, a Western intellectual had managed to enjoy simultaneously the two pleasures, normally thought incompatible, of being both a communist *and* a fascist; or rather (since it was out of the question to enjoy anything to do with fascism) the pleasure of using a contraband archaism in half-deliberate violation of an interdict.

But doubtless these comparisons are too ideological. Perhaps what we discovered over there was quite simply, via the hot immediacy of the Word, the obscure physiology of belief enunciated by St Paul: *Ex auditu fides*. Faith through hearing. To believe *in* someone you have to hear them, if possible not alone: close contact, the physical touch of voice on eardrum. To believe *that* something is thus or thus, all you need to do is read or look in silence. Anyone rising from the *credible* to the *believable*, from weakly held deduction to fully dynamic adhesion, is practising the Pauline adage: he is *listening* to the muezzin's voice floating down from the minaret, the preacher's from the pulpit, the leader's from his platform. He becomes all eardrum.

Don't forget that in ancient Greek the same verb designated hearing and obedience. *Upakouein*, to obey, means literally to hear from below. Of course one can hardly imagine a tribune getting an audience in the palm of his hand by shouting up at it from below. Perched on a high wooden dais, behind his desk with its row of raised microphones, Fidel loomed over a pit packed with subjugated listeners. To me he remains a *voice*, an intonation I only have to hear accidentally on the radio to be gripped by it anew.

*   *   *

We Europeans, pasteurized and homogenized, raise our eyebrows at all this picturesque truculence. At these kings of *pronunciamento*, these kiss-curled Soulouques. The small size of that Caribbean country and its modest standing assign it to inside pages, befitting the baroque offspring of a shattered communism. Quite wrongly. Fidel Castro is not the fanatic people think. He is recounting our own forgotten history. That this should seem eccentric to serious people is really the measure of the amnesia that prevails 'at the centre of the world', in our overdressed and as it were deodorized societies. What we forget – *repress* – is war.

As there are both war and peace, so there are two chiefs. Two Mohammeds in one: the preacher of God's mercy in Mecca is not the military leader ordering the slaughter of Jews and idolaters in Medina. In France, I frequented for ten years a ruler of great physical courage who disliked war, uniforms, Manichaeism, staff officers, the secret services and crude distictions between friends and enemies, instinctively avoiding these things and manoeuvring with smooth and consistent brilliance. In the Caribbean, for almost as long, I frequented another who disliked peace, shades of grey and badly cut tunics, tolerating these things only with difficulty. Mitterrand and Fidel Castro, president and *Comandante*, lord of peace and lord of war. Mecca and Medina. Planet of day, planet of night: does everything depend on the conditions?

El Comandante (the one and only, with the definite article) should have made us remember that 'La guerre, c'est moi' came before and was the basis of 'L'État, c'est moi'. Of course guerilla warfare is war from the old days, from before 1914, 'small war' born in Spain (where its ungraspable amateurishness threw Napoleon off his stroke), without heavy weapons, artillery or aviation. Not industrial and technological war, butchery between collective capacities rather than individual wills. A younger sister of feudal war. A matter of heart and soul, almost of single combat, in which everyone tests his own valour against others (and this ideal, archaic form of war, in Cuba, had been remarkably short and not especially bloody). To call the Commander-in-Chief the president would have been to insult and demote him. For forty years the Cuban leader has worn fatigues, boots, Sam Browne belt and pistol, only laying this uniform aside in recent times for foreign visits, two-piece suit and tie then making their appearance as a pledge of correctness, a sort of down payment on the hoped-for certificate of good conduct, to outwit the liberal adversary. Diplomacy and the dollar made the suit necessary (Castro being quite capable of taking up golf to force the gates of that club for suave big game, the 'international community').

He is a born conspirator with the art of being contrary. He is always the first to conspire against the governmental teams he has placed at the controls, distancing himself promptly from any minister who seems unpopular. As a result he embodies for his subjects both the state and protest against the incompetence and insensitivity of its bureaucrats. Like Philippe le Bel, Louis XI or Henri II in our own country, the populist king attacks the aristocracy on behalf of the common people. He may have accumulated a list of titles that would make Stalin, Mao, Franco or Duvalier blench, but the army chief far eclipsed the head of the party, of state, of government and the hundred other institutions he headed for the sake of form. His private residence in Havana has now become a military camp, the camp of the 'special troops'; in those days it was still a travelling camp, constantly on the move from one 'safe house' to another, without an escort of gunboats at sea or limousines on the road. Castro had still hardly emerged from behind Fidel, a king without pride or ceremony, without pomp or hauteur, like the Renaissance monarch Louis XII, who received the ambassador Machiavelli without making him wait. The country is his castellany, the state his inheritance: he administers it as a latifundist administers his hacienda. Supreme proprietor, master of measures and timetables, he keeps a staff of sergeants, provosts and foresters; officers and regional secretaries are his vassals, chairmen and ministers his aides-de-camp; the national budget, which is not publicly debated or controlled – does not even have accounts – is his Privy Purse; the Court, his HQ; his second in command, soon to become vice-president and vice-first secretary, was and is his younger brother Raúl. Feudal grandees surrounded the princes of the blood. There was no private or family life, no house, no small parties. The Chief was neither husband, nor father, nor son: he was Chief full-time. His love affairs, forgotten; his mistresses, Cuban and foreign, innumerable but scattered and anonymous; illegitimate offspring of the royal bed, whose numbers are uncertain (there are said to be eleven at the present time), kept at arm's length. There was a single fixed point in the capital: Celia Sánchez, his lover and secretary in the Sierra Maestra, at whose house he resided when in Havana. A small fierce bony person, diligent, discreet and like him never seen out of uniform, who ran his rear base and maintained the line of communication with the civilian in charge. While the Great Uncatchable restlessly prowled the island without programme or timetable, a jeep for a horse and Kalashnikov for a sword, distributing alms and largesse to the poor who besieged him with supplications.

The *escolta* consisted of ten or so *guajiros* in olive-drab without special insignia. When you sat in the back seat of his car your feet rested on and among a jumble of automatic weapons; and on the top floor of Celia Sánchez's aggressively functional house in *calle once*, where he used to sleep on a metal-framed bunk in vest and underpants, we would eat our breakfast within easy reach of the arsenal piled on the floor under his bed. Because you never know, do you? Apart from this detail and the communications equipment in the next room, the *Jefe* lived like a student in digs, amid bare walls and a joyous shambles of books and papers. His personal security was still quite relaxed, based on complicity and mobility. The Chief was elusive, not yet in the style of a despot living in his fortress under heavy guard (the thousand men of the battalion responsible for security of the *Palacio*), but that of a guerilla who 'bites and runs', vanishes without warning in the opposite direction to the one he has just indicated, with random changes of route further down the road. Unpredictable, purposely, and instinctively unpunctual. No fixed itinerary, no timetable: the magnificent informality of a *condottiere*. A half-hour meeting could go on for sixteen hours, while an official visit might be cut short without explanation. Formal civilities were left to a president of the Republic, Osvaldo Orticos, a pleasant-mannered jurist content to play the polished, stoical front man. No one went to bed before three or four in the morning, a habit of guerillas who lie low in daylight and travel after dark. The state's clocks were set by his waking hours as normal ones are to the rising and setting of the sun. This meant that there were two daily rhythms: the orderly and predictable one followed by the technocratic ministers, department heads and senior officials at work during office hours, running everyday business; and another, without agenda or timetable, for the comandantes who – they too – could never be located, most of whom had no well-defined function, but who possessed the two visible attributes of delegated sovereignty: a beard and a pistol (the latter sometimes carried at the belt under the *guayabera*, sometimes ostentatiously visible on the hip). In that flying head-quarters, to which foreign ambassadors and dignitaries, even Soviet ones, had practically no access, a minister in civilian dress cut the lowly figure of an esquire or shield-bearer. Such commoners, men who had not put their lives on the line at the proper time and place – in the purifying Sierra, not in the corrupting cities – got their simple due: the paperwork of decrees and decisions, the drudgery of sucking up to 'fraternal countries' which – with the mysterious exception of Bulgaria – were viewed with unrelenting scorn. Not even the Soviet Union was sacred: 'a giant country run by midgets', Fidel used to call it, not without insight and in a tone of decent regret, leaving me to conclude that a small island run by a giant must be preferable. Fortunately, to make up for Kruschevs, Mikoyans, Bulganins, and so on, there were still memories of Stalingrad, the partisans, Marshal Zhukov and the battle of Kursk (the greatest tank battle in history) to secure for the 'old-time' Soviets a leading place in the heroes' worldwide roll of honour. A historical primacy maintained by epic movies from the Mosfilm studio (which Raúl Castro used to have shown in his private cinema) and edifying novels translated into Spanish, like Nicholas Ostrovsky's *And the Steel was Tempered* or Boris Polevoï's *A Real Man*, used for evening readings in our barracks. The Red Army absolved the Soviet Party, Kruschev's withdrawal in the October missile crisis, in an inexplicable abdication of will, having confirmed the congenital pusillanimity of the civilians, the overfed bureaucrats, who had the final word in the Eastern countries. It goes without saying that the second circle – the old Communists – tended to see the first – the original 26 July men – as a *camarilla* of 'irresponsible petty-bourgeois elements', amateurish firebrands. Catapulted into the *Jefe*'s inner entourage over the heads of these officials, I was more in touch really with the decision-making process than the administrative details, especially as Cuba was not a country that burdened itself with normality (managing, for example, to survive for seventeen years without a constitution). It is not difficult to imagine the sort of thing that might have been said about some 'little protégé', some foreign freelance from an imperialist country, who was not even a Party member, being projected into the inner circle over the heads of these protectors of orthodoxy. I do not include among these apparatchiks Carlos Rafael Rodriguez, a cultivated and cosmopolitan former Communist leader who at that time was number three in the régime, after Fidel and Raúl. Like a lot of ex-Stalinists, he was a good deal more tolerant of heretics than late-model Bolsheviks.

Born of the fortunes of war and chance, that still-improvised monarch was not crowned at Reims or Westminster. He did not cure scrofula. He had no truck with Christ, the Virgin or the saints. But he had his own transcendence, the Revolution; his own great deeds and predecessors; his lineage and historiographers; his privy councillors, his dukes and earls, his liturgies, his largesses, his majestic pleasure, his 'secrets', his dungeons and iron masks, his special orders, his Bastilles; his inexhaustible goodness of heart and his bad advisers ('If Fidel knew about that it could never have happened' being the country's most popular refrain, from shanty to villa). For people do not call him Castro, they call him Fidel, as they used to call Louis or Henri by their first names, the virtual ubiquity of sovereigns ensuring a sort of familiarity that enables them to be designated in this way. Certainly this king is a man of the sword and not of the law. The basic laws of the kingdom do not dominate him; he can do what he likes with them and they can do nothing to him. He is a king *in statu nascendi*, drawing his sacrality from his personal exploits and not, like a Christian king, from a pre-existing state or tradition. He is a pure war king. Is it so strange after all, a rebel ending as king? War tends to create monarchs and the word rebel derives from the Latin *re-bellum* : 'he who restarts war'. Any war that continues beyond a certain point is a monarchy approaching. Let a successful captain but say to his comrades: 'The war's over, let's move on to other things,' and there it is at the top of the agenda. (Republicans have a form of courage that I lack. They alone – Washington, Clemenceau, de Gaulle – are capable of reclosing the doors of the temple of Janus.) 'The king is a maker of war as a cobbler is of shoes,' said the sixteenth-century Spanish Jesuit and historian Mariana de la Reina.

At the time of the Tricontinental *monarquía* would have seemed comic or out of place; but *guerra* was on everyone's lips, the word heard on every crossroads. The record has retained the 'missile crisis' of October 1962, the frisson of the decade. On the spot, nuclear vertigo was experienced as just another thing to be faced, not necessarily any worse than the others. My friends described it almost as a faint and distant memory. Our Cold War over there was hot, dirty and energetic, and had started in 1959 before there was any talk in Havana of Marx and Lenin. First the CIA blew up the cargo ship *Couba* in Havana harbour, killing eighty people; bombs were planted in cinemas, cane fields were set on fire, sugar factories sabotaged; then came the landing in the Bay of Pigs, with preliminary bombing of airfields; weapons were parachuted into Escambray, in the middle of the island, where three thousand 'counter-revolutionaries' were being given a hard time as the new Rebel Army; Mafia teams were sent from Miami to assassinate Fidel, glamorous woman spies were set on him in airport-novel style: all acts of aggression that were not committed by the *comandantes*. But although they would probably have preferred to do without it, this 'low-intensity warfare' came to fit them like a glove. As well as being their sole unarguable speciality, clandestine warfare confirmed their pre-eminence, while bringing the salt of the earth wonderfully into step with a new plebeian nobility that owed everything to the Chief. The whole island could become a military camp, and the olive green uniform (the colour of palm leaves) its symbol of support, its collective icon. And apart from the fact that the periods of pluralism in Cuba had been too short, and too absurd, to implant a liberal tradition or any nostalgia for one, the ingrained habits of clandestinity were unlikely to facilitate any move in that direction. Even in France, as the Resistance showed, an underground organization is never democratic but vertical: there are no written statutes, no time to consult the rank and file, to meet, to work things out. Too much democracy in underground warfare means death or disintegration. The head of a network or movement is a *boss*, not an elected leader required to explain his acts and respond to the wishes of his electors. He works through trust, nerve, personal authority. And the ruling group around him must necessarily have the character of a *clan* – in the case of an enemy or competitor known as a *clique* – while repression and the threats of infiltration and betrayal reduce the leader to 'the solitary exercise of power'. *Dura lex sed lex.* Veterans of a clandestine struggle, wherever it may have taken place, very rarely become good democrats who respect due processes. From the inside, that continuing state of clandestine war, along with the determination, swiftness of decision and compartmentalization it demanded, made us see the absence of freedom as natural, even desirable.

An aristocratic ideal can perhaps take shape more easily behind an egalitarian discourse than in the bourgeois cult of ability and celebrity, as if the ritualized celebration of the 'masses' aroused in each individual, through a spirit of contradiction, the desire to stand out. The contribution of this fortified vanguard to the communist mainstream (influential among Third-World liberation movements raised and trained in the island between 1960 and 1990) had been not the *abolition* of stern egalitarian hierarchy but the reversal of its poles, replacing doctrine with action. A heroic-sentimental demiurgy: to receive, all that is needed is the will. Ordinarily, in Russia and China, leading Party clerics controlled the hierarchs of the (Red or People's) army and promoted engineers and technicians, exalting dams, canals, petrochemical plants and cosmodromes. The tropical equivalent of this technico-scientific *hubris* (beyond the means of a poor or small country) was the macho-Leninist cult of the armed superman, of which the Japanese samurai-movie star Toshiro Mifune, idolized in a Cuba starved of Gary Cooper and John Wayne by the blockade, became the exemplary incarnation. 'The best swords are those that remain in the scabbard' (the wise *ronin*'s remark framed by Kurosawa as the final moral of *Sanjuro*) had not registered. *Valentía* came above clear-sightedness, embattled nation eclipsed toiling country; and politics, more a matter of *cojones* than prudence, was a continuation of war by other means.

Hence the amount of time devoted by the blue-bloods to physical exercise, shooting competitions, spear-fishing and hunting, all hobbies of their *primus inter pares*, Fidel. With the power of the mind annulled and that of gold banned, ideally there remains nothing in the lists but the sword. It writes History in a language of virile exploits that the clerics, holders of the written word, will explain to the people later by means of lectures, lessons, quotations. In feudalism the political and military functions were not separated, as they are in democracies where the military is the 'sword arm' of the thinking head. No political commissar to accompany and supervise the head of a military unit. Civilians had to obey the guerillas: in Bolivia, Che always insisted on the subordinate role of the Communist Party, something utterly heretical in traditional terms. After Guevara's death the Soviets made unceasing efforts to restore the primacy of commissars over constables.

The knights of old did not themselves cultivate the land from which they lived. At the beginning of the revolution their tropical descendants, many of whom were former agricultural labourers, imagined that they too would be exempted from productive toil, as from fiscal and economic constraints, especially as the notion of taxes had disappeared and most of the urban services were free or virtually so: telephone, hospital, accommodation very nearly, education and electricity. As minister of industry, Ernesto Guevara strove to get revolutionaries interested in economic production by clothing it in warrior prestige. He did this by militarizing the vocabulary and even the staff: cane-cutting 'brigades', worker 'contingents', production 'battles'. And by sending the soldiers of the Rebel Army to do 'voluntary labour' as cane-cutters. By means of such fatigues – ritualized, almost liturgical offerings of sweat – the state managed to reconcile the doctrinal primacy of 'productive labour' with the moral supremacy of the combatant, and Marxist 'science' with popular mythology.

In that bucolic monarchy without legists or mediating bodies – in simplistic terms a dictatorship pure and simple – the men of power inhabit a space without shade or nuance, harshly black and white. In places where militants can only subsist as courtiers, individual careers are characterized by violent fluctuations, sudden stops and starts, high and low moments with no apparent cause. This produces men gnawed by anxiety, without plan or programme, deprived of a safe middle altitude between flying high and crashing. On the higher levels of the pyramid it is access to the summit (or lack of it) that makes the difference between life's losers and triumphant winners. *Estar en la viva* (being in the loop) and *tener acceso* (having access to Fidel) conferred a quasi-supernatural, highly precarious status that reflected not the official post or social rank of those so honoured, but wholly unpredictable and decisive personal contacts. It placed on the rack the five hundred-odd important uniformed individuals who seethed over the upper slopes, striving not to *have* this or that, but to *be* someone or other. Primacy depended not on the visiting card, titles having no real significance (membership of the Political Bureau did mean something; ministers, directors and Central Committee members played cosmetic roles), but on a single magical faculty: being or not being one of those who saw *him*. An unexpected fall did not move the climber from 'in' to 'out' (as in those relatively benign magazine articles about fashion) but from Being to Nothingness. Such thunderbolts – sudden, irrevocable, quickly known to all Havana – could cause years of depression, and few of those struck by them survived unscathed. A lot of leaders who had lost access in this way later committed suicide, from illustrious individuals like (President of the Republic) Osvaldo Orticos and Haydée Santamaria (heroine of the early days, legendary chairwoman of the *Casa de las Americas*), down to obscure serving ministers who had been abruptly and humiliatingly unplugged.

The scramble for intimacy with the *Jefe* became, for the successful, a race for the precipice. How can we explain this paradox of the *libido dominandi* without positing a death impulse? Only by pointing to the enchantment that no one raised to the heights can escape. Once the new favourite has gained access to the holy of holies – games of chess at *calle once*, midnight volleyball in the gym, shooting competitions on the range at dawn, picnics on the corner of a table at breakfast time with French wine and cheese – daily life there quickly becomes so easy and familiar, so ordinary and relaxed that, apart from the change of pattern (sleeping through the day until three in the afternoon, not really getting moving until dinner time), he feels that nothing very 'enchanting' has happened. The favoured individual is surprised to find an impalpable gulf opening between himself and others: family, colleagues, friends. They have understood that he is within the magical – or accursed – force-field of great secrets. They instinctively scent the perils of bewitchment, of upward aspiration, discerning more clearly than he does the pitfall that awaits the one thus miraculously blessed: disgrace, banishment without a word or worse – dungeons, suicide, degradation – simply because the fool has let slip an ill-chosen word or made some blunder (or merely been reported as doing so to the supreme Chief by a rival, in tones more of sorrow than anger). Friends soon start to avoid the future leper and lower their voices in his presence: he has become 'holy'. Fascinating but alarming, a man apart, at risk from mood-swings as well as catastrophes. All vassals allow themselves to be possessed by this curse. The *Jefe* is a man like others, disconcerting in his simplicity, who gets excited over nothing, like a child; who takes a sudden shine to some unknown and keeps him around all the time, takes him everywhere *por arriba y por abajo*, from evening till morning, until by imperceptible degrees the honoured one lets himself go, drops his guard. He

may to succumb to 'vainglory' (as Loyola called it), by becoming boastful in front
of a rival awaiting just such a chance. He may blurt out on the telephone when
asking a personal favour (something utterly trivial, a small amount of foreign
currency, a late-model Lada, permission for a cousin to travel abroad), to a
minister or understrapper who sounds uncertain or reluctant, an encouraging
'Go ahead, I was with the Chief last night'. A few days later, without warning or
explanation, the sky will fall on the presumptuous fellow's head. The *Jefe* no
longer shows any sign of life. He has become invisible, unfindable. That is when
the dropped vassal – *comandante*, minister or diplomat – discovers the ontological
abyss that separated him without his knowing it from the man whose friend,
whose right arm, whose alter ego he believed he had become. He discovers that
men need God but this particular God, proverbs notwithstanding, does not need
men. And that everything rests on that dissymmetry. But too late, for once fallen
he will never rise again. Back on the plain, all he can do is try vainly to climb
back up the slope by asking, casually, on some anodyne pretext, for some
plausible intercession with the *Palacio* from a more or less indulgent intermediary
(who will, however, be very careful not to take phone calls from the infectious
one). Eventually, among the former *compañeros* he meets by chance, a few months
if not years later (at an embassy or a reception, or on some platform), he may
well manage, dangerous though he has become, to corner one and ask in an
offhand way if Fidel has received his message of explanation, if everything is
OK, if the misunderstanding has been cleared up. But the use of the name Fidel
(the one used by ordinary *Fidelistas*, 'Castro' being used only by declared
enemies) alerts the intended intermediary, who looks away in embarrassed
commiseration. For it is proof that the outcast really has become a stranger: in
the immediate entourage, at the true heart of things, the *Jefe* is referred to in his
absence by a gestural periphrasis, the equivalent of the four letters used by
Hebraic scholars to indicate the unpronounceable name of God. Two fingers pass
close to the chin suggesting a beard, or touch the shoulder to evoke the silver star
on the epaulette. That is the current style of the archangels with human faces of
whom it is said, in hushed tones, that they 'work directly with Fidel': members of
the *Despacho* and the *Grupo de Apoyo* (the Office and the Support Group). Current,
or rather former. For these gestures gradually lost their distinctiveness as a result
of being imitated by the common herd (everyone does it now to indicate the
Supreme one). Another way of displaying one's connivance with Upstairs (*allá
arriba*) had to be invented. Through reverence, ecstasy, fear or collusion, or
through all of these, the celestial militia of *ayudantes* always employs a periphrasis,
a code name that changes with fashion, from one interlocutor to another: the
inexorable obsolescence of passwords. *La Iglesia* for example; *El Hombre, El
Uno* . . . thus, in the Old Testament, Elohim or Adonai, to circumscribe the
location of the prime Subject. *Omnis potestas a Deo*. All chiefs, said St Paul, come
from and represent God. Just admitting it out loud lightens the heredity, and
such authorized catharsis, reducing or even eliminating millenarian terror, is the

major difference between the governing entity of today and its theocratic
ancestor. The satirical use of the title 'God' by journalists and song-writers
in France, to designate with polite mockery President Mitterrand, underlined *a
contrario* that he was only a man like others. The name disarmed the thing itself,
warded off its return, released the wish for it. A real God, intolerant and
punitive, in the image of the primitive horde's Old Man, has power of life and
death over his creatures, who are not advised to make witty remarks. For a
member of the entourage to call the Commander-in-Chief 'God' out loud
before witnesses would have been a sign of suicidal insanity, as well as a rigorous
objectivity which the rest of his life would not have been long enough to expiate.
Not only affection and piety, but the omnipresence of microphones (rightly or
wrongly assumed by everyone, even his intimates, to be planted in the house, the
office and the car), stimulated the liege's capacity for poetic metaphor in
referring to the suzerain, shutting earls and esquires alike into the indirect
discourse appropriate to negative theology (a Supreme Being that can be
designated only in terms of absence, beyond any human or positive determination).

God gets angry but never laughs (nor does Christ). That is the deepest
difference between democratic and autocratic divinity: I have seen Mitterrand
laugh heartily on many occasions, to the point of shedding tears, when listening
to a funny story or some piece of absurdity (the sort of thing that Roger Hanin, a
witty man and warm friend, used to tell him). For a king, laughing in public
means revealing himself, stripping himself bare. Having himself a very dry sense
of humour, François Mitterrand made this confession of weakness with a good
grace. I never saw Fidel (or Che either) laugh, pass on a good story, recall a
comic film. Knowing, having always known, that laughter is sacrilegious,
therefore regicidal, the *Jefe* regarded gags with horror and jokes with suspicion.
It was not a question of propriety or etiquette, but of metaphysics. A seeker of
the Absolute possessed by the supreme Cause cannot even consider allowing it to
be relativized by a *bon mot*. No one can distance himself from the sacred, still less
laugh at it. In religious regimes, the weighty interdict from the top on
caricatures, satires and parodies (compensated among the rank and file by
an underground cult of derision and damaging epidemics of good stories, a sort
of spontaneous, clandestine anti-tragic defence) made seriousness compulsory;
but at the very top it was natural, obvious and so to speak superhuman. It is not
omnipotence that makes God, it is omnisufficiency. That rigid entity is a
universe in itself; there is no *outside*. Such inward closure on the self, indispensable to the sacred (which without it would be exposed to the risk of creeping
incredulity), makes for *closed* hierarchs, closed in the same way as a society, a face
or a door. Fixed, sure of themselves, both feet on the ground, masters of
themselves and of the universe.

The mortal gravity of immortals. Whose faces crack from an excess of poise.

*   *   *

Old soldiers have medals, annual banquets, pensions, a ministry. But for 'professional revolutionaries' there is no veterans' association, no unknown soldier or eternal flame. It is a short-term contract (Lenin, who invented the thing and the term, did not supervise its development), a job whose *career pattern* is tiresome when not fatal. Painters and Bordeaux vintages improve with age. But staying in one place and being promoted spoils a revolutionary. The veteran will turn tyrant or pirate, bureaucrat or delinquent (or any combination of these). If the underground combatant ever achieves his aim his tunic will be plated with gongs, his skull covered by overbearing headgear, his tongue coated in fat and turgid words. By failing to die, by staying afloat on the ebb tide, the Rebel ends as a Godfather. And the liberation movement, a mafia. So too for the rank and file: if it avoids the work of mourning, it will change over the same period – between ten and thirty years – almost without being aware of it, from an esoteric aristocracy into a parasitic lumpen class, as emergency military courts become local assizes and political decisions mutate into common law. At the beginning, for the cause of good; at the end, to survive.

While there was still hope, along with some semblance of organizational support, it had robbed a bank or two to get money for weapons, for the support network, to pay off associates in neighbouring countries. To minimize risk it had taken to kidnapping the odd inoffensive industrialist for ransom; and more profitably still, cooperating with narcotraffickers for a percentage. Each downward step is negotiated without difficulty. At what point does illegality become criminality, a guerilla a desperado, 'revolutionary levies' a protection racket? In such rampant underground wars, never formally declared or won or lost, the insurgent can easily persuade himself that the profits will come in useful later, when the struggle is resumed. The statistical chances of success – if the 'seizure of power' can be termed a success – being of the order of one in a thousand, there must be 999 'revolutionaries without revolutions' wandering the urban jungles as free electrons (against *one* government soon to begin exiling, liquidating or corrupting its own heroes). Th *ex* then becomes a problem for society. In Colombia, the reinsertion of insurgents into legal life causes the sort of problems we have in financing the social services or keeping the inner cities quiet: the state and the Church have both launched 'reintegration programmes', with limited success. In Venezuela, one president of the Republic financed out of his own privy purse the purchase of *fincas* and shares for unemployed petty warlords. And he knew exactly what he was doing, so deeply can the idealist's degeneration into a gangster eat into a society. The metamorphosis of Sandinista and Salvadorean *comandantes* into unabashed businessmen gave many people food for thought. *Perdieron los principios, los valores, el sentido de la lucha* ('They lost their principles, their values, the desire to fight'), commented, rather scornfully, my old Guatemalan friend Ricardo, a leader for many years in a guerilla army still active today. This decomposition is almost a physical phenomenon: returning to the profane world seems to cause the missionary to fall apart, much as a spacecraft's jettisoned booster motor burns up on re-entry to the atmosphere.

'Resign! Resign!' This supposedly hostile cry shouted at an erring minister by parliament, I would willingly echo in a votive sigh, a supplicatory coo, to persuade the Man of History to return to the perfection of his own being through abdication, exile or suicide: some positive catastrophe. The request should be addressed, in particular, to war kings who in any case, for functional aesthetic reasons, should not make old bones; while peacetime kings, or most of them, take on with time a patina of old ivory which improves them (a Mitterrand is at his worst at 30, at his best at 60). For a long time I hoped, like most of his old supporters, that Fidel would resign one day or – better still – manage some sort of immolation in action: the opposite of cyanide in a ruined bunker. A lot of Fidelistas hoped – for they did not want to watch Castro degrading Fidel and consigning him to the oubliettes of an intransmissible legend – that Castro would emulate the Swedish warrior king Gustav-Adolf, killed while leading his troops at Lützen in 1632: the *Jefe* hurling himself on the barbed wire at Guantanamo, like José Martí felled by a Yankee bullet as he charged the Spaniard with sabre drawn. This picture-postcard vision somewhat discounts the realist's sense of self-preservation: good politicians take better care of their physical health than their posthumous images. That is why in the end Castro, who always remembered to secure his rear, won the battle of positions and lost the battle of dreams: the antithesis of Che, whose shortcomings as a politician finally served him well. No matter that he chose to enter legend to escape from personal and political impasses: the Guevarist saga saved the revolution from foundering in a moral morass. What could be more clownishly sad than an old beard, perorating amid the rubble on the youth of the world? The substitution of the actor's 'number' for old-style declamatory music-hall singing frustrates our selfish demand for proper style and comportment (in other people); Castro has not played fair in this respect, while Guevara satisfies us because, once 'astride his Rosinante', he never dismounted. Time has degraded the Monarch, and made the Crusader sublime. Rather unfairly, given their relative competence and performance: Che couldn't be bothered with *follow-up*, he liked starting things but to tell the truth soon tired of running them. But there is a higher justice, the inverse of the 'reason of state' although just as influential, that might be called the reason of the weakest: it is the loser who wins.

'*Mourir pour les idées oui / mais de mort lente . . . / Car à forcer l'allure il arrive qu'on meure / Pour des idées n'ayant plus cours le lendemain . . .*' ('To die for ideas yes / but a slow death . . . / For by forcing the pace you can die /For ideas out of date by next day . . .'). Is Brassens just fobbing us off with words? Che's ideas may still be spine-chilling, but they are no longer current. He forced the pace, but there he still is, more alive than ever. His silhouette still walks among the poor, his poster is still popular with the rich who know a romantic hero when they see one. Like Kennedy in his West. Never growing old, because murdered, like the Argentine and the American, or deposed, like Bolívar and de Gaulle: what better passport to the beyond? Slow death is a renunciation, the wire cut before time, a consecration that marks the forehead with a sacramental sign. What is the point of prolonging a reign by a few years, if the name loses its radiance a century sooner as a result? Old chiefs become attached to the petty pleasures of power, the delights of appointing, promoting and sacking, making and unmaking: are they unaware that such protracted indulgences ought to be discouraged? (Mitterrand took something of a risk by standing for a second term as president, not to press forward a governing idea or pursue a great quarrel, but merely to demonstrate tactical mastery of seduction and manoeuvre.) What the physical individual loses, his myth gains a hundredfold. On the world stage, the lead roles are the worst, since in political action (more than any other subject to entropy), no one can win by 'achieving his objectives', 'fulfilling his contract' or even 'making his actions live up to his words'. Even the luckiest, who can be counted on the fingers of one hand, have not managed as Bolívar did to escape the realization of failure, the final what-was-the-point. Among politicians the ultimate split is between those who succeed at failure and those who fail at it (by trying to stay too long). De Gaulle did not establish 'participation and national independence' in his lifetime; Che did not achieve his 'continental liberation war' or Allende 'socialism in freedom'. But the failure of their very different dreams helps us to nourish dreams of our own, as their death helps keep us alive.

It seems appropriate that the French democrat and Cuban autocrat should have met in Paris, in the autumn of their careers. What they have in common is that they *dragged on*: posterity has every chance of remembering them both in shades of grey. This judgement is less moral than aesthetic: unlike the academic centuries (the century of Louis XIV, for example), today's taste is for sketches, life-drawings rather than finished and varnished canvases; for aphorisms, snippets and fragments rather than polished orotund prose; lives cut short in their prime, oaks felled before 40 rather than deserving centenarians. In politics, as in painting and literature, there is no feeling of completeness unless something is left unfinished, as if in this domain too *finished* and *truncated* meant the same.

To understand the extreme unimportance of ideology in governing the conduct of its greatest champions, all we need do is consider the opposite courses followed by the two main comandantes. People do not choose the crown of thorns – or the crown either – because they are Marxist or communist. Depending on culture and individual temperament, that doctrine can embrace accommodation with circumstances – endurance at any cost – as well as supreme love of solitude, the Spartacus way. At the crossing of the two roads Fidel and Che met, as (later, and in more bourgeois fashion) did Mitterrand and Mendès France: the eternal split in the political vision of the world does not prevent the cunning and the intransigent from meeting and even cooperating (although never for long). The two Frenchmen were rivals and not friends, while

Argentine and Cuban made a tandem of complementary opposites, fraternally united although from different families. Fidel lived the horizontal life of a man who took care of business, Che the vertical one of a dreamer.

Quarrel, divorce, exile: rumour made it a replay of Stalin and Trotsky. The Relter and the Paladin, the impudent and the imprudent. Reassuring, that: a familiar scenario. But misleading. As chance would have it, I was myself the last messenger between the two companions in arms. Before my departure for Nancahuazu, Fidel talked to me privately for an entire night about Che, showing the mixture of tact, pride and anxiety that an elder brother might feel for a younger about to start an adventure: one whose defects he knows well, only loving him the more for them. And I heard how Che spoke about Fidel before my planned return to Havana (after a detour through other countries), loading me down with messages for him, both personal and political (his radio transmitter had stopped working). With unquestioning devotion. Of course, in that abandonment to his own devices of the former right hand man, there are aspects that remain puzzling even to the survivors, of whom there are three. However, I can bear witness that there was never a break between Che and Fidel, and that their contrasting sensibilities did not damage their relations of allegiance. If mystery there is, that is where it lies: in that nomad's inflexible loyalty to the only sedentary chief he had ever recognized. It hangs on psychology, not ideology. Before he met Fidel in Mexico, Che was a lever without a fulcrum, which would never have managed to lift anything if the Cuban had not provided a base on solid ground. Something like that leaves a debt. Weaned from his adolescent leftism by a pragmatic *caudillo*, that landless outsider owed him no less than his entry to the real world, and the chance to prove himself in it.

Culturally, they were opposites in everything. Guevara was first and foremost a man of the Book; *criollos* are people of oral tradition, resistant to synthesis, to organization, to logical sequence. A narrative, localist, anecdotal mentality to which the Argentinian's European-style education and rational, slightly melancholy coldness did not predispose him. Fidel, who reads nothing but history (obsessed as he is by historians in the future and his own posthumous image) and for whom theory has never been a problem, has no interest in debating ideas and never listens to an adversary's argument. Studious and keen to base his approach on the truth, Che used to study opposing arguments, and was careful to distinguish the objective from the subjective, not just the useful from the useless (the method was obligatory, not the result: you could go wrong, but should at least have tried properly). When still very young he had devoured Jules Verne, Conrad, Lorca and Cervantes; he had learned French and English; he read economic treatises and took notes. He used to invite heretics to Cuba (the Trotskyist Mandel, the Maoist Bettelheim) to hear what they had to say. In Bolivia, almost at the end of his strength, he still carried books on his shoulder.

Earlier he had made himself a small library, hidden in a cave next to the food supplies and the transmitter: medical books but also Trotsky's *My Life*, short works by Mao and the poems of León Felipe. A heavy rainstorm damaged everything, and he gave the bringer of the bad news a ferocious tongue-lashing. We all believed there would be years of coming and going, as around a Chinese-type red base. Among the things he had asked me to do was to bring him some books on my next trip to complete his reserves. I remember that the list began with Gibbon's *Decline and Fall of the Roman Empire*, proof enough surely that he thought he had time ahead of him, once his rearguard was stabilized. Gibbon's opus, completed in 1788, was a mere distant school memory to me, rather like Voltaire's *Le Siècle de Louis XIV* (I have not read either). To Che it appeared relevant. And now that historians are analysing the decadence of the American Empire, this incongruous interest seems to suggest a certain foresight.

A ruminant of the written word, then, but devoured by impatience. Unwilling, or unable, to take his time like more adept managers of collective expectation. Not giving a damn really whether anyone understood him or not; not bothering to acquire the means to win the 'masses' over to his point of view, as politicians do. Not even his own lieutenants: he never explained orders, briefed the men, asked them any questions or invited them to speak. In this sense he was more despotic with his own people than Fidel. In the Congo and in Bolivia, he kept subordinates completely in the dark, keeping not just his plans but his motives to himself. A strategist, not a tactician. He aimed as far ahead as possible, and paid no heed to distance or terrain. 'Launch two, three, several Vietnams . . .' But how could Vietnam be reproduced in the Congo or Bolivia, so far from the paddy fields and Confucius? How could you get Africans and Latinos to dig underground mole-runs, to remain motionless in a hole for weeks breathing through a straw? How could you repeat even the Sierra Maestra anywhere else? Batista had no troop helicopters, but his colleagues had hastily acquired them following the Cuban Rebels' victory.

Always a beat ahead of the music, Fidel said of him. Yes, always in a hurry: to face enemy fire, take Santa Clara, enter Havana, redistribute land, break off relations with the US, bring communists into the government, publicly accuse the Soviet Union of neocolonialism, invite Jonas Savimbi and Holden Roberto (those shaky allies) to Cuba for training without looking twice; to rush off to Tanzania without even informing its legal authorities of his arrival; to face everyone with a *fait accompli*, without caring whether 'the objective and subjective conditions are appropriate or not'. Che, who politicized everything, was not an expert in politics; and on this point, in a sort of spoken confession that he made in my presence one night in 1967, Fidel had demonstrated irreproachable lucidity. Getting the timing right is a lay responsibility: the century's regular clergy couldn't spare the time to try. His own aim: to help New Man into the world with forceps, in a few decades. Disorganized individuals who left the queue instead of waiting their turn with God were stigmatized as 'leftists' and expelled from the Church. The Argentinian had enough contempt for doctors to risk excommunication, 'taking his own impatience for a theoretical argument' quite openly, without subterfuge.

Che liked to compare himself with an early Christian in the catacombs, grappling with the Roman Empire in the form of North America. After refuting the idea that Cuba was a 'historical exception', and convinced – as we all were – that 'the Andes Cordillera will soon be the Sierra Maestra of South America', he staked his inheritance on the Congolese rebellion. In 1965, more or less on impulse, he took a hundred black troops – he thought colour made people 'African' – to make war in the hinterland of Lake Tanganyika: the escapade was a disaster, and Mobutu took power without firing a shot three days after the Cubans had gone home. His companions, under orders to follow him, hardly knew whom they were fighting or whose side they were on or why. Che attributed this discomfiture to the personal ineptitude of his local allies, Lumumba followers grouped in a shadowy 'National Liberation Council' who lounged in hotel rooms in Paris and Dar es-Salaam issuing phoney victory communiqués. After that he went to plant his cross not far from Argentina, the land of his mother, of his fiancées and tangos, where he would have liked to die. Another miss. His supporters promptly blamed moral betrayal by the local communist leadership: anything goes, to protect the historical metaphors that serve as the private motives of 'refounders'. No matter: the Pure in their catacombs despise expedients, detours and men as they really are. They head straight for the worst. Che was good at short cuts but knew nothing of what Christians call the economics of salvation. From Venezuelan baptism to Bolivian calvary, he went straight at it without pausing for thought. As one who sought death to escape the labour of mourning.

He was 24 and a pretty offhand medical student (he used to call himself *matasanos*, killer of the healthy) when he found his road to Damascus in the middle of the Venezuelan Andes. 'Verily, verily, I say unto you, the hour is coming, and now is, when the dead shall hear the voice of the Son of God: and they that hear shall live.' (John V, 25). The patrician internationalist St Paul, born in the year 10, announced that the Advent would be in the third decade of the first century. The upper-class Argentinian born in 1928 was hopeful that it would come before the last third of the twentieth century. A voice from the shadows, a slightly mad stranger encountered at night in an Indian mountain village at the end of that iniatory journey, had 'with a mischievous child's laugh' (as he noted the next day in his travel diary) given him the Glad Tidings: 'The future belongs to the people which, step by step or at a stroke, will conquer power here and everywhere on earth.' Like a missionary discovering his vocation, he moved from vaticination to fantasy then and there.

I saw his teeth and cunning expression as he anticipated History, I felt his handclasp . . . and now I knew that when the great governing spirit delivered the enormous blow that would divide humanity into two opposing factions, I would be on the people's side. And I knew, because I saw it engraved on the night, that I, the eclectic dissector of doctrines and psychoanalyst of dogmas, would charge howling like one possessed to storm barricades or trenches, I would bloody my weapon and, mad with fury, cut the throats of any vanquished who fell into my hands. And as if an immense fatigue were repressing my recent excitement, I saw myself fall, immolated in the authentic revolution that standardizes individual wills, pronouncing the edifying *mea culpa*. I could already feel my nostrils dilating, savouring the bitter odours of powder and blood, of the enemy's death. My body was already tensed for battle, and I was preparing my whole being as a temple that would respond, with new vibrations and new hope, to the bestial howling of the triumphant proletariat.

This was an illumination worthy of the 'fanatics of the Apocalypse', a mystical visitation like the ones experienced by the Lutheran heroes of peasant revolts. Everyone's thoughts wander extravagantly at one time or another. Generally these vengeful fantasies are forgotten on waking or on leaving the darkened auditorium as people return to 'serious matters'. The visionary, the all-or-nothing seer, differs from the ordinary dreamer in not rubbing his eyes or trying to return to earth. The nocturnal vision becomes his aim in broad daylight: 'To raise armies of internationalist proletarians, all united under the banner of Human Redemption.' Che raised the banner and the armies did not come; but the game was not yet lost, he said. Stubbornness was needed; victory would come later. And was it really even necessary? Buckling on your sword is what makes the crusade, not taking Jerusalem. 'What does it matter where death surprises us, as long as our war-cry has been heard?' And his was heard: in Nicaragua, Salvador and a dozen other places; thirty years after his death, the Mexican Zapatistas echoed it once again. Now it is their turn to put their ears to the ground, trying to detect the decisive vibration. And when they are killed? Others will rise at the back end of some valley, invoking the names of their predecessors. Carrying the torch in their turn.

The way of the cross had started out as a road movie. You have to travel to find the truth about yourself . . . Prince Siddhartha too had had to break out of the cocoon. Anyone will draw closer to humanity when far from his compatriots. In the two years – 1951 and 1952 – spent wandering the continent from *pampa* to *llano* on an old motorbike with his pal Granado, a leprosy specialist, Ernesto Guevara, an asthmatic rugby player who could run like the wind, made three discoveries: that there were Indians in America; that there were proletarians bent double in the mines; and that fortunately there were communists everywhere, so you could hold your head up. One very cold night, sheltering in a hut at Chuquicamata in northern Chile, Ernesto lent his blanket to the unknown miner sleeping beside him. He wrote in his travel diary: 'It was a day when I felt as cold as I ever have in my life, but never closer to the human species which is so strange to me.' Among that species, Castro was like a fish in water. Guevara stayed on the edge or above, an outsider, but subject to furtive flashes of affection. As if he had made himself into his own citadel. Two commanders, two styles of command, two visions of the world: the conspiratorial and the sacrificial. Sarcastic and undemonstrative, Che secured men's loyalty by giving as few signs of affection as possible, while Fidel captured them with communicative exuberance. Fidel trusted in lyrical contagion, Che in the power of example. The Cuban could tell the difference between a cause and a programme, between what doctrine demands and what reality permits. He was a politician who intended to endure. The Argentinian really preferred the impossible to the possible. He was a mystic who intended to die. His apotheosis is not explained solely by his handsome profile and 'hero appeal'. It is sudden death before the age of 40, a Christ-like precocity, that makes an artist, politician or star stand out from the common run (what would Jackson Pollock have been without his accidental death–suicide, or James Dean, or Valentino for that matter?). Che was not an angel blasted by a stroke of fate. He did not snatch his death: he had been incubating it for ten years.

Where power was concerned, his main purpose was not to conquer it, still less to conserve it. But to read into this indifference a Robin Hood or romantic caped rebel shows a certain ignorance of the subject (good and necessary though this may be for idealization). By inclination and on principle, the real individual was unarguably far harsher and less sympathetic than his power-seeking elder. Less demagogic than Fidel, and much less democratic. The fine photographs by Korda and Burri have left us a sensitive dreamer, when in reality gentleness and kindness were not among his salient characteristics. And what a fertile misunderstanding it was, in 1968 turning that believer in no-holds-barred authoritarianism into an emblem of anti-authoritarian revolt from Paris to Berkeley. A global wave of permissive nudist sensibility, lauding to the skies a corseted puritan. A return to 'ambulance clericalism' had replaced the militant at the top with a medic, a sort of *Médecin du Monde* before his time, but one who, after landing in Cuba in 1956 with the armed expedition, inaugurated his biography with an emblematic gesture: laying aside his medical kit to pick up the rifle of a fallen comrade. The posthumous simplification of complicated lives defines in every era the work of legend (the complementary opposite of the work of mourning). The natural effect of time, 'the great sculptor', has been assisted in this case by three factors: popular 'epic song', official adoption and posters in the West. In Cuba, the hero was made the keystone of the state religion. Schoolchildren used to recite every morning: *Todos los pioneros seremos como el Che* ('All us pioneers will be like Che'), and militants: *Sus enseñanzas fortalecen nuestro trabajo* ('His teachings fortify out labour'). He became *el hombre sin manchas* (the unblemished man), *el modelo del nuevo hombre*. These official liturgies detract not at all from a genuine and spontaneous popular affection. An entire continent has imbued the armed hermit with its nostalgias and longings. The people love him. Did he love the people? Yes, and humanity too: the idea rather than the flesh and blood, the mass rather than the single unit.

Every legend is a collection of misunderstandings, and this one is no exception. The apostle of 'resistance to bureaucracy', when Minister of Industry, preached ultra-centralized planning with administrative control of production and management. After he replaced 'material incentives' – the more you work, the more you are paid – with 'moral incentives' – the more you work, the more you are honoured – the system became languid in the lower levels and overblown, hypertrophied and inefficient in the upper ones. Under such conditions a managed economy is more or less synonymous with an all-powerful bureaucracy. Trying to industrialize an agrarian economy at a gallop, by interfering with the flows of raw materials and finance, led to widespread bankruptcy among small enterprises and threw the sugar cane industry into disarray. Failure on both fronts. A 'libertarian, indulgent, open-minded' Che, contrasted with a cruel and dogmatic Fidel? When in 1959 Fidel sent to the firing squad – the *paredón* – five *esbiros* from the former régime, Che would happily have shot ten. The death penalty was not a thing these war chiefs agonized over: in proper wars, especially guerilla wars, summary execution awaits traitors and deserters, at all times and everywhere. Capital punishment came naturally to them, through what Diderot would have called an 'idiocy' of their profession. But there is a difference between dishonouring enemies or rivals before standing them against a wall and the volley without phrases or calumnies. Che restricted himself to the second. But it was he and not Fidel who in 1960, on the Guanaha peninsula, invented the 'corrective labour camp' ('forced labour' would be more accurate), not, it must be admitted, without going to try it out for himself. The purity of exterminating angels: Che would never have tolerated homosexuals, deviants or 'crooks' in his entourage, as Fidel did. Political training, more solid and long-established in him than in the older man, made him resemble Nechayev ('the revolutionary is hard on himself and should be hard on others') rather than Tolstoy. 'I have no wife or house or child or father or mother or brother or sister. My friends are my friends when they think politically as I do,' he wrote in one letter. And that young Franciscan who wanted to cure the lepers of Peru, who evoked at one time the ideal revolutionary driven by a deep feeling of love, left as his testament a long cry of funereal hatred, 'efficient hatred,' as he called it, 'which makes a man an efficient, violent, selective and cold-blooded killing machine'. Islamists say the same thing with more flourishes.

The difference between the political guerilla and the 'heroic' one is the difference between an indulgently majestic Prince of the Church and an anchorite clinging to his discipline to escape the temptations of compromise. Or a team captain, centrist by necessity, and a left-winger who will insist on playing his own game. The Cuban may have been a dictator, but he was more willing to negotiate – more subject to the reality principle – than his lieutenant. In an adoptive country, therefore without final authority, the Argentinian was never able to show his true governmental mettle; but I am sure he would have made a more trenchant and drastic, less fluid and supple Almighty than Castro. Being further from the centre of things, he did not have to trim, or face down the imperial adversary eyeball to eyeball. The art of politics – dividing the adversary and gaining time – was not his strong point. In Cuba, that inside-out Machiavelli seems to have made enemies everywhere in the shortest possible time: among old Stalinists who loathed him as a 'leftist', the bourgeoisie alarmed by a 'communist' and the mainstream, which disliked him as an over-radical sectarian (and a 'foreigner' to boot). After that he descended, a lonely gladiator, into the arena – Congo, Bolivia – to make war on the United States *and* the Soviet Union, armed with a few muskets. Uniting against him both empires, all the local Communist Parties and all the local armed forces: a combination not easily achieved. All the extremes, versus a single extremist who did not deign to seek any form of support from the centre. One does not need to be much of an expert to recognize this misanthropic exploit as a true masterpiece of political anti-art.

Che the anti-Prince: that was fine by us. It was his his foreignness to the political game that thrust him into the political memory of the time. The combat he waged was not one of ambition but redemption. He viewed his personal war not in a prudent and calculating way but morally, as some see a civil war. A valiant knight who wanted to remake the world's soul, not modify its map. So his was a holy war, extremely limited in means, but *total* in its lack of precision and the absence of negotiable aims or possible areas of compromise, which could only end with the annihilation of the enemy or, failing that (more likely actually), himself. A religious guerilla war, with will for a credo. That most celebrated adept of revolutionary war was, at heart, wholly uninterested in its soberly realistic uses, the ones favoured by Asian contemporaries like Mao, Giap and Ho Chi Minh.

It was himself he had it in for. Che was his own worst enemy, and there lies the tragic aspect of his character. He did not like other people – except for his mother, Fidel and two or three schoolfriends – because he did not like himself, having spent his childhood grappling with a frail constitution and incurable asthma. He 'pulled himself together' early in his adolescence with the aid of rugby and many mortifications of the flesh. Hermits and saints learn early to punish themselves and they prefer obedience to freedom. Self-mastery through will, the noble face of masochism, was carried by Che to extremes of formalized asceticism. In mastering his own recalcitrant body he had learned to master others by redirecting that practised hardness. The physical is decisive, inborn. Fidel, that force of nature, does not have to try: a *criollo* Depardieu overflowing the screen, identifying so well with others that they identify with him. The born leader is hysterical as a mirror. Che did not have his solidity or breadth of bearing, or his fluency, or his geographical warmth or tropical cordiality. The shrewd try to make up for this sort of deficiency by learning the rudiments of public relations. Che's pride would not let him stoop to the flourishes and grimaces of communication which made Castro, a propaganda genius, into a TV star. Documentarists complain that there are few film images of Che in the Cuban cinema institute's archives; no one else had ordered the cameramen not to film him, it was the choice of a self-destructive man busy 'constructing socialism' who liked to chasten himself by cheerfully yielding the spotlights, the whole comedy of power, to the *Jefe Maximo*. Celluloid only caught up with him after his death, to transfigure him. There are one or two photos of Che taken soon after his capture: half-tramp, half-troglodyte, hair unkempt and feet wrapped in rags, he is totally unrecgnizable. To convince foreign opinion that it really was his body, the CIA men and Bolivian military cleaned up the body, dressed it in suitable clothes and touched it up with makeup to give him back his old face. That Christ-like cadaver from which a legend emerged – eyes open, head supported by a plank, stretched out on a cement slab for display – was offered to the world by his enemies. And although in Cuba he never in his lifetime, outside the most politicized circles, enjoyed the same broad popularity as Camilo Cienfuegos or Fidcl Castro (himself at first less loved than Camilo, who died in 1960), he projected a charisma *a contrario*, by distance. To the power of suggestion, warm and voluble, he rather ironically opposed the power of laconicism, which is just as effective in putting the entourage under tension. Electricity can pass between men in a short-circuit.

In a word, Fidel was a very sympathetic but not very admirable man, Che an unlikeable but admirable one, far less amiable and forthcoming than the *Jefe* with associates and subordinates. He was the opposite of the unscrupulous revolutionary for whom the end justifies the means, but there can be something cruel in the passion for integrity. Insensitivity, 'inflexibility', the superhuman face and inhuman obverse of the same coin. What I witnessed in Bolivia is wholly in keeping with what I have been told by veterans of the Congo and the Sierra. With his own men, the 'demanding leader' and man of 'implacable and rigorous discipline' did not refrain from abuse of power, and with an ill-concealed sort of sombre jubilation. The purity hardened with the years and he became increasingly cold and distant. To send an unarmed recruit to the frontline with orders to get a weapon from the enemy, using a knife or his bare hands, was traditional: he had done it in the Sierra Maestra. But to threaten with the firing squad as a deserter some honourable old combatant, just for stumbling during an ambush and losing his rifle in the heat of action, indicates bad character. To sanction a peccadillo – the theft by a famished and exhausted man of a tin of condensed milk – not with four hours' sentry duty that night instead of two, but to three days without food, is even more 'rigorous'. So is humiliating an inexperienced peasant boy in front of the whole unit to teach him to march properly. Making his companions walk barefoot in the jungles of the Congo because 'the Africans manage all right' is not without an element of cruelty. As was forcing men who had slept with black girls to marry them immediately . . . a puritan's caprice perhaps, but it drove a man already married in Cuba to suicide.

When an old companion died Che kept his feelings to himself, giving no external sign of compassion or sorrow. 'A scratch,' he would shrug when someone was bleeding. His murderous tongue-lashings, his much-feared *descargas*, brought tears to people's eyes. I once saw him, in front of all the men, demote 'Marcos', Major Pinarés, the head of his vanguard, and call him a *comemierda* because he had in Che's absence ordered evening tattoo in the central camp before the appointed hour. As he never allowed those he was verbally abusing or punishing to speak, or gave them a second chance (unlike Castro), resentments and tensions, especially between the Cubans and the more sensitive Bolivians, built up at Nancahuazu, but could not be vented for fear of further scoldings.

An infinite internal distance separated Che from his men in Bolivia, like a wall of silence and fear. 'I can't stand that guy any more. He's impossible, or he's gone mad. He treats us like unclean urchins. Ask Fidel to send me back to Cuba,' Marcos said to me in a low voice after the altercation, during my spell of guard duty. In Cuba he had been a full major, a member of the Central Committee and governor of the Isle of Pines, often known as the Isle of Youth. Down there in the jungle he sobbed like an angry child. Marcos was killed soon afterwards and his body eaten by wild dogs; Benigno survived. He is nearly 60 now. He always gave Che total loyalty. Then a peasant youth in the Sierra Maestra, he had seen him arrive in his hut a few days after the landing, when Che was still simply the guerillas' official doctor, and thereafter followed him everywhere until his death. I asked him if he could remember a single sign or gesture of affection towards him from Che. He thought for a long time. 'Yes, once in Bolivia, at the end of September. I'd got a bullet in my shoulder, and a high fever. I could only fire left-handed. He mouthed off at me, and then he took me by the shoulders and gave me his cigarette ration. I asked him why. "You're the wounded one. You need them more than I do." Nice of him, wasn't it?'

What were the feelings that made his men stay attached to him? Fear and admiration. Fear of his *descargas* and *castigas*. Admiration for his courage, his uprightness, his character. Vexations and rebuffs came as if to cement a sort of veneration. 'Che doesn't send people to their deaths while staying in the rear. He goes into the frontline with his men. He can go out and treat the wounded under fire. He tells things as they are. He's intelligent, and speaks well, although he uses a lot of gross words. And when a tiny piece of sugar – a Bolivian *chancanca*, a hard russet-coloured loaf – had to be divided among twenty, or two hard-boiled eggs, or a *choclo*, a boiled cob of maize, he gave everyone an equal share, and his share was the same.' In the forests of Zaire his only privileges were a cook for him and his staff, and a box of cigars which he shared willingly. In Bolivia, they were a thermos of bitter coffee and exemption from guard duty. His aide de camp, Tuma, used to help him hang his hammock. The moralist did not cheat. He hammered himself and others with the same compulsive energy. Strained solidarity to the limit, and would say yes one day, no the next.

People have spoken of mental cruelty. It should only shock the confused who look for light at night or heroes with no negative side. These lightweights forget the double nature of martyrs: sacrifice and sacrificer, suicide and homicide. And that men 'capable of dying for their ideas', as people unthinkingly put it, are just as capable of killing for them: as a general rule death is given and accepted with the same insouciance.

Stoicism, says the moralist; *sado-masochism*, the psychologist replies. Both are valid. If perversity consists in making others suffer for the painful contradictions we cannot resolve in ourselves, then what champion of Justice would not have needed a shrink? We know nothing of Christ's psyche, evidently much idealized by the gospels; and what expert has examined St Paul, Ignatius Loyola or St Theresa? If Che had met his Freud the twentieth century would have lost a Messiah. How many great men, how many saints of this or that credo would be left, if they had all had to spend some time on the couch? The painter Degas recalled that his mother had taken him as a child to visit Mme Le Bas, widow of the great Convention member, and had been piously outraged to see portraits of Robespierre, Couthon and Saint-Just on the walls. 'They were monsters!' she exclaimed.

'No,' her Jacobin hostess had answered calmly, 'they were saints.' The antithesis is pious but misleading. They were undoubtedly both. If there are *idiots savants* why should there not be saintly monsters?

The theological virtue of Hope can camouflage a secret despair. What God could tell the difference between a suicide and a sacrifice? It is always possible to envelop one within the other. That was Che's supreme politeness: he did not kill himself, he allowed himself to die.

In Cuba, political suicide has letters patent dating back to independence. The trail was blazed, not without a certain ambiguity, by the two founding heroes of the nation, Carlos Manuel de Cespedes, head of the Mambi or independentist army that freed the slaves in 1868, and José Martí, the poet-liberator who fell in 1895 in a cavalry charge against Spanish infantry. The tradition was carried on in 1951 by Raúl Chibas, leader of the 'Orthodox Party' and the young Fidel Castro's first political master. He denounced the corruption of the régime, but who believes a politician? People made fun of him. So he shot himself through the head on radio during a live broadcast. People believed him then all right, but too late. Castro has not forgotten the lesson. He is a shogun, not a samurai. Born to command, and thus to carry on living. However chivalrous you may be, however aware you are that 'a dead body is honourable, a prisoner isn't', experience shows that you 'may emerge from prison one day, but from the cemetery never'. Without pointless fuss, Fidel had surrendered after the failed attack on the Moncada prison, where sixty-two of his men had died; and in the Sierra, brave though he was, he never exposed himself unnecessarily. Che at the same time was dodging bullets at Alegría del Pío, at El Hombrito, at Santa Clara, taking risks that Fidel, surely with reason, thought pointless. He had the vocation. The beauty of death. That fascination of the Spanish ascendancy in which the genes of Tertullian, the Church father, mingle with the oxblood of bullfighters. Martí, the father of the Cuban nation, died in agreement with a profession of faith that one of Franco's supporters, Millán Astray, could have taken as his own: 'I believe in death as the support, the leaven and the triumph of life.' That sort of vertigo is the moral luxury of marginal characters answerable only to themselves and posterity; it is not recommended for serving leaders. The antipathy between the adventurer and the militant, which is not a fable, can also exist between the hero and the ruler.

Certainly he did not open his veins, he was no Werther. Che was murdered, on the orders of three Bolivian generals, on a nod from the American government. Che did not talk about suicide, or even think about it clearly (as Schopenhauer liked to do while seated at a groaning table). He was all of a piece in his actions, or rather in the absence of initiatives, the fatalism (a word he had long treasured), the routine, apathetic stubbornness, the *empecinamento* that marked his last two months in the Bolivian jungle. His doomed conduct began much earlier. Without looking as far as the Sierra Maestra, or the suicidal speech in Algiers, the first trace seems to have been his decision to go directly from the Congo to the Andes, despite his great ill-health, without even passing through Cuba to recover. Fidel managed with great difficulty to persuade him to drop this idea, but in August 1966, with incredible casualness, he agreed to leave for an unexplored part of Bolivia, on the sole basis of a hurried verbal report from his aide 'Papi', without any political, geographical or social surey of the terrain, without trying to set up any sort of support network in the region or to recruit a single Bolivian from the region (and when Alto Beni and Chapare, both more suitable regions, were inviting him to come). It took me twenty years to break the taboo against admitting the paradox – corroborated by a mass of other indices – that Che Guevara went to Bolivia not to win, but to lose. That was what his spiritual battle against the world and himself required. Some find regrettable his failure to mention this detail to the Cuban and Bolivian companions who accompanied him; it seems likely that his unconscious had left him equally in the dark. It is true, however, that those living stepping-stones to Calvary have been too easily forgotten, purged moreover from biographies, photos, tele-films and albums: thirty or so majors, captains and lieutenants willing to operate from a liberated zone in the Andes for many years, who vanished without trace long before their time. The unjust darkness that enfolds those faceless spectres, even within the Guevarist legend itself, to me indicates a measure of self-sacrifice perhaps even greater (in its tolerated anonymity) than that of Fernando, alias Ramón, alias Che.

October 1967. Twenty-two footsore men: seven Cubans (two badly wounded), seven Bolivians (three unwell, one crying out for water) and two Peruvians (one wounded): frightening spectres in rags. Dogs barked at the sight of them and people fled. The column of semi-conscious men limped through hamlets that seemed deserted. On one occasion it camped for the night in the middle of the road between two villages 5 kilometres apart, taking no precautions. Che sought the peasants out, ran after them and told them who he was, knowing that when he left they would denounce him. The Bolivian army could plot their progress almost in real time. One imprudence followed another. He did not bother to cure his blisters, which slowed the column's progress. Not because his will had weakened, but because he was applying it to ensure a swift and clean finish. He let everything slide, walked in a straight line, ignored obvious dangers. Apparently indifferent to deaths, capable of leaving a wounded man bleeding on the ground for an hour to punish him for failure to execute orders. On 20 September his exhausted men begged to be allowed to stop, find shelter, recover their strength, treat the sick and wounded, gather some bananas and cobs of maize, dry some beef. He replied: *No hay tiempo para descansar* ('There's no time for relaxation'). He was set on taking the large village of Muyopampa, quite unnecessarily, simply to buy medicaments at the *bodega*, when a discreet errand by two men would have been quite sufficient. His oldest associates, veterans of the Rebel Army, Orlando Pantoja, Benigno and Pacho, went to see him. He looked at them sarcastically.

'Let's get out of here, Fernando.'

'What's the matter, scared? Let's keep going to the end.'

'What end? Where?'

'It doesn't matter where. We'll see afterwards.'

'After what?'

'Fuck off.'

Che continued on his way. He was trying in fact to reach Valle Grande, to buy supplies and medicine, then head for the department of Sucre because that had been the plan six months earlier. Everything else had changed, but not the plan. He marched on. No one had boots. Nato had made him espadrilles that were too big for him: soles cut from a car tyre with buckskin straps. He was vomiting; the sulphurous water had given him diarrhoea. Their water-bottles, watches, canteens and belt-buckles glittered in moonlight. They still had the strength to urinate on fine earth and smear polished metal with the resulting mud. But their machetes and weapons still clinked. Che made them stay in inhabited areas. It was pointless to go to ground.

'Wait a bit,' he told his companions during the last days, with the hint of a smile. 'Who knows, perhaps an *angelito* will come down from heaven without warning.' Paratroopers, a rescue expedition . . . why not? In the *Chanson de*

Roland, God sends an angel to the dying knight at Roncevalles, surrounded by Saracens, to 'bear the soul of the Count to paradise'. This time, though, God abstained.

And that skeletal corpse, exposed in the Valle Grande morgue to the obscene probing of camera lenses, somehow embodied the two funerary ideals of Christianity: the sacrificial victim dying to expiate the sins of his people, and the paladin immolating himself in silence for his Charlemagne, like Count Roland, who refrained to the very end from sounding his ivory horn.

For those who come to the republic through revolution, a shadow will always darken the glitter of the forum. Bastille Day, electoral euphoria, the excitement of promotions and appointments: you can – should? – enjoy all that without banishing a gate-crashing aftertaste, reminiscent of the *memento mori* whispered by slaves into the ears of triumphant Romans. Even the most limited revolutionary experience shackles the Capitol-squatter to the Tarpeian rock. What made my friends exultant used to fill me with gloom, like a bad omen. The suicides of Bérégovoy and Grossouvre horrified them; I regret to say I was better prepared. Yet I must confess I have not yet recovered from the great Latino slaughter of those leaden years. In me it evokes slightly nauseated melancholy, like an over-generous ossuary whose occupants had gone there, so to speak, a little too readily. All military butcheries arouse, when they are over, the same dismay at the ruin of human lives. And in comparing these guerrilla wars with the two world wars Latin Americans may feel they have escaped lightly in terms of numbers. But although victims of the *revolución* are numbered in tens of thousands rather than millions, the deliberate nature of the carnage compensates, if I can put it that way, for its smaller scale. *Militant* and *military* come from the same root. It is quite normal for a killer against whom the insurgent is waging total war to try to massacre him and his associates in return. What is less understandable is the sight of friends killing themselves and each other in the enemy's absence; the attrition by suicide, fratricide, parricide and infanticide of revolutions seen from the inside raises the appalling spectre of a sort of sacrifice within the sacrifice. Killing may be an ugly necessity; killing each other is going too far. I can more or less accept (in the absence of images, which would make it unbearable) that my old training comrades, the Guatemalan poet Otto René Castillo and his companion Nora Paez, were captured at home in Zacapa, tortured and burned alive by the Guatemalan army in 1967. I still cannot accept that my *socio*, my friend Roque Daltón, a very great poet of modern Salvador steeped in humour, insolence and joie de vivre, should have been shot through the head in 1978 by the very young chief of a rival organization, at a safe house in San Salvador, soon after he had arrived in the country to launch the armed struggle he preached in his books. Nor that 'old man' Marcial, the Salvadorean leader of the FPLE, should have taken his own life in Managua, after the murder of his comrade and rival Ana María by some of his own men.

Perhaps revolution in the modern age, in its various aspects of suffering and militancy, will one day become part of the long-term history of the death impulse, extending the sacrificial tradition of Isaac, Samson, Jesus, Blandine, Joan of Arc . . . A cynical sociologist might say that this school of suffering served as an ideal meeting-place for suicidal temperaments in Latin American capitals, not unlike the top platform of the Eiffel tower or the roof terrace of some Tokyo skyscraper.

In peace time every society chooses its own Minotaur; and that one, taking it all in all, is less absurd than the Automobile which in Europe exacts every year – a statistical sacrifice without accompanying faith – its tribute of flesh, like a percentage promised in advance to our industrial and mercantile machinery. A 'bourgeois' psychologist would nuance this comparison by suggesting that a human type less favoured by objective history would be more tempted than others by a nihilist ideal. Suicide would thus be a last and doubtless unconscious transfiguration of rejection by the environment into exemplary immolation. The loser's apotheosis, in simultaneously noting and sublimating an impasse. The outside world doesn't want him? It is he who doesn't want it; he dismisses it contemptuously, and himself with it. 'Pou qui peut poum n'est plus pou',[5] as the surrealist poet said. Suicide in that case would be the supreme *act* of black humour for people who lack it (few revolutionaries have that sixth sense, the exception of the Mexican Marcos proving the rule). Barbey d'Aurevilly, an ultra-royalist and dandy, believed at the end of his life that nothing remained to him but a choice 'between the muzzle of a pistol and the party of Revolution'. That was in France, at the end of the nineteenth century. A hero of the twentieth might have told him he could have both, and that that is how to transfigure a *revés en victoria*.

4

Disconnection

My blind spots, the nation and hatred – Dangers of happiness – Breaks don't have a timetable – Cuban metamorphoses – Families, I love you – A fuite en avant – The struggle between master and slave – Bad cess to foreigners – An agonizing trial – The forgotten culture of war – Acknowledgement of a debt

New Year 1971: there was nationalism, and there was hatred. These two irrefutable observations, which I could have made on leaving my monk's punishment cell, brought Mass to a close: *Ite missa est.* If the political animal were not a rabid lunatic, I would have left the stage without insisting on the rest of my due. For are they not the basic chemical ingredients of History? No experiment seems to be able to manage without them in the end, their *opposite* being worthless in science and art (even though individual artists and scientists may succumb to it, for the flesh is weak). I discounted them, and they burned my fingers. They did not fit into the range of ready-made wishful thinking that served me as a pass-key, those sketchy and ephemeral plans with important-sounding titles like 'global strategy'. Just absorbing those two banalities cost me a lot of contorted effort. Indeed I am not sure I have really absorbed them even now. I may pass for an acceptable patriot these days, but I still have trouble with hatred.

It was in prison that I became free. A quiet emancipation, wholly intellectual. Between four walls, preserved from the emotions of communal life (the great advantage of solitary confinement even in the doggiest of days), I had ample leisure for a policy review. The 'national question', to give it its official title, had kicked us in the teeth. It had killed Che and made it clear that guerilla warfare, practised as an export product, was ineffective.

So what had I learned that so changed things? Essentially, that my blood group (if I may use the metaphor) was not Latino. This led to the shocking deduction that the Bolivians and Cubans had failed to agree even in the guerilla struggle, and I as a European had had found it difficult to be accepted by the *kambas* and *kollas* of the Altiplano, because the revolution did not constitute common ground, like a great motherland for the stateless. The French verb *naître* (from which the word 'nation' is derived), meaning 'to be born', is falsely active rather than more correctly passive as in English or Latin. What I am, irrevocably, was formed before me and in my absence. I inherit a History that I may try to remake or unmake, but that I did not make. Supranationality is not a matter of volition. One does not choose a community like a watch in a shop window. And I was beginning to see those Marxist-speaking sons of Bolívar as patriots who lacked self-knowledge. Not quite all: some did know, like my friend René Zaveleta, who had been minister of mining in La Paz in the Paz Estenssoro government. Before joining the guerilla camp he had often told me: 'I want steelworks for my country. Among other advantages, it will lead to the birth of a Quechua Proust. Without blast furnaces there can be no madeleine biscuits.' I had not previously seen the connection between steelmaking and remembrance of things past, although from a sufficient distance it seems obvious: forgetting industry is a privilege of the industrialized, as despising money is for the rich. *Altos hornos para todos* : 'Blast furnaces for all'. Despite its anachronistic flavour – the ecological objections had not yet been formulated – I would willingly have supported the slogan: primitive accumulation of capital is the starting point for the workers' trade union, parliamentary debate and the precious archive of museums and libraries. All peoples had a right to these things. It had become clear too that those Cuban, Chilean and Bolivian volunteers dressed up, in internationalist missionary red, reservoirs of pride and memory that were essentially indigenous (much as local adepts of 'world culture' now bestow that grandiloquent name on the national culture of the US, which they confuse, as imperial provincials will, with the world itself). Basically those guerilla wars, those armed struggles, were protests against the absence of the republican – or indeed *any* – state: falsified elections, stifled trade unions, puppet parties, biased justice, non-existent sovereignty. In essence their demand was (and still is, in Mexico for example) that there should be a nation, with a set of essential rules for its conduct. So what was I against, what negative feelings drove me to act? A fascist-style hatred of 'democracy'? Obviously not. Hostility to 'capitalism' as a mode of material production? Not that either: caring not a fig for economics, I knew too little to analyse the prevailing iniquity from that angle. My background, in which Indo-China, Algeria and Bandung loomed large, had erected scarecrows called 'imperialism' and 'colonialism' (both terms currently out of circulation). No doubt the others were discredited by association since *capitalism* (another vanished bogey), as a social system, was obviously implicated, while a *democracy* that exploits, deports and bombs foreign villages looks very like, if not a total fake, at least a half-lie. So of what did a transplanted European's 'anti-imperialism' finally consist? The common denominator of the Latinos in my camp was *nacionalismo de izquierda*. 'Left patriotism' was thought appropriate on the oppressed peripheries but denounced as chauvinism, blind and dangerous tunnel vision, in sovereign countries. The doctrine forbade in the northern hemisphere what it encouraged in the southern. But had not the Jacobins of 1793, the Communards of 1871, the Resistance of 1944, called themselves 'patriots'? The same incoherence affected notions of the 'great man'. There were no heroes, except elsewhere. The proletarian nations had a monopoly of the sublime breed, to suck the blood of the bourgeois ones. So it seemed perfectly normal to dismiss the whole idea of the man of providence – neither God, nor Caesar, nor Tribune – and march in step with local panjandrums, never wondering for a single moment whether the rare bird might be found at home . . .

Until 1967 I was ashamed of being French. It was not as bad as being a Yankee, a suspicion to which my *gringo* blondness exposed me. I took good care to mark my distance from all things American by speaking Spanish in a thick French accent. Of course Carnot and Robespierre could not really stand with Lenin and Trotsky, but in anti-conformist circles Asterix had the advantage of plebeian seniority, although short on proletarian authenticity. Along with the Commune and the *Internationale* (written by a compatriot, Eugène Pottier), the 1793 precedent ensured that one's student papers were indulgently marked. A flagstaff bearing a Phrygian bonnet dominated the *plaza de la Revolución* in Havana, and I had heard the *Marseillaise* sung in Spanish by armed Bolivian miners marching at the tin mines of Siglo XX and Huanuni. The extension, not of the boulevard Saint-Michel to the sea, but of the Vercors resistance to the Andes, was not the product of my imagination alone, and more than one monoglot Latino tried, on hearing where I was from, to pronounce the universally known words 'partisan' and 'maquis' (naive emblems of Frenchness now replaced among non-francophones with 'croissant' and 'parfum'). Their reflex was flattering to the national vanity. Living on the credit of one's passport in this way had a fraudulent side: any expatriate rogue could draw on the prestige those far-off glories had paid into the French account, none of it his by right. But after 1960, de Gaulle, Jean-Paul Sartre and Brigitte Bardot formed a handy, portable trio that the wandering Frog could usefully flash in the slums of Bogotá or La Paz. Even if ignorant of Gaullism, philosophically hostile to existentialism and sexually fixated on skinny brunettes, any migratory Gaul came sooner of later to embody this Holy Trinity whose immaterial attendance swathed him in a sort of aura, a glow of indirect glory. In those days a lot of us benefited, involuntarily for the most part, from a refraction which the French sunset has now brought to an end. Does not every passing foreigner seem the bearer of his country's shadow? A Soviet citizen in Paris might twitter like a sparrow, but still resounded in those days with the baritone thunder of a Red Army choir, just as today the most geekish American shimmers with subliminal reflections of Neil Armstrong, Ted Turner and Clint Eastwood. We could say that today's Frenchman has reverted to his real scale: citizen of a small canton of Europe, itself the western wing of the new Middle Kingdom between the Atlantic and the Pacific.

Strangely, the hints of May '68 that reached me – via the press, letters and the radio – did not bring me closer in spirit to my native cobbles, but rather repelled me. Although I was reassured to see that good traditions – barricades, emphasis, red flags – were still very much alive, the anarchist psychodrama had nothing meaningful to say. Despite elements of respectable old-Marxist finery, the carnival, at first sight punitive and puritanical, smelt of heresy; it was about playing without hindrance, not about dying for the Cause. Those Californian seasonings, the games with desire and growth that made the thing unprecedented, had a whiff of devilish counterfeit about them. These kids were too amiable, too nice. Too lacking in experience, in serious reading. My instinct was sound, for they were flinging wide the doors to let the American videosphere into the Old World; those noisy brats were trailblazers, and I belonged to prehistory. Like a decadent collector accumulating terracotta, Louis XV armchairs and Etruscan urns in his decrepit Roman palace, an old owl who has come to shrink from the sunlight and tumult of the piazza, I was becoming the sort of antiquarian adventurer who is eventually put off adventures by an exaggerated sense of his patrimony.

For one still shackled to the archaic duty of expiation, the sacrilege of 1968 lay in the absence of human sacrifice. No blood had been spilled. Revolution without deaths was the life of Christ without Golgotha, a whodunnit without a corpse: bargain-basement History. What good is a faith without martyrs? How could our Moloch take seriously that impudent pastiche, whose new-minted ministers of the cobblestone – unlike the guillotined guillotiners of 1793, the shot shooters of the Commune and Guevara himself – had shirked the double role of Minotaur and devoured victim? It is a very long time since I stopped inveighing against that game of dedramatized signs – at least in France – to which, in the name of leftism, the waggish side of Vallès's *l'Insurgé* served as an introduction. It is easier to accept when one is no longer revolutionary, a word that twins naturally with reactionary. The blimpish point of view was only marginally enlightening, on the volatility of the movement and the future inconsistency of this memoir. The absence of sacramental bloodshed (sacrality and sacrifice being linked) was to restrict the decennial commemorations of 'May '68' to purely cultural homage, producing nothing but brilliant debates of ideas in the papers and on the air, as if the event referred to had not achieved milestone or cornerstone status in the national unconscious. A few loyal souls in Paris are still driven by a compulsive sense of blood-debt to celebrate the Commune, the Resistance and the execution of Louis XVI (at the mur des Fédérés in Père-Lachaise cemetery, on mont Valérien and in the place de la Concorde). May '68 has champions and philosophers – Foucault, Deleuze, Baudrillard and 'everyone who counts' – rather than plotters and obsessives; as if the event only meant anything to intellectuals (and not much to them). As if it were engraved on our minds and not in our flesh, unable to generate the freemasonry of sworn avengers that follows each appearance by the Grim Reaper.

In 1969, by a sort of telepathy, a left Gaullist almost unknown to me, Philippe de Saint-Robert, gave my partner a Gaullist profession of faith to bring me on her next visit. I answered immediately, braving the censor, with a letter I can

certainly reproduce since he has already done so (after keeping it private for
some time to avoid doing me harm). Those critics who in 1990, to celebrate the
conventional idea that intellectuals recant in the end, referred ironically to my
'tardy conversion to Gaullism', had not registered that it was already twenty
years old. There is consistency in my ideas, even if they are not very many or
very new.

Camiri, August 1969
Dear Philippe de Saint-Robert,

*I have received your Jeu de la France, and send my thanks after a delay that the
circumstances and my cellular regime will, I hope, excuse. This letter itself may seem odd to
you, coming from a stranger, from so far away, when almost everything would be expected to
oppose us after what you might call 'all that has happened'. In fact, I have wanted to meet you
personally for some time, after seeing your articles here and there. But while your book has
undoubtedly introduced us, a letter is not worth as much as a meeting, and I have dropped the
idea I had of sending you a sort of account of my reading, which I will therefore leave in its
rough state, for my sole use. The whole question is too important, occupies too much of my
attention, to be dealt with in sketchy fashion: I am talking of course about the idea and fact of
the nation. To you, the idea and fact of France. For me too, I'd like to say, if only that were
plausible; even though there is a savour to the exile in certain struggles that, unlike me, you have
the good fortune not to know about. You say I believe in reference to Louis Aragon's war
poems: 'the ones that saw beyond the nation, but saw primarily through the nation'. A fine,
simple expression, that touches me deeply, for what it's worth, but that above all expresses in
its own way the authentic internationalism whose formula is sought in every corner of the
earth, everywhere that nations are struggling to be born, feeling involved in a struggle that is
identical in essence, but being waged elsewhere. You have some pages on the nation that, apart
from their rather classical beauty, touch a deep chord. I dare say they will serve me as texts in
the future, if I am allowed to publish one day.*

*It seems to me a pity that you did not extend certain philosophic and historical lines of
reasoning which, if developed, might have taken the slightly bald edge off some assertions. Your
rejection of what you call 'ideology' implies the existence of another, just as 'ideological'. The
nation may be salutary and permanent, but it is not an abstraction without history or social
content. There is a France that exploits, pillages and kills: Indochina, Algeria. There is a
France that liberates, thinks and gives life, increasingly as it recovers the independence that
(it's true) de Gaulle had started to restore to it . . . but how far and for how long? Painful
questions that I have been turning over in my den for months. But I do not want to go deeply
into a subject defended by its complexity. Not because of a taste for compromise. Perhaps you
will know one day that I don't always mince my words, and that my passion for 'France', for
the fairy-tale princess, for 'Freedom guiding the people', is as demanding as your own. One
thing is certain: it is high time for anyone who does not understand that the economic and
technical unification of planet Earth will be accompanied by an accentuation of its national
particularities, who does not grasp this astonishing dialectic, to be branded an imbecile once
and for all. Even if he be socialist, pacifist and globalist. How many contemporaries who*

think themselves modern will edge backwards into the twenty-first century still bearing
illusions that date from the nineteenth . . .

Everything that you and your friends will be doing to save what is essential from the
shipwreck looming over us, that 'certain idea of France' implying its independence and the
maintenance of its real sovereignty, and consequently implying its support for the sovereignty of
other peoples; your action and perhaps your organization can count on one more sympathizer,
an ordinary young Frenchman who, because he loves his country and its people, went to
Bolivia. Everyone plays, as he can, in his own fashion, the game of France.

Had I become a late-season bumpkin? A low-epoch modernist rendered
obsolete by the transnational new wave? Ridicule has its uses: being so out of
date gave me several years' start on the children of May in discovering archaisms
specific to the postmodern era. Metropolitan leftists still thought of themselves as
Chinese, 'German Jews', Palestinian fedayin, Vietnamese *bodois*, Bolivian guerillas or, if Trotskyists, plain old international proletarians. I knew already that I
was nothing *but* French, or at best European, and that no one could escape that
shrinkage in the wash, that unwelcome amputation of ubiquity. Some would
find later, depending on the case, that they had become practising Jews at *yeshiva*
or Bretonizing Bretons in Quimper. *Yarmulke* or oilskins, blood will out: there is
no way round its finiteness. After leaving prison in 1971 I met a visiting
Trotskyist compatriot in Santiago de Chile. We discussed what could still be
preserved of a 'Gaullian' margin of independence in the American orbit.
Without making an issue of it, I mentioned the disconcerting persistence of
nationalist reflexes, and said it might be a good idea to give them a second look.
In this he scented the old territorial song, a brightening of the chauvinist flame
liable to undermine any hope of planetary strategy. 'Nationality,' he told me, 'is
just a geographical accident. You can't base anything on an accident, let alone a
project for human liberation. Nations, don't you see, aren't very important.' I
refrained from telling him that Planet Earth was an astrophysical accident, that
he and I were biological accidents; and that this did not prevent us from soothing
sore places on the terraqueous ball, and on our little persons. Every death is an
accident too, but that does not mean that everyone's end becomes a news item. I
did not push the parochial spirit to the point of telling him that everything that *is*
is accidental, but still occurs 'somehow, anyway'; that there was crude stuff,
unavoidable and irrational, in the most refined people and that it had been
called destiny since the Atridae. One is always discredited by a systematic person
for comparing a contingency with a finality, a sordid *somewhere* with the Utopian
everywhere. He will concede at best that you are picturesquely absent-minded,
accepting your right to be in error: no one is perfect. The fact remains however
that the *place* and the *fact* are offensive to the Correct Idea, which prefers the law
of nowhere-in-particular, the rectilinear neatness of plans. The *idée fixe* deducts
contingency from a luminous first principle, shoulders the accidental into the
margins as if it were a remnant of savagery to be thrust beyond the pale. The

opaque, the undulating, the oblique, the silt of time, the weirdness of things and the animal side of human beings: these have no place in the Radiant Cities. The Great Clockmakers are there to eradicate them, nowadays with the aid of calculators and computerized graphics. In the face of all these good *reasons* (quickly joined by markets, satellites, computers, the facts of globalization), I put that fat *faux pas* the nation back in my pocket. Better to furl the flag than get it torn.

Hatred did not dawn on me, as the idea of nation did, after long distillation, although it is a passion every bit as obscure. It came as a sudden and very physical discovery on the day following my arrest in the village of Muyopampa, dressed in civilian clothes, after being identified by deserters as the foreigner 'Danton' whose presence in the maquis had so intrigued them. It introduced itself to me without ceremony or warning in the form of a heavy blow in the solar plexus (leaving me not hurt but suffocating), followed by a regulation bashing from a team of NCOs, apparently beside themselves with rage, which ended only with the fortuitous arrival of a captain. Several of their comrades had been killed in an ambush a few days earlier, and the sergeants were taking their sense of helplessness out on me, spontaneously slaking their thirst for revenge, eye for eye, tooth for tooth. Just when they needed one, they had caught a scapegoat who suited the purpose in several ways: foreign, unarmed, responsible for who knew what, and representative of the Enemy. To hate is to hate all others in one. The days, weeks and months that followed were a dive into that palpable element, a black and viscous oil I had never tasted before, and which I had never suspected of driving the small machines that theorists and makers of models for society draw diagrams of on paper, without meaning any harm.

I was totally unprepared for this chapter. A cleric without notoriety is not an *object* of hatred; nor was I a *subject* of it either as originator or vehicle. Marxism is a culture of antagonism, not vengeance. I had been caressing a virginal Utopia: violence without hatred, an immaculate conception that exists only in people's minds. Holy war, in which the Infidel is execrated for his ugly mug, his whole attitude, preaches unalloyed hatred. Just war, for rational secular reasons, only has it in for impersonal wrongs: imperialism, colonialism, fascism. I had espoused the struggle between an abstract entity and its opposed double, Revolution against Oppression, without rancour, without considering the names, bodies, eyes, behind those two Great Transparencies; and I had grossly undervalued instinctive solidarities, the heat of action. Romeo loves Juliet, but *the* Montagus hate *the* Capulets; these family affairs lie in wait for us at every turn; only nomads can dodge the communal reflex by slipping across the surface of things, leaving no trace. In duels, the man who most hates the other is more likely to prevail. In the race to fanaticism I had started alone, a serious handicap. I needed a few days to catch up, to rise to the level of the feelings I was supposed to have. To raise my own gut response to the level of collective representativeness attributed to me, a little too generously, by those impulsive torturers.

The walls of La Paz and other Bolivian towns were soon covered with bills and *pintadas* reading *¡Muera Debray!* (death to Debray), not all posted by the authorities; war widows and the families of soldiers killed in ambushes organized marches demanding the criminal's head; francophile editorialists compared the careers of the three Frenchmen best known for their depravity: Landru, Dr Petiot and the vile creature bearing my name. From my cell I heard drunken men – I do not recall any women – shouting: 'To the stake!' Later, climbing out of the prison van outside the military court, the wall of spitting, distorted faces and shaking fists. Such in summary was my baptism, my 'welcome to the club' of obsessives and lunatics always stirred up by political struggles (and even more by religious ones). No one can spend long in the spotlight without sooner or later being execrated by total strangers. I had dedicated myself to the shadows, then been forced to seek the headlines in self-defence: an unanticipated breach of principle from which I have never really recovered. Malevolence can figure on the debit side of a career plan, but my internal accounting system had never allowed for it. Party and government leaders quite often lose their lives in hatred country, under the bullets of lonely individuals overexcited by the ambient atmosphere; more often perhaps than at the hands of rioting mobs in front of red-splattered walls. I learned a lot about what lies behind decent behaviour and respectability from reading the *Mercurio* – flagship of the Chilean press, roughly equivalent to our *Figaro* or the *New York Times* – of 12 September 1973. That austere journal of reference, on the day following the military coup, made its front page a poster featuring the photos of twenty left-wing personalities 'wanted dead or alive'. The main organ of the Chilean bourgeoisie saw nothing wrong in their being tortured and shot shortly afterwards. My friends Perro Olivares, Jaime Barrios and Claudio Jimeno, all socialists, teachers and advisers of President Allende, had already been summarily executed, with others, behind the Moneda palace. That too seemed perfectly all right to the bishops, bankers, senators, doctors and bosses of the England of Latin America. Since the 1930s and the Occupation we have grown unused to such savagery, but it is still the lot of Southern countries, even educated and prosperous ones like pre-Pinochet parliamentary Chile.

Hatred of the bourgeois, the West, the Yankee, is an abstract thing that quite often masks a lack of curiosity and a certain intellectual laziness, sedentary characteristics. I was too fond of travelling to have caught it badly. As for self-hatred, one can live with (or even *on*) that old scar, that familiar discomfort. The hatred others bear us is less easily tamed. It is a disconcerting blight, ever-new and never-ending, that sort of hissing stridency signalling visceral aversion to someone's name: I heard it again in my own country in May 1981, unchanged after fifteen years, when normally level-headed individuals got wind of my appointment to the Élysée, in signed notes from academicians, electoral epithets, scaremongering articles. Press cuttings, anonymous letters, insults in the street: every passing day, backing the victim against the wall. Not forgetting the supportive friend who conveys the message despite himself: 'You've no idea what I have to endure, old fellow, because of you . . . but don't worry, I'm standing firm.' When you *are* a bête noire, you end by slipping into the part. Sometimes I would like to change my skin. Out of the question to blame plots hatched in the shadows by bad guys, like Jean-Jacques in victimized mode. There are natures that catalyse loathing and acrimony, it's as simple as that. I enjoy stirring things up further by exposing the idolatries of my own circle, putting down some TV starlet, pile of situationist trash or much-admired lagoon. I took on the facile reputation of a grumbler to give myself a little merit. However thick one's hide becomes, it is impossible to get used to the self-confident and stereotyped animosity with which highly estimable individuals continue to gratify me without having seen me or read anything of mine; or to that diminution of the self, baptized 'sadness' by Spinoza and called 'depression' by everyone else, that eventually results from repeated rancorous maulings. Every day they gnaw away a little more of our ability to dare and to deviate. My prose is reputed slapdash by the literary tribe. Wrongly. Of course I know that if you dish it out, you have to be able to take it without complaining: the law of *guerra spirituàle*, which I accept. But without denying myself a measure of polemical jubilation – the inevitable outlet for a writer's will to power – I have always tried to focus on the demolition of ideas, clearing up the rubbish, while avoiding the low pleasure of denigrating individuals. Nothing is more foreign to me than personal attacks, shooting people down in flames. I only review new books for journals if I can say something positive about them. I have published two collections of critical pieces, entitled *Éloges* (Eulogies) *I* and *II*, panegyrics on Tintoretto, Courbet, Claude Simon, Muglioni and the great French republicans. They are never mentioned, but when I published a few ironic pages *Against Venice*, to explain how very happy Naples used to make me, I was instantly promoted to chief thug and first villain. Since people hate me, they want me to hate myself. Sorry, but auto-allergy has passed me by. Politics is a complicated world ruled by a simplistic wisdom summarized in the ancient Greek precept: 'Love thy friends, hate thine enemies.' The opposite is more fecund: see the faults of your friends, learn to recognize the virtues of your enemies. I apply this advice first and foremost to myself. When I don my detractors' spectacles – impelled by the sympathy I feel for most of them – I share their aversion to yesterday's cynic-arriving-to-try-out-his-system-on-Indian-guinea-pigs, and to-day's richly-paid-troublemonger-making-a-career-on-the-other-side. Those two spivs make my gorge rise, but I don't recognize myself in them. I know myself well enough, on the other hand, to avoid social symbols I have decided to be against, for any encounter with the real individual is sure to make me fall into his arms. Those who were my enemies (had I but the tenacity to round them up) would end as my best friends. Anyone who has become a minor celebrity in self-defence knows that even turning his back on public life can never free him from that ugly and damaging passion. It is the servitude of the public man, who in compensation can count on the support of his fellows. A writer or philosopher, a solitary, has no such lifebuoy, the backing of 'his own', for the intellectual party disdains the *esprit de corps* of its electoral rivals. To swim alone against the tide he must therefore resort to hatred as a source of energy: a desirable extra that boosted Zola, swashbuckler though he was. 'Hatred is holy,' he wrote. 'It is the indignation of strong and forceful hearts, the militant disdain of those angered by mediocrity and stupidity.' Nothing great is achieved without hatred, Hegel might have written in a survey of our driving passions. But that energy source is not present in my cellar, I lack the pamphleteer's long wind. Small angers are but bread and milk, and I lack the assiduity to hate methodically, one at a time, the indefatigable army of the hateful.

Landing in the Chile of *Unidad popular* after coming out of prison in January 1971, I almost forgot the all-important rancour. Everything was smiling: the future, the women, the eucalyptus trees. And Salvador Allende himself, who liked laughter, good Macul wine and nice alpaca suits. I feared that 'socialism in freedom' might end by capsizing, but it never occurred to me for a single moment that the event would be bloody. It displeased Allende, that prediction of failure, based purely on electoral mathematics and pretty harmless compared to the knives already being honed in the shadows. I voiced it without malice in our first conversations, one of which was recorded for the gallery between Santiago and Viña del Mar, his summer residence (Miguel Littín later made a decent documentary from the footage, despite repeated technical incidents). With engaging pride the president, whose manner was friendly, informal and unpretentious, showed me the photo of Che on his desk inscribed: 'To Salvador Allende, who is going to the same place by another route'. We thought this meant 'to the revolution', not 'to suicide', an interpretation that would have seemed outrageous at the time. The Chilean socialist leader, legally elected and with growing popular support (a relative majority becoming an absolute one within a year), was on a roundabout route to death, and the country at large cheerfully heading for a bloodbath. Anyone who did not experience the southern summer in that first year of the Popular Front has not known the sweetness of life . . .

The temptation of happiness was a new idea subversive to the mystique of armed struggle. The vertigo was sensory, stemming from my recovered freedom, the change of air, the lilting accent and pleasant urbanity that now surrounded me. Was it the white wine, the shops, the lifestyle, the high-heeled Lolitas in the smart areas of Providencia, the upper-middle-class suavity of bourgeois Santiago? The savour of that welcoming country carried an appetizing hint of France. After the dry and hard Altiplano in landlocked Bolivia, imprisoned by ice, rock and adobe, Chile's pastel-coloured wooden houses projected a sort of feminine grace, a cosseting, wholesome, spring-like charm. There was something gay and light-hearted in the atmosphere, as surprising to an habitué of the steppes as Tuscany to a Bavarian, although the grey and windy cold of the Pacific Ocean lent a rough Celtic edge to that Italy of Latin America, an echo of Ireland or Finistère. The 1973 coup d'état put a bloody stop to the well-behaved jollity, which reminded me as a Frenchman of our Popular Front summer of 1936, or anyway the image I had formed of it: nothing sombre or savage in that holiday-mood Utopian upsurge, no asceticism or grandiloquence either. The left-wing groups, much preoccupied with love affairs, exuded a naive confidence in the future without the sour note of death-dealing catch-phrases. 'Democracy is an exercise in modesty,' Camus said. He was a nice fellow too. Allende never spilled blood or imprisoned or exiled anyone. His Chile was not a single-party state, had no political police, no armed militia. What passes for greatness in a revolution is often just barbarity dressed up as religion. Chile was a country too civilized – or too sensual – to slide into ferocity, although the collective superego of the left, and Allende's too, were caught in the force-field of the legends. But the socialist leadership's way of life agreeably contradicted its fire-and-flame perorations. On reflection, the compromise third way – the 'Chilean way' as it was then called – provided a perfect decompression chamber for one intoxicated by prophecies. The local extreme left wanted to see it as a resumption of the old saga, but it was much better than that: the wish for revolution as a mobilizing passion, but without the communist system of authority and supervision. An idealized formula that sounds like bringing the sea to the mountains, or Europe to America; and that is just what Chile is like, a place where the mad geography of a long mountainous strip of land has placed sun-bathed beaches at the foot of eternal snows, a contradiction offered in demi-tint to the gaze, to the skin in caressing breezes. 'Socialism in freedom' is sweet and sour, *dulce de leche* after a basket of urchins and oysters, a menu much appreciated in those parts. If happiness is a democratic idea, invented in Greece by the first cities of free men, the long visits I made to Chile between 1971 and 1973 accelerated my secular education. Subversion within subversion. They very nearly dechristianized me. I emerged 'employable', reformist, acquiescent, alert, without the slightest desire for 'fundamental change'. Apart from the parliamentary debates, newspapers pulling in all directions, joyous chaos in the streets and offices; apart from the relaxed morals and doctrinal eclecticism, everything in that magnificently feminine country transmitted the libertarian and pagan message that it is not suffering that saves. Last-stand heroes, volunteers for the gibbet should keep out. He who starts to believe in happiness in politics will betray the revolution sooner or later. The politicization of happiness that began in the Enlightenment century was a two-edged weapon whose early puritanical deployment, around 1793, masked more pleasure-seeking uses. Saint-Just had the right approach here. Being cured of unreality or brought down to earth exposes devotees of secular religions to utter abandon. Every springtime of the soul brings another unfrocking.

That country of moderation, wisdom and optimistic pleasures was nevertheless most savagely afflicted by class hatred. ('Universal History is not a place of happiness. Its periods of well-being are blank pages, for they are periods of concord deficient in opposition . . .') The period of (relative) concord lasted three years, and the Hegelian 'opposition' took the wholly unexpected form of bombings, murders, torture, exile, disappearances and mass graves.

Radical-socialist in his way of living and governing, and radical, full stop, in the way he signed off, Salvador Allende (if it is permissible to include such a great gentleman in this intimist, albeit fairly edifying, Madame Tussaud's) has come retrospectively to occupy his place in my gallery of sacred monsters, with Castro and Guevara on the way in and Mitterrand at the other end, near the exit. That lord of transition resembles the first two in his samurai's death and trenchant convictions, and the latter in his democrat's life and episodes of foxy zigzagging. The ambivalence detracts from the shine of the individual, most unjustly forgotten, as it were erased, from the annals of a technocratic left intimidated by its great shades and eager to forget a past superior to its present. No lying in state for that social democrat immolated on the field of honour. No worldwide myth took shape either, probably owing to the absence of photographic evidence: the sacrificial victim left no Christ-like, redemptive mask, no iconic poster. The Chilean military whisked everything out of sight, careful not to repeat the mistake of their Bolivian colleagues by cleaning up and exhibiting the remains. In biased and totally inadequate tribute, there remains in my personal *Bildung* a sober and discreet figure, slightly apart from others, occupying as it were the mid-point between a war leader or inspired, obsessional, merciless great man and a wily conciliator: close to the happy medium, more inclined to go to the law than resort to violence, but able to pick up a weapon when the time came.

To this prodigal clemency from the left, the right replied with the most obscene brutality. And Allende himself, an anti-hero to guerrillas of the time, died on 11 September 1973 like a Roman hero: he shot himself with a Kalashnikov in the wreckage of his office in the Moneda, which was being bombed by the air force. A way of telling the faction attacking the presidential palace that the junta would not have the satisfaction of displaying him alive. Something like: 'I'd rather not be forced to ask for my life, because you would be quite capable of sparing it.' That stoical Freemason, with his well-fed notary's paunch and the manners of a senator from Lot-et-Garonne, passed into a higher category at the decisive last moment. A fine exit is a hundred times better than 'transforming life into destiny'; it transforms destiny into will. But this sumptuous gift was received unwillingly by Allende's people. His daughter Beatriz, who reached Havana a few days later having escaped from the palace before the end, told the crowd gathered in the *plaza de la Revolución*, in the *Comandante*'s presence, that her father had died in combat, killed by 'soldiery' (the term for enemy troops). *Muerto en combate* was the label of official heroes. She had been misled by an inaccurate account, but since you have to be a victim to be counted among the Just, it all fitted together well enough. When the truth emerged not long afterwards, militants tended to look away and go on elaborating the assassination theory. Where there is taboo there are lies. Only several years later did the Chilean left admit the sublime gaffe, in coded terms and with embarrassment. Poor Beatriz, a doughty militant who had not wished to infringe an unwritten rule, herself committed suicide in 1976 in Havana, leaving a letter to Fidel Castro which has never been published.

Who can remember the exact moment when he fell *out* of love? You can remember the date when a gesture perhaps, a look or a smile, said 'I love you' for the first time; but the day when you first thought privately 'I don't really love her any more', not to mention the one, always after the event, more painful but less decisive and incidentally in no way essential, when someone says to you 'And by the way, I don't love you any more': those dates are not written down in some internal record. They sneak treacherously away from the summary. Do we flee their presence or their memory because they represent a tolling of the bell? We certainly experience these separations on some level as irremediable losses of substance, irreversible diminutions of vitality that might almost have been called, were there not already a masterpiece of the same title, 'days in our death'. To have been born several times implies as many deaths, but we would rather think about our renaissances than the successive deaths that make them possible. In this way we accumulate in memory a shameful list of muzzled abortions, our discarded doubles still struggling vainly back against the current. Each of these alter egos, aligned like a row of small white crosses in a neglected cemetery, might remind us (if we would let ourselves listen) of a vanished belonging, a family no sooner formed than dissolved. We hurry past this alley of discarded *mes*, of *wes* that never took shape, for fear of having to remember all the dubious expedients we employed, when cutting the umbilical cord to each little community whose comforting warmth had led us into making another false start. Whether the magnetic field of the coterie had been political, artistic, esoteric or anodyne (you might say Trotskyist, surrealist, Freemason or simply friendly) we retain the embarrassing, shabby impression that we sneaked away while no one was looking.

How do people stop belonging to a group? Not often in the catasrophic manner of someone falling off a train. Or rather, while an inner part of the traveller, what we might call the reasoning part, may have *disconnected*, another part, more secret and stubborn, continues instinctively to run along the track after the train, which its logician twin has just deemed to be going the wrong way. Laboriously negotiated passages from suspense to sympathy, then to resentment, finally to indifference, mark the stages of a *disincorporation* analogous to the fading of the amorous trance into detachment, a process that can take many years; meanwhile, what we call the *political consciousness* rushes busily about, teeters, argues, gesticulates, in perfect illustration of Rouletabille's advice: 'Since these mysteries are beyond us, let us feign being their organizer.' Erotic or political, the reconstituted history of a separation of bodies, as absurd as falling in love, a to-and-fro of sudden withdrawals and revivals of the flame, of undervaluations and relapses, seems to suggest that the only way out of one frenzy is through another. However anxious we may be to represent them as rational, separations are as inexplicable as *coups de foudre*, and the end of a love affair with a group, gang, party or individual is even more mysterious than its beginning. With the *comandantes*, getting clear took me a good ten years, a delay of which I have no cause to be proud.

'What remains of our loves?' Mainly, astonishment that they ever existed. What exacerbates the discomfort, and inhibits us from unravelling the slow loss of belief, is the bitter realization that we have striven desperately to kick in an open door, through which the indifferent or ignorant pass easily, without a thought. Imaginary chains are the heaviest, and it is humiliating to have worried for years before concluding, drenched in sweat, that 2+2=4. I was flabbergasted when François Mitterrand, whom I accompanied to Havana in 1975 (in a group that included Gaston Defferre, Lionel Jospin, Edmonde Charles-Roux, André Rousselet and Didier Motchane), after a tedious formal meeting between the French and Cuban delegations at which Fidel had spoken continuously for two hours, murmured in my presence in a disdainful, fatalistic tone, hardly even irritated: 'Of course we could hardly expect anything else from a *dictator*.' My new father had been dealing with his mail, keeping up with current business, as the Cuban LP droned on. That word made me shiver. For days I struggled to come to terms with its brutality. *Dictator* (I kept saying to myself), bit superficial, surely . . . what about the blockade . . . the local idiosyncrasies . . . the country's historical culture . . . etc. The fact is that it takes a very complex effort of optical readjustment to see the nose on the face of an 'ego ideal' so familiar that one has stopped looking at it. By that time, though, I was prepard to discuss the word, as it were to envisage it. Ten years earlier I would have shrugged it off, imputing it to the 'enemy's' gross malevolence. Not that the word had never entered my head, in connection with some arrogant assertion or barmy statistic: such flashes, though, quickly forgotten, signals slumbering in the memory, small marker pebbles left by a providential internal Tom Thumb, but unable to tell us much until we reach a safe haven.

Leader to populace: 'I will surprise you with my ingratitude.' Populace to leader: 'I will surprise you with my love.' We must leave it to historians to work out whether the changing nature of mass movements has modified the 'hero instinct' or the 'group mind'. What seems certain is that specialists are much more interested in 'the birth of love in the West' than in its extinction. We don't do much better with our little internal Wests.

Every point in the network communes in the worship of the Boss, the one who makes the connection between all and each and through whom cohesion comes to strangers separated by everything else. Centre of all beings and axis of the

world, people vied with each other to win or retain his love (nothing is ever
certain) and suffered a constant and obsessional fear of losing his protection. Of
being undeserving. Of disappointing. If that happened, you would be driven
from the group and life would lose all meaning. At Camiri, physical isolation
exacerbated the repudiation vertigo, soothed only by occasional messages, nods
and winks. So I have never known a greater euphoria than when, on my arrival
in Santiago de Chile on New Year's Eve of 1971, my friend Coco Paredes, an
Allende intimate and head of the Chilean police, handed me a telegram from
Fidel assuring me of his affection and pleasure at my release. Or rather only one
greater, the next day when I was dubbed: Ariel, the America Department official
responsible for Bolivia, called to present me on behalf of Piñeiro, not without a
certain solemnity, with new caste insignia in the form of a 9mm Star automatic,
Spanish-made. 'The CIA and the fascists still feel at home in Santiago,' he told
me. 'At least with this you'll be able to go out.' I kept that pistol for ten years,
until the generalization of metal detectors at airports.

In February 1971 I returned home a prodigal son. Not to France yet: direct from
Santiago to Havana. In Chile I had been on leave; now it was time to report
back to Supreme Headquarters.

The tousled chief I had left was now a *Líder Máximo* buttoned tightly into
brand-new truths. Our first interview – an ordeal of mutual readjustment – took
place not in his office but at the *Casa de seguridad* in town to which I had been
taken directly from the airport, and where he visited me the following day. I still
have in my mind's eye that olive-green monolith framed in the doorway, newly
impermeable, pharaonically massive; and an awkwardness, a shared embarrassment: we were no longer quite in tune, *abrazos* notwithstanding. Perhaps I was
the embarrassing witness to an outmoded period, an unwanted souvenir. He
started extolling the sagacity, the supportiveness of the people from Moscow. I
remembered our last nocturnal private talk four years earlier, his exasperated
complaints about the Soviets and their local representatives, their paltry
concerns, their suffocating appetite for control. What had been restless or
anxious about the man seemed to have congealed and stiffened. That feverish
individual had become set in his stature: as if the king's second, theological body
had absorbed his carnal one. He represented, he embodied. Everything at once:
Me-Party-State-Proletariat-Nation-Humanity, fitted one inside another like
Russian dolls, but constituting a leaden mass obstructive to mental agility. I
could not call him thee and thou any more: the formal plural simply imposed
itself. Those who have found the keys to eternal power glow with a sort of
internal sacrality that religious historians call the 'numinous'. Seized by totemic
solemnity, my companion was well on the way to being certain of everything,
and deaf to everyone.

I had retained the image of an unsure, muddled, questing revolution; on my
return I found a rationalized, hierarchical and ceremonious system of govern-

ment. Less impassioned, more imposing. My interlocutors had become *officials*: the usual fate of adventurers plunged into the adversity of power, when the heavy graces of the state fatten a group of pals into civil servants with assigned places, separated by protocol, interchangeable roles, an organizational diagram. The growth of the rebel into a head of state had here produced fast-forwarded bureaucratization (tropical hothouses shorten germination time). The mutation of the marginalized into potentates was far from complete, although the first companions were no longer allowed to share the *Maximo Jefe*'s tent. Soon the former comrade (etymologically, one who shares the same bed) who, in the Sierra Maestra, had sometimes slept under the same blanket, would be obliged by regulations, when in his presence, to stay ten paces from the Commander-in-Chief, at attention, with eyes lowered. He would have to wait for the *Maximo* to address him before opening his mouth. The good-natured *caudillo* of 1965 (at least to my inexperienced eyes) had not lived in a reserved area where every passer-by in civilian clothes belonged to Security; he had not yet had the three armoured Mercedes saloons, identical so that no one could tell which he was in, or the hundreds of special troops deployed in the neighbouring streets, or all the traffic lights preset to green on his chosen route, or the accompanying ambulance, or the food-taster, or the cameraman recording every move, or the bulletproof vest. His friends had been able to get into his office (on the rare occasions the *Jefe* was there) without having to leave their pistols, Swiss army knives and nail files in the ADC's office, then enter a long brightly lit corridor – a disguised security lock, video-monitored by a hidden member of the escort – ending in a closed sliding door that only the Chief, informed by microphone of the names and titles of the petitioner, can open from the inside by remote control; then at last, in an office secure against nuclear and chemical attack, the strictly time-limited audience can begin.

A different man, in a different country. Soviet starch had been ironed into the *criollo* insouciance. Midway between dying fervour and papier-mâché, the regime like an overfed python was making heavy weather of digesting its reverses: Che's failed 'sortie', the defeat of the guerrillas abroad, the failure of the ten-million-tonne harvest, the bankruptcy of the agricultural plans. I made a round of my friends to pick up the threads, questioning them tactfully on the past four years. Their accounts gave me some idea of the electrical disarray that had presided over the lost 'great battles': the Struggle against Bureaucracy, the Revolutionary Offensive, the Giant Sugar Harvest. Militarization of the economy had passed beyond the rhetorical to affect the organizational levels. Fidel had disbanded the ministries and sent the *comandantes* into the provinces to take direct control of production from *Puestos de mando*, fixed command posts set up from scratch. The 'apparatus' generally seemed to be a copy of the Big Brother model. Why this volte-face? Major Serguera, my friend 'Papito', who was one of the very first Fidelistas, former ambassador to Algiers and a francophile, made no direct reply to my naive question. Smiling sadly, he went to a bookcase, leafed through Max Weber's *Economy and Society* and without a word handed it to me opened at the page headed: 'The institutionalization of charisma'. The Sovietization of the state made it possible to stifle the small and still-turbulent military nobility. By bureaucratizing the former 'Rebel Army', replacing its original three commissioned ranks – lieutenant, captain and major – with Soviet nomenclature, and subjecting everything to an artificial Party equipped with the usual decorative attributes – congress, Politburo, Central Committee, etc. – the war king was getting rid of nonconformists, people whose obstinacy or purity of heart prevented them from lying. Thus moulded, that revolution – still in full sap – was being groomed for the premature senility of its East European counterparts. Like those brand-new towns in South America of which Lévi-Strauss observed that they 'pass from freshness to decrepitude without ever becoming old', twentieth-century revolutions will have gone from adolescence to sclerosis without enjoying a period of maturity. A sunlit dawn, a long winter, a blighted spring, a black hole: the steep slope of 'real socialism' was also that of many individual communists. But it seems quite a usual fate – I would not exclude myself from this group – to make the leap from fervour to boredom by way of lucidity. Surely everyone knows one of those enthusiasts who have slipped round to the other side of the horse, who was once a big idiot stuffed with certitudes and now, on the verge of middle age, has become a shrewd fellow who doubts everything.

Allende was more like America's uncle than its spiritual father, and it was as an impertinent young nephew, affectionate though sceptical, that I visited him several times, the last in August 1973 a few days before the drama. I had a daddy on my back already, the same one that bestrode thousands of adoptive sons (each of course believing himself to be the favourite child, the chosen foreign disciple). And when you have managed to find a father, that rare and threatened species, you have to try him more than once before discarding him.

I love families . . . too much, indeed. The revolution, I have since read, was an attempt to break away from the paterfamilias. What could I have been thinking of? In a lamentable misconstruction, I had made it as a revolt *in support of* 'the' Father (one's biological progenitor having nothing to do with this). So deprived of admiration and subjection that I sought them again from the patriarch. Our Father who art in heaven, give me here below an individual father, upright and severe, a giant who scoops me off the ground, sits me on his shoulders to see my midget siblings from his full height. I was acting the child to leave childhood behind, but how could I break away without someone to join elsewhere, all the more inspiriting for being foreign to our world? The gift of the self augments us by raising us to the supraterrestrial heights where the Eponymous sits enthroned: the Fidelistas' Fidel, the Lacanians' Lacan, the Mitterrandists' Mitterrand . . . and the Christians' Christ. The Liberation clan had given me this supernatural (if not downright unnatural) family, braving the inevitable fact so pithily summed up by Napoleon III, who knew a bit about inevitability: 'One endures one's family, one chooses one's friends.' After all, I owed my replacement castrator to my own merits: yet another reason for hanging on to him.

The roundabout of affiliations, which breaks one family to make another, is more bitter or amusing – doubtless both – from the left. The other side gambles everything on the Economy, a Greek word designating 'all that happens at home', while the old right exalted obedience, birth and properly run families (the reactionary ideal consisting essentially of transforming a people into a big family). The left, by tradition, rejects the values of nature and heredity in favour of individual freedom and the general will. The difficulty arises from the fact that this rejection of the natural has to be embodied in substitute families, no less suffocating than biological ones: parties, societies or associations. Very occasionally, by chance, there arise times of war to demolish these restraints; then other, new ones are assembled by main force: networks, underground movements, paramilitary groups: *common law* households, so to speak. Throughout my imprisonment the Cuban 'apparatus', that small, warm-hearted and uncouth family, had been my point of reference, my home port, sending me regular instructions and encouraging messages by various routes (usually my woman companion). It was working on an escape plan when, in 1970, the advent of a left-wing government in La Paz made the plan redundant. The community of shared risk is the most committing of all: voluntary as a contract but unifying as a tribe.

Disaffiliate, kill the Father, acquire another, reaffiliate, kill again . . . There it is, the happiness of Sisyphus: in the quest for a perfect society, communing and not communicating, that magic circle of which the ashram and the kibbutz seem (from a distance, if you have never visited one) to give the closest image. That banquet where all hearts are opened is not just a mirage, for I ate at its table on New Year's Eve 1967, in *plaza de la Revolución* in Havana: a hundred thousand Cubans feasting elbow to elbow on *congri*, beer and songs. Anyway that is how I remember it. This casting about for a *free family* – something pessimists will think a contradiction in terms but that I cannot help imagining as a reality carelessly mislaid, therefore retrievable tomorrow – makes militancy resemble a prolonged adolescence. We want to be accepted, taken under supervision, to wrap in tutelary warmth the solitary we refuse to be, the forlorn creature it would cost us so much to become. To this fine phantasm we are prepared to sacrifice our small sovereignty, our semblance of dignity. The effort of mourning soon becomes tiring; one accommodates to the idea of not being loved, of veering about unsupervised, at random; one replaces *compañeros* with friends, just a few; one learns to live alone without dwelling on the days of glory. Becoming a grown-up, in short, means no longer going to meetings in the evening, choosing the lesser of two sadnesses: staying at home alone, and sitting frigidly in the middle of an exalted group.

Of course this cliché about 'murdering the Father' does give one something of a leading role. As if one had been a particularly bloodthirsty son. All I really had to do was notice that they had died, one after the other, without needing to hurry matters along. My father-figures committed suicide morally of their own accord, like grown-ups. Althusser ended a murderer; Castro a tyrant; Mitterrand blandly acquiescent. This is where I close my proclamation, to move on decently to the obsequies. My report: a register of obituaries.

Living divided, dividing to survive: the time-honoured position of ambivalent sons, swimmers between two waters. In the Stalinist sphere, the schizoid singer and paranoid potentate form a classic pair (say, on the grand scale, Ehrenburg and Stalin, Aragon and Thorez). On my own humble level, I split in two without duplicity: my intelligence was no longer engaged, but my heart still was. It has its own tactics, the heart, its rearguard actions, its ruses. It knows without knowing. It doesn't want to know. It knows perfectly well but all the same.

Elastic defence: you abandon an untenable forward position for another to the rear, apparently more secure, and take stock. In 1968, the Commander had endorsed (although in evasive and circumlocutory fashion) the invasion of Czechoslovakia by Warsaw Pact troops, and this disappointment – conveyed to me by my woman friend during a visit to Camiri – made no small contribution to my rediscovery of my condition as a European: a *flouted* European. I sent out a letter to the *Jefe* to apprise him of an upsetting, though localized, disagreement. Henceforth, I said politely, he would only have jurisdiction over Latin America, and over my own person, since I was stuck there; but Europe and the rest, about which he knew nothing, were all right without him. That first break with unconditionality allowed me to sit more or less on the fence. Soon after leaving prison I was surprised by the 'Padilla affair' (the enforced self-criticism of a good Cuban poet), which forced me to extend these mental reservations. European protesters had the advantage over me of only having spent a few days in Havana; appalled, these intellectuals spoke of an upsurge of Stalinism and did not hide their bitterness as former sympathizers. I chose to act the idiot: wasn't the whole business just idiocy? The instinct of self-preservation. A closer study, a more detailed diagnosis, might have led me stage by stage to realize 1) that I had done nearly four years of jail for an error of judgement; 2) that logically my comrades, including Che, should have been my adversaries; and 3) that I was ripe for the funny farm myself. But it was too soon for me to accept the first point; the second, even now, I instinctively exclude; only the third has always been acceptable. Passing through Paris in 1971, I called on Sartre in his studio in boulevard Raspail. He was alone. He opened the door looking haggard, tottered about finding me a chair and listened carefully to my defence of a bad and lost cause: revolution under siege, cock-up without true significance, don't play the enemy's game, etc. When I had finished he said that Castro had already changed from the man he had met when writing 'Ouragan sur le sucre' ('Hurricane over sugar') for *France-Soir*, he was edging gradually over to the oppressors' side, all that was reviving bad memories of the Soviet Union and co. I did not dare reply that 'all that' revived very good memories in my case, that the highest educational standards in the Latin American continent were well worth the internal exile of one poet. Or that Castro was a choirboy compared to Mao Tse-tung, whom the Maoist Sartre allowed to be idolized in his presence. We parted vexed with one another; he was twenty years ahead, I was ten behind. That was our first and last private meeting. So Cuba wasn't a land of happiness and freedom? Big deal! Happiness, I retorted, is for prats; and freedom, for the rich. May Heberto Padilla and his friends forgive me. I was not on my best form.

The 'heart' contrives to put itself in step with the reason. I accordingly paid lip-service to critical intelligence by writing a self-criticism 'focused on the future', in stereotyped language. It was *La Critique des armes* (1973), three volumes containing accounts and analysis of the failed 'foquist' guerilla campaigns in Venezuela, Guatemala and Bolivia, based on research, interviews and as-sembled documents. The thing appeased my registrar compulsion (no disaster without a prosecution, no assault on the sky without a diagram of the ladders and a description of the clouds). Arid and pointless, the enterprise took two full years and was a total flop: too militant for the merely curious, not militant enough for the people involved. They were quite right not to read it. Analytic rationality has never done anything for the cause of peoples.

I resumed the tradition of going on mountain marches with Fidel. I remember surprising him one evening with an exaggerated line in Fidelism. At the time he was very taken by Japanese gadgets: a quartz watch with minitransistors, the very latest in camping equipment. After stopping to make camp in a clearing near a spring, he unpacked from his *mochila* or rucksack an ultra-modern hammock, nylon awning, clean clothes, a mess tin and a flashlight, all in lightweight materials, and ranged them on the grass listing the advantages of each article. After the demonstrations I could not prevent myself from saying aloud: 'In short, when the *guerillero*'s pack has gone down from 25 to 12 kilos the world will be in a new phase.' The *Jefe*, who hated word-play, made a face and hastened to curb my loyal enthusiasm. 'Danton, you're going faster than the music,' he said, but without contesting my theory itself. And he went to the spring to calculate how many minutes it would take to fill an empty water canteen. He had the gift of serious childishness. A mischievous urchin, but always methodical.

The best remedy for incipient atheism is devotions. During those years I went back into training. It wasn't all over in Bolivia; Roque Dalton was going to El Salvador, where it was all about to recommence. People needed to get ready. La Gringa set me an example: that beautiful and upright German woman, a militant of the 'Bolivian Liberation Army', had just returned from Hamburg where she had executed a senior Bolivian police torturer, and would soon head back to La Paz to be killed in her turn. She, Giangiacomo Feltrinelli (the publisher of *Doctor Zhivago*, who had been sent to La Paz by the Cubans in 1967, soon after my arrest) and I formed a trio, and attended a training course together at Punto Cero. Giangiacomo was as useless at chemistry as I was, and a thousand times more unreasonable in politics. A few months later his shattered body was found at the foot of a giant pylon supplying electricity to Milan, where he had made a bungled attempt to apply our course notes. He used to tell me about mad plans for landings in Sicily, a maquis in the Alps, sabotage, which I did not take seriously. 'Don't be ridiculous,' I told him privately as we fiddled with our wires and batteries on a mattress, 'this sort of thing's no use in Europe, don't go getting the era wrong.' It was obvious that these techniques were for use against American dictatorships. He gave me a silent, myopic look, smiling gently, spectacles balanced on his nose, convinced that fascists were at the gates of Rome, that the 'blacks' were plotting a coup d'état and a Mk. II Resistance was going to be needed. Revolutionaries live on metaphors, and die of them. That generous soul had followed André Breton's advice to 'give up everything'. Abandoned his publishing house, his millions and his mansions, to set up in rather patchy clandestinity as a proletarian; to recreate *partigiani* who would sing *Bella Ciao* as they had in the good old days. To die like others before him on the battlefield of analogies. All honour to him.

What retained me was not a pact with the devil but a debt of gratitude, the weight of collusion. Only my Cuban comrades knew that I had lied throughout my trial. My defence was that I was an observer, a journalist, a visiting useful idiot. It did not really stand up, but I am very gifted when it comes to acting the halfwit, and it kept Havana out of the frame. In reality I had carried a weapon and taken part in the first ambush; I had fired, I believe without killing anyone; I was not there to interview people but to follow orders. General de Gaulle had cabled Barrientos. But the Cubans did far more than the French to orchestrate my rescue, promoting solidarity campaigns, inflating the affair and giving credence *urbi et orbi* to my cover role of wandering idealist. You never know what evil may stem from good. By trying to save me my friends had unintentionally barred every exit to Che. The military did not fail to weigh the repercussions that could follow news of a live Guevara in their hands: my own case, while not the determining factor, may well have had an effect. I gave a detailed account of the politico-legal imbroglio in *Les Masques (Masks)*: pointless to do so again, or to recall the unhelpful background role played by Bustos, the Argentinian arrested with me. My promptitude, I believe, is explained by the disproportion between the fuss surrounding my case and the very minor function I had fulfilled. I had not deserved all that honour, and needed to catch up retrospectively.

You can never predict the consequences of what you do or do not do. I learned only recently of one curious sequence of cause and effect. In the summer of 1966 I went to explore the Alto Beni in northern Bolivia, broken country very suitable for guerilla warfare. I was spotted by some old acquaintances, and the communists heard I was there. The CP secretary, Mario Monje, quite rightly concluded that Fidel Castro had been lying when, seeking his help in getting Che into Argentina, he assured him that the guerillas would only be passing through his country. My presence had helped the communists understand that Bolivia was really the prime objective: why, otherwise, would a 'Cuban agent' have been surveying a zone in northern Bolivia, when the frontier with Argentina is in the south? The small clandestine PCB leadership immediately started scheming to manoeuvre Che towards the exit, by getting other Cuban agents to choose a zone of operations in the far south of Bolivia, an empty desert region, an utter rat trap about as contra-indicated as one could imagine.

That is what responsibility is like, the real thing: something you cannot answer, and that you discover twenty years afterwards.

Havana, 1973, 1976, 1979. The Latino Comintern having foundered, like the guerrilla offensive, there were no more escapades as excuses. It was high time to look at what was happening, at what I did not want to see, not at what was going to change everything tomorrow. During those years of 'revolutionary ebb-tide' I at last managed to understand clearly the unease I had felt on every visit to the island, and the curious impression that, in a society ostensibly focused on the future, individuals did not seem to have one. While in capitalist countries equality of opportunity is a materially unattainable ideal, too obviously under-mined by the unequal conditions between town and country or different quarters of the same town, *feudal* inequality – the pure dominion of man over man – is even more dishearteningly total.

Money, or the Party. Two fetishes, two lures: economic in real capitalism, political in former real socialism. Where money rules some hope is permitted, for the game is always open, there is some margin; where the Party rules the game is closed, and the margin signifies definitive exclusion. The reign of *numerus clausus*. To live in style you have to be a Central Committee member, and this membership is decided on high: no one controls his own life. Communist society was a society of status or caste, in which access to things was decided by people: the feudal cast of countenance. In Cuba all powers were concentrated in the *comandantes*, military, political, economic and spiritual. In the capitalist physiog-nomy, access to people is decided by things, and the paths to success can vary: when one is barred you can try another. Our dependences are anonymous and, more importantly, dissociated: if my banker refuses to extend my credit, a minister can still receive me, and the editor of my newspaper publish the content of his readers' letters. In a country where one head controls all bodies there is no way round the hierarchy, it's all or nothing: money, influence *and* renown, or none of them. Hence a line of separation essentially not between rich and poor, but between powerful and weak, big and small. 'In the Carolingian vocabulary,' Duby writes, 'the word *pauper* designated above all submission to power; its opposite was not *dives* (rich man) but *potens*.'

Of course these were not caste or ordered societies in the exact sense, with pre-eminence and distinction conferred at birth. The kinship between the communist and the Carolingian lies in the moral basis implicitly advanced, in Moscow and elsewhere, for the divide between the potentate at the top and the anonymous individual lower down; whereas that between rich and poor in our societies is seen as a factual condition. In any case, scaling the dominant heights was not a realistic ambition for a subject of real socialism: not even something that could be attempted in a systematic manner given the abrupt, often whimsical changes of line decreed from the top. Miraculous ascents were balanced by equally unexplained disgraces. Statistically, a bankrupt small businessman has a much better chance of rebuilding his credit than a sacked communist petty boss of struggling back to the surface. A poor man in our societies may envy a rich one, but has no reason to genuflect before his moral qualities; for the capitalist winner has won a lottery, whereas the man of marble is supposed to be *made* of marble: no lottery or gambling there. The powerless feudal subject envies, but must also admire, the *potens*, whose justificatory discourse connects with the universal compulsory religion, giving the Great Man the added advantage of supposedly embodying the small man's values. The result is weak social mobility in a society blocked, not by dysfunction, but at source.

Cuba's 'internationalist duty' served, up to a point, as an outlet for the hopes of those at the bottom (fit males of military age at least). There came a point, in the 1970s, when the external safety valve of expeditions to the Holy Land to fight the Infidel was democratized, with crusade privileges hitherto enjoyed by special forces extended to the regular army. In exchange for a plenary indulgence granted by the *Líder Máximo*, several hundred thousand recruits and officers were firmly invited to head for sanctified overseas lands in Angola, Ethiopia and elsewhere. As Knights Templars they left; as derelicts they returned.

The misadventures of these missionaries recall irresistibly the chapter in *The Phenomenology of Mind* entitled 'The struggle between master and slave', a bravura passage whose soundness they illustrated in the process of defending themselves. The key word of this famous odyssey of awarenesses is one much used in Cuba: 'prestige'. Among revolutionaries it was declined like a verb, active and passive. I measured its full weight of life and death when, in our camp at Nancahuazu, 'Marcos', *Comandante* Pinarés, retorted to Che who had just humiliated him publicly, calling him a coward and sissy: '*Mejor muerto que desprestigiado*' (better dead than discredited). In a sense, the two men were replaying the drama of recognition dissected very accurately by Hegel 150 years earlier. Permit me to indulge in a little philosophy, not for the pleasure of scholastic comment but because in this instance it cuts deep. A consciousness, to become self-aware, must gain recognition from another self-aware individual. The human is distinct from the animal in that human awareness of life extends beyond life, and the human desire to be recognized by an Other is stronger than the wish to survive physically. Man is certainly a wolf to man, but a spiritual wolf. The animal wolf struggles for life; the spiritual wolf struggles for death, when that is the condition for being recognized by his Master as an equal or superior. By staking his life, the prestigious individual demonstrates that he has been liberated from the first of the servitudes, enslavement to life. He stands as a free man, in contrast to the base individual who refuses to subordinate himself to the Cause (for example, by accepting dangerous missions from the Commander-in-Chief), preferring the petty existence of a toiler who deals with the resistance of things to transform, day by day, the material conditions of his existence. In the vassal aspiring to sovereignty, risking death is part of an unconscious strategy of domination, for it is valour in faith and blood that establishes the Master as the Master of serfs. But the question of self-sacrifice does not end there. The believer in 'Patria o Muerte' relates to death, and is thus an essentially *moral* being; the *gusano* (an epithet for 'villein') relates to things, he is an *economic animal* wallowing in the universe of need. He trembled with fear at the idea of losing everything, and fled from that fear into work. For the slave works, learns a trade, hustles, tinkers, traffics, slips away to Miami, gets a job, starts a business. Meanwhile the delegate Masters, the commanders who owe everything to the revolution (in other words the Chief), travel to Venezuela, Ethiopia, Yemen, Angola, Nicaragua in quest of his imaginary recognition. And the survivors who make it back home to Cuba find themselves penniless at 50, colonels and generals with three eggs a week, two litres of petrol a month and a fridge sabotaged by power cuts. A reserve general could be seen panhandling not so long ago outside a 'diplomatic shop' for foreigners in Havana. Meanwhile the Miami cousin arrives in the house next door for a visit, arms full of presents. When he left, in the *Mariel* boat exodus of 1980, his cousin the general – then a captain – had been at the departure dock, in mufti, throwing bad eggs at the infamous, despicable traitor, one of the thousands of 'revolutionaries' bussed in to raise troop morale and feed foreign news cameras. Now, ten years later, the one-time 'grub' can strut about lording it in his old neighbourhood. He even slips his former persecutor a hundred-dollar bill, the equivalent of a year's salary or pension to the unhorsed knight. Now the ex-villein can humiliate his former Master, who inexorably becomes financially, mentally, materially dependent on him. At the same time the retired samurai (or the jailed one, if his lord and master wishes to keep him out of sight), discovers that the way of mastery was a blind alley and that of servitude 'the true path of human liberation' (to borrow the words used by my master Jean Hyppolite in his *Genèse et Structure de 'La Phénoménologie de l'esprit'*). He discovers the vanity of the ideal of prestige he had made his own, to win recognition from his peers, but more decisively from the Master of masters, the Commander-in-Chief. Its vanity, or rather perversity; for now that he is nearly 60 he begins to perceive that the desire he once had to fight and die was something breathed into him by the absolute Master, that the magic was not really his own, that its ultimate function was to satisfy the supreme being's insatiable desire: desire to be the spectator of the lives and deaths of his subordinates, to revel through them in his own power. The *Jefe* has elaborated the sacrificial concept of the world into a national religion, while favouring a more sober and conspiratorial approach as his own guiding principle. A lot of his subjects have died of this official credo; he has lived on it, a professional manager of other people's sacrifice. But unlike the spiritual master, the Master of bodies has a chink in his armour: he has no *immediate* access to his power; it is mediated by others who believe strongly enough in him – and it – to be willing to serve him and die for him. Even more than maestros of religion, learning and the arts, the Master of the sword is a trustee who dominates on credit, through the reverence in which his victims hold him. He is their debtor, as God really is of human beings, who would have done away with him if they were not believers.

In 1958, a very young peasant took up arms in the mountains. In 1965 he went to Africa with Che, and in 1967 he accompanied him to Bolivia. Having survived with the rank of colonel, he beat up his next door neighbour for trying to take refuge in a foreign embassy. Some years later, realizing that he had been swindled, he recovered his rebel's soul, laid his uniform and pistol aside and went home to plant tomatoes on his farm. 'The best answer to this form of power is non-power,' he told me the other day. Benigno is a certified hero of his country, the survivor of ten dangerous missions, who has now returned to his plough. Nothing like Gandhi or Cincinnatus, but a courageous and lucid soldier-peasant who has understood what happens when someone refuses to *disarm* in a last-ditch effort to retain the job of chief: you march in support of a Bolívar and end in not-so-comic opera. He will no longer listen to the blockade as an excuse, he is bored by the constant redefinition of the Enemy, he despises national defence as a police expedient. It is one thing to establish an emergency dictatorship to make war, and quite another to make war in perpetuity to legitimize a dictatorship-for-life. To make this distinction from the inside, when you have not been to university or read Hegel and Hyppolite, may well require twenty years of rumination. My own access to the best authors did not enable me to do much better.

Presidents, generals, cardinals and spies know that it is more difficult to make peace than war; to evacuate troops from a territory than to send them into it; to get an agent out than to infiltrate him; to unfrock than to ordain. Old pros take good care not to warn the youngsters: they have to learn for themselves that it costs more to disengage than to engage. I was no longer a tenderfoot, but I still wanted to go back into service: another proof that in these matters we are not governed by common sense. Logically, after my half-intellectual, half-physical discovery of the nation and hatred, I should have *quit*, and respected the principle *Errare humanum, perseverare diabolicum* by doing something else: put my knapsack down, gone to the library, turned the page. But I didn't. Although by now I had almost no ideas in common with the *Jefe* and his people, on a personal level I still had close sympathies with them. Close enough to take me to Nicaragua in 1979 to bear arms in a Sandinist uniform. No one pressed me to do this, least of all the Cubans who did their best to delay me in Havana, from where the operations were being directed. In the end I arrived in Managua on the day of 'victory', with nothing left to do but take part in 'mopping-up' operations against Somoza's national guard which had retreated to the north of the country.

One can do a thing carefully and conscientiously while unconsciously aware that it is idiotic; inversely, the unconscious can be allowed to dictate actions that the conscious mind would reject. If a revolutionary is a person animated by confidence in the future, certainty of being right and clarity of outlook (to an extent he will find it 'frightening' when he has stopped being one, but that at the time seems entirely natural, proof of great mental health), by the 1970s I was already too perplexed to lay claim to the title. Although where Europe was concerned I now took an openly reformist line, and although I made my self-criticism conscientiously, I continued to preach revolution in Latin America. In all bad faith (which does not exclude superficial behavioural good faith). The reason, I believe, was that I was confronted by two feelings from a region darker than the one where our convictions are knitted, ravelled and patched together (awareness and feeling in harmony would be too good to be true): survivor's guilt, which presses you to make pledges, and fear of abandonment, which discourages you from leaving. In the end I did manage to leave, a step at a time and without too much agony, as I gradually threw in my lot with more natural (if that is the right word) adoptive fathers, Allende being soon followed by Mitterrand. While stripping one king bare I was robing another. Kings die like fathers, but paternity goes on for ever. To tell the truth I could not cry: 'King Fidel is dead!' until I was able to continue with equal piety, in the same breath: 'Long live King François, his oak and our rose!' One spectre drives out another; thus do militant souls survive.

These rearrangements at the summit might be seen as signs of immaturity; or they might reflect the questing of an obstinate will to live. To stop believing, to disconnect oneself, is to die a little. You have to restore the link, extend the lease to palliate the endless adjournment of promises. Nancahuazu, Santiago, Havana: you think you have arrived, but each landfall is just a call to take on water and supplies before weighing anchor again, for better or worse. In 1965 I had followed the surge of hope from Europe to the Third World; in 1975 I left in the other direction to safeguard my remaining faith, transferring my expectations from the Third World to a socialist republic in Europe, an explosive charge lodged in the heart of the old world. 'Though the night be long, comes the dawn.' This astronomical reassurance (much used by Brecht) for years protected me from terminal disillusion: the moment of emptiness endlessly conjured up by our superstitions, when we realize that Godot is not coming, that there is nothing to wait for either *there* or *here*. The dawn of adulthood, it seems: the end of fine certainties, of risk-taking, of hallucinated love. A generalized withering. The scales fall from your eyes, the slippers come out of the cupboard. Yet another disillusioned individual settling down to gaze back emotionally on youthful pranks already being marshalled for the memoirs. Who then calls himself a 'committed observer' to get the best of both worlds; we venerate that courtesy of nations, a sententious disguise for desertion. Poor us

Varadero, 1979. Despite his name, Luis Alberto L. is French and was born in France. He arrived in Cuba in 1957, joined the Rebels soon afterwards and fought with Che at Santa Clara. I first met him in 1961, when he was a first lieutenant working at the armed forces political directorate. He used to give lessons on the ministry terrace, using Politzer's manual. He left the army in 1968; the Party thought him 'libertarian', uncontrollable and vaguely suspect, but he was still Fidelist at heart, and practised psychoanalysis at the National Hospital. Tired of the ambient spy-paranoia, he told me he wanted to go to Nicaragua. Although I wanted to go there too, I advised him to go back to France instead. He said he had no attachments there or, he added, any other motivations; he hoped the Central American revolution would prove more open, more welcoming to outsiders and marginal elements. 'Perhaps,' I said, 'but hurry. It won't last.' He agreed, with a rather sad smile.

Nothing, not even the argument that it serves upholders of the status quo, can rid me of the idea that collective agitations, however variable in visible outline, obey a tidal rhythm as simple, unalterable and recurrent as the gravitational pull of the sun and moon on the sea. Among the 'brazen laws' that work with the regularity of a pump, like the way profiteers succeed mystics, the coalition of appetites following the communion of the faithful, none is more depressing than the warm welcome extended to foreign sympathizers followed, some time later, by their relegation to the margins, the outer darkness or the grave. There is no regression more often repeated – from Paris 1789 to Havana 1959 – and less studied by historians of revolution (whose favourite zone of darkness this xenophobia is) than the territorial withdrawal from the human species, the retraction of vows of universality, that follows the appearance of naked chauvinism. The Sans-Culottes of 1790 adopted the Venezuelan Miranda, the Prussian 'friend of the human race' Anacharsis Cloots, and 'citizen Paine'; three years later they were all dead or on the run. In 1920 the Moscow Bolsheviks welcomed with open arms supporters from Germany, France, America, India, etc.; they became the first oppositionists, and the first to be shot. The empty shell of the Comintern was not finally dissolved until 1943. When threatened, the motherland no longer sings the *Internationale.* Children of the world revolution recognize each other as brothers; but in national witch-hunts the first distinction made is between cousins by marriage and blood brothers.

I watched the law of the family prevail over the law of affinities in the Caribbean where, as crisis followed crisis, the thousands of volunteers for the new legions of Bolívar were inexorably expelled, starting with Guevara the Argentinian (whose letters of farewell were published prematurely, making any return to Cuba impossible). The two dual-nationality Frenchmen serving in the Rebel army did not last long once the guerrilla phase had ended. The process in Allende's Chile was more muffled until the military junta, to make its massacre less unacceptable, put the spotlight on 'foreign mercenaries'. In Nicaragua the Argentinian, Chilean and Salvadorean 'internationalists', even the Cubans, were sent home, more or less politely, to assuage popular feeling. But why look so far afield? What fate did the Spanish Republic have in store for the International Brigades? And the French Resistance for Spanish maquisards, Polish Jews from the MOI, 'unpronounceable names' posted in *L'Affiche rouge*? What traces have they left on our street names, in our school textbooks?

Volunteers and adventurers who join a foreign insurrection because it speaks to their hearts as a struggle for all humanity are soon wandering like zombies between a country of origin which rejects them and an adoptive country where they are distrusted. Generous souls who have given everything, but whose names do not appear in listings of the public debt. As if some no man's land of the memory were the sepulchre every people assigned, in all good faith, to creditors it had not chosen for itself.

July 1989. People called them *los Jimagua*, 'the Twins'. I had made friends with them in the summer of 1961 when, Castor and Pollux in olive drab, they used to drive around Havana in a raspberry-red Studebaker convertible, in enviable company. They were rich US-educated brothers who, after taking part in the urban fighting of '26 July', had thrown in their lot with the socialist revolution in preference to easy careers and continuing privilege in Florida: a pair of irreverent and cultivated anti-conformist sportsmen who donated their yacht, seaside villa, light aircraft and fortune to the Cause, daredevils who introduced Fidel to underwater fishing, water sports and hunting, and generally the most exhilarating of companions. I met them again in 1966 in the corridors of the Tricontinental, then again in the guerrilla warfare training schools. They were among the prime movers of *Tropas*, the elite unit of Interior Ministry 'special troops', outside the normal military hierarchy, intended for external interventions: the equivalent of French marine commandos or US green berets, but with political training. Those 500 men, later increased to 2,000, were regarded as a sacred battalion and never used for internal security. It was a 300-man *Tropas* unit, rushed to the Angolan capital Luanda via Algiers, that just saved the town from falling to the South African army. Tony and Patricio spoke English, not Russian, and no Soviet advisers were admitted to the 'special forces' (or, incidentally, to the 'America' department, where giving information to the KGB was regarded as a crime). The pair were Fidelist in spirit, communist by necessity (or rather, like nine Cubans out of ten, by chance), and answerable directly to the *Comandante en Jefe*, whose adoptive sons everyone thought them to be. Of course they were never given written orders. With 'the Twins' you could be stripping an Uzi machine pistol one minute and discussing a Miró painting or Norman Mailer's latest the next; they were combat divers who loved to paint and read, and Tony had married a young philosopher at the university. Those high-living sophisticates made the grubby academic bolsheviks I knew turn pale, but I liked them a lot.

They were not chosen to accompany Che to the Congo (because they were white), or later to Bolivia, their guerrilla expertise being urban rather than rural. We met again in 1971 just after my release from prison; they were in Santiago organizing rear bases for neighbouring guerrilla campaigns. The two ever-genial corsairs – holders of letters patent from the king himself – moved on to one 'internationalist mission' after another. In the years that followed I saw them at work in Nicaragua, where they ran the southern front, and in Jamaica; and they were seen – or rather not seen – in the Lebanon, the US and other places. Until the day when Tony was brought home and immersed, on Fidel's express orders, in another secret activity: state contraband. As an official of the *Moneda Convertible* department of the Interior Ministry, heading a section called 'Naval Operations' whose function was to bypass the American blockade and acquire as much hard currency as possible, by whatever means. Reconverted from armed missionaries into import–export operators, something between commercial travellers and back-shop smugglers, 'the Revolution' now required them both to bypass the law in any way they could. Cocaine offered by far the best ratio of profit to risk; and when eventually they were threatened with exposure by Washington, Havana acted pre-emptively by sacrificing some pawns. When you 'play with men', as Napoleon called it at Las Cases, some of them get eaten. And in the twinkling of an eye the pawns of that whiskered Capablanca, himself a keen chess-player, were swept off the board and into the soup.

So Tony and Patricio de la Guardia – one a colonel in the intelligence service, the other a brigadier-general and former chief of staff of the Interior Ministry, to give their meaningless official titles – were among the accused in the dock at the 'Ochoa trial'. Dressed in mufti – chequered jumpers – and with a distant look in their eyes, facing a bench of field officers in uniform. Tony was shot, at the same time as the admirably brave and smiling General Ochoa and several others, for 'drug trafficking'. Patricio, against whom the prosecution was unable to bring any evidence of an 'offence', was sentenced to thirty years in jail.

All the musty regalia of exorcism were unearthed from the crypt in the service of the Prime Cause: the court-appointed assistant advocate who began by apologizing for having to defend a dissolute scoundrel; the interminable, mind-numbing dreariness of the prosecution case; adjournments of the trial for top-level consultation; and the accused with downcast eyes, acquiescent, having the Chief's promise of their lives in exchange for appropriate behaviour in court. And I used to think such lunacy of interest only to the historians of dementias long played out and already judged . . .

Afterwards, retrospectively justifying the death sentences in public, Fidel did mention *los Jimagua* in passing, but claimed he could no longer remember exactly what it was all about.

By coincidence I was in Moscow on 11 July 1989, the day after the trial, for a Franco-Soviet ceremony to mark the bicentenary of the French Revolution. Half the Politburo was ranged on the stage of a seedy theatre in front of a distinguished audience. Official speeches. After Thierry de Beaucé, for the Quai d'Orsay, I spoke on the fate of revolutions and 'how to finish them without betraying them. Our own answer was the Republic. Dear Soviet friends, now that counter-revolution has arrived among you, as it always does after a revolution, why not build a republican state in your turn?'

Marseillaise, TV, red roses. The two delegations spilled out of the auditorium into a corridor no less shabby. I buttonholed Chevardnadze, the foreign minister, and Alexander Yakovlev, head of ideology inside the Politburo and inspirer of *perestroika*, and asked them to intervene, at least press for a reprieve. They turned their eyes heavenwards. 'We haven't got any real leverage these days, and Castro's frightfully haughty. He just does what he wants.' I argued some more: perhaps I had been misled by the broadsheet press constantly referring to Fidel as a 'satellite'. But I insisted in vain. My interlocutors – and who could blame them? – had their minds on other things. Moscow would do nothing.

And who else would take any interest in an old-hat remake, a 'Moscow trial' in the year 1989: hardly serious. How could decent-minded Europeans be persuaded to linger over an off-season masquerade? The ones who believed it, the grumblers, simply shrugged: they understood only too well. The young could not get their minds round it, it was just too much to believe. And in Latin America, where justice is usually a parody and summary execution common-place, that 'wayside incident' hardly raised an eyebrow.

By the time I reached Paris Ochoa and Tony de la Guardia had been shot. Before walking to the wall Tony, with tears in his eyes, said to the men in the firing squad: 'Make sure my sons don't become soldiers like me, because I've been betrayed. Let me serve as an example at least.' This emerged afterwards because in a country of secrecy everything is filmed: love in bedrooms, death in the open air.

The difference between the communist Saturn and the Jacobin one is that with the first, children sacrificed to the Cause are required to thank the Father for the just punishment with which he means to honour them, at such cost to his own happiness and peace of mind. There are several indications that Ochoa and his co-accused faced their friends' firing squad despising Castro but retaining – a paradox of prolonged enchantment – the image of another Fidel in their hearts. Hearts blown apart by the bullets of that same *Jefe* whom Tony had served, had loved to distraction. And who afterwards watched (because you never know) the videotape of the execution.

Since that date I have referred to Fidel as 'Castro'. No animosity motivated this change of name. It was effected with sadness and in silence, as in the wake of a private disaster. I cannot be sure that I have aged more gracefully than my former mentor (who is surely more exposed to the disfigurements of age than a marginal memorialist would be). You have to take care not to hate yourself through your defunct fathers.

Mexico, 1990. I understand why Latin Americans, friends like Gabo and so many others, still sympathize with the rebel country (of course they do not have to live there) and with the *Comandante* grown grey in harness. García Márquez does what he can to humanize the inhuman, but judges it to be family business, closed to the spoilt children of human rights, impenetrable to didactic Europeans. I do not say he is wrong, even though such attitudes seem to me hopelessly backward, out of phase, indefensible: proof that I have become, as he says, desperately French. Lucid perhaps, but inoperative.

From the inside, in private, you do not see yourself ageing. A couple that stays inside its bubble (of ideology or culture) remains young, for you only discover your age in the eyes of others, when you change your surroundings. Moreover the passage of time is a snare, offering itself to the politician as a friend when really it is his worst enemy. One injustice among the many in that profession. On the one hand, endurance is seen as a gauge of seriousness and obstinacy as a sign of professionalism; the brief incursion is the mark of the irresponsible amateur. On the other, we are always quick to vituperate slowness in relinquishing the reins, presidents who hang on interminably. They ruin our lives: longevity gives the game away. Not only does it flaunt a decline that we would rather not see (and that is especially unbearable in others: our own decline we bear more willingly); it reads aloud to us from a repugnant Book that militants, with their sound instinct for self-preservation, try hard not to hear, an amoral Book with a plot that drags on for generations, making it easy for us, on our mortals' time-scale, to escape its conclusions. This Taoist anthology, facetious and harrowing, is the *Book of Changes* (the manual of political know-how). Derisory though it may seem to most of these gents, to me the Cuban story has become a summary in sound and colour, an object lesson, in a law far harder on those who would change the world than those who flexibly manage it. Joint ventures, foreign bank accounts, offshore and under-the-counter trafficking: thirty years on, the spiritualist state of the 1960s has engendered a society more materialist than our own, where everything unconnected with *divisas* and *ganancia* is collapsing into ridicule. In Cuba as in China, as if overcompensating for his stolen youth, the ex-communist now swears by the greenback, with all the naked zeal of the recent convert. The guerrillas wanted to kill the dollar in people's minds, and in return the dollar is killing them, outright.

The rich should perhaps not be too quick to celebrate victory. What culture has ever escaped a mauling from what it represses? Thinking only of war, the 'totalitarians' were laid low by economics; trying to make the New Man, they erected a Golden Calf. How can we be certain that our liberals, who think only of economics, will be able to cope with war tomorrow when it returns? As in the Gospel that tells us the last shall be first, twentieth-century tail-enders could then make a comeback as pioneers of the twenty-first. Things already scrapped could be recycled in futurist ways.

Can any exemplary meaning be read into this slow swerve from the red into the black? In less than thirty years the *Patria o Muerte* of the early days has become more like the *¡Viva la Muerte!* of Franco's generals (as the 'rapid response brigades' invented in Havana to terrorize demonstrators might easily be mistaken for Mussolini's *squadristi*). While an ultra-revolutionary has become a conservative ultra, a Cid Campeador taken on the air of an Ubu. The early oppositionist will say that the worm was in the fruit from the start, that the totalitarian autocrat of 70 was inside the authoritarian swaggerer of 20. He might add that the post-communist era will itself be his worst punishment, that here is a fine case of the biter bit. The logic of the perverse effect, serving the so-called reactionary tradition as a universal rhetorical pretext for avoiding reforms and leaving things as they are, but whose experiential reality is undeniable. An over-intense 'anti-imperialism' will end by securing twenty-first-century Cuba to the empire; even before the end of the twentieth a lot of Cubans were dreaming of Miami, and when the tyrant has died the people of Havana are going to applaud the stars and stripes along the Malecón, as those of Tirana and Prague did earlier. Prostitution, inequality, jails, dollars . . . Alcázar has replaced Tapioca, Castro Batista, and tomorrow back again, *eadem sed aliter*. For the *Book of Changes*, like all tragi-comedies, has a light-hearted and in this case illustrated version: Hergé's *Tintin and the Picaros*.

In the school textbooks of 2190, the merry-go-round in that Caribbean island will be the object of a footnote: 'Oddities of the twentieth century'. But my mentor will still head one list in the *Guinness Book of Records*: in terms of absolute power, he beats Franco and Stalin hollow with the longest dictatorship of the twentieth century. Deciphering this technical exploit will surely cause headaches among future doctors of political science: a *caudillo* in an age of managers, becoming at 70 virtually the doyen of the planet's heads of state, he has survived ten assassination attempts, five internal disasters, any one of which would have finished an ordinary petty tyrant, the collapse of his foreign supplier and protector, the (obsessive and counter-productive) hostility of the world's most powerful country just next door, and finally the exodus of his *balseros*, so eager to leave that they brave sharks and cyclones perched on air tanks.

No accounts department could ever reveal what is most important in the background to this record: the hundreds of thousands of broken, humiliated, ruined lives; the corrosive omnipresence of informers and petty spies; the exiles, deaths and arbitrary detentions; the prodigious waste of people's sincerity and enthusiasm; the endless repressed exasperation, the despair piled on despair, the double language and double game at every level of the pyramid. Like Brazilians, unlike Russians, this Afro-European people had no real gift for suffering, but strong affinities with *danzón* and the rumba, superstition, physical love, gambling, banter and rum. Harassed by total war and the single party, it put on uniform, back to front, and then – in its genuine majority – displayed astonishing tenacity and dash over many years. Castrism was unstinting with prison (35 thousand suspects rounded up in two days after the Playa Girón, to nip any fifth column in the bud), but hardly ever used 'torture' in the crude Latin American sense (replacing it with an indirect, psychological version in the style of *Darkness at Noon*). Until the Ochoa trial, purges did not involve liquidations: in this respect, the blockaded fortress deserves the regard of Gulag historians. But the monopoly of information, the dismemberment and then levelling of civil society, the close supervision of bodies and minds (Committees for the Defence of the Revolution, set up in 1961 during the state of siege, keep an eye on every neighbourhood) – all the musty family secrets of a police state – could never have made governmental indifference and penury acceptable to so many people for so long. That called for the mobilization of their dreams and hearts on a scale unknown in Eastern Europe; it needed a great dramatist. Like an unmarried woman of 50 repudiated or despised by her former lords and masters – first Spanish, then American – the island at last believed itself beloved by a superman, and gave itself to him as if in revenge. The principle that 'To govern is to persuade', dear to Hobbes and Churchill, in this instance takes the apparent form of romantic attachment to a teller of tales, midway between bird-catcher and conjurer. For a quarter of a century, a hulking brute of stage and state held a somewhat frivolous and inattentive population spellbound, breathless, glued to its seats in a big sweaty auditorium. By presenting the *Revolución*, that grandiose and inert façade, as a thriller with narrative twists, the American star held 'his' people captive, eyes fixed on an epic drama of which he alone was writer, set-designer and director. The everyday life of ordinary Cubans may have been worse than mediocre and largely uneventful, but at least there was open-air cinema in the plaza de la Revolución. Everyone used to await the next 'speech by Fidel' as if it were the *n*th episode of a big-budget politico-police TV series. 'What's he going to come up with next?' 'Who's killed whom now?' 'Who are the good guys and the bad guys this time?' The unfolding melodrama makes it possible to forget how thin the cows are. But as the promised fat cows never arrive, the performer has increasing difficulty in getting across the footlights, the audience starts to doze, to become restless and slip away (but without quite daring to boo and whistle). The magic seizes up. Enough claptrap. What can Caesar's inexhaustible brio do for empty bellies? What televised *circenses* can replace *panem* on the table?

War exhausted a Castrist monarchy that was already too small and too late (just as it bled Philip II's Spain, the greatest power of its time). One day the Antilleans will tell us how companionship becomes mafia and paladins sleazy businessmen. How the *caballero andante* gradually mutates into the *jinitero* (a squire who lives off tourists by selling them girls and rum). How the mechanization of heroism, the droning of *Patria o Muerte, Socialismo o Muerte, Marxismo-leninismo o Muerte*, the vulgar chronographs of the 'heroic guerrilla', the North Korean slogans, enabled a neophyte business culture to take gradual shape behind the façade of rhetorical idealism. Edifying memories of Knights Templar of the hammer and sickle, perpetuated by the hagiography and iconography on constant display, now serve merely to sugar the pill. 'Our heroes (Camilo, Che and the rest) shed their blood for you, you are in their debt; and with only a bit of rationing, a few power cuts, the odd empty pharmacy, the loss of a couple of jobs, lousy wages and exclusion from hotels and beaches reserved for foreigners, you're getting off lightly.' Things may have fizzled out there rather, but to the tradition of the heroic gap between discourse and behaviour, the 'big lie' so characteristic of our time (and always at its most flagrant where discourse soars to lofty heights), that Caribbean island has made a valorous and distinctly original contribution.

Paris, 1995. Remorse? Regret? Repentance? I hear the accusation. Along with the flower of the Third-Worldist intelligentsia, I can be said to have endorsed that murderous illusion for a whole decade. Not altogether with impunity: secret agent, *franc-tireur* or flanker, I paid my dues for the totalitarian magic with several years in jail. Which does not absolve me of all responsibility.

Totalitarian. It is impossible to squeeze the *compañeros*, my youth and our dreams into this word which is too *wholesale*. The retail individual cannot recognize himself in it. Valéry said that a theatre audience becomes 'a giant more stupid than its parts'. The same is true of the contemporary Leviathan: appalling when seen as a *whole*, from behind and above; appealing from below when considered in its constituent parts. To the aerial photographers who, with the sort of precision we have come to expect of them, confound fascism and communism in the same 'totalitarian' portmanteau, I offer no factual reasons that might enhance their 'definition'; Paxton, Kershaw and other historians have already taken that soft-watch notion apart. Without rehearsing the philosophic and historical arguments, I can say that confusion of these *isms* arouses in me a stubborn feeling of injustice, while dozens of faces met along the way file through my memory. I fall suddenly into dreamy silence on hearing those hasty, loose-woven panoramas, because I remember the superior human qualities of the militants who kept the inhuman machine running. It is a fact that the men and women I admire today usually passed through the far left in their youth, however unsullied they may have been by politics. As if there had been selection of birth characteristics. Quite a long list, from Julien Gracq, writer, to Georges Charpak, physicist, by way of a hundred or so lesser names. Even today, if I find myself in sympathy with a stranger of my own age met in a train or aircraft, there is a 90 per cent probability that at some point months later I will discover by chance, without much surprise, that they too have 'been there'. But the select group of 'former Party members' is insignificant compared to the throng of honest and upright figures of all nationalities that parades through my mind when I hear the ill-famed word 'communism' (while the well-famed 'social democracy' and 'centrism' evoke unattractive images of paunchy notables and yuppies in three-piece suits). Consider the absurd reflex of a rambler in the French countryside, soaked with rain, staggering under the weight of his rucksack, when told that the inn proposed for the night is full and he is going to have to find shelter with locals, or in a barn or shed. Even in 1995, he mutters anxiously to himself as he trudges after his companions: 'If only there were a militant, a pal, retired or even still active . . . I'd certainly be able to knock at the door, there'd be a crock of red, I'd be able to rest at least.' More than once, when lost in some corner of the Auvergne or the Ardèche, I have regretted not having a list of local communist militants in my pocket. I would mentally add Christian militants and members of charitable NGOs: none of those people would set fierce dogs on strangers who opened the garden gate. And at dinner time they would probably say that enough for four was enough for eight. This is not a type of argument that the political sciences regard as acceptable; which suggests to me that learned doctors who pass quickly over such matters cannot be very serious.

With the gilded legend of old-time revolutions and the pivotal role played in our Judaeo-Christian imagination by the persecuted (whose main persecutors can abuse all the more freely when they retain a persecuted image from their own early careers), the 'human factor' explains the majority of conversions to an intrinsically dubious cause. The point is that to *judge* a social system one has to consider it in person, from all angles, piece by piece. But to *believe* in it one has only to come across *a* marvellous individual, or several, who act as spokesmen for the distant *ism* and dissuade the sympathizer from opening the file in a sober, thoughtful manner. This is where revolutionary faith converges with religious faith, in the mechanisms of adherence rather than in the aims pursued. Like revealed religion, 'scientific socialism' was a seed that germinated on contact with human soil. The divide between St Thomas's *Summa* and the taking of monastic vows was as great as that between Marx's *Capital* and the plunge into militancy: hence the redundancy of reasoned refutations of 'Stalinist' dogmas, which were of no more concern to what we used to call 'the ordinary fly-poster' than theological controversy over the double nature of Christ to a Little Sister of the Poor. It was surely companionship and personal association, not textual analysis, which only came afterwards, that led even the most cerebral individuals, the best supplied with arguments, to plunge into the icy waters of partisan calculus.

How simple everything would be if communism had just been a machine for making prison camps! The curse (or the blessing, I am not sure which) is that between the crimes it produced fraternity, self-denial, optimism, courage and generosity. A corrupting and uplifting machine for making people worse and better than they are. For making them happy, for happiness lies in struggle, and stupidity too. Like any mobilizing collective emblem the red flag was a notable school of bravura and imbecility. From this point of view, sierras and high plateaux were for me the cause of regression on the mind side and advance on the heart side. The latter amply balances the former, in my private accounts.

Do I dare make a statement of my debts, all weighed and measured? If I owe my first begetter, Louis Althusser, my importunate interest in truth, it was the second, Fidel Castro, who led me to the turning point of rigour. Who put my finger on a disconcerting truth that Raymond Aron was teaching at the same time, in a peevish and academic way, to the sons of my country's solid bourgeoisie: 'Political action is a response to a situation, not a theoretical exposé or expression of feeling.' Only my tutelary tyrant would have added: 'Action is there to respond to a situation of *hostilities*.' The professor would have understood that perfectly: in the lineage of Machiavelli and Clausewitz, it goes without saying. To the seigneurial family decorously honoured by my two ferrymen I will refrain from affiliating Che, although he too was no choirboy (no more of one I daresay than St Sebastian, or Baden-Powell). Nevertheless Guevar*ism* – rather than the over-heroic deviationist himself – introduced me to orthodoxy: not monetary but warrior. This runs through all epochs. 'Polemos, king and father of all things,' said Heraclitus, scorning Eros. I envy those with the good luck to live without frontlines, and these days incline to such innocence. But I still cannot much value a political culture that is not a culture of war. A scouring, corrosive culture, anti-demagogic (anyway in periods of prosperity), repellent to men of ideas and bad for your reputation abroad. I am in no sense an expert on strategic matters, but nothing else in politics seems to me worth a conversation. Apart from my simple interest in 'defence matters', this arises from a vision of the world that is not particularly pleasant, and uncommon among leftists whose utopias tend to be too amiable. The decade of the *comandantes* immunized me against that woolly idealism, soothing as old lullabies to the well-meaning, constantly discredited by the facts but still used as a soporific by each generation: international arbitration, collective security, peace forces, preventive deployments . . . juridical Europeanism has given that outlook a new gloss in recent times. But the Eurodelirium of the liberal *fin de siècle* – 'Europe equals peace' – has always seemed precarious to me. Distant lands gave me a glimpse of the sombre logics of power, opened on life a shutter of death which I have never been able to close.

The very idea of war seems old hat to the global civism now favoured by opinion. This generalized superciliousness can thrive now that our means of destruction render international relations abstract, like the act of killing which, terrorism apart, only materializes for us on a large scale as a flickering televisual reflection in the depths of our domestic caves. Our military–industrial complexes have depersonalized the warrior function by incorporating valour in weapons systems, indexing military capacity on the gross national product, placing the engineer above the brawler. The nuclear pacification of the developed world since 1945 has completed the transformation of the great captain into a calculator of odds. Nothing could be less 'warlike' than the silent underground and submarine deterrents that enabled the rich world to live in peace for half a century. A few dives out of Brest with our *Force océanique stratégique* made me aware of the astonishingly peaceable character of nuclear vigilance. The role of a missile-launching submarine is not to spit lethal fire but to trail detectors in silence at a depth of 300 metres to pick up 'signatures' and analyse them with computers. Does this very high technology have emollient effects? Who can say that the nameless mass of potential horrors has not undermined the real honour of our societies . . . The advance of military technology being accompanied by an equivalent regression of martial values, there is perhaps an inverse relationship, in the long term, between the destructive power of weapons and the moral prestige of the soldier (which may thus have been in steady decline all the way from the Greek hoplite to the fire-control officer sitting at his console). The archer was a threat to the mounted knight, the crossbow trumped the sword. The spread of firearms – mortars, culverins, muskets and arquebuses – overturned a chivalrous society based on armour and hand weapons; today the new instruments of empire – surveillance satellites, AWACS intelligence aircraft – have taken over from the nineteenth century's armoured steam warships and quick-firing guns, making expeditions with 'zero casualties' (on the US and allied side) theoretically possible.

In their hegemonic relations with other civilizations, our fortified democracies stake everything on technology, shoring up the spiritual, where we are weak, with the material, where we are strong. Against the Koran, the Tomahawk missile. Islamist suicide commandos do the opposite (making a virtue of necessity, given their limited equipment). The Westerner relies on his tools to save his stake and his skin. Today's computers and space technology represent a military leap forward at least equivalent to the revolution of the fifteenth and sixteenth centuries, which produced 'bastioned' fortifications, musketry and square-rigged warships. This enabled our ancestors to block the Islamic thrust of the classical age, first at Lepanto, then outside Vienna. The rich of what was once Christendom have reason to expect something similar from today's prodigious weapon systems. All the same, one cannot help suspecting that, despite their 'superiority' in humanist values, Westerners, with their predominantly feminine 'life-affirming' mentalities, may find themselves on the spiritual defensive when faced with the 'death-seeking' posture of phallocratic societies with strong beliefs, those said to be underdeveloped. The intolerance of over-developed societies for loss of human life helps explain the tragi-comic paralysis of great powers when facing resolute micro-states, determined bands or 'fanatics' (that word so often used to make thought unnecessary). But with nuclear deterrence useless against the weak, and air strikes often prevented by landscape and camouflage, we could witness a disconcerting return to land mines, small arms, hand-to-hand. How long can our democracies 'keep order' and safeguard their 'vital interests' without paying the blood bill? The question revives an immemorial operational problem, one to which mercantile individualism has no answer: if nothing is worth a human life, why go and get killed? What was left of a great 'totalitarian' power of 260,000,000 inhabitants – the USSR in Afghanistan – when by the nineteen-seventies its *babushkas* could no longer endure 3,000 body-bags? What is left of the unrivalled 'superpower' of 250,000,000 inhabitants, when it has to withdraw its troops from an African country because eighteen infantry are killed in an operation? Today more than ever, in evaluating the power of a state, it is sensible to avoid being dazzled by its gizmos and armadas, and assess instead the attitudes of its young people to death and what role God plays; whether or not there is a heaven.

'UN peacekeepers', multinational gendarmeries and other laborious constructs are no more than false good ideas that we use as escape clauses. There are a dozen good and complicated reasons for the congenital feebleness of these UN 'forces', but let us tiptoe prudently around the most obvious: peace troops, who have no 'motive to act', are never going to feel that they ought to die for someone else's juridical settlement. I refer not to individuals, of course, but to the ethical substance of our societies (from which most of these contingents come), whose high average life expectancy, low birthrates and ambient scepticism cause the death of a citizen on what used to be the 'field of honour' to be seen as a moral scandal, or worse still a political gaffe embarrassing to the government.

We very nearly persuaded ourselves that Mars had died at Hiroshima, and that Hermes the messenger, the new strategist, would serve henceforth as the arbiter between peoples. Did not the Soviet superpower, all girded with bombs and tanks, collapse like a house of cards? It is a plain fact that power at the millennium is more a question of wavebands than tons of steel, more of speed than land area. In the computer age, the light outweighs the heavy and a ten-point stag has less chance of leading the herd than a tineless pricket. The parameters of supremacy have mutated (as Michel Serres discerned) along with the scientific and technical paradigms; this is attested by the continuing ascent of the two countries defeated in the Second World War, Germany and Japan, as well as the collapse of a technically backward and over-militarized false giant. Wars seem to have changed too, becoming economic, cultural, technological, even narcotic (drug trafficking represented as war by the South on the North). Are we to conclude that only the backward have time to waste on military concerns and budgets? Postmodernity seems to be setting Carthage, with screens and dishes, against Sparta. As if our societies had endless time to toy with the religious question: to what do we attach an unlimited value? For what, for whom, are we prepared to pay the supreme price?

It is banal to recall that 'the earliest state structures grew out of military organization', and that the distinction between friend and enemy defines the collective. Nevertheless, political bodies dislike war and do all they can (as they did in 1940) to delay the moment of truth. One has to sympathize: it is embarrassing when the 'art of living together' threatens to culminate in the art of mutual extermination. It is not fascist to question Aristotle from Clausewitz's angle, to search out the wolf in our political science manuals, that wolf that used to be communism and is now the Muslim thrust at the heart of the atheist West. Who can guarantee that this is just a passing aberration without a future, or that the reign of economics will soon banish it for ever?

Although their worship of weapons and heroes went beyond reason, the *comandantes* and Latin American guerrillas opened my eyes to the human scrimmage. Thanks to them, I cannot now see a period of peace as anything but a phoney war. If war is bad and peace a relief, there follows a rule of behaviour: do not want war, like the fascist, and do not believe in peace, like the slumberer. It is easy to become somnolent: peace has the perverse quality of seeming normal and natural at the time, while a historian may well regard it as an interesting but precarious interlude (between 1500 and 1800, 270 years of war in Europe; between the year 1 and 600, 587 years of war in China). Blinded by our proliferating juridical structures and the belief – ever-fresh, though ever contradicted by the facts – that commerce and industry reduce 'bellicose passions', our post-war democracy dreamed of dissolving the use of force in a jurist's dominion and a flood of supermarkets. It sought peace insurance in legal codes, economic groupings and growth rates. The Helvetized European has thus become justice of the peace of a planet in disorder, but ignorant of the background to the case and the rules of the game. He averts his gaze from the barbarians at the gates, forgetting that he is himself the product of a past very like the present of those 'fanatical' and 'tribalized' groups. The best proof that the Christian West still exercises (while awaiting replacement in the driving seat by Confucian Asia) the spiritual regency of our madhouse is the dissymmetry between its dominant position in the deployment of legitimate ideals and its distance from the laboratories of truth represented by hunger, insecurity, conquering faith and war. In such areas, distinct from the exact and natural sciences, the global reputation of our ideologues cannot always mask the unreality of the ideas being debated. It is to the post-1945 mastodons of the industrial North with their libraries, professors and archives, their calm and silence, opulent grants and helpful assistants, that the impoverished two-thirds of the planet have entrusted, willy-nilly, the task of developing standards of reference. But protected by the selfish order of nuclear deterrence (peace in the centre, wars in the marches), sheltered by an unprecedented parenthesis of peace, the new generations in our countries have become foreign to all that is fundamental and recurrent in the accursed order of the collective. With its moralizing, openly pacifist intelligentsias, protected by its circumstances from any unhealthy preoccupation with things military, the 'First World' and Europe in particular, preoccupied with its new Scandinavian religion, no longer has the historical experience appropriate to its speculative capacities. We cannot last indefinitely as the thinking, judging and grading centre of the planet while remaining at the periphery of its torments: and the eventual apprenticeship will be costly. This bottleneck to our boundless regulatory plans seems to me to render pointless the printed elaborations piled in thousands on the bookshop counters, more apt for bookish commentary than observation of facts. An adept of the old masters of wisdom, one who in Machiavelli's phrase prefers 'the actual truth of the thing to his imagination', may find some relief from this turn-of-century sedimentation in the resumption of the old train of horrors: wars, alliances, frontiers, ruses, armistices, all the usual sound and fury. Nuclear proliferation, like the crumbling of 'peace by law' in Europe itself, will have at least these advantages: it will rid us of edifying speeches and speed the return of hard-core philosophy and high-pressure romance. Without the Napoleonic slaughter, would Hegel, Stendhal, Schopenhauer or Tolstoy ever have seen the light of day? We need not despair of the future.

If I may now return from the History men make, on which everyone is free to have his own ideas, to the one that has made me, on which I am entitled to more certainty, I find on the threshold a sultan of the isles. Had he kept me under his hand that bushy-bearded Scaramouche would have devoured me without ceremony; but if he had not brought me down to earth, I would never have emerged from my wimpish Sorbonnery to engage with the nuts and bolts disdained by great authors: commissariat, armament, logistics, machines. Thanks to which, more interested in 'how it works' than 'what it means', I finally abandoned bellicose matters after a final relapse, in France, out of technical curiosity. I have called 'the why of the how' mediology, and that is where I am now. The malice of perverse effects: a logorrhoeic individual pre-armed me against logocentrism. A chimerical, earthy, ferocious and subtle creature of the Caribbean set me at odds, thank God, with the Parisian *bel esprit* and New York radical chic. A yokel I am, and negligible I remain: the taste for *realpolitik* – not being but doing – the reality instinct, a sense of detail; the capacity to endure hatred, contempt. Other minds in flight have fallen back to earth by more honourable ways: the Resistance, a medical thesis, a diary, *a sous-préfecture*. What can I say? Lovers in the clouds cannot land by themselves; an ogre served as my shock-absorbing angel. It isn't proper history, but it's my history. Sorry, there's nothing I can do about it now.

Notes

1 Special class preparing students for entry to the ENS.
2 Star pupil, most academically successful student.
3 Castrism or Latin America's Long March.
4 Long-established military and teaching hospital.
5 'Louse that goes pop's louse no more'.

Part Two:
Governors

Investiture

Really it was the monk Joachim de Flore (1130–1202) who addressed the planet on 21 May 1981, in one of those mysteries of the impromptu. Stuck with the job at the last minute, I had picked the millennium-old Cistercian's brains before putting the sacred flame (in sixteen-point characters on three A4 sheets) back in its place the previous evening. To a battery of cameras in the banqueting room of the Elysée palace, in the voice of the newly elected president of the French Republic, the Calabrian cleric proclaimed with great formality the advent of the 'third age'. This would be the good one: after the Old Testament, then the scourging of the Son, reconciliation with the Holy Ghost. The chosen people had been dragging its feet in the execution of the Divine plan. To make up for the lost millennium it was going to have to take double mouthfuls, so crucial is it to 'the nature of a great nation to conceive great designs'. It is all there in black and white in the investiture speech of the spanking-new head of state. The country (I had specified in writing) '*ought to* light the way for the march of humanity'. For a good reason: the country of *Les Misérables* was repossessing its family heirloom socialism, the legitimate offspring of the Jacobins, appropriated in 1917 by unpolished *moujiks* and again, post-1945, by famished aboriginals. Rome was going to be back in Rome at last. But at this point our celebrant almost irritated me by straying from the parchment: in the reading, that *ought to* somehow melted down into a limply virtual '*can* light the way . . . ' 'To this end,' I had written in the palimpsest, 'France can count on herself.' This time, my spokesman accommodated himself in reverse: *ought to* instead of *can*. Those approximations, those little amendments: incorrigible, decidedly. All right, call it a slip, forget it. Amid the general euphoria, I forgave our dragoman these trivia – need I recall that to do something is to make do? – even when he saw fit to interlard the illuminist's ternary warp with consensual humanist clichés for which I take no responsibility: things like 'the path of pluralism' and 'confronting differences while maintaining full respect for others'. What could such concessions matter against the grandeur of the backdrop: a political majority that coincided at long last with the social one? What really counts is the framework, the sacred word behind the flourishes, the medieval prophet's mystical trio[1] (soon to spearhead the Hegelian triumph of the Mind). Falling back from America to Europe as if from Charybdis to Scylla, I found myself (predictably enough) in the back seat. Jules Verne one minute, celestial Jerusalem the next. Just as the New World, an empty space illuminated from the front, is an ideal place to try out the sort of new ideas that emerge from fervent summers – Jesuit *reducciones*, Fourierist phalansteries, Che's *hombre nuevo* – so the Old World, whose present is illuminated by the past, is a place for recapitulation, ideal for the mature age that comes along in autumn to harvest very old inheritances.

The end of time is a three-beat waltz. So on that inaugural day (as the *Journal officiel* might say, but does not), redeeming France was starting 'the *third* stage of a long journey, after the Popular Front and the Liberation', sealing a '*new alliance* of socialism and freedom' representing 'the *highest* ambition held out to the *world* of tomorrow'. Yes, the Angel of Judgement would get the carnivorous primate out of its rut. The final lap had begun, and that rainy May was going to put the industrial centuries in perspective. After the capitalist moment, 1850–1920, first setback, and its totalitarian negation, 1920–80, second setback, here at last was the *negation of the negation*, of which the planet had almost given up hope: socialism in freedom, 1981–2981, even if it cost the lives of a detachment of scouts (us). France, the 'third people' after the Jews and Christians, was going to lead Babylon to our common final truth. In these dialectical odysseys, you always find yourself back at home by the end of spring, bruised by long tribulations (less pointless in hindsight than they seemed at the time). In the back row, a passing gatecrasher with lowered eyes and sphinx-like smile, I listened smugly as the esoteric grace-notes of the eternal Gospel resounded under the TV floodlights and chandeliers. A revival of faith? The flame still guttering? The celebrant officiated gracefully, without apparent shyness. He had asked me for 'a sermon with a bit of mouth to it'. And that was what he got.

He was the only one who did get it: no one else listened to the thing. Blockbusting, super-colossal and ripsnorting though they be, our written buy-back bids pass unnoticed. The next day's press hardly mentioned that peal of bells. Locally, the universal order of the day passed straight over the heads of the gnomes ranged in a horseshoe pattern about the presidents of the Constitutional Council and the Republic. I am afraid the tumult inside their skulls that day concerned other things. 'Why wouldn't Marie-Claire Papegay (the president's secretary) take my phone call yesterday? How do I stand with Pierre Mauroy? If only they'd told me he was going to be prime minister! And my office: what floor . . . how many buttons on my intercom . . . and the car, CX or Renault 25? . . . God, I hope the snapper's still there when I grasp the Beloved's paw . . .' Such are the thoughts that moil in the brains of important men ranged like a row of shoving, jostling schoolboys in their playground. They were too overjoyed just at being there to hear a word their Messiah said. Murmuring like a prompter from behind a screen of notables, I had thought myself pretty hip. As the aide handed those three pages to the Enthroned One, standing at his microphone, I laughed up my sleeve at my cunning. And when he stuffed them casually in his pocket to move on to serious matters – back-slapping and gossip – I *wept* up my sleeve at my innocuousness, already discerning that in the beginning was *not* the Word, that those fine pledges out of the mists of time were strictly without importance, wasted sweat: 'words, words'. A single image, they say, is worth a thousand of them. And of that tricolour *introit* there remains a single frame, a thousand times reproduced, of an embrace between two leaders of the Republic, one departing and one arriving. Who, in the end, had exploited whom? Had I used my megaphone to spread the message, or had he got his pen-pusher to help him make a noise with his mouth (that obligatory formality for democrats on parade)? Who uses whom – the ultimate question in politics – had just bagged another bumpkin.

'My vocation is political only in so far as it is religious,' François Mauriac puffed one day. 'I engage with problems here below for reasons from on high.' Repatriated to on high, God's witness had left everything here below to junior staff paid off at seven-year intervals with the Légion d'honneur; and the reasons, little changed since St Augustine's time, to us, clerics without a clergy. Our job was to overhaul the seized, rusting lift between heaven and earth. I was no longer certain that the socialist-republican repairman would come, but this was an ideal opportunity to find out, here and now among children of Michelet, the last direct bloodline from 1789. If I had controlled relations between earth and ether I would not have guaranteed a radiant future; Michelet was playing his last card here below. The pill was sugared that day for local consumption. Far from surfing on their elated mood with that coded profession of faith, Joachim and I had intended it as a last warning, a statement of what was really at stake, no more and no less. There had been a genuine change of majority! After two fiascos – sado-communist in the East, maso-Third-Worldist in the South – it was time for the West to get its act together. Once our plenipotentiary was safely headed for the Arc de Triomphe and the flame of the unknown soldier – always amuse the gawpers – in an open-topped Citroën SM, with a still-shiny prime minister at his side, I tried to put Bérégovoy in the picture, for he had muttered something about Léon Blum and the summer of '36. 'This isn't a new beginning,' I insinuated as we climbed the grand staircase with bronze palms built for Murat, king of Naples, 'it's a rounding-off.' 'If you say so,' replied the new secretary-general of the presidency a bit tipsily. He jerked his thumb at some big black clouds. 'They'll get soaked, poor chaps. You going to the Panthéon this afternoon?' Big History too is made up of misunderstandings. But he wasn't wrong: the sky was threatening.

It was a bit late, let's admit, to save the Hexagon, Europe and the human race. The Sèvres plates and silver-gilt forks at the blow-out that followed the royal enthronement – emotion is famishing – only half distracted me. We had arrived like turds on the sacrificial altar, electorally victorious but religiously bankrupt (for despite Jack Lang's choirs from the Opéra, and a lunch for 200 with 'the cream of the world's intellectuals and artists' – Melina Mercouri, Julio Cortázar,

Gabriel García Márquez, Elie Wiesel, William Styron, etc. – the underlying feeling was no more red than it was festive). Although not located anywhere, an atmosphere (I have since realized) vastly outweighs a programme in due and proper form. I still imagined that somewhere between Grace and disgrace a sort of recovery might be managed, with the aid of a judicious shove or two, following the happy capture of la Pompadour's Paris residence. We were the trailblazers, and the agnostic masses would thank us later.

The air was getting heavy. Roused by the *Ode to Joy*, Jaurès wished his successor good luck from the depths of his crypt. The repressed wish for public misfortune that gnaws even at the most well-meaning people was about to mature. A cloudburst voids a storm too long desired. At last, when the garden parties were over, the worst could begin: insurrection in the smart quarters of Paris, military mutinies, burning the Tuileries, provocations by the special services, war in Spain, terrorist acts . . . Who would have predicted a gradual foundering in ordinary political sleaze? Allende had parried the blade for three years; the strategic stakes may have been paltry, but the CIA had taken them seriously; half his cabinet had been shot and the rest put in concentration camp. How long would we remain unscathed? Even a year would be a miracle; but long enough to show the way for others to follow later. With heavy heart I watched my little office colleagues clustered round scattered celebrities, all overjoyed at arriving in the centre of things without a doubt in the world. Playing at resting their buttocks on periwinkle-blue silk-upholstered Empire armchairs, smugly eyeing the glories in carved and gilded wood, the beauties and geniuses over the doorways, the oval-framed portraits in the salon des Ambassadeurs, the biblical tapestries, the giant amphorae in the winter garden. They seemed unaffected by the scent of blood that hangs about thrones: neophytes, sure that they would not be splashed, clambering into the cart with the shining faces of newlyweds. My own bore the grimmer look of an old fiancé of débâcle: veterans know that you don't take standard history lightly. In the same way that high office 'takes over' the dubious character who accedes to it, a Shakespearean dénouement would soon overtake the constituted bodies who, brushed and polished as if for a review, stood around the Elect discreetly jingling their stars, medals and ribbons. How many of us would survive the coming coup d'état? Small men, as all are who prefer success to glory, those bemedalled adolescents had nothing to lose by waiting: our destiny would be greater than us. (I refrained from warning the old Fourth Republic men from behind whose backs I listened to my mystic lamb's homily. Those happy fellows hadn't a clue: they thought they were back in the timeserving days of René Coty and President Queuille; and I knew we were on the eve of a Paris Commune Mk II. To each his own spectres. Theirs at least had some idea where they were going.)

'Be a good fellow: don't show your face too much. It'll damage us,' a young colleague muttered in my ear a day or so later. 'You know very well you don't belong here.' I acquiesced willingly. He was thinking already of opinion polls to come. There were rumours of communists in the government; only errand boys, juniors and extras perhaps, but this was the limit. 'Our American friends' were making rumbling noises, with Vice-President Bush threatening a Paris landing in person; our opinion leaders were seeing red, and the 'President's men' trying not to be noticed. 'This is no time to complicate things,' one murmured. An énarque, but sensitive to public anxieties, he reminded me that I had 'a serious image problem'. Normally this is tempered by my sense of decorum; this time, I had thoughtlessly shown my face to the courtyard through the tall window at the top of the cloistered staircase, at whose foot were gathered reporters who might see me. I withdrew immediately to avoid compromising them, and my collea- gues were grateful.

Not long afterwards the first secretary of the Socialist Party assured a journalist bothered by the presence of a dangerous Marxist among the pre- sident's 'close advisers': 'He's just a personal friend, among many others, to whom no political significance should be attached.' I understood that this accommodating man would go far. Jean-Pierre Chevènement, with Gaston Defferre, was alone in treating me with sympathy at that time. A man of character who would have difficulties.

To general satisfaction, I thus found myself consigned to the most remote and exiguous cranny of the first house of France. A corner room at the back end of a labyrinth on the services side, far from the decisional sanctuaries overlooking the silence of the park. This cul-de-sac suited a fantasist charged with semi-official and parallel functions touching on relations with the Third World (itself a media cul-de-sac of no interest to anyone else in the entourage, for good reasons). My superiors rejoiced in the belief that they were slapping me down; in fact they had returned me to familiar haunts: cell, attic, cellar. That hierarchical attribution of dens was just what I needed: an exalting whiff of solitary, which only bothers 'relational' types. I am shy at parties, I stiffen in front of lenses, champagne gives me hangovers and I long to flee when there are more than ten people at dinner. These things have advantages.

Chance favours the meek and the agoraphobic, and it made my place of exile an Ali Baba's cave. The last (as prophesied) became the first in the depths of a cramped grey labyrinth (since redecorated), for our Palace of Supreme Har- mony, behind the shop window of state chambers, is more like a *sous-préfecture* in the Aveyron than a fairy castle. Wandering the corridors, back staircases and mazes of hidden attics, I had discovered by chance that the famous 'red telephone' linking Moscow and Paris, the only nuclear capitals in continental Europe, like the one between the White House and the Kremlin, was just a teleprinter stuck away in a broom-closet that smelt of disinfectant. The disen- chantment! The bitterness! You children who tremble before the mysteries: stay out of the holy of holies.

My neat, unfindable little office connected with another glory-hole, a

stripped-out former bathroom, whose very existence was unknown to our higher
dignitaries. In this adjoining bin, something between a mail office and a
temporary storeroom, there arrived by unexplained routes all the information
that irrigated HQ hour by hour: notes from advisers, telegrams from the Quai
d'Orsay, defence dossiers, flimsies from the hidden lairs of intelligence. These
arrivals in TTU (*très très urgent*) envelopes ended up there, slumbering in ordinary
cardboard files fastened with string, piled inside an ordinary greenish metal
cupboard with an ordinary suitcase lock, to which Mme C., keeper of documents
for the international section, jealously guarded access. The ultimate repository
of secrets superintending the storage and classification of this perpetual manna
was a small grey-haired lady of no apparent distinction. The most important
individual in the Republic, unknown to all, travelled to and from work by metro.
Since Vincent Auriol's time she had seen a good few people come and go under
the faded gilt panelling: nice people, you understand, distinguished, people
you've heard of, with entries in *Who's Who*. Older than most of the House
secretaries, who had fled back to their old departments to escape rape by the
helots and the spectacle of the coffers being pillaged by levellers, she stayed at
her post like a Blandine of the supreme magistrature's archives. For a while she
managed to dissimulate her stomach-heaving anxiety, I believe with the
laudable intention of bearing witness for posterity (a posterity which, when
the natural hierarchies had been restored, would take the severe but just form of
the High Court, or perhaps some special tribunal for the sort of crimes to be
expected from power-crazed socialo-communists). A conscientious reader of
Paris-Match, the *Quotidien de Paris* and *Le Figaro*, especially the hair-raising
warnings from M. Jean d'Ormesson which she would underline in red crayon
in the safety of her bunker, she was manifestly aware of the justice-dealing
possibilities of her observation post. She savoured these in advance with brave
determination, although they sometimes made her dizzy. Like the eye of God in
Nazi Germany obliged to swap the cassock for SS uniform, that invisible grey
mouse, unfailing in her duty of discretion, trotted back and forth across the
carpet feeding papers to the 'diplomatic cell', blank-faced amid the bustle of tail-
coated and lounge-suited flunkeys, eyes open and ears pricked against the
moment when she would be called into the witness box. We saw a good deal of
each other, she and I. Indeed we exchanged civilities several times a day, as the
absurd layout obliged her to cross my office to enter her own. By an extraordinary piece of good or bad luck, the sort of double-edged coincidence that
could bring a later accusation of passive complicity or commendation for
bravery behind enemy lines, the little shepherdess of the legal state was forced
to frequent the den of a wolf, a mole, an extremist – let's utter the word, an
ideologue – infiltrated into the highest circles (her favourite rags kept reminding
her) by the KGB.

For the first month or two, she forced me to retreat with a terrified, hostile
stare when I ventured to peer round our padded communicating door in the

hope of circumventing her vigilance. She alleged all sorts of emergencies and priorities to avoid responding to my indirect, probably over-diffident memos requesting sight of documents. Until the day when, after a prolonged and subtle approach campaign (which I would rather not go into), I used my fist brutally enough – only on the table of course – to extract a crucial concession: the location of the drawer where she kept the key to the cupboard of dangers. From that day forward I could stick my nose freely, day or night, into all the secret defence files, heavy with several years' worth of notes on the so-called 'East-West' strategic matters that had caused such speculative hysteria: SS20, Pershing, cruise, MBFR, Atlantic Alliance, Warsaw Pact, balance of forces; not to mention the files on the USA, the USSR, West Germany, NATO, WEU, EEC, ANZUS, ASEAN, and so on. Like M. Seguin's little goat, the resolute Mme C. had surrendered, uncovering the pots in which the future simmered. A glutton in the kitchen. Like a bad cook at Maxim's when dishes return uneaten, I tasted them all, ignoring the fences between military and civilian, private office and secretariat general, advisers on this and advisers on that. This unexpected advantage of a stoically diminutive strategy of advancement, like the ones followed by Ignatius's disciples or the Queen's musketeers, made me the best-informed man in France on the state of the world, for the data reached me immediately after the generalissimo himself (or at most a day later). For unlike the head of state (or foreign minister or director of political affairs), with their crammed schedules of formal duties, idle civilities and pointless journeys, I had all the time in the world to read, annotate, compare and combine. From person-to-person meetings, industrial summits, Franco-American correspondence and internal French consultations, the substantive marrow reached me promptly in raw verbatim form, unedited and uncut. In the heart of things because kept away, I was everywhere at once, stuffing myself with the real, slaking my thirst for figures, graphics and minutiae. My personal observation satellite orbited the earth every twenty-four hours. I could change the orbit at will, jumping from basic *notes* (ten to thirty pages, not read by the 'decision-maker' who only has time for one or two) to ambassadors' *end of mission reports* (they never go upstairs either) to *diplomatic telegrams* (three collections a day) and unheaded *flimsies* from the services. For one unplugged by orders from on high and reconnected out of carelessness, the intoxication of power showed as a sort of craving for knowledge far beyond the perimeter of my official duties. With it went the certainty of arriving at the finishing line abreast of the Palace's first eunuchs in accordance with the philosopher's saw: 'Know so as to foresee in order to be able.' That school memory sweetened my banishment to the palatine suburbs, far from the 'divan' on the garden side where decisions were taken at the rate of one per minute. On the time-for-reflection side there was at least a consolation: peering through the window at the beautiful women of the faubourg Saint-Honoré fastening their Hermès scarves.

*   *   *

All right: if I had been ordered back to church by the Ostrogoths, I would climb by main force to the role of 'master of offices' inside the barbarian kingdom. One day the history books would describe me as having been to François the Prudent what Cassiodorus once was to the emperor Theodoric (or for modernists, Commynes to Charles the Bold). I would civilize technocrats, cover economists in classical scholarship, build an archaic Christian Noah's Ark behind the backs of number-crunchers and spinners of 'strong signals'. As the sixth-century Praetorian prefect had used hairy, illiterate Nordic looters in heavy gold jewellery to spread Holy Scripture and literature across the empire, so I would drench the establishment of audit commissioners and publicists in St Augustine, Auguste Comte and André Gorz. And my latterday Theodoric would be able to say proudly: 'Other peoples have weapons like ours, but only the sovereign of the Romans commands eloquence.'

I would set about it *pedagogically*, by correcting the prejudices of the governmental elites, countering opinions distorted by bad priests of the media with the authority of the thing itself, the real truth, the bedrock of history. I could only proceed indirectly. I would have the ear of the man who had the ear of the people, government (so to speak) by ricochet: the old paradox of the longer but quicker way round. I dislike speaking to no purpose, especially to my peers. Friends and enemies (even the closest of all, your humble servant) have often accused me of neglecting the 'grass-roots', ignoring rank-and-file nonentities. But in listing the distasteful leanings of the lickspittle – the itch for honours, the taste for luxury, for anything flash or gash – they omit the desire for speed. Going straight to the top saves time, and the adviser is a man in a hurry. 'I will be asked whether I am a prince or legislator, since I write on politics. I reply that I am not,' wrote Jean-Jacques Rousseau, that plodding reformer, 'and that is why I write on politics. Were I a prince or legislator I would not waste time writing about what ought to be done; I would do it or keep quiet.' By attaching himself to a man of action, the thinking reed believes he can recover the time wasted on ten or twelve *Democracy 2000* papers, and go silently into action, subsumed in the rolling fire of decrees. In joining the miserable race of courtiers (as would-be members call it) the committed volunteer bypasses words by a daring and quite economical short-cut (but at a cost, usually to others, that only becomes apparent later).

'Ability to produce maximum results at minimum cost': the civic *minimax* principle is as old as the city and philosophy. 'It's too late to act on something,' Malraux once said, 'one can now only act on some*one*.' This despairing observation holds good for all time. It took Plato to Syracuse, Aristotle to Alexandria, Seneca to Nero, Descartes to Christine, Voltaire to Frederick II and Malraux himself to the great Charles: even the top acts kept an eye on the end product. The first written record of this bad productivity decision is to be found in old man Plato's Letter VII, where he explains his positive answer to Dion's letter inviting him to Sicily to work for his uncle, the tyrant Denys II, as a decision counsellor.

When I was wondering if I should set off and accept this invitation or make my mind up somehow, what really tipped the balance was that if I was ever going to attempt to realize my ideas on law and political organization, this was the moment to start. In effect, *I had only to convince a single man, and that would suffice to bring about the advent of Good in all things.* So it is in this attitude of mind and resolved to achieve this task that I left Athens, not for the motives attributed to me by some, but principally through fear of then becoming in my own opinion one who is nothing but a fine talker, otherwise incapable of resolutely pursuing an action.

I agree entirely with the motives of the detainee of Syracuse. Let it be said that Plato and Debray have finally come together. A release to AFP would be appropriate.

I have never been able to communicate. That cuisine has recipes of its own which are beyond me. It is my Achilles' heel. I explain myself in Latin, my winks cheer no one up, my sentences wriggle like sea serpents. Fortunately, there are those elected by the people to speak demotic to the people. Weak in this homely area, I had gone to the Castle to use those volume-sales technicians as translators: the mayor-delegate and his image advisers would relay the True to simple souls. They knew how to twang the strings, those guys, how to soothe and shock. They would be our telex operators. From behind the scenes we would feed the programme to professionals in making things known. How the message would spread was their business. For 2,500 years now, we people of learning have had no function; but in the same way that others have hatred or plague, we have the vocation to separate true from false, to pin down mirages, to confront naked reality without blinking, rain or shine.

A scribbler with ideas is shot straight into the stratosphere, the glib bourgeois cliché runs. A philosopher – one of the worst sort, materialist and critical – is not the type to fall for 'fanciful literary politics'. We have a motto in our profession: 'Don't daydream.' There is something sad about it. A philosopher is someone who does not want to lie to himself. The problem (as can be seen from this very text) is that no one makes History without doing so a lot, *in petto*; and that a militant who does not daydream is ready for carpet slippers (or perhaps dancing pumps). I had my track record of tomfooleries. Reasons from on high being familiar to me from church, what I wanted to dismember was problems here below, in general and in detail. Out of asceticism. Our Cretan palaces are not just the nests of hitmen and sinecure-holders our troubadours depict; Minotaurs have dwelt in the labyrinths for 10,000 years. They rub your nose in the harsh realities that have to be embraced, a lethal ordeal for ideologues, those phrasemongers who dislike having their backs to the wall (a position I favour: no chance there of sounding off like some editorializing babbler who dreams of leading without concretizing, and prefers grandiose social plans to anything small-scale). What was at stake was the *real*. *Hic Rhodus, hic salta*. Reality – like the imagination – has an unforgiving way with show-offs and prattlers. Its mechanisms demand precision. Stand a bullshitter in front of an interministerial conference for eight days and he will be cured of blah-blah for ever, or burst into tears and run home to mummy. The Jacobin by contrast cuts straight to the quick. He is a practical man.

The device 'The truth, the bitter truth' appears as an epigraph to *Le Rouge et le noir*, attributed to Danton. That had been my pseudonym in Latin America. Perhaps I was scaling new heights of impertinence by taking on the once-prized but now much-decried role of 'adviser to the Prince' (the opposite, unless you are blinded by stereotypes, of the 'courtier', who hopes to please by sugaring the pill). Those courtiers of public opinion, the bought-in intellectuals, are there to pluck at the heartstrings of the populace: I would leave the broad principles to musketeers of verbiage. Danton's truth is a razor's edge, blunted by unsanctioned 'free opinion', sharpened by the terrifying constraints of practical action. I would toil unemotionally for twelve hours a day on nothing but raw events, dealing with the things themselves. From the mud and shit stored in that cupboard of secrets I would extract, by screening and distillation, lapidary feasibility studies. You have to be laconic to govern.

In this lunatic asylum (I thought, poor madman), our elective kings need to keep nursing assistants in the back yard to recall them to the flouted order of reality. I had saddled myself with the uncomfortable mission of defence counsel for the long-term in the courts of the ephemeral, advocate for both past and future (the widow and orphan of our videosphere), my Prince's shield against twilight electronic sorceries. There would be no betrayal of the truth in serving the state, for I was being paid (modestly) to lay gold nuggets of the possible at the feet of its chief. To escort my champion through conferences and ambushes, not intoxicating him with lyrical chatter but slipping distilled notes, telegrams and files into his pocket, an updated world-summary on two sheets. My bondsman's pen would be his fiery sword. Long-term strategy calls for people with precise reflexes, steely souls impervious to gibes and *banderillas*, capable of hacking openings to the future through the mediatic smog. Stendhalian concision, hardness of edge, would be far more harmful to the established disorder than Sunday-supplement admonitions and anathemas.

I would operate stealthily, eschewing facile effects, *in full knowledge of the facts*. Complex, the real, as people often say, but rational: the chaotic torrent of news hides intelligible long-term trends, little-known but constant relationships between different sequences of phenomena. I would disentangle these connections, extracting from complicated data underlying simple causes; I would travel to observe Africa, Asia and Latin America with the naked eye; I would expose the underlying motives of tyrannies and terrorisms; I would investigate in person and send assistants among the tribes, collate their reports, ponder alternative views and summarize the options; I would pinpoint, with documented chron-

ology and statistics, those places where the common man was growing restless or
angry under the promptings of his generous heart. An eccentric boffin, remote
from Saint-Germain vanities and electoral hassles, master of codes and clocks, I
would give advance warning of tomorrow's wars between nations, religions and
civilizations. I might not be able to guide the multitudes directly, but I could
instruct my Lord on the right path to follow. He would take the lead, stepping
over the mediatized agenda of his ministers with an Olympian stride. Sometimes
there would be a shy hint of his gratitude; he would summon me to his sanctum
in the gilded salon that the General used as an office; I would sit sideways as
intimates do before the Cressent desk, violet-wood and red Morocco, my blue-
grey eye and furrowed brow heavy with cares, but alert as always; then in veiled
but tender words, looking up from my latest note (heavily annotated in
presidential blue), he would fuss about my needs, my tactical rear (for as well
as 'every letter deserves a reply', he often said that 'every service deserves a
recompense'). Blushing, I would murmur with lowered eyes: 'I'm only doing my
duty, President. I love the Republic: allow me to serve it accordingly, as a citizen
I mean: without hope.' He would look up, intrigued; he would insist, offering
one after the other, in ascending order of importance, the Medal of Arts and
Letters, a seat on the Economic and Social Council, the villa Médicis and a job
at Gaz de France. At this I would stiffen, turn from crimson to white, draw
myself up haughtily. 'Do not think to buy my services, my Prince: they are free.
Let others have the sinecures: needy men are not lacking. Perhaps it will always
be impossible to separate love of the common good from the desire for social
honours.' On this stentorian *Quousque tandem Catilina* I would rise proudly to my
feet, signalling with angry brow the scorn inspired by his disrespect for humans.
He would be left open-mouthed on the green velvet seat of his Regency chair.
And I would withdraw silently to my apartments with the majestic sadness of a
misunderstood Colbert.

That was not exactly the way it went, in reality, when the time came for me to
bow out. But what is reality these days? Read the accounts that strain all the
bookshop counters and you can see that each former something-or-other does
things his own way.

Have I the right to address serious things in the tone of a little jester? Of course
not. Tipsy illusion inspires opening fanfares and lends all beginnings a touch of
soaring flight, of baroque toccata. I know that political morality and philosophy
demand a responsible tone: so be it. But at Court, more than elsewhere, truth
comes from the mouths of buffoons, and the clownishness itself reveals the
primary misdirections woven into our Folies-Machiavel and flights of ambition:
the puerile lining of our three-piece suits, what you might call the psycho-
comedic components of the Power question. I will soon indicate more crudely by
what stages I descended from the Paris Commune to the Palais-Royal, degenerated from a Cassiodorus into a Courteline, transshipped from caravel to

galley. Doubtless I should first explain what earlier drift led me to embark, for what voyage; and what captain justified such presumption on my part. He was called François Mitterrand and was president of the French Republic from 1981 to 1995; other suzerains had or may have had more panache and charisma, more vision – or less, who knows? – but he was the one given to me by very ancient dreams, and by my time and place of birth. You do not choose your life. You give free rein to your time, your impatience and your king.

Was he a good king or bad? Others can argue about that. In my view, he was certainly a great lord.

2

A Lord

The road to Sauveterre – Le temps des cerises – Vertu and virtue – A better geographer than historian – The culture of imbroglio – Gold and lead

Well before the end of his mandate, the 'François Mitterrand portrait' had become a competitive civico-literary event, an obligatory exercise in magazines, on platforms and at dinners. Hardly a single man of letters has not been egged on by his fellows – and after fourteen years refusal is difficult – to trot out his 'Mitterrand story', much as the old-time schoolboy was asked on 1 September to 'describe the high point of your holidays'. Now it is my turn. Has that bottomless barrel not yet disgorged all its shadows? I only have small things to add, but solid, like the lees in a precipitating wine after long fermentation. My cellar of memories is so made that sourness diminishes with the passing years.

I base my presumption on a few documents, and on distance. I have kept my 'agent's papers' by me, in deliberate violation of rules which, for lack of a Republic, were no longer enforced. The beachcombers of the national memory would dislike me less if the autographs in my possession had not appeared on anyone's death warrant. There is no travel diary: dissatisfied with the little that happens to me each day, ever-impatient for the morrow, I could never discipline myself to that masochistic listing of minutiae. And what would I have had to put in it of any importance? A 'drawing-room favourite', not an office one, excluded from the councils of the great, I did not have to follow affairs on a daily basis. His immediate associates saw the president every day. From 1981 to 1988, I was in the second circle of 'those who can see the president when they want, and talk to him about more or less anything'. The 'commandos', the 'flying squad', the 'musketeers', the gossip columns called us, not inappropriately. The 'special advisers' were placed outside the hierarchy, with direct but irregular access.

The distance that comes with the fading of resentments restores a sort of half-amused, half-exasperated equanimity. Inexplicably, François Mitterrand long treated me with distant indulgence (and I him, excuse the symmetry); our 'ideological' break, at the beginning of his second term, did not affect my persistent fondness for the private man, a libertine admirable for his elegance and courage. His indulgence was not that of the father for spiritual sons like Fabius, Lang or Attali, and my fondness not the one I bear for François de

Grossouvre or Paul Guimard (the lifelong companions I have known best); our relations were more those of friends who are complicit for a time, and whom everything tends to separate but the refusal to give each other up. This saves me from the ex-employees' temptation: retrospective vengeance, on paper, for all the things they did not dare say in front of the Master at the time.

It says a good deal about the period and the individual that the record of his principate should have come to consist mainly, in the public mind, of X-ray views of the Prince on duty and at home, and of his soul and conscience. Of all the kings who made France, none has guided so closely the hands of portraitists, biographers and radiographers. In our country the writer is never far from a Narcissus, and what is written soon becomes public. The extraordinary thing about that man of the pen was his final metamorphosis into a man of image, monopolizing the screen with his states of mind and live confessions, director-producer of his own ego in countless news reports, films, interviews, books and dialogues. Where de Gaulle spoke of France, Mitterrand spoke of himself. The general was not interested in himself. His inner recesses – if indeed he had any – left him, and us, indifferent. Mitterrand reassured us by being like us: a common concern for the self united the man in the street with the head of state. In 1969, de Gaulle ended thirty years of History with a two-sentence press release and went straight home without ever seeing a journalist or appearing on television again, remaining parsimonious with words to the very end. In 1994 his successor mounted a farewell ceremony that lasted a whole year, transforming the current news into a private diary. He involved us in his family life, his adolescence, his encounters, his old friends. He groomed himself deftly for the Pantheon, erasing mistakes, covering tracks, selecting witnesses, re-editing friends line by line, filming confidences, cutting firebreaks (even going so far as to authorize his former special adviser to photocopy state secrets in violation of decency and the law). Speaking openly of his feelings, his approaching end, his physical suffer-ings, the beyond; interrogated week after week by journalists: 'How are you, monsieur le Président?' 'How are you standing up to your treatment?' 'How do you feel about your approaching death?' This mediatized obscenity seemed natural to everyone, or nearly, and the outcome was a very fine exit (so far had the sacred republican things, the function of president, already suffered audio-visual humiliation over the 'miserable little pile of secrets'). I had attached myself to the state in 1981 in the naive belief that institutions are there to rise above what Hannah Arendt called 'the futility of individual life', the everyday banality of mood and whim. Is not this elevation, which depersonalizes obedience as well as command, the reason for being on the side of Law? One had to get used to the overturning of principle by televisual deed, as well as the presidential taste for public introspection. Supreme power now lays bare, through the technical constraint of transparency, all that is apolitical in a professional politician. The longer the reign the more flagrant the striptease becomes; by the end of the second seven-year term that cruel disrobing had reached abyssal depths of refined sorrow and pity. And that gallant Don Juan on the brink of the grave, defying morality, the nation and his friends, lent himself with provocative complacency to the exposure of his past. Like a magnifying glass that gains power over time, a prolonged reign inflates oddities into defects, defects into vices and finally into a crisis of confidence. We are all secretive, manipulative, tangled, tortuous, amnesiac, hypocritical, etc. But we can hide our game (or failing that, ask for mercy), because in the final analysis none of us has presided over the destiny of France: not as long as Louis-Philippe or Napoleon III, but longer than Napoleon I between Brumaire and Waterloo. Perhaps what is most pitiless about high office in the videosphere (where *private* is no longer the opposite of *public*) is the way it expropriates a public man from his own life while he is still living, as it were nationalizing his privacy: his organs, his cancer, his address book.

What made me attach myself for ten years to that suzerain who was not my type? I have as much right as the next person to answer this question, for there were quite a few million of us asking it one way or another, at audit time.

Without my years of exile I would never have thrown in my lot and my imagination with the General's former adversary, or invested him with the high mission of equalling the grandest of the shades, a flashing Jaurès/de Gaulle cross. Arriving from Chile in early 1973 with a message from Allende to his French equivalent, I was taken to see him by a common friend, a woman. He was holding a meeting in Pau for some local election or other. The man I found was a social-Catholic tribune with a vivid, even emphatic, way with words, and over supper that evening he displayed a powerful, concise and trenchant mind, and a habit of switching abruptly from sincerity to sarcasm (or in his writings, from elegy to blackguarding) that threw newcomers into confusion, and had the advantage of putting off the lukewarm. The next morning he invited me to join him in his car, and we spent the next three days as a joyous team, visiting every corner of a smilingly complicit south-west. I was discovering a cantonal France hitherto known to me only in theory from books and wall maps. I had landed at last and was having the time of my life, as overjoyed as Lindbergh at le Bourget. That Third Republic France of stout councillors, town-hall schools with balconies, farmyards, war monuments and Jules Guesde arm-in-arm with Giraudoux: something I had dreamed of but never really seen. I was so starved of Frenchness that a red-and-white checkered tablecloth, a steeple with a weather-cock or a well-rolled *r* was enough to put me in touch with the promised land.

These hallucinations will seem idiotic to anyone who has never left, because you have to leave your motherland to learn through your body what country has moulded you. Nations are the opposite of paradises – all lost – in that they exist only when found, and are valued only when they have been mislaid along the way. Occupation, exile, long journey: so little is needed to make the discovery

that almost anything will do. In the empty winter streets of Vancouver or Puerto
Montt, the highways lined with hoardings and supermarkets that pass for towns
over there, a European will suddenly remember that there is a strange zone on
the planet where people are still abroad after six in the evening, sitting in pubs
and bistros talking about things from the past; and that this region inhabited by
time is called 'Europe'. I willingly forgive those whose path has never taken them
past blue Breton shutters or dove-grey Paris roofs for trumpeting their disdain
for the Frog and cock-a-doodle-doo. The essence of a nation, that vanishing
point that retreats as we advance, that taunts us, keeps us moving on an Odyssey
endlessly resumed and failed, is nostalgia; but of a sort that no school, family or
book can teach us. After years living among grossly inhospitable vowels,
consonants and diphthongs – how the Spanish *jota*, the *s* and *z*, had made
war on my tongue, rasped my throat, exposed me as an outsider! – I revelled in
the deep joy of gambolling effortlessly in my mother tongue. In canton after
canton, Mitterrand talked about people, battles and landscapes; the valleys and
glens we passed sprang to life with his stories, fragments of history great and
small, from the last elections back to Henri IV; he talked about his grandparents,
his genealogy; he gave me back the French youth I had missed, with the bonus of
a new geography. I restored myself on his back, at his expense. He was no
Penelope and I was no Ulysses, but that *Gallia narbonensis* with live commentary
became my Ithaca: this is the place, you've arrived, you're not leaving. Ten years
earlier, I had had to choose between my mother and Justice; would it be possible
to reconcile them, to glimpse equality at home, in French? I don't suppose
Mitterrand gave a damn for my myths, my mother and the rest (language
excepted), but he said yes to me, by not replying no to my unasked question. He
would be the one, then: nothing impressive, just the mediator between Mme
France and her millionth orphan.

Crystallization took place somewhere between Jurançon and Béarn. Like the
salt-caked tree branch in Stendhal's *De l'Amour*, the leader of the Left emerged
from this plunge through Aquitaine 'garnished with an infinity of mobile and
dazzling diamonds'. Fresh from the fraternal, exuberant, shoulder-thumping
humanity of places like Santiago and Caracas, I might have found his rather dry,
correct, formal and straitlaced delivery disconcerting; but my unconscious,
already smitten, was undeterred. It instantly decorated his face, outline and
name with the thousand perfections scattered between the terraces of Pau and
the hot springs of the Béarn, on the Sauveterre road: dells, torrents, beech-
groves, vineyards, shooting-lodges, the French-style gardens of the château de
Laas, old moss-covered bridges over the Oloron, fields robed in maize. My
provinces at last found by – revealed to – a little Parisian who knew the Andes
ten times better than the Pyrenees. That carnal, quasi-biological France was
shadowed by another, which I knew better and had never lost: the impalpable,
dreamed France of memory and History. Between the eye of the narrator and
the face of Albertine, 'the generative centre of an immense construction that

passed through the plane of his heart', were interposed so many indefinable sensations, sweet and painful, that no photo of the beloved could convey them; nor could he discern later her changed appearance, for she was 'like a stone after a fall of snow'. Between my 30 years and that grave 50-year-old, already dogged (the class enemy has no pity) by murky hints of Vichy associations, guillotined Algerian patriots, the Suez expedition and the Observatoire affair[2] were similarly interposed nebulous Épinal prints and yearnings too long repressed: a whole Milky Way from a village 14 July celebration to Renoir's *La Marseillaise*, Jean Moulin's sash, Walter Benjamin's round spectacles and the barricades of August '44, all glowing in the distance like Bengal lights . . . complete with smoke. Twenty years on, in September 1994, I saw him again in the cloister at rue d'Ulm addressing the students on the bicentenary of the École normale. In that old gentleman, his face drawn with suffering, ordinarily aged, ordinarily presidential, chest stuck out like all old chiefs, I no more recognized my one-time underground ferryman of heroes than the young Marcel who, on seeing the photo of Albertine, the celestial creature of whom his friend has so often spoken, realizes with consternation that a man he has always considered of sound mind is in fact utterly deluded. Not that Mitterrand had changed all that much; it was just that the snow had melted. That is how it is with affairs of the heart; and the so-called public ones, which at base are hardly public at all, are by no means the least poignant.

In the militant scrimmage, amid the unselfconscious and virtuous optimism that suffused the meetings and dinner-tables of the 'left' (before the loss of faith, in the late 1970s, which made the pre-Solzhenitsyn era seem to us like a fabled pre-war period), our champion maintained an ostentatious distance, marking himself out from the surrounding fuss with a sort of caustic and chilling calm. A product of natural shyness or 'class origin'; nothing abnormal there, I thought, Blum suffered from the same infirmities. Those signs of defensive self-sufficiency, perhaps involuntary or even painful, seemed to me to betoken something very French, a supplementary proof of authenticity: the progressive movement in France has always been led by grand-bourgeois class traitors. I was on familiar ground. 'You aren't a militant just because you want to be. If the self comes first, you're excluded for ever.' I knew that curse of birth well enough to excuse it in another. In any case, that self-centred socialist did not pretend not to have an ego, nor was he going to trade it in for a sacrament or sermon in his new church. There was no threat of hysteria. That internal weightiness seemed to me to augur well: at last, a bourgeois who played fair and didn't mislead the populace.

'The French', said Paul Thibaud, a sharply hostile critic, 'can see that the individual's hauteur has no other referent than a destructive and all-consuming idea of the self.' Half the truth: without the other half, the adventure that started at Épinay in 1971 would have petered out at ministerial level. Although the idea our chief had of himself pre-dated the one we had of him, and was wholly independent of it, it was not destructive or devouring but on the contrary pleasant, even graceful. He invited one and all to bounce their own referents off him. It is the doctrinaire who clings to his own image and tries to order the world around a fixed idea of himself. Rigid, abrupt egocentrism makes for ordinary, infertile paranoiacs: the classic despot. Mitterrand was an obliging and productive egocentric, for he never made his ego into a closed dogma: it was open to all. Many commentators are too inclined to see him as a character in a novel, forgetting what distinguishes fiction from treatise and who the author is in this case: the *oeuvre* is his own character, and his heroes have been invented to fit, all interconnected and all different: right-wing nationalist, *maréchaliste*, Giraudist, Gaullist, Third Force, anti-communist, authoritarian anti-capitalist, indulgent liberal, Europeanist, *Union sacrée*. A novelist is in control and does not identify with his creatures: being all his characters at once, he is not any one of them, and each speaks with his own individual twitches, accent and vocabulary. A good fiction writer is always sincere: he makes the convictions of each of his many doubles entirely his own, enabling readers, depending on their own experience and elective affinities, to identify with one or more of the characters without invalidating the rest. The story of this life was written by all of us; if there was 'lying' involved, we are its co-authors. Every militant, every associate, every elector even, could plug his own little history into one of its segments, project his own film onto that adaptable, swivel-mounted screen. The faceted mirror (or lark-mirror, depending on your point of view) that this leader managed to construct out of the successive slices of his life, offered with an effect of subtle if finally passive generosity, enabled all our narcissisms, both shared and individual, to converge and amalgamate with his own, to such effect, in 1981, that he passed the '50 per cent barrier'. That egotist was to collectivize the enjoyment of power, by projection. There was space on that mobile screen for almost all the dreams, all the narratives, all the imaginary egos of the time, from the 'French State' to the stock exchange society, via the consular Republic and social democracy. To each his own international scenario, defence of the West, support for Israel, Atlantic solidarity, the alternative Soviet alliance, help for the Third World, French independence; but just one screen for all. I am you. And he is us: an effective belief mechanism that in 1971 helped the federator of the socialists, the unifying Mystery, to gather about him everyone from antediluvian Marxists to neo-Californians; enabled the victor of 1981 to harness pallid *psychorigides* to his chariot alongside sparkling bronzed athletes; so that the incarnation of united France, in 1988, could combine hip anti-racists with nostalgic Pétainists in the 'Mitterrand generation' that emerged at the second ballot.

Usually, a reflective character does not permit this play of reflecting surfaces. The extraordinary thing about that singular introvert was the alliance of a dense and hard ego within, ceding only the barest minimum to passing circumstances, with a quite pliable exterior. It made his political fortune. The recipe may be more or less raw or developed depending on individual chemistry, but the general rule holds that in a democracy the chief is a composite entity, like the electorate. France is not homogeneous; it may be tending that way now, but thirty years ago the process had not advanced far. Given the interlinked tangle of interests and collective fictions that coexist in a population, anyone wishing to be elected by half his compatriots plus one is more or less obliged, statistically, to write off a good third of them (equivalent to more than half of his own side). The ultimate feat is to engineer a *rotating third*, so that those disappointed in the morning are satisfied in the evening and vice versa, airing resentments and preventing the build-up of explosive pressure. 'The politician betrays either his electors or his country's interests,' the well-known adage runs. This president was exemplary: from one side to the other of public opinion, by a sort of two-stage alternation, every type of sensibility could imagine itself by turns expressed, nurtured and betrayed. In my own interior film, the final freeze-frame came ten years later on a serving head of state, now inactive in a style incompatible with the mandate I had secretly given him on the terraces at Pau; and not for another ten years did I understand the logic at work behind that style. The delegation of images has these sluggish moments. Crystallization comes in a flash, love dies in stages like a gangrenous limb.

Too much has been said, it seems to me, about cynicism and lack of convictions, in a decent man who sometimes complained, with reason, that he was not believed when he said that he believed deeply in what he was doing, heart and soul. People read ambiguity into a succession of superimposed sincerities, the latest inevitably casting a shadow on its predecessor; they see as a labyrinth a sinusoid made up of incompatible straight lines (which he was almost alone in managing to connect end to end): was it his fault that his half-century was so sinuous? That great accompanist of his time espoused its caprices and tendencies so earnestly that he was incapable on any given day of uttering a hint of contrition for the previous one. He absolved himself every time, for he had been sincere and wholehearted throughout. Put simply, no new conviction operated to the detriment of its predecessors; they just piled up, one on top of another like generations in an age pyramid. Originally a right-wing anti-Gaullist, after 1958 he recycled the credo of his youth into a left anti-Gaullism with greater breadth and content, but without modifying his earlier reflexes and networks (much as a new house can be built from recycled materials, or a second novel woven around characters from the first). To the novelist there is no contradiction, for there is nothing about Père Goriot that disparages cousin Pons, nor does *Lost Illusions* invalidate *A Harlot High and Low*. His life was like a dashing nineteenth-century novel cut through the centre of the twentieth, a novel of education and disillusion. Of adventure too, but only if the word is given its full meaning. To the *militant* the essential thing is the goal, and his person is secondary. To the *adventurer* the goal is secondary, all objectives being disposable because subordinated to his person. The adventurer cultivates negativity; the militant works in disciplined fashion on an order open to all. That tenacious individual was certainly not ruled by a cause. But in his tolerance of other people's illusions, his readiness to espouse the different aims of different periods, he may have invented a new figure: the positive adventurer.

I had returned from America with a big incomplete novel swirling around in my head, too baroque for the national mood: extreme-left Gaullism. The Republic styled by Michelet, with words by Trotsky: the country's affliction. Life is made up of misunderstandings, and so is France: his smelt of earth and the dead, tranquil, sure of itself, impenetrable; mine was an unstable, wandering little fairy that exercised no physical attraction because it existed only in the mind – the dago mind for preference – but had to be checked every day because it could vanish at any moment. Mitterrand listened to my delirious ravings, amused, too polite to set me straight; not long afterwards, for the campaign of 1974, I published in *L'Unité* a paean to my red princess France, flouted by a bourgeoisie that had gone Vichy and worshipped money and America: the Red Butte answering Mont Valérien in advance. My new friend made no comment on these patriotic intemperances: proof that we understood each other almost without words, instinctively. He and his escort of young 'straights' did not really seem to be on that wavelength, but so what? We know that a man is not what he thinks, it's the ABC of materialism. Being both Patriot and Montagnard gave me a head start on those Girondists. Dialecticians call this phenomenon 'convergence of opposites'. When two adversaries meet in single combat, they end by resembling one another. David becomes Goliath: pointless to argue, it's the law. Anyway my new hero had made a fair start in terms of panache and effrontery: what could be more Gaullist than his rejection of Gaullism in 1958? And was not his period in the wilderness a dissidence, since all the grandees of the Fourth Republic, except Mendès, had foundered in sleaze? Bogged down in 'the forces of money', de Gaulle did not have 'the social base for his political project'. In my view only the left, innately disinterested and forcefully backed by the workers, could fill that blank space, the independence of peoples, squatted for the moment by the paunches of the Pompidou era (an interregnum too ridiculous to be anything but temporary). So we were going to drive out the usurper. A government that returns to power after a quarter of a century of voluntary opposition is there to make *History*, not just politics. That was my Mitterrandist bet in 1981, as it had been in 1974.

I liked to think I was no longer wet behind the ears, and the time, still Marxizing, favoured serious-mindedness. Even so, the occasional ugly thought would arise to disturb this Pascalian voluntarism. I knew very well I had not voted for the long-toothed schemer in the 1965 presidential campaign: the Union of Communist Students, in rebellion against the Party, had thought 'that opaque character' unsuitable to represent the 'toiling urban and rural masses'. The francisque[3] might be a calumny and the Observatoire a provocation, now unmasked. But what about 'Algeria is France', and staying in the government after Ben Bella's kidnap? What about acquiescing to the legal murder of the Algiers communist Yveton, who had not killed anyone? I knew too much about all that, and too little; I knew and didn't know; I didn't want to know. Our desire and the atmosphere of the moment had erased the centre-right grandee, the raghead-basher, the militant Atlantist. The unloved one had no need even to retouch his own past: we would do it for him. He didn't hide anything, he just telescoped time: jumped from 1941 to 1944, from the successful escape to the balcony of the Hôtel de Ville listening to de Gaulle, whom he had held by the leg, he told us, to prevent him from falling off. His recent travels in Allende's Chile and Mao's China, his quotations from Marx, Che and Althusser, the twisting course of a muddled time, covered over the traces and confirmed the metamorphosis of 'opportunist republican' into cunning socialist. By this time, anyway, such wet-blanket objections were only being raised by the 'soft left', on which I had turned my back in 1965 by joining the high authorities of Historical Effectiveness, who don't make omelettes without breaking eggs. People might well have preferred a Savary, say, a Daniel Meyer or Mendès France; but you don't win territory in Godfather country with good conduct badges. Just as man can only triumph over nature by obeying its laws, a bourgeois can only triumph over *his* nature by yielding to it. Where would be the virtue otherwise? It's from manure that roses grow. Our Charentais, that tenacious pioneer of the Apocalypse, would sooner or later bring about political and social storms that would either temper him or break him; never mind Nasser or Neguib, the new socialism was coming, with him or over him. In my own case, these dialectical reasons were accompanied by a sly and haughty enjoyment of my role as squire to the Black Prince. I knew a day would come when the White Knight would drop his disguise, reveal himself to the doubters of the moralizing left as the 'man of business of the universal mind', mediator between the history of France and the True Socialism he now represented. With shrewd compassion I had taken the leftists' antihero under my wing, lining myself up for a sublime role in the last-minute rehabilitation of the misunderstood hero. I savoured in advance the gratitude my dozy little comrades were going to feel when the class struggle came swarming all hairy out of the ballot box to grab them by the throat. All they had to do in exchange was drop a voting slip in first: not dear, for History with a capital H.

The 1970s, that time of electoral defeats, was our *Temps des cérises* (love of failure being a left-wing virtue). How beautiful 1981 looked from the courtyards and plane trees of 1973! The Republic is said to be merciful to its prodigal children, but its institutions in those days were less so: national education closed its doors to me; no newspaper or journal would employ me except as a freelance; I was high and dry. Mitterrand alone received me without asking questions, without caring what people would say. That marvellously imprudent moderate was always hospitable to orphans of lost causes; of the far right after the

Liberation, of the far left after May '68. God is ambidextrous by job definition; and the left hand is just as bold as the other, although it produces more ingrates (loyalty being a right-wing virtue). It takes a good measure of intrepidity to practise what the experts call 'recuperation'. I was grateful to that old solitary for opening his small family to a younger man. It was hardly an order of chivalry or a holy family, but it doesn't take much to keep me warm. A curious entourage, which I did not yet realize was only one among others. Third-wave Mitterrandists (I was from the sixth), while awaiting ninth-wave experts and eleventh-wave énarques, had formed a Youth Guard of ambitious individuals still in their thirties, many of them former members of the Convention des institutions républicaines, fresh-moulded from the Épinay congress. The wide age gap protected the Prince against shadows from his own past and the rancour of those evicted: there were no sensitivities to nurture, no long memories to be feared, no competition for the limelight or deals to be made. The young wolves could wait. Budding killers are easier to live with than proper rivals, less threatening to one's confidence. As a Blanquist turned radical socialist I enjoyed that temporary brotherhood whose tone was free, robust and lively. I was not accustomed to the good-humoured ferocity of free political animals conspiring in private. Mitterrand was at his best, quick and disillusioned, in closed committee, freed from *isms* and poses. He cut straight to the bone: balance of forces, physics of ambition, logic of interests and alliances. That hissing cruelty, those unadorned glares and brisk swipes, gave me confidence: the laconicism of captains. Talkers always disappoint, when their backs are to the wall.

I had arrived at the right moment. That small *circle* was too professional, and already too close to the corridors of power, to be considered a *chapel*, like those *consciousness-raising groups* favoured by the amateurs of the intellectual left; but still far enough from its goal and fresh enough in heart to be a *camarilla*, tightly focused on its rituals and access strategy. Later I would taste the bitterness of the passage from *gang* to 'President's Household'; but the period when a *clan* has not yet beome a *seraglio*, with good faith and good humour still prevalent, offers working companionship at its best. People are warmed up without being tiresomely alert. The absence of hierarchic signs prevents major squabbles and jealousies; the community of illusions creates one of individuals. My innermost thoughts being demented rather than tactical, I felt no needless anxiety. I had never dreamed of entering the Socialist Party, and had no constituency committee or electoral fiefdom to worry about. A network, then the masses, without a party to get in the way: ideal for a marginal individual in need of company, but too experienced to take programmes seriously and too proud to fit into an organigram.

In 1974, as in 1978, the people, the real people, gathered in large numbers behind the 'representative of the Common Programme' (a title that pained our champion but did not bother any of his close associates). The herd generates a well-known form of involuntary snobbery. Just as in art we deem to be beautiful any object, picture or statue before which people gather, so in politics we attribute all the virtues to the individual who provides us with a community. People are so fearful of solitude that they admire anything that enables them to be together: the joy of assembly almost justifies the existence of parties in itself, as well as ensuring their unending survival. Campaign meetings in 1995, when the big issue between right and left was 'VAT versus employer's contribution', generated as much heat, mobilized as much youthful generosity and fervour, as the ones in 1974 on the issue of old world versus new, capitalism or socialism. On the left, supply is diminishing, but demand stays the same. Hope, too. The so-called 'end of politics' can never prevent honest hearts from dilating on contact with others, whatever the circumstances, and the 'great moments' of militant youth recur generation after generation, signs of a drive so deeply rooted that it discourages rational investigation of motives and aims (which are not really all that important). Those collective levitation exercises that climax every seven years in a presidential election, and the big springtime 'demos', would have left me only the best of memories if they had not resulted in a government. For just as the march to power binds militants together and fills them with joy (which, Spinoza tells us, augments the power of being), so its exercise disperses teams and fills individuals, separated anew, with a sadness that diminishes that internal sense of power. After 1981, each bee in the Mitterrandian raising suddenly found itself crammed into the back of an alveolus called office, in that hive of vertical combs, honey unlikely, queen invisible, that we called the Château. 'I don't want a cabinet,' the barely elected president told us in his office, still Gaullist with its Gobelins carpets and Boulle furniture. 'I haven't got an entourage. As an entity, it shouldn't exist. There are individuals who lend their assistance, and that's it.' The Prince's first ingratitude: scattering the retainers.

So far as his own sense of importance is concerned, the scribe's best time is before, not after, the victory: the dominion of a wooed beauty before her surrender. Whatever the régime. Bolshevism made much of all its theorists until the October coup d'état; Mussolini did much the same in Italy. Men of ideas are precious to the pretender, irksome to the winner. They are the same people, but necessity is a stern taskmaster. To gain the throne you need a lot of general ideas on the future; to retain it, you need as few as possible. Particularly in France, where, as Balzac said in 1840, 'a special man can never make a statesman, he can only be a cog in the machine and not the motor'. That is why the support of 'intellectuals' is more necessary to a campaigning politician than to a victor in power, although he may still need them sometimes to decorate formal dinners. An opposition keeps things moving with seminars, manifestos and plans; a government, with prefects and finance inspectors, succinct minds. To put it more nobly: there is a time for social plans and a time for balancing the budget. The party leader has to make people dream, the head of state has to make them do things. Different duties, different needs. Hence this paradox: a party leader's accession to the supreme post, which ought to broaden his outlook and give him a more elevated view of the human condition, leads in practice to a sharp and inexorable narrowing of the winner's horizons and throws his favoured gurus, who have ceased to be useful, into technical unemployment. By the time I started my official career as an adviser, on 21 May 1981, I had already served my purpose; all I was good for now was assuaging that taciturn character's guilt and sticking semi-colons in his speeches. Since he disdained the first of these things as much as I did the second, our association was not going to last.

Not that I was particularly thin-skinned. In France, between 1960 and 1980, any 'left intellectual' (never my species) was something like Hercules at the crossroads, obliged to choose between Vertu and Luxury, Mendès and Mitterrand, Duty and Power. The bulk of the moral left followed the straight path of renunciation, with incurable lassitude usually setting in after the age of 60. A wilier, more serpentine path was only open to twisted individuals, who had a bad press. A Mendès man turning Mitterrandist was betraying his principles; a Mitterrandist going over to Mendès was sulking. By the end of the seventies the betrayers outnumbered the grumblers. Life in the the desert is drawn naturally to the oasis.

The fall of the dice had favoured the latecomers, and the dilemma in 1973 was less Cornelian. Since all that repels the principled intellectual is pleasing to me, my bad tendencies imposed the bad choice on me, without any agonizing. A matter of tropism. 'PMF' only merited respect, with nothing visceral or compelling about it. The superego could only bow to that conscience of the Republic, that Concours général prizewinner inscribed on the roll of honour of his time. His intellectual antecedents were the same as mine, the Enlightenment and the Republic; his profile rationalist and rigorous. But the unconscious jibbed, finding in that figure of the Just Man, the totem of the élite, something insipid, unsexy; too clean. Was it his 'moral tutor' side, the heavy father? The limited attraction exercised by a virtuous individual who avoids great risks? Austerity, uprightness, honour, expertise, all present . . . but safety, too. Morality made political never amounted to a policy, except for a few months at Matignon. History has given its – unjust – verdict. Mendès France was a valiant man who founded neither a republic, nor a party, nor a doctrine; a rebel who did no lasting harm to any established interest. As if he excused himself from acting, was more political scientist than politician, too much of an Antigone for my taste (and not enough of a Creon). It is difficult to assess the relative importance in that melancholic of reluctance to succeed, which is entirely honourable, and a sort of will to impotence, which is less so. It seems to me, from a distance (for I have not met him), that that model student, who cannot have spent many afternoons in the cinema, had more intelligence than psychology. FM was not a 'golden mind', all right. But he seemed to me less spiritless because he dared to go for it, to accept communist votes, to talk revolution in public and police surveillance in private. Above all I saw him as having a more varied surface, more biography. Mendès was too principled a man to fool with the pen, look into the dark areas of the picture, butter up the rabble, chase pretty women. A rigorist, too taken with ideas and indifferent to forms, insensitive to contrast, to the marginal and the outsider. The Landes forester's taste for original people, and the freedom of his private life, blinded me for a time to his more politically commonplace, classically calculating side. Mendès may well have possessed greater originality behind a more conformist exterior. Whatever the reasons, my instinctive dislike of beautiful souls drew me towards the friend of writers, those ruffians who go straight to the point, to life at its blackest, and turned me away from professors, people who beat fussily about the bush with measuring instruments. So the embrace given by the older man to the younger, under the blazing chandeliers of the Elysée, after the end of the era had been announced, looked to me like *vertu*'s homage to virtue.

Favoured by his earlier death, with fewer of the blunders that accumulate with longevity, the memory of Mendès (among purists and virgins anyway) has long cast a shadow over that of Mitterrand. But let us be fair. Although both symbols of the French left during the last half-century were of historic stature, and disdained vainglory, neither managed to sound the little note of heroism in people's hearts and the world at large, like Saint-Just or de Gaulle. Mendès could have been the General's grand vizier; but to invent his own legend that tempered man would have needed 'a small vein of madness', a dash of irrationality, a barmy and beautiful dream. The fact that some devotees draw parallels between a sage and a genius shows that the effort to be serious can drive political scientists mad. No one attains the sublime without skirting the ridiculous. De Gaulle was something of a fruitcake: he heard voices, talked to the dead, referred to himself in the third person. A great man is a heavyweight oddball with enough staying power to outlast the sniggers. The heroi-comic epic of free France began with drolleries. When René Cassin, before signing the first juridical convention uniting Britain with the three destitute refugees of Carlton Gardens, asked de Gaulle 'What am I signing on behalf of, General?' and heard the reply: 'In the name of France, Cassin!' he glanced around to make sure that no normal individual was within earshot: they would have been thought barking mad. De Gaulle was famous for gaffes and extravagances, up to and including his 'Vive le Québec libre!' in 1969.

Our advocate may have been almost too intelligent, but he turned out the least intellectual of the Fifth Republic presidents; here the pack-saddle galled me quite early, from 1983. 'The intellectual is one who orders his life around an idea' (a lofty definition, but technically correct), and in this respect he lived in disorder. He seemed to be insensitive to ideas themselves. The aesthetic world-vision I had found so seductive in the observer quickly repelled me in the actor; art for art's sake, in this setting, is an aid to endurance, not creation. We were both victims of a misunderstanding. I had thought he played the tactician for tactical reasons, when really it was his character. I had thought his opportunism planned, when really it was just his fate. I had admired his impatience with verbosity, but now suspected that he was resistant to any long view of History. Unlike wisdom, sagacity does not follow its own advice. But sharpness, quickness of eye, give a short-range lucidity: a bad point seems as good as a good one. Anti-intellectualism is, so to speak, too serious a thing to be left to mere empiricists. In his case it had seemed to me to indicate courageous freedom of mind, leavened with dandyism and guile: really it expressed an allergy to deductive exposition, and I am afraid to the very idea of truth. On his side, because I wrote speeches for him with rhythm and punctuation, he thought himself flanked by the classic figure of the '*normalien* who can write'; but I did not so much 'write' them as sweat blood to translate urgent visceral ideas into prefectorial lyricism. Basically, he took me for a littérateur resuming his career after a brief digression through the exotic. 'You'll see, Régis, when you're at the Académie . . . yes, yes, don't protest . . .' I did protest, and he laughed, although not unkindly. To each his profession. Mine was to polish phrases and earn my cocked hat.[4] Any convictions I might have, or worse still any organized view of the world and History, were seen either as a supplementary attraction (return to previous box) or a dangerous caprice belching toxic smoke (see below, box headed 'ideology'). To that cast of mind, a philosopher is always just a blocked writer. Happy in the company of people of letters, for their incisiveness on details and flexibility on basics, he imputed my asperity to moodiness, vague misanthropy and over-sensitivity, apparently unaware that, while words can take any form, ideas, like rocks, have corners.

His passage through Vichy and quite numerous contributions to the 'theoretical' reviews associated with Pétain's 'national revolution' had surely vaccinated him against doctrines, burning his fingers so badly that he regarded any general idea as a dogmatic aberration. That is a partial explanation. But behind the period phraseology of his first contributions, made in 1942 and 1943 to the *Revue de l'État nouveau* and *Métier de chef*, one already discerns something that became a constant: an organic rejection of the tool for making History known as 'abstraction', veiled by a sort of carnal mysticism. 'The error derived from my history books,' he wrote during the Occupation, 'which had taught me to number the motherland among the ideals, gradually led me into abstraction. And robust, proud features soon became colourless and mummified as a result.' Thirty years later the lover of the soil – now officially socialist – was still to the fore, classing friends of the Idea with the elves and fairies: ' "A certain idea of France" . . . the expression is General de Gaulle's. I don't like it. I don't need an idea of France; France is something I live.' This antithesis between the cerebral and actual experienced reality, between cold and warm, is an adolescent's cliché: a month or two of final-year philosophy would have taught him the difference between reason and system. But since Barrès, authors on the sensitive right have viewed the philosophy class as a place of perdition, and republican schoolmasters as castrators of energy. Our rootless young man had not discovered his Renan; he was a 'little savage' in the raw, unrestrained by formal teaching, who could give free rein to the 'cult of the self'. Instinct is natural, argument artificial. That contained savagery – a bourgeois heritage – gives rise to a sceptical and contemptuous concept of the profession of politics, thought to have no concern with Truth except as an instrument for dealing with the dangerous or the specious. 'Either the truth is what I believe and impose on everyone,' this thinking runs, 'or the truth is what suits me and can be used; fanaticism or opportunism, garbage either way.' The reasoning of literary types who know the human soul and won't be conned by a bit of reasoning. Not without flavour, but not very knowledgeable: in effect, they navigate by line of sight and dead reckoning or go with the flow. All very well for coasting from port to port, but on the high seas instruments are needed.

One telling detail should have alerted me: in the concentric circles of his friends of fifty, thirty and ten years' standing there was not a single 'higher déraciné', leading academic, researcher or teacher. University was seen as a parking-lot for the young where only mediocrities took root (Jack Lang's theatrical side somehow obscuring the law lecturer). Squeezed between religion and literature, the austere world of Education was foreign territory to Mitterrand, along with secular rationalism and the disinterested pursuit of Truth. When visiting Germany he chose to see Jünger rather than Gunther Grass; and he spoke with great earnestness of seers, Indonesian healers and spoon-benders. A spiritualist really, whose unscholarly schooldays had left no visceral respect for the republican mystique. This he viewed as one social matter among others, like health or housing; another segment to be managed, watched over, pampered: part of the profession of president. Men dedicated to conceptual thought as a surgical instrument for grasping reality, clearing undergrowth and breaking new ground, he saw only as crass pedants or doctrinaires, Diafoirus or Robespierre: a cast of sensibility that sees any philosophic view as a violin or a guillotine, a pious hope or an imposition. In the first two years at the Elysée I organized for his benefit a series of informal working dinners on specific themes, with appropriate 'leading intellectuals' including Fernand Braudel, Simone de Beauvoir, Louis Dumont, Pierre Nora, Claude Lanzmann, Pierre Vidal-Nacquet, Michel Foucault and others, and meetings on sensitive parts of the world – India, the USSR, Islam – with suitable specialists, historians and social scientists. They were gloomy occasions. On his guard, terrified that someone might slip him an *a priori* between the fruit and the cheese, he eluded all discussion of fundamentals. The stilted social occasions that resulted were neither exploitable – photographers being absent – nor profitable in other ways . . . 'we'll see when the time comes'. So we reverted to the merely agreeable – Françoise Sagan, Antoine Blondin, François-Marie Banier – stylish anecdotes, charm and causticity, the true roots; and evening receptions for the Tout-Paris of arts and letters, a banal responsibility yielded to the minister of culture, a talented procurer. I had failed.

That reader of *La Table ronde*, *La Parisienne* and *La Revue des Deux Mondes* was never going to manage *Les Temps modernes*, *Esprit* or *Le Débat* (no one expected him to go as far as the *Annals*, Herodotus or *Mots*). The path of learning was blocked: no more broad perspectives or long views, just sophists of the 'new philosophy', slick rightist pamphleteers, questing minds with flair. They would get the leading roles and the jobs.

The Society of Jesus could have prevented all this, but alas, the priests of Angoulême[5] and the Marists in rue Vaugirard hadn't been up to it. Define, classify, distinguish, order; proceed by stages and divisions; contrast, cancel out, compare: these principles are taught from childhood by the Jesuits. They are the stuff of a classical education, something that literary man (contrary to legend) did not possess to any serious extent. The promising eldest son had been abandoned to the faculty of law and his own talents: too much finesse, not enough system. De Gaulle *did* have a Jesuit style, clear, incisive and contained, with – despite the grand manner and booming delivery – the language of a soldier, devoid of double meanings and exploitable fogginess: indicating a rational organization of work, a stable command structure with hierarchical levels, coordination by a chief of staff and attribution of responsibilities to the competent departments. The profession of arms requires these things; pettifogging can manage without them. Without military training or managerial culture, Mitterrand was unable to make up his deficiency in abstract education with practical experience of matters demanding clarity. And could only follow Lamartine willy-nilly: 'the style is the man'. I know what I am talking about, having absorbed the ignored-surveyed, the shameless-prudent, on the job. As chief clerk for professions of faith from 1981 onward, responsible for the effusions at Cancun and elsewhere, for diplomatic responses to the tiresome Third World, after a little practice I shifted from an oratorical style to a buttonholing, almost intimist one. By the end of the first term of office I could churn out kilometres of pure Mitterrand non-stop. In the usual setting of 'probing' press interviews: written questions submitted in advance, answers sub-contracted to an underling, photos of the President with the big-name journalist under the trees to prove the whole thing's authenticity. I also wrote for a leading magazine, before his re-election, a long confession, supposedly oral and transcribed from a recording, complete with sighs and other incidental business, which the president read out verbatim without changing a single gasp or 'er . . .'. Direct from clone to client. Slalom without hitting anything, repeat yourself when necessary; leave every door open, dot dot dot, you never know; zigzag, fly overhead, suggest; theme and variations, flourishes, dodges. Don't knock anything, don't undertake anything; no edges, a featureless surface, fluid, nebulous. And let every statement on page one be balanced on page two by a contrasting one that cancels it. So that any quotation taken out of context can be countered with another that contradicts and complements it, not a denial exactly but exactly like one. I am in no position to cast the first stone at my elusive boss. I could never have sidled under his shadow if his false-bottomed luggage, his subterfuges, had not reflected a side of my own character. In the final anlysis he was my other self, my magnified foxy double, my alter ego in the forum. It would be too good to be true if philosophers were made of stone and only had pure ideas

No one governs innocently, but some govern in depth. A de Gaulle grasps things at the root, a Mitterrand by the leaves. To have principles is good; to return to first principles is better because it clears a path for principled conduct. Convoluted wrangling over morality has distracted attention from the important thing: the shortage of radicalism. Perhaps those who dwell on the 'shady' aspects are allowing shadows to distract them from the reality. No lapse of memory, no black mark escapes the bloodhounds, except perhaps the connection between lack of principle and lack of rigour; between the cult of personal caprice and 'general culture'. What was taught under that heading to law students in the thirties – as to present-day candidates for the main oral at the ENA – was practised verbal dexterity in wielding a few well-bred generalities lacquered with all-purpose humanism, flexible, accommodating and imprecise. A bit thin to satisfy a strong appetite for understanding when everything is going awry. Thanks to the stalag and the occupation years, which emancipated him, our budding chief was able to thicken that watery soup with experience of chaos and some private reading. But intrigue and manoeuvre preoccupied the writer manqué soon after the Liberation, and nothing was consolidated. This forced growth produced a mixed personality, sententious and mordant: vigorous expression, approximate thought. He would skip straight from a wickedly-observed novelist's detail to some pious generality drawn from the press or 'folk wisdom'. To hear or read that acute mind was to oscillate between pure gold and cliché, longing for a stop somewhere between Jules Renard and Ecclesiastes to breathe more practicable mid-range novelties. There is nothing like a banality, of course, if you want to seem profound: 'give the time some time' got a lot of coverage from media apparently unaware that the Spanish saying *dar tiempo al tiempo* is a catchphrase no undergraduate from beyond the Pyrenees would dare write down in black and white. In the more important international context, sententious hauteur came up with the 'eternal opposition' between Persians and Arabs, the harshness of empires towards the weak, 'France is my motherland, Europe is my future', 'The balance of forces between East and West, the sole key to Peace', and so on. But what, for example, is meant by 'forces': military weaponry? Goods, inert forces? Economies and cultures, live forces? What does 'balance' mean, and how is it calculated? Was not deterrence of the strong by the weak established precisely to supersede notions of balance as arithmetical parity? What does the West mean, in reality, and the East, historically? A 'cultivated man' does not question the *doxa* of his time and place; he does not dwell on the prevailing commonplaces that serve as arguments but are not argued about. Examining the meanings of words, decon-

structing the obvious, rethinking the usual from new angles, are distractions
from more urgent matters, lead to paradox and affront common sense. Keeping
prejudice at arm's length is not 'politically profitable', but it is precisely what
distinguishes the successful politician, half a century later, from the History-
maker. While one modernizes the answers to unchanging questions, the other
changes the problematic, and bounds forward into the next century. De Gaulle
shocked people by examining the causes of continental drift; Mitterrand
restricted himself to its effects, and reassured them.

Lawyers are not designed to discover new worlds or wage war on the frontiers.
The legal fraternity exploits existing codes without forging new ones. It finesses,
temporizes, comes to understandings; discreetly negotiates the least damaging
outcome in a corner of the court; gets people out of trouble, one by one, case by
case. No overall vision; no questioning of the way things are done. Not much
imagination, plenty of knavery. A culture of urbanity, leading to the belief that
people are caught by words, and bulls by the tail. This particular jurist never
hung up his gown: nor did he need to practice, for legal pleading was in his soul.
His foreign policy was not the continuation of war (which he detested) by other
means, but of the Bar, that source of so many talented and adaptable individuals
for whom entering politics was just a matter of passing from the courtroom to
the Court, from one accommodating Bohemia to another. That was what
people did under the Fourth Republic; but the orthodox man of that period was
seen, in the official circles of the Fifth, as merely a heretic. He was not a rebel but
a laggard. I mistook one for the other.

It is not surprising that a lawyer and established notable, while joining in the
stupid and ephemeral refrain of the moment that life should be 'changed',
should never have broken, in his heart of hearts, with the frame of reference of
his own background. In international policy, de Gaulle could play the nomad
because he had freed himself from the formulaic attitudes of his time; the
sedentary Mitterrand, friend of familiar hillsides and more of a geographer than
a historian, equivocated and came to terms. He would rather influence things
with secondary effects than smash them with prime causes. *Against* abuses, *in* the
system: give the Marshal a Gaullist tint without breaking with Vichy; encourage
a more evolved colonialism in black Africa without risking actual decolonization;
temper American arrogance by joining the NATO herd; moralize the money
that pollutes everything by flattering the stock exchange and launching Tapie.
'Yes but' was his natural downward slope. He had managed to climb back up it,
to his credit, saying no to de Gaulle in 1958, and spending twenty years in
opposition. In 1981, on the eve of a decisive vote, he shouted his opposition to
the death penalty from the rooftops: proof that that tactician had convictions.
Nevertheless that maverick of the established order ended as a conforming anti-
conformist. Emancipated bourgeois are like that: half-original, churchgoing
rebels. They have more than one household, but go home to sleep. They leave
without making a clean break, separate without divorcing: for the family is

sacred (and convenient). Lead private lives both heretical and orthodox. Some do end by taking the plunge, burning their bridges, but he kept a pied-à-terre on the other bank (Rubicon? Never heard of it). What some saw as cynical, deliberately ambiguous language seemed to me the product of an almost physical, and social, reluctance to burn his boats; the partial schizophrenia imposed on semi-dissidence by de facto powers, skills and available opportunities. Atypical within the stereotype, with an instinctive ability not to go too far, a Lamartinian given over to intrigue inspires others with the same ambivalence that inspires him. An alternation of hopes and disappointments on the left; of anxieties and reassurances on the right. While they live, everything around such people is mitigated, support and opposition both: nothing in their conduct really inspires enthusiasm, or seems seriously deplorable. Their supporters would not risk death for them, and nor would their opponents, to bring them down: the two balance out. Only simpletons, who have not understood properly, remain uncompromisingly for or against. Differences within the consensus are not without short-term advantages, enabling the opposing camp to be divided and disparate elements to be added to one's own: teachers plus bankers, nurses plus big bosses, rap singers plus sedate citizens. Posthumously, though, and in the long term, this ambiguity has an inconvenient side.

Transforming a weakness – eclecticism – into a strength requires self-control and a measure of application. Two virtues, which are also techniques, are needed as well: compartmentalization and indifference (the first regulating action, the second feeling). However gifted the invulnerable character may be for these things, their combined exercise amounts to a daily ascesis: a training of body and soul that makes politics one of the fine arts, and raises the virtuoso performer almost to the level of a Marcus Aurelius, less the empire and the *Meditations*.

Ordinary senior officials or heads of state do not need this personal discipline, because they separate their political from their private lives: a natural separation once the State has become distinct from the family, as it did in our part of the world between the feudal period and the arrival of centralized monarchy. Our democrat was like a Valois: from antechamber to bedchamber, from boudoir to office, the seraglio was omnipresent and unavoidable. This is called 'personalizing relations'. By entangling service with allegiance, it generates a surrounding atmosphere of psychodrama, while the race for posts in the nebulous entourage is simplified into a race for proximity. A weekend at Latché, Whitsun at Solutré, Sunday evening at rue de Bièvre, put you one up; not being there set you back three squares. There was permanent tension at Court, uproar in the House. In that somewhat perverse, randomly recruited emir's retinue formally known as 'the President's Household', there were no clear frontiers between chancellery, harem, escort and private office, so that advisers, whether male or female, soon started to wonder if they were there as experts, bodyguards, confidants, poets, chamberlains, jesters, favourites or objects of erotic interest. The murderous traffic-density and uncertainty could cause depression, nervous breakdown, suicide. Some went mad, most feathered their nests; an élite served.

The example came from the top. If the Prince had been the heartless calculator people thought him, his office would have been staffed only by experts and administrators. It was more like a Noah's Ark containing the worst and the best, because that clansman (rather than statesman) always – dangerously – mixed the personal with the functional, collusion with practicality: a cold man influenced by emotion for the best and worst of reasons, loyalty and nepotism. He drove the whole lumbering apparatus on a loose rein, looked the other way, evaded, forgave. A friend would have had to chop up his parents to find himself barred from the Court. François de Grossouvre, a follower from the bad days, towards the end of his life conducted a feverish campaign of denigration around Paris, a tissue of informed gossip and resentment, fact and fantasy. But he kept his car, office, apartment and telephone in the Palace until his final revenge: an accusing suicide under the nose of his too-remote suzerain. I believe it was from delicacy and goodness of heart that the master of the house, fully informed, kept him under his roof to avoid humiliating him. The reflex of a Godfather perhaps, but a generous one: there are such.

When a life has become a nexus of so many live wires, any false step can cause a short-circuit. One has to make contact and insulate at the same time, to insulate on entry and restore the connection on leaving. The watchword in a shambles of that sort is 'divide and survive': trying to please comes second, and actually *ruling* is a bonus. If Badinter found Bousquet at the same lunch, Omar Bongo ran into Mother Teresa in the salon or a Grand Master of the Freemasons met Brother Roger of the Taizé community in the vestibule, a cock-up had occured. But the chief needed all those irons in the fire, because each was good for something and would have (or had had) its moment. For everyone to take part in the game, each pawn had to be able to see itself as the player's special pet, the only one privy to his real thinking. Hence the meticulous care with timetables, seating plans and itineraries: accidents happen so quickly. A presidential day was like a Marivaux play, a *Così fan tutte* of collusive comings and goings, the sigh of padded doors opening and closing in turn on an ill-lit office, mask and bergamask, carp and rabbit, a picaresque farce of voluntary metamorphosis, divine role-switching: Jupiter perfecting himself as a double. Supreme power means maximum replication, the ultimate enjoyment: being everywhere at once, being many, a thousand-eyed nosy parker savouring sidelong in the mirror the endless receding rank of his own mocking doubles. Playing *Amphitryon* every day stimulates the vital forces, the Nietzschean intoxication of the ubiquitous and elusive superman. The resistance agent, that adept juggler of contacts and false identities, meets the President rushing from Defence Council to love-nest, televised ceremonial to rascally escapade. So the most visible man in the country becomes the most secret as well; every head of state enjoys the pleasures of the conspirator, and Mitterrand was as happy slipping from castle to castle as the young Morland, pedalling quietly between networks on his bike.

Was it from that era that he had retained his very Mauriac taste for the whispered hint, the instruction muttered in a corridor, the capital word-in-your-ear? Awkward in conclave, stiff at ceremonial dinners and big meetings, he was liberated in private, laughing and relaxed in *tête-à-tête*. I will always remember how that utterly contained president, in the front hall of the Élysée as the guests took their leave after a working dinner, would signal from a distance with a crooked forefinger or mutter with a furtive jerk of the head: 'Stay behind a minute, would you, Régis, I've got something to tell you . . .'

Only a half-skill, though, in the long term: the bullshitter is always at risk of drowning in the stuff. The Feydeau labyrinth may exit into a cul-de-sac, the attempt to hang onto all the strings can leave a man hopelessly entangled. The 'Greenpeace affair' was a tragi-comic example of the harm too much secrecy can do even in secret activities. Not so much in this case the operation itself – a half-witted idea, deploying disproportionate means, quickly blown to the Auckland authorities by a random imponderable – as its extended unveiling, a slow strip-tease which held the country spellbound for six months. By carpeting the five or six people concerned with this production the President could have defused the whole imbroglio in twenty minutes, but the clean-up never took place because it would have involved explicit face-to-face discussion. When I expressed astonishment at this failure to an informed friend, a general with privileged access, he hinted smilingly that the boss would have found such a meeting acutely embarrassing. Instead, he dropped hints – different ones, several days apart   to Lacoste, the head of the DGSE; to Hernu, the Minister; and to the head his own staff. The result was that each man expected the author of this disorder to sort it out; believing that the others were in the know, none of them dreamed of interpreting the presidential half-silences. That subtle game of hide-and-seek grew into an episode of criminal stupidity, eventually blamed on 'anticipation' by hapless, distant 'Pacific admirals', allegedly of liberal outlook but very stupid. The same deficiency of method arises, in diplomacy, from a monarch's resistance to the 'debriefing' required by any administrative apparatus. Normally, after a private meeting with a foreign equivalent, a head of state or government informs his minister and staff of what has been said, so that the essential details pass down the chain of command to the ambassador concerned. Our secretive president would emerge from these meetings as if nothing had happened, leaving his diplomats in the dark. They had to try to wheedle crumbs of information out of the interpreter and note-taker (himself sworn to secrecy), and were reduced on one occasion to cornering a Japanese understrapper the next day, just to get some idea – in English – of what the French president had agreed, rejected or proposed with the prime minister of Japan: humiliating, and unprofessional. Withholding information, an old feudal expedient for amassing or retaining power, is a contagious vice, turning advisers and some ministers into low-rent creatures of mystery who strut about cloaked in shadowy importance. Imbroglio and entanglement became the collective culture at the Elysée, in direct contravention of modern decision-making and communication practice. The logicians who were then working on a projected French-style 'National Security Council' came up against that *non possumus*, so visceral that it would have seemed absolutist to Louis XIV: to have my hands free, and no obligation to anyone but myself, I need to keep my lip buttoned, accumulate as many secrets as possible and only listen to advice in one-to-one privacy. Distance is the ABC of command; enigma for its own sake is majesty on the cheap, much less clever than it looks. Nietzsche said that real nobles are 'speakers of truth, who have no need to dissimulate'. Great politicians who are just great dissimulators don't make very great lords.

With indifference – that agnosticism of the heart – we touch on the most private, the ultimate zone of darkness, where we lose our footing. This non-feeling does not hinder friendships, loves, attachments; on the contrary it multiplies them, accumulates them without cost; by keeping them at a distance, under control, it renders fidelity less costly. Avoiding that dependence on the affections that governs emotional individuals facilitates a certain perseverance of the heart, as the absence of involvement makes for accurate assessment of features in a terrain. Our leader had mastered the difficult art of attaching people to him without attaching himself to them. Hooking people out of curiosity, letting them go out of fatigue (the effort of seduction leaving the heart empty), that angler simply did not care in the final analysis. His sovereignty disdainfully equated the candidates for this or that prize: him, or someone else . . . ? The same smoothing process was extended from individuals to situations, from situations to objectives, all equalized by pride: it's all the same, one thing is worth as much as another. A soldier of the Wehrmacht and a soldier of the maquis: brothers in courage and patriotism. White or black, Pétain or de Gaulle, right or left, what's the difference? Neither approval nor attachment: you pick things up, put them down, pass them by. And you stockpile people, just in case. Among ordinary mortals, indifference stems from indolence; or it increases with age like a *taedium vitae*, a foundering process. But in that imperturbable, ever-energetic character detachment was an *insolence*, and a source of energy.

When an agitated old man made a scene by announcing that he was going to kill himself if he continued to get the cold shoulder, the president listened in silence throughout and then answered shortly: 'Rest assured that I shall come to your funeral.' Or so Grossouvre told a confidant on the eve of his suicide. Whether true or imagined, this piece of laconicism is worthy of the ancient world and the stoical concept of behaviour. The wise man acquiesces to passing events. Exempt from any possibility of falling, the emperor views with the same eye glory and the absence of glory, health and illness, the living friend and the dead one. Aiming only at self-mastery, the master otherwise sticks closely to respectable behaviour: honouring the gods, attending to business and burying friends. By fulfilling his duty of *apathy*, the stoic sharpens his will; he consents to this or that action, but does not want to be bound by it or restricted to it. Careless of what does not depend on him – fair wind or foul, the betrayal or loyalty of associates – he safeguards the innermost self that depends on him alone. 'That alone belongs to you: playing to the full the character you have been given.' Indifference feeds the 'actor's paradox' defined by Diderot: 'It is not the heart, but the head that does everything. The sensitive man loses his head at the slightest unexpected circumstance; he will never be a great king, or a great minister, or a great captain, or a great advocate . . . In the great comedy, the comedy of the world, the stage is occupied by emotional souls; all the men of genius are in the audience.' That thorough, insensitive soul played his part on both sides of the footlights: tribune of fire and flame on the boards, cold-eyed sceptic in the stalls. Talleyrand gazing coolly up at Gambetta: these two half-lies together comprised the truth of a man. Duplicity! cried *vox populi*. No, dissociation, replies Diderot: a representation split in two. Read Retz, who advises that one should appear to take an action that others would accuse one of not taking, but without taking it: that is how he called Condé, his enemy, to his rescue; and that is how Rocard was promoted to the Matignon. Mitterrand, apolitical at heart, practised throughout a policy of the head: that was his genius, and his limitation. Could he admit even to himself the depths of unbelief hidden behind that detachment from himself and others? He was moderate in everything except nihilism, his only radical principle.

Longevity dissolves. Who, *exactly*, will be entered in the records? Not the founder of anything. Nor a Just Man. A great character, curiously elevated by meagre deeds. Great in firmness of soul, endurance under punishment, setbacks surmounted; and in the paradoxes of his own personality. La Bruyère baffled! For what classical moralist's microscope could pin down the cautious swash-buckler, the centrist *condottiere*, the delicate boor, the careless calculator, the shy swaggerer, the blundering virtuoso and so on? The oblique man jangles our preconceptions, disarms antitheses, substitutes *and* for *or*. Decipher it for yourselves, my dears; I have served my time.

And we – the hussars, the old sweats recommissioned for an Italian campaign – loved him, and all the more because he did not love us. Prancing with impatience we followed that Kutuzov hallucinated as a Bonaparte, because he promised us the wide steppes, that we would cross the Alps with him to join Fabrice in Milan and tumble duchesses at Parma. We gave our faith to that man who had so little of it – certainly a convinced European but a socialist by hazard, who got elected in 1981 on a socialist platform, not a European one, and drifted thereafter on the surface of things. Finding itself at the end of that Long March – 1965–95 – in an inner Charente brought final disillusion to an inattentive generation. 'We were dressed for a different destiny': not for a

career, let alone that return to earth. Should people blame him for that
humiliation? Moderate-left radical socialism may be bad for the soul over time,
but at least it respects lives and bodies. The crusaders had ideals and so had
Lenin; Mitterrand perhaps not. Fortunately, in a way: it brought fewer deaths
and pointless sacrifices. When the Absolute is lacking, heroism is absent, but so
are calamities, and the dark side remains benign, under that debonair, legalistic
and tolerant satrap no one was killed, kidnapped or proscribed. There was no
torture, there were no iron masks, no dungeons. Telephone tapping and
nobbling the judiciary were about the extent of it: not very wicked by Princely
standards. Let us leave canting moralism and our more or less vainglorious
disappointments there; we had been stood up many times before. Let us look at
things coolly. It is saddening to watch a genius of action foundering in
ineffectuality, a great wrestler reduced to appearing in a provincial arena
by failure to embody anything larger than himself. Most upsetting to the
amateur of emotion is the sense of extraordinary means deployed in the service
of ends as commonplace in Europe as democratic 'cohabitation' and 'alternation', seen as a way of sharing the exposure among the élites, turn and turn
about. The original intention had not been to occupy a wing of the baron's
castle, but to build another one without a barony. 'History will do me justice,'
he used to say in his last days. 'I have ensured alternation in the State.' Yes:
within the existing mould, leaving the matrices of the single party intact. So left-
wing notables now sit on the Trilateral and the Conseil d'État, draw attendance
fees, edit newspapers, dine at the Siècle with other careerists. Much good may it
do them: those who elected them certainly had other aims in mind. Two terms
gave enough time for the liberal establishment, inside and out, to co-opt 'new
strata' and make new conformists out of former dissidents. A positive record:
but for whom, and for what? Our war aims in 1974 and 1981 were not really to
establish the 'spoils system' and job rotation, plus a strong franc and total press
freedom (freedom, that is, for money to control the press). Merely to usher the
trade unions of the Fourth Republic across the threshold of the Fifth, to
reconcile the brewery and the château, the Orléanists with the Bourbons, to
replace 1960 growth technocrats with 1980-style technocrats of global accoun-
tancy, was it really necessary to mobilize the whole panoply of hope, with fifes
and drums?

De Gaulle had a thousand years of history on his mind. Mitterrand had
Mitterrand: not nothing, but not enough. He called that slightly truncated
autonomy 'freedom', believing in effect that a free man is one divested of
overriding values and aims, when really the opposite is true. The man who
knows he can make use of anything (including ruffians) loses all taboos, is
catapulted beyond good and evil. But the fact remains that means without ends,
faithless pragmatism, only make half a programme: Che had the other half. I
had passed from faith without method in one continent to method without faith
in the other. It is too late for me to find a third ideal man to reunite the two

pieces of the tessera. The present political lull is unpropitious, for a great man, in politics, always results from the encounter of a great character with a great circumstance. On the left, which is my side, I see no one of the first rank able to effect that conjunction of dream and reason (Freud would say: of the pleasure principle and the reality principle) that de Gaulle managed by subordinating the romanticism of the ends to the classicism of the means. The candidates are a bad production run, or trapped like starlings in a net. All that effort and compromise just to circle back to the divorce of the two kingdoms, source of the uneasy conscience that inspires the intellectual left, and that I had done my best to avoid by plunging into the dirty waters of efficacity. Such perhaps is the destiny of the contemporary left: a proud species that emerged in the nineteenth century from the crossing of Revolution as myth with the Book as instrument but is now a technical anachronism, doomed to disappear in the global ecology of the videosphere. We had listened to our own yarns, we were living above our means in the imagination. Like France in the world, the left in France since 1945 had been travelling first class on a second-class ticket. A Charentais inspector had turned up, affable and shrewd, and we had returned without fuss to the right compartment. No more special French case, no more arrogance. And no more religious war. Appeasement, modesty, relaxation. At last: a democracy like the others! One turn for the left, one for the right. Phew! That socialist president had delivered a last generation of socialist dreamers from the century of lies that had done us so much good.

Great men (since that is what we call small men who serve something bigger than themselves) leave their fidelities behind them. Mitterrand took his to the grave; or we will soon take them to ours. Ego without transcendence, will without purpose, he will enter posterity as a long-tailed meteor. Political adventurers, unlike literary ones, are comets without tails: this one will have few posthumous followers, but I believe it would be wrong to make him a scapegoat for our lost illusions without questioning their original validity. Declining fervour may be the price we pay for the mistakes of our time. Was it he who let us down, or the whole political thing, through him? Was Mitterrand the illusion, or politics itself? And wasn't it *our* illusion? Peddling dreams is not illegal like influence trafficking, but it does more harm, and to entire populations. We entrusted our follies to that adaptive genius, and he gave them back to us transformed into base lead: external trade balance, Enlarged Market and ERM. But were our own heads filled with such pure gold? We cry that we are betrayed, robbed. 'Our dreams, give us back our dreams!' Is it sensible to carry on dreaming, given the realities? Is not political activity ultimately a trivial matter of translating hope into management, the absolute into small change, as a photocopier by covering a surface with dots transforms a colour original into a monochrome print? *Traddutore, traditore* . . . but without that betrayal our history books would have a lot of blank pages.

I liked the seducer, the countryman, the friend; the State Narcissus not so much. The private dynamic, not the public and consensual vacillation. But in the final analysis I am grateful to that leader, who disappointed many, for disappointing me too. I will even give him credit for some very belated realizations: we should not render unto Caesar that which is God's; politics as national religion is ending; it is not healthy to confuse a priesthood with a profession. There are more degrading professions. This one consists of getting elected, knowing how to wait, shaking people by the hand, dining in restaurants, pulling strokes, networking, making defensive countermoves, uttering agreeable platitudes in studios, reviewing the press twice a day and hunting in a pack. My misunderstandings cost me dear, but I feel sorry for the future, because the day of the prudent professional has arrived: and sadly, professionals, however highly trained and aware, lack imagination. In politics as elsewhere, only outsiders produce new ideas. With the last round of every presidential election becoming a contest between two old énarques, we can expect some very mournful duels.

Let us play safe in summarizing that period (I am afraid it will not count as an epoch) by assuming the worst about the protagonist. Borne along by the tail-end of a millenarian breeze, surfing on the last wave of revolutionary hope raised in France by May '68 – final gasp of recycled nineteenth-century religion in the twentieth – exploiting the old egalitarian Gulf Stream more freely for not being part of it himself, and therefore not mistaking words for things ('changing our way of life', 'breaking with capitalism', 'Common Programme', etc.), a perspicacious cynic joined the flow and, being obstinate, followed it all the way. He should have subsided along with it in about 1983. To stay afloat, that socialist metamorphosed, via the Europe myth, into a reluctant liberal, finding his feet one more time on a flat political foreshore at the extreme edge of the century. Thanks to that human bridge, a Calvinist left that had fallen one republic and two technical revolutions behind the times managed to pass in a single generation from 1848 to the New Deal, from Marx to Roosevelt. The socialist sphere jumped in fifteen years from tendency to 'stable', from militant to supporter, from programme to opinion poll, from vanguard thought to management, from conviction to opinion, from planned economy to personal ambition. In 1980 people still talked about bosses, not entrepreneurs. By 1995 the socialist expert no longer said 'the working class' but referred to 'the labour force'. One might have hoped for a less brutal transition, better controlled and above all more open, but the left has a human core unbreakable enough, immortal enough, to survive such a loss of weight, albeit at the cost of part of its soul. And incidentally, the diversion may have been necessary, a way round the uncrossable swamp of dead words. For not only France was involved: the hangover was international, and the Mitterrand era the French form of a universal dedramatization, more eloquent in France than elsewhere only because it was the European country seen, since Marx, as the 'homeland of politics'. We suffered the backlash of a planetary crash diet, but Spain, Italy and the whole of Latin Europe were hit just as hard at the same time. And now we are all lighter, physically and morally. Such would appear to be the general content of that purely individual and therefore empty will, the truth about our illusion; or if the absolute Truth of an episode does not exist, enough at least to make it possible to rise again, for what that is worth. 'Pray do not set these verses to music,' Victor Hugo told his posterity. A modern statesman should enjoin his not to scribble Ideas in the margins of his activities. 'No speeches', Mitterrand's last will and testament specified accordingly. In keeping itself afloat for fourteen years the French ex-left pulled off a remarkable political success, and suffered a no less remarkable philosophic setback. The one paying for the other. It has given us no new reasons to live, and taken away some of the old ones. And since when (it might reply) has the role of a government been to give people reasons not to kill themselves? We are not in 1793, 1848 or 1944 now. And who can really argue? There are churches for people worried about the meaning of life. Each to his own catechism.

Worthy representative of an unworthy *fin de siècle* (but what century ever lives up to its beginnings?), involuntary carrier of a message extending beyond it, the misadventure of those years of wind undoubtedly merits a reading in the manner of Hegel, but with bowed head. That will diminish its importance, but also its bitterness. The non-spirit of the universe also has its men of business. Like Hegel, who, after the battle of Iéna watched the essence of the world pass under his window on horseback, I will be able to tell my grandchilden, with a crooked little smile, that I sometimes watched the essence of a world without essence pass under the window of my office, his bulletproof Renault 25 crunching over the white gravel of a *cour d'honneur* past the red plumes of the Republican Guard.

3

Advice to Younger Generations

Start early in the morning – Whatever happens, no zeal – Professional detachment – Blunders of the subtle – Only the imaginary is real – The limitless value of sham – Corruption is no big deal – One-horse race – On the proper use of cocktails

You who will live on when we are gone: what do the miscalculations of an old lunatic matter to you?

Listen: I am not some morose old buffer shaking my white locks over yet another bulletin of defeat, nobly and lugubriously for the collusive effect. You know that my soul is not pure enough for the obsequies, that my files are too empty to add my own Memorial to all the others. All I want is to help you.

What can you learn from something that was no big deal? Nothing very thrilling, as you already know. We can ignore the hubbub of councils, conferences and summits; all that is common knowledge; photocopiers and copyright have put custom well ahead of the law (which used to hold that thirty years was the proper interval), so that this morning's defence secret is sure to be on TV by the evening. A few practical hints on 'the art of prudence' will probably be more useful. The young do not need specialists in the bittersweet to dissect dead meanings out of History, they need circumstantial intelligence to help them make their way through the shoals of life: like standing orders that have to be passed on at the changing of the guard. Cheerfully, obligingly, to help budding Mazarins fulfil their destiny, I now assume the role of a veteran tradesman, nursemaiding the apprentices for the honour of the trade.

Why Mazarin? Look again: a master artisan, and a key work. Not much needs to be added to the fifteen axioms and five precepts of his *Breviarum politicorum* (1683). With issues so subtle and unchanging the publication date matters little, but every period forgets its Latin and needs to be reminded of it. So start by learning the unloved grandee's irrefutable 'axioms':

1. Act towards all your friends as if they were going to become your enemies.
2. Where there is community of interests, danger arises when one of the parties becomes too powerful.
3. When you are anxious to obtain something, let no one perceive it until you have done so.

4. You must know an evil to be able to prevent it.
5. What you can settle peacefully, do not seek to settle by war or litigation.
6. It is better to suffer moderate damage than, in the hope of great advantages, to advance another's cause.
7. It is dangerous to be too unyielding in affairs.
8. The centre is worth more than the extremes.
9. You should know all and say nothing, be gracious to everyone and give your trust to no one.
10. The best position is at an equal distance from all the other parties.
11. Always maintain some mistrust of others and rest assured that their opinion of you is no better than yours of them.
12. When a party has many members, even if you are not of that party, do not speak ill of it.
13. Be suspicious of that towards which your feelings draw you.
14. When you make a present or when you give a feast ponder your strategy as if you were going to war.
15. Do not permit anyone to approach a secret any more closely than you would permit a prisoner determined to cut your throat to approach your throat.

Perhaps I should also remind you of his basic 'precepts':

1. Simulate.
2. Dissimulate.
3. Trust no one.
4. Speak well of everyone.
5. Foresee before acting.

You may think this breviary dry and old-fashioned: extend, stiffen and modernize it if you can. Obviously the experience of a humble and marginal adviser will not help much, but no footnote, however trivial, is superfluous to this *vade mecum*, cobbled together by each generation and forgotten by the next, until it too follows timeworn paths and timeworn maxims to rediscover America. Even though it is vain to expect some lesson from History and in this context each newcomer thinks himself a pioneer, I would feel bad if I did not fulfil the elementary obligation of lobby veterans: help my juniors to save time on the paths to glory. I do so on the sole authority of our best teacher: failure. It may be thought that mine was merely banal and predictable. Of course: the ruin of aulic counsellors has been programmed for twenty-five centuries, descent from the heights into prison, opprobrium or ridicule. Nilotic scribe, keeper of the seals, seraglio writer, court intellectual, toady of princes, understrapper, scullion: the increasingly scornful names lofty souls use to denote the unhappy individuals who try to give the intellect a role make the historical tendency clear: a downward slope. I do not despair of seeing it reclimbed some day, by young people devoted to the public good and ambitious to play a great role in great events, or dressing up their ambition as devotion (which God will recognize his own?). Let us leave the soul supplement at that and opt for some complement of information. The new blood should do the opposite of what I did – I who played a subordinate role in commonplace events – to have the best chance of success.

The golden book of melancholy has no blank pages left, but so much the better. Open your jotters, take technical notes: they are the only ones worth having.

1. *Start early in the morning.* No other prescription is required for those wishing to 'do cabinet' (the term used in France for a president's or minister's personal staff). Corridors and antechambers cause premature ageing, another reason for starting early. Age limit: 30. Increasing life expectancy in the West being accompanied by an equivalent decrease in the age of governmental personnel, *nomenklaturas* get younger all the time. Some are alarmed by this, objecting to the spectacle of 'twentysomething whippersnappers giving orders on matters they know nothing about to experienced administrative directors'. Indeed, the sight of chieflings whose only training has been a stroll through the fields during a spell in a *préfecture* short-circuiting the proper channels at will, scheming all day long and unable to hold a ten-minute meeting without taking three phone calls to show how important they are, is more than a little disquieting. But despite the probability of petulance, youth is compulsory for a lot of reasons.

For a start, a young proletarian gives a better yield than an old one (for it is a proletariat *sui generis* that populates the outbuildings of palaces). The output of a cabinet dogsbody on fatigue duty belongs solely to his boss. Ideas, speeches, travels, contacts, reading, all go to his immediate hierarchical superior, the *directeur de cabinet* or secretary-general. Subordination to him defines the technical adviser; and transmission by hand of the finished product to the minister or president defines the special adviser, the favourite, the 'damned soul'. To him goes any material or moral benefit from the work of his subordinates. Hence the decisive importance that should be attached to the location of offices, the most advantageous position being as close as possible to the chief, among the last links in the chain of transmission. That is where the plus-value extracted from the exploited individuals lower down the chain is converted into power. This condition might seem more acceptable for a trainee priest, but in any case working for someone else, for no apparent return, comes more easily to a mad dog than an old pro. For the latter is less tolerant of waste; and it is a fact that no profession is more prodigal of energy than militancy and politics in general. It is not over-fanciful to liken it to a giant Jacques Tinguely self-destroying machine, but one made of human flesh, rattling and shuddering in every nerve and sinew, consuming vast quantities of time, thought, sweat and self-sacrifice to produce virtually nothing. Input considerable; output variable to put it politely. Beyond a certain age, when time starts to run short, we become more aware of the succession of losses, more inclined to calculate, to think of the cost. If you prefer the nobler metaphor of a steamship, we could say that the obscurity and arduousness of the work done in the engine room contrasts uncomfortably with the striking personalization of the results on the bridge, when you aren't in first class and have to work in the coal bunkers. Hence the importance of securing a fief or mandate as soon as possible, so that you can stroll nonchalantly about the promenade deck with the gentry. Or if glamour is your thing, envisage a modern government as 300 little seamstresses slaving in the dressing room for five top models who know how to swish around under the spots, but don't give a fig for the cut of the dresses or the complexities of high fashion.

At 25, you can shelve the question of descendants the better to share the present and future glory of your Lord. By 45 you are wondering what happened to your balls and starting to fantasize about replacement therapy. Immorality sets in, the ego thinks of itself, of fleeting time, days and nights eaten by the wind, the risky and squalid lengths to which you have gone to secure jobs (ambassadorships, portfolios, directorships in quangos and state enterprises) for pals who continue to complain endlessly, entire weekends wasted in unlikely, sterile meetings to argue about reforms that will never take place; the thick confidential report on audiovisual reform that the President commissioned from you a.s.a.p. – giving you to understand that the other, official report making a fuss in the media was strictly for the gallery – that devoured your whole spring and summer, that you delivered by hand in September on the day promised, and that the president chucked negligently into the back of a drawer, remarking that this terrific Italian chap called Berlusconi was going to sort all that out for us. These things make you more miserly, less of a soft touch. You count your change. You drag your feet. You deteriorate.

After that a young wolf suffers less from the ambient wickedness, having developed long enough fangs to look after himself. National palaces are hostile and cruel places, jungles more ornate than others but equally subject to harsh Darwinian struggle. A lot of the bloodshed goes on during Sunday visits to the Loire châteaux, where the carnivores in charge parade their offspring on the day of rest. Being evicted at the last minute from a trip you have organized yourself, from a restricted lunch to discuss an issue you have been asked to deal with, from a consultation to discuss an initiative of yours; having ideas stolen, seeing your note bearing your superior's signature, getting the blame for a press leak organized by a rival to discredit you . . . endless is the list of ordinary affronts. It explains the comic persistence (and obscene disproportion) of 'tabouret squabbles' in the true and unvarnished history of any reign, absent though they may be from text-books and official records. Omitted from state memoirs, too trivial or familiar to be mentioned once you have retired from affairs, this is nevertheless the real and unvarying sauce base: an interstitial and conjunctive sourness. Those most affected end by becoming unaware of it, as the ear ceases to be aware of a continuous bass accompaniment under the melodic variations of a concert piece. No one could imagine the affronts and vexations suffered in a working day by an Important Person or high-level aide. The prime minister discovers that Jaruzelski has arrived in Paris by reading the paper; the foreign minister has short-circuited him and left informing him to the president, who has not bothered. Insult. The president notices while watching television that his deputy is contradicting him in coded terms. Having just appointed the man, there is nothing he can say or do. Insult. The secretary-general of the presidency discovers by chance that the boss is holding important meetings behind his back. Insult . . . a full programme of insults, in a seething nest of vipers, every day that God makes, from the top of the heap to the bottom. All concerned simply swallow, say nothing and wait. It takes a young stomach to digest that and start afresh the next day. In the plainclothes army of a state bureaucracy, where a sort of egalitarian and laid-back bonhomie prevails between high-ups and foot-soldiers clothed in the same three-piece suits, these hierarchical mini-cruelties seem especially stinging, studied and pointed.

Finally, on getting home at about nine in the evening after ten meetings in succession, the younger Turk will be better able to overcome, night after night, that impression of sickly vacuity, as from an hour of zapping back and forth between a dozen moronic TV channels; that impression of exhausting stasis inspired by the unending treadmill of politico-administrative labour; the suspicion that pervades you at nightfall that the crucial activities over which you have sweated blood since seven in the morning are insubstantial, ineffectual, irremediably aqueous. Like the interdiction of thought that goes with administrative overwork, the impossibility of fulfilment in a sphere where no one sees the end result of his actions carries a taste of ashes that, after a certain age, tempts you to follow Seneca into the bath. The young endure it better.

2. *Whatever happens, no zeal.* Don't jump the gun when the decisive moment comes, a new president, government or parliament. In fact that is the very moment to avoid antechambers, telephones and entourages. If you have already acquired some social visibility (better than a name, a track record or a work: a *face*), guard it jealously. Pull out of the game just when Tom, Dick and Harry are jostling for a piece of the action. The later you enter the lists, the better you will be received. Hide your goals, and your convictions if you have any. Be what you are: an uncompromising man of principle, far above the mêlée. Remember where enthusiastic and resolute support for a partisan cause lands most 'good militants' and 'loyal supporters': in the stables or the kitchens. While 'centrists', reputedly soft and wavering, swan about in the drawing room accepting honours and sinecures. Those anxious to serve can use the back stairs; you should enter by the front door. It is a general rule with parties or governments that the last to arrive, those hardest to convince, must be kept happy by all means. Hence the importance of not belonging to a clique, stable or tendency: you will already be

'marked', so not eligible for the best jobs. Any faction arriving in power seeks to pay its dues and show broad-mindedness by bestowing favours on non-members. This democratic obligation gives new validity to the prescient cardinal's axioms 8 ('The centre is worth more than the extremes') and 10 ('The best position is at an equal distance from all the other parties'). If by chance you have a known weakness for one or another, pull a wry face, state your conditions and get yourself seen, but stay away: they will come looking for you. Show your face on the small screen, your name in the prints. Desire is mimetic.

Notice the contradiction? First I say: 'Read Tanizaki, love the darkness, the veiled, the obscure depths of back offices', then I say: 'Flee the dark, be shrill and noisy.' It is chance itself that is fluid and swirling. Hence this advice: advance yourself in the dark but bear in mind that the dark does not pay. If you ever have to choose between a regular press column, a solitary Atlantic crossing or slim volume of haikus and a job as a secretary of state or occult senior adviser, don't even hesitate. Do not yield to the desire to be at the centre of things, the fear of missing the bus, the lure of the arcane. Do not put on colours and a number just for access to the other side of the walls where, you imagine, big secrets are simmering. You can influence events in there better from outside; in the videosphere (where *in* and *out* have permutated), working on a colour magazine will do you far more good than polishing a well-informed confidential note. Your best bet is to increase your luminosity as quickly as possible. The footlights lead straight into the seraglio, which threatens in turn to cut you off from the bright lights of the city (if you take the traditional rules seriously, put the state first and observe proper discretion). Our time has turned the 'honest dissimulation' recommended by the great Jesuit masters upside down. These days it is common prudence to be seen with journalists, singers, starlets, songwriters, TV presenters and publicists; and a bit unwise to cultivate the friendship of middle-ranking civil servants and administrators, let alone teachers (those blind alleys). Your luncheons, your dinners, are precious. Cultivate the first, avoid the second, the news will get around eventually.

Think about it. 'Administration', etymologically, means 'going towards the *minus*', lesser people and activities. Career security is bought there at the cost of guaranteed obscurity. It may be an error of ambition, in a still-fresh will to power, to associate yourself with public power, when the *de facto* powers are becoming private. And our public law powerless. By joining what is too readily termed the 'decision-making class', a member of the intellectual class risks sacrificing his main accomplishment, the ability to make minds supple and construct opinions, to the duty of discretion. The Prince himself, permanently plugged in to the papers, radio and TV through his press department, twitches and vibrates in response to any clamour outside the walls. He will pay more attention to a signed newspaper leader than a note placed silently on his desk, for the front page read by a million people carries a social weight he must take into account, while a note that will be read by him alone poses no threat. It will have only the importance that its solitary reader is willing to give it; it will make no sensation; it remains in his power, at his discretion, discreetly to hand; if he makes nothing of it, it will have no effect. Sooner or later he will have to answer a repeated public objurgation, a substantial current of opinion, an 'expression of genuine feeling'. But what does the Master owe the individual he has chosen to hand-feed and carry him? Nothing at all. So speaking into the president's ear may not be the most effective way of *having* his ear. The Master depends on public opinion; become an opinion leader and the Master will depend on you. People pay court only to those on whom they depend. Those with easiest access to the Palace these days are not the people you would expect: they are those who traduce accredited Palace officials on the small screen or in the prints and who, unlike their victims, are actually believed.

If you already belong to the élite whose members comment on current events, avoid espousing any cause but an elevated one, to which there can be no possible objection (democracy, freedom of conscience, rejection of fatwas and genocides). Keep your distance, be a Great Conscience. Temper your urbanity with genuine aloofness. Make your editorials without indulgence, barely polite, slightly bantering. Then the president will invite you to a little private luncheon, a favour reserved for the leading tenors of the adverse camp; then ministers of state will call you by your first name at cocktail parties, draw you confidingly by the arm into an alcove for a long private chat, in the full sight of all and to the great chagrin of enfeoffed knights and squires. You will become an objective in the 'continuing battle', to be cajoled, neutralized and if possible converted. At this career crossroads, with mutual seduction reaching fever pitch, the Great Conscience must imperatively stiffen, refuse to surrender, receive confidences without making any return. For a man of the pen worth his salt, hiring his services to a grandee is a good way of ensuring that he will never become one himself. That is the real art of being a man of principle: exhibit your talents without parting with them. Let yourself be seen as a 'dependable man' and you are out of the game. Let the acolytes be 'dependable' (that deadly word). And remember: unconditionality is for boobies. A fool wears his heart on his sleeve, a shrewd person keeps it hidden and only shows his teeth. Treating all issues individually, the visible personality gains by remaining in public the enigmatic, irritable, unpredictable and difficult creature he has always been in private. Open-minded on the death penalty, obstinate about the Middle East. Full of appalling incomprehensions and divine surprises. With women or Consciences, only the unsecured and unexpected are worth much effort: loyalists do not need to be stroked. A serving president hardly glances at the memos and faces of his people, and listens to them carelessly; they are won over in advance, so no really new information is expected from them. He focuses his attention on known adversaries, because opposition makes people shrewd, as loyalty makes them slightly stupid. He sets his sights assiduously on a 'recruitable' golden mean, and is intrigued only by individuals who cannot be completely won over. Publicists call this teasing behaviour the 'duty of independence' (some prefer 'irreverence'). You will recall that this attitude of rebellious suspicion, marking the Conscience's superiority to the ordinary state employee, was recommended to *The Courtier* by Baltasar Gracián under the heading 'Know how to cultivate other people's expectations'. 'One should not show everything on the first occasion. It is good practice to match one's forces to the needs of the moment, and discharge what is due to public expectation day by day.' Those seventeenth-century ecclesiastics were decidedly sharp. Nothing is to be taken for granted by the Prince or the public: neither their strength nor their weakness nor your conscience. When they open their arms to embrace you and their shadow makes a cross on the ground, let it stay like that.

Need I mention the fate reserved by all régimes for devotees from the earliest days? Eleventh-hour arrivals scoop the pot every time. It would be cheering if the people who went through the suffering *also* received the honours; if survivors of Vercors or Buchenwald had been given portfolios at the Liberation; if republicans exiled by the Second Empire had come back to harass the Republic of the Juleses;[6] or if socialists from 1960 were running socialism in 1990. But these would have been dangerous precedents. Never forget this primary truth: just as the guerilla in the sierras does not come out on top in revolutions or the working scholar become the big-name intellectual, ministers pregnant with the future are not recruited from among old militants. The political galley operates in two tempos, on two levels. You have to pick the right moment, if you know whether you want to be a captain or man the sweeps.

3. *Keep your faith moderate. Stay professional.* Do not get too full of your subject, carried away, ill and sleepless. Only amateurs get excited. Professionals maintain a slight distance, thus remaining mobile, available, hands free for the next job or portfolio. Strong feelings make you drop your guard, get flustered easily, invite mockery, fall into traps. Desensitize yourself. Pay attention to the winners' style. 'There are three things I'd like to say.' Or again, to introduce a longish intervention: 'Just half a minute, if I may . . .' Cool, dry and precise. Do they give way to anger, to indignation? Do they hurl themselves into a task body and soul? They take part in an 'exercise' (that eloquent diplomats' term). They have an easy bearing, gazing about in a manner vacant but alert, invulnerable, not jovial but airy, like their remarkably clear and uncluttered desks (it is his immaculate work that identifies the chef in a kitchen). In any high-powered gathering, graduates of the Ecole d'administration can be recognized easily by a sort of private frigidity that makes them genial, efficient and brisk, somewhere between bustling and offhand. That cold-blooded expert remains cool where others, vehement with feeling, become vulnerable. When he is a minister it will not bother him in the slightest to go straight from a meeting in the suburbs to supper at Maxim's; to deliver a lachrymose speech to the wretched of the earth half an hour before an uproarious dinner with a group of robber barons. The

absence of an inner flame facilitates this splitting or detachment, which it would be wrong to see as an infallible sign of insincerity or dandyism: it is more a matter of caution in broken terrain and often, given the ambient level of external aggression, a defensive armour. There is no point in starting early if you then wear out your horse. Putting too much soul into your life will stop you from going far. A man possessed is clumsy, a haunted man dangerous. I will make you unlearn fervour, Nathaniel.

Don't be too conscientious either, people will think you an amateur. To be taken seriously in that milieu, you must take nothing too seriously. I learned this too late, and so started (and finished) badly. In 1981 I took my job to heart like a greenhorn, with positively Boeotian enthusiasm. I wanted to do well. Knowing something about my subject and nothing about administrative methods, I buried myself in the work without leaving my office (instead of taking journalists to lunch), approaching it with the earnest determination of a newly qualified cabinetmaker. Appointed a special adviser on international affairs, I did every-thing I could to put myself on an énarque's wavelength, absorbing his outlook and lexicon by devouring lectures and treatises ranging from the *Précis de redaction administrative* and the *Manuel du protocole* to specialized texts and the files of *La Documentation française*. No one has an inborn facility for finely turned notes and compellingly stacked files; it has to be acquired. So I attacked what I believed to be my duties with a yokel's earnestness. I was such a bumpkin that I even tried to *make the point*, putting on paper three months after starting work the concept I was developing of a possible coherent approach to the Third World (as it was still called), with proposed initiatives, graded and linked region by region. A classic thirty-page memorandum covering objectives, costs and advantages, methods and means. Coming into the open in this way seemed to me to answer a triple duty of honesty (this is what I really think), transparency (are we really in agreement?) and efficiency (for the good of the service). I sent my dissertation upstairs, where it vanished into a black hole. I had acted in the hope of eliciting some vague directive from On High, some sort of faint tinkle in response. After that, I imagined, I would be able to proceed in full harmony (or simply go back home, if it turned out that the bee in my bonnet kept me too far from the Chief's music stand). There was no response until, a fortnight later, in answer to my direct questions, I was given a benevolent, embarrassed presidential smile: 'Interesting, yes, er . . . time will tell, eh?' Had he even 'taken note'? From the Quai d'Orsay, by contrast, a copy of my text came back two days later, annotated in the margins and sprinkled with *yes*es and *no*es backed by intelligible arguments: the minister had gone through the paper paragraph by paragraph. Alas, the domain was reserved, I served the suzerain; the lord of the Quai's hands were tied but . . . Claude Cheysson was a *polytechnicien*, incompatible really with the trade of *politicus*. A rather trenchant fluency, an enthusiast's manner, individual ideas, an open but abrupt personality and an absurd uprightness made him trample daily on the cardinal's precepts: 'Do not expose or declare yourself in anything'; 'Princes wish to be aided but not surpassed'; 'If ever passion seizes your mind, let it do no harm to your work, especially if it is important.' Where a great steward is excessively competent and lacking in psychology, the manner can harm the thing itself. Such four-square minds hold that there is no problem that cannot be solved by proper working methods (when the artist knows that there is no problem that 'cannot be dealt with adequately by an absence of decision'). Where a preoccupation with finesse prevents some from uncovering their batteries, the Ecole polytechnique's geometrical mindset, combined in this case with a deficiency of cunning, often made that incautious man say what he thought and do what he said. Openness is perhaps the ultimate in diplomacy, and good strategy, for tacticians run into difficulty where ambiguity ends. On the inside, however, tactics is everything. So his ignorance of *conseils généraux* and disdain for the literary would soon deprive the post of his professional excellence, score and book having fallen out of step. The constructivist approach of his minister may have embodied method in Descartes' sense, but the head of state's was an impressionist one, straight out of Verlaine: '*And nor must you ever go / Choosing your words without some carelessness / None is more precious than the doleful song / Where indecision with precision joins / Like fine eyes flashing from behind a veil . . .*' So many veils, indeed, that the gaze was hidden and the road sometimes missed. The first manager of foreign relations in the first term was poised to conduct foreign policy unceremoniously, face to the wind. That over-explicit, self-confident mind lacked the true *art* of misunderstanding: skill in reviving it, if ever by mischance it gets dissipated. Was he unaware that being too much ahead of events would arouse prejudices and powers against him? In any case our Prince took the view that external affairs ought to be subordinated to internal ones. And presently a gifted intuitive replaced that provoking logician at the Quai d'Orsay, like a cello replacing a bugle.

The absence of guidance from my boss to help me find my way through the fog brought this realization: a great professional has no time to waste on small boys. Tactical and strategic orientations, even those touching on his area of responsibility, are decided at the top. Enquiries among my better-placed peers soon revealed that everyone at the Elysée was in the same situation: wandering on a loose rein, no road map, destination unknown. The new head of the secret services for example, a friend of a friend carelessly appointed on the basis of nods and winks, was left entirely to himself. He never received from the head of state even the most basic 'focusing' directives, general guidelines or regional orientations, and was forced to refer to traditional prejudice and the newspapers to identify friends and enemies. To tell the truth everyone knew already that to continue as a modest branch of the Great Leader of the West would be the least risky option, a change of chiaroscuro leaving the underlying interests unaffected. An advantage of untrammelled *laissez-faire* is that it can promote recycled conditioned reflex and reformist cant both at the same time.

On reflection, it seems to me that this silence on the goals being pursued not only suited the personal style of a very experienced individual, but gave away a universal secret: the stupefying amateurishness of professionals, who all believe that their decisions are the fruit of careful scheming, matured at length on paper. In reality they are made on impulse, during mood-swings, on the basis of old resentments, whims and obsessions. An old friendship from the *Préfecture* days, a word in someone's ear from a cousin or sister-in-law, Buggins's turn, a nice country house, are the sort of things that appoint the heads of public establishments, ministries or administrative directorates; more reliably anyway than assessment of a CV, a work or a character. This applies in big choices as well as small, when defining the general line and when bestowing favours. The practitioner of the art navigates by intuition, he claims; by instinct. At random, more like: following his nose, testing the wind with a wet finger, bluff and bluster. At close quarters, it seemed to me that amateurs are more inclined to weigh things up and consider underlying goals. Such deep focus hampers the necessary mobilities and polyvalences. You may have noticed that the ministers of that period who left a mark – Badinter, Cheysson, Lang – were neither elected nor interchangeable. Their ministries were their lives; they had thought about the job for years and seized it with both hands. The 'pro' by contrast is a jack-of-all-trades able to switch with light heart and untroubled mind from Culture to P&T, or from Justice to Health.

4. *Do not be too subtle.* Be suspicious of cultivated and erudite persons (and too bad if rule 4 seems to contradict rule 3, as rule 2 does rule 1: it will teach you dialectics). It is a fault of subordinates to pay too much attention to pros and cons. Assistants are more intelligent than chiefs, which is of course why they are not chiefs. What, in their heart of hearts, did Plato think of Denys, Machiavelli of Lorenzo, Turgot of Louis or Diderot of Catherine the Great? That they did not know what they were doing. Yes, and that they were doing it anyway: others were just talking about it. Learning is a tree whose fruits wither early, and weighing too many factors is damaging to decision, like excessive lucidity to love. The ability of some graceful little goose to propel the bewitched poet to new heights of sophisticated song is equalled only by the way a yokel at the controls can elicit learned effusions and maxims cast in bronze from the intellectual. Between Laura and Petrarch, Odette and Swann, exists the same moral distance as between Lorenzo de Medici and Machiavelli or Charles X and Chateaubriand; between the blockhead who acts and the ventriloquist who writes. Only rarely is there a period where text and commentary are on the same level (de Gaulle's perhaps being one of them, with a Mauriac or Malraux able to deal with the original on equal terms). Just as it is absurd to want to be more responsible than the bosses themselves, we ought to admit that there are hidden depths behind the apparent superficiality and brisk detachment of decision-makers. It is to them that we owe the thoroughness and despatch with which good governments conduct business. (And there were countless cases in which

vain individuals mistook their chief's benevolence for indifference. Mitterrand would often say of someone: 'He's interested in that stuff. Find him something in that area – not ceremonial, something with a salary.' What mattered was not the job but the friend. The latter, alas, did not always understand that the president was only simulating interest in his new job to be nice to him. Soon he would complain: 'The president isn't really interested in what I'm doing. It's just a bone he's given me to gnaw.' How could one tell him that the Master had acceded to his wishes out of pure kindness of heart, just to give him pleasure, and that the inner workings of the state were none of his business?)

Intellectuals have a different sort of intelligence from decision-makers, whose placid exercise of authority needs the backing of an unthinking, audacious side that reacts instantly to events. 'You engage and then you see,' said Napoleon, author of 'War is a simple art and all in the execution'. You know already that what distinguishes the appealing but hollow discourse of men of ideas from the harsh but complete discourse of men of action is acceptance of the consequences of what is wanted. A peace-through-legislation idealist does not see the contradiction (as Blum did not in 1936) in wanting militant solidarity while avoiding military engagement. A pure heart on the 'moral left' can protest simultaneously against 'American imperialism' and our own arms sales, for he will not have worked out that a country that produces arms must sell them if it can, and that if it did not produce them it would have to get them from the imperial supplier, *thus* falling under its sway and *thus* extending its dominion over the rest of the world, clients and allies. I will credit you with this minimal realism, since without it you would have gone into a university or monastery. But allow me to draw your attention to a less obvious point. In the final analysis, we don't know what we are doing because we never know what tomorrow will make of what we did yesterday. The jolt of a perverse effect is as unpredictable as a favourable outcome; no one foresees the far-reaching import of an insignificant decision, or the insignificance of a grand and formal one. These uncontrollable slippages justify an expeditious approach. The important thing about a signature is that it is signed. After it, there will be time to see what happens as a result; before it, things just happened. Pointless to encumber yourself, *alea jacta est* and let what comes come. That is how lack of culture serves as the statesman's ace in the hole. What will seem to you to be 'weakness of arguments' in the sovereign is really the distinctive sign of sovereignty. If its holder has the bad luck not to be an utter lout, he will have to vent his peculiarities in exotic reserves far from his daily stamping ground.

'I would not be king,' Louis XIII said, 'if I had the same feelings as individuals.' Respect the simplicity of kings. If you must have complication at all costs, let the *trompe-l'oeil* of the public stage do its work. This theatre derives much of its credibility from the involuntary conspiracy between wings, stage and auditorium. Resting actors, delayed-action strategists, devote themselves off-stage to stuffing afterthoughts into the narrative of their hazardous 'strokes'; in their memoirs, they (or their incense-bearers) will talk about their vision for the future, their deep knowledge of humanity, the 'small inner voice'. The spectators in the balcony, seeing only the upstage flourishes – single currency, treaties being ratified, pregnant gestures – cannot begin to imagine the whims and last-minute panics that preceded these faits accomplis as zero hour approached. Frontline newsgatherers, supposed to know what goes on behind the scenes, could not admit that the wings of the reign were bare of grand designs, that their little eavesdroppers' secrets were valueless, without devaluing themselves. We like to believe that the politicians at centre stage 'play a hidden game'; in this we estimate them too highly; most do not have a 'game'. This does not prevent a game from being sketched in, over the years. As walking consists of a series of falls prevented by stepping forward, a strategy is a series of last-minute tactical recoveries, or a sequence of *fuites en avant* placed end to end (as the builders of the 'European Union' showed us: each major step, from the 'enlarged market' to 'monetary union', then the 'common foreign and security policy', resulted from a throw of the dice to escape from the previous bad decision). The passage of time has the almost mechanical effect of reassuring us retrospectively, by inserting causes and reasons into the dull administrative porridge and grafting on any aims that fit. Trust in the observer's spyglass: it will add multiple intermediate shades, cunning and sagacious, to a scene that at the time, in too merciless a light, appeared contemptibly crude and trivial. Do not imitate the ethnographer who grows indignant on hearing an explorer dismiss as 'primitive' a threatened Brazilian tribe whose mythological subtleties and highly intricate kinship system are beyond the understanding of conceited westerners. Be astonished rather by the orgiastic inventiveness of the analysts and political scientists who, doubtless to satisfy the clientele's passion for refined dishes, work hard to 'complexify' on paper what amounts to a string of unforeseen events. All those subtle high-fliers looking for something behind the appearances, reading the random gropings of an empiricist with the eye of an Agatha Christie! Written History will perform the retrospective miracle of transfiguring a 'success' into a win at liar-dice or chess. 'Pragmatism' is certainly a virtue, and 'instinct' and 'flair' genuine talents. But be aware of what these fig-leaf words conceal: hustling and disarray. A government – a cork adrift without a chart on an ocean whose contents and currents are unknown – is reputed competent if it stays afloat. So it can replace a knowledge of things with a well-tempered character, the sort you would need to face down a fortune-teller called Conjuncture with the mask of a chess Grand Master.

Bear in mind that the most startling interpretation (the one that makes us cry: 'What a scenario! You couldn't invent it!') will be the most often advanced, even if it is the most reassuring. The *a posteriori* reenchantment of the past gains credit from our spontaneous tendency to measure causes by effects. Given our Pascalian mottoes, it is vexing to have to admit that Cleopatra's nose or Grouchy's lateness could have caused the birth of one empire or the end of another. Feeble of us, I grant you. But what could be more bruising to our self-esteem than the historical study establishing that the Sarajevo assassination of 1914, the trigger for a monstrous butchery and all that followed it (communism, fascism, and so on), was the act of a free electron teamed with two hotheads, none of them 'manipulated' in any way, and not of a shadowy, coherent plot carried out at arm's length by the Serbian or Russian services? There was no one behind Lee Oswald. And what was Gorbachev thinking about, when some scatterbrain coined the word *perestroika*? One false step and an avalanche occurs: who can believe it, on the opposite slope? The greatest secret of all, and the hardest for a lover of mysteries to reveal, is that there is no secret; the hardest thing to accept, for the believer in manipulation, is that there is no one pulling the strings, no one working the puppets: no synarchy, no secret international committee, no murky entity plotting in the shadows.

5. *Be realistic, believe in symbols* (and not in 'reality', as I did). Concerned with the truth, I got everything wrong. Do not believe in facts, reason, the essence of things. Reality is a technical category that changes with our machines, and our machines are no longer those of Mazarin's time. Reality, for a postmodern individual, is the media, and facts are images of facts. My realism was a backward one: I wanted to serve the republic as others had earlier served the revolution, by employing the means of the possible in the service of the impossible. That is what the enlightened realist did. Changing conditions have dethroned him: this is the era of the bluffer in the spotlight. Never mind *La Documentation française*, cultivate your contacts. A man who is reputed important *is* important: take care of your reputation, rather than your plans. In fact it was ever thus: people are governed not in accordance with the reality of things, but with the representations of reality that a society forms for itself. These are matters not of diagrams and figures but of love and hate. Representations of the adversary are satanic, those of the protector angelic. Make your contribution to this mill, without looking too closely into the file. In politics, two plus two making four is the beginning of the end. Let me give you an example.

In about 1983 I started to wonder what was meant concretely by the term 'Gulag' in the USSR of the time. The televisual and generally accepted figure in France was 3,000,000 detainees. After a great deal of deciphering, cross-checking, travel (to Moscow among other places), interviews, computations and donkey work, I came up with an approximate total figure of three thousand 'political prisoners' for the twenty-five republics of the Union (which of course tried not to admit that the category existed). I wrote it down in black and white, and two rags accused me the next day of being a KGB media asset charged with disinforming the French. After the fall of communism, the new anti-communist Russian leadership published the real figure: 300. In your universe, being properly informed halves a man's value. Look at the bad reputation surveyors, statisticians and recorders have in well-informed circles ('Horror is not a matter

of numbers, you know!'). Do not make a fool of yourself with precise facts
gleaned from sound sources. Real History has one rhythm; our images have
another. Keep time with the second of these, and do not risk losing the beat.
Mentioning the reality of the Gulag in France between 1930 and 1960 put you
at odds with the reigning intelligentsia; and so did describing it in 1980. When
there were 6,000,000 prisoners in Stalin's USSR, Soviet embassy receptions
were all the rage in Paris; under Brezhnev, with only a few thousand left, no one
would dream of being seen at one. Not until totalitarianism was on its last legs
did it become necessary to be fiercely and unambiguously 'anti-totalitarian'.

In politics, where no one is only right, it is no more rational to stay rational
than it is realistic to align oneself with reality. The world should be taken at its
face value, although – or rather because – its 'cover' hides the reality. And you
should not inform, but communicate (the two 'exercises' are rigorously opposed). Distribute your time and energy in the manner of a humanitarian
association or anti-cancer campaign, brand-name intellectual or statesman in
the videosphere: one-third for the work, two-thirds for getting talked about. Do
not forget that there are only two routes to the position you want: Lot-et-
Garonne or *Paris-Match*, an electoral fiefdom or a strong image. Look at the way
the TV state works, and do likewise: four colour shots on the front cover,
editorials on the first pages, echoes inside, with surveys and factual items filling
the gaps. 'Relational' material on top, facts lower down. The first duty of a
government is to *massage* the public, to supply it with pleasure, with the
superfluous; an agreeable pal, not a heavy father. What is demanded from it
is not knowledge but acknowledgement (placing collective action, in all its
stuttering archaism, in the religious rather than the scientific domain). The
communicator functions like a priest, a tribal sorcerer; the purveyor of facts
disturbs people by needlessly upsetting their certitudes. Tailor supply to
demand.

Was it the inner joy of serving a great cause? The absence of television, make-up,
opinion polls? In Latin America our weapons were pathetic, our plans crazed,
our considerable efforts without much effect, yet when I mull over those years
now they emit an aura of seriousness, something authentic and luminous. And
there were truly radiant moments, times when physical well-being verged on the
unreal; the magical sensations I remember from a solitary exploration on foot of
the mountainous jungles of Bolivia in 1966, a few months before joining
Guevara. From my passage among 'men of power' in France, a 'serious'
situation in a country of repute that counts in the world, I retain – perhaps
because the body had so little to do with the transaction – no memories of pure
or full joy. Despite the interesting foreign visits, the wealth of information
gathered, the vanities of petty importance, I cannot rid myself of a sense of
artificiality and emptiness. Mauriac used to say that in politics one cannot be
happy twice . . .

Now that my 'political divergences' from my then friends, quite sharp at the time although soon blunted, have become part of the thin surface memory that records in us the chronicle of fleeting time, there arises from those pinkish-grey years, like a Scotch mist or the steam over a washbasin, a tenacious impression of sham, but of a kind more *fallacious* than *fraudulent*. It surrounds those people and that slice of life, overworked and driven though it was, in an odd miasma of tarnish, too upsetting to be compensated after the event with a fine melancholy (the authorized penance for 'baneful wanderings').

I believe that quite a lot of us staff veterans and one-time sub-ministers have the same difficulty, which is not at all as people imagine. The sensation of embarrassment, of inglorious confusion, that I retain from those bureau-cratic macerations (along with everyone else, it seems to me, who has had to do with the daily conduct of public affairs) does not come from involvement in or knowledge of 'dirty business', despite the murky reputation of the side-corridors of power (the 'antechambers', the 'seraglio') that makes us associate 'reasons of state' with lurid schoolboy images of villainy, dark machinations, louche intrigues (this 'affair' or that nowadays replacing the poisons, iron masks and secret committees in novels by Dumas and his ilk). Close scrutiny dissolves this romanticism before your eyes. Think, rather, of the way a person might feel at daybreak after a masked ball in dubious company, when the time came to remove the masks and capes: the feeling of having made a spectacle of himself in a bad-taste show. A carnival of studied kindnesses, a staging of magnificent gestures, a deluge of fine speeches put together by others: the absolute opposite of the effective crimes that had been going to spice, for the best of causes, a shadowy 'epic of the national energy' of which, regrettably, not even a chapter unrolled before our eyes (as we watched from the dress circle, when not actually on stage in full savage's costume). I see nothing unworthy or scandalous in a courageous and circumstantial lie, for example a newly elected president's decision not to reveal his cancer. Even under the cover of transparency, such evasiveness is not a hanging offence. That imitation big secret, good for something at least, might almost rehabilitate the real-false passports issued every day by warming up the house, bringing grist to the the media mills. When 'the shadowy side of government' is mentioned these days I cannot help adding silently: 'Yes: *Chinese* shadows', which makes it feel worse. Not: 'What a hole I got myself into,' but 'What a joke it is, all that stuff.' Ponce ponce, blah blah, hey presto, there it is.

It would be useful to have as an excuse the old and respectable 'reason of state' (whose supporters seem to become fewer by the year). That would assume that some reason had been noticed somewhere, connected through some link with a state. The surprising thing about the big and small technicians of that artifice-mill is not their amorality but the shoddiness of the flim-flam they produce. The cardboard men of the communicators' music-hall (Mitterrand was

certainly not one, and neither were the small square of great stewards who kept
the machine going around him, in anonymous and already obsolete dedication
to the service of the state) seemed to me less interesting and perhaps more
morally suspect than the bloodstained figures of literary melodrama (from a
romantic point of view, of course). 'The Elysée' – and I imagine the White
House, the Kremlin or any other place where central mirages are confected
was a magic lantern, updated with audiovisual hardware and a wide spectrum of
'special effects'. The televisual state recalls the Reverend Robertson's famous
fantascope rather than the stage hypnotist Mesmer and his jar, so thoroughly has
the gaudily meretricious come to predominate over other sorts of simulacrum.
'The art of causing spectres and ghosts to appear' bore in the eighteenth century
the engaging name of fantasmagoria. Today we call it politics. It seems
extraordinary in fact that that hysterical daily brew of arc lights and tele-
prompters can elicit anything beyond an 'OK, entertaining, granted, but not
very serious, all those yarns of yours'. True, my taste in cinema runs to Lumière
rather than Méliès: I wasn't designed for the TV state.

Auditory memory: a pervasive rustle and swish, the opposite of guns rumbling
or the tumult of storms. More the sound of barrow-boys fluffing up the
merchandise, engaging in primary falsification by 'presenting a piece of material
to the best advantage by making it appear to contain many thick folds' and thus
seem to the casual shopper longer than it really is. Hustling is a trade, not as
difficult as people make out. After a year or two you learn the knack, and on my
humble level, for my own guidance, I came to identify four levels in the
huckstering scale, in ascending order of importance:

1: Setting up, with fanfare, a top-level *crisis* or *anti-terrorist cell, contact group* or
   task force (a 'crisis cell' at the Quai d'Orsay is someone in an office with a
   telephone, who receives telegrams and AFP despatches on the subject in
   question, classifies them meticulously and wonders what to do with them).
2: Appointing a *roving ambassador* or *personal envoy* from the president to a given
   region (his reports will be ignored, but he will be 'taking the pulse' and
   'keeping in touch'); mounting an *emergency humanitarian mission* (with a lot of
   TV crews).
3: Big-time spectacular international *summits*, with American music and
   prefabricated communiqués; the Council of Europe's *common declaration*
   (instead of action); *big-name reports* on the urgent problem of the day
   (administrative reform, television, drugs, assize courts, inner cities, etc.)
   that no one, least of all their intended readers (president, prime minister,
   ministers and so on) will look at, but that will spawn valorizing ceremonies
   (seminars, relaunches, statements) featuring prominent figures.
4: *Supreme Council* of this, *Consultative Committee* on that, a *Nobel Laureates'*
   Conference in Paris around the President, *World College of Creative Artists*.
   Level 4 is nearly all 'Culture and Communication'. The ultimate in flim-

flam: *culture* completely cut off from the *civilization* of which it is, or ought to be, only a support. The more insubstantial the exhibition, the greater the clamour around it: articles, lead story in late-night current affairs TV, magazine covers. Take away the spotlights and studio audience and all that remains of these prestidigitations is a slight draught, soon gone.

For the 'Elysian staffer' in charge of one of the twenty amenity windows disposed in an aureole about the central rainmaker, the bait is a daily grind resistant to glamorization and devoid of glitter. It consists mainly of receiving petitioners and lobbyists by the bucket, ten or fifteen a day, listening or pretending to, taking ostentatious notes and sending the timewasters about their business delightedly clutching a soothing, analgesic missive couched in due and correct terms. On level zero, the level of the ordinary special adviser – your rank-and-file infantry conjurer – it becomes a game of pass-the-parcel, an unending three-card trick, the petitioner shuffled rapidly from one office – 'sorry, we're not dealing with this' – to another. Looking harassed, the cornered official points down the corridor to the lair of another – 'who will be able to give a case like this the attention it deserves'; he in turn will deplore his colleague's error, and hurry the fellow on to yet another under-secretary. All of this makes a lot of work in itself. Few people have any idea of the astronomical number of obsessive bores who 1) have an urgent, vital, almost insoluble problem and 2) have the front to take it up in person with the president of the Republic, as much from ignorance of the proper channels and administrative mechanisms as from a touching faith – which would be laughable if it were not millennia old and indestructibly magical – in the omnipotence of the curer of scrofula seated under his oak. So each little vicar of the sacred royalty then signs a standard letter, not forgetting to send a copy to the wronged petitioner seen a week earlier so that he will know what is being done about the scandalous injustice he has suffered. The interested party, who does not realize how uninteresting he is or know the code signs for pain-in-the-arse-file-and-forget, will dissolve into effusive thanks and oaths of eternal gratitude. The standard letter from the senior adviser to the under-secretariat of the ministry being 'informed in the most urgent terms' ends with an imperious-sounding: 'Please keep me informed on subsequent developments concerning this matter to which, as I have had occasion to remark in the past, I attach the utmost importance.' Where the eternally grateful one sees the mark of singular generosity and a 'focus' altogether-amazing-at-such-a-senior-level, the addressee will have no trouble decoding the exhortation to 'keep this fellow out of my hair from now on'. The under-secretariat concerned understands the abyss separating the velvety 'Please keep me informed . . .' (not to be confused with 'Would you please . . .', addressed to equals rather than subordinates) from 'Do not fail to keep me informed . . .', the velvet glove pulled back from the iron knuckles to discourage the lower orders from dawdling. Just one level higher – level 1 – is the letter 'signed by the president', on headed paper (sensation guaranteed). There are three or four of these a day, on the general model: *Monsieur le Président* (or *Doyen, Député, Ministre, Secrétaire Général* or simply *Cher ami*, depending on who the high-level petitioner is).

Since learning, with great interest, of your concerns over the problems of (insert summary of matters raised), *I have asked one of my closest associates, Monsieur X, who follows these crucially important matters at the secretariat general, to seek further clarification from the Minister.*

I hope the difficulties that have arisen will be resolved to the satisfaction of the different parties concerned, and in keeping with the best traditions that have always inspired the Republic in this area.

Please accept, Monsieur le . . ., (choice of handwritten civilities, signature in blue ink).

During official visits the make-believe routine will need to be augmented with a slightly (but not excessively) personal, as it were heartfelt, note. This produces timeless allocutions, like the one delivered at the memorable reciprocal dinner given by the president of the Republic at the French embassy in Brasilia for the unmemorable president of the United States of Brazil: 'Allow me to tell you, Mr President – dear friend – how very greatly I value the words that you have just pronounced. Our meeting will be recorded as an important date in the annals of relations between our two countries. Relations that are modern, close and trusting, corresponding to the nature of our two countries, of which your capital offers so admirable and striking an image. It is to the message of friendship and trust you bear, Mr President, that it will be incumbent on us in future to give the response it calls for, that it deserves, that it – why not say so? – demands. So I would like to raise my glass', etc. (I was over 40 when I rendered this signal diplomatic service to my country, but I will brook no allegations of senility).

If there exists a shared professional secret, a slightly shabby connivance between all members of the international tribe, left and right, East, South and West, it is probably a conviction that it doesn't take much to keep the punters amused. The fact is that at heart most of us, subjects, citizens or militants, are a pretty good audience. Throwing dust in our eyes works every time, or nearly.

Having myself laboured inside the rabbit-hat, and even though the dividing line between fraud and music-hall is a blurred one, I am not about to denounce the aces of mystification. It would be demagogy to accuse them of being forgers and horse-dealers fleecing simple folk. A conjurer fleeces no one; he is not a thief; he works to order, like stunt and special effects people in the cinema. Of magic, flourishes and tinsel we can never get enough. Governmental illusionism is a substitute fairyland that compensates for the relative absence of belief in the supernatural. Secretly everyone is whispering to his president, minister or parliamentary deputy: 'Take me in, but in a way that I can believe. So look to your tricks.' In other words I only half believe it, but I expect a good show.

You can see now how very wrong I had got things, to approach them in the spirit of a 'critical mind' dedicated to rooting out the fake. For our duty in fact was to fabricate sham, to keep it in trim, in a word to *ensure* it: all in the higher interests of the market economy.

6. *Be resolutely democratic*, and not delicate (or republican). Have impact. Join the scrum, put yourself about. Think celebrity, not excellence. That is the only worthwhile standard. It is your firepower. It will be counted in your favour at the first glance, and you will need it at the front to survive. While doing so, do not forget to execrate Stalin's famous question at Yalta: 'The Pope: how many divisions?' Nor to observe that the moralists who appear most outraged by such cynicism practise it themselves, not towards the Holy Father (who, as everyone knows, is worth a hundred divisions) but the first person they meet: 'How many votes did *he* get?', 'What's his exposure?', 'How are his ratings?' On the answers to these questions, so deeply incorporated by our peers that they are not aware of asking them, depend the length of the interview, the warmth of the handshake, the extraction of a book from the pile on the desk or an invitation to lunch: in short, the level of consideration. Perforce: since it cannot all be given to everyone, there has to be a criterion. It may also be sensible to see that instant weighing of humans, that art of classifying the living at a glance as heavyweight, middleweight or lightweight, as the most reliable definition of political 'sense' or 'flair', which you would do well to acquire as early as possible. 'So what can I use this man for?': this pragmatic and pertinent question is our common denominator. It converts easily into a modernized 'how many divisions' adapted to the nature of the forces in play during a period of peace: how many electors, readers, viewers? What quota, audience, percentage? What influence, what credibility in his own field? That will allot your working time. I attributed to distraction or fatigue the fact that in 1981, not long before the elections, the sole candidate of the left, at a warm reception where he was to meet his support committee, immediately picked a satirical TV animator and a celebrated songwriter out of the throng. He spent half the party talking privately to these two headline acts from the spirit of the time, avoiding (not carefully: instinctively) the nameless university professors, classical actors and obscure poets, all spiritual authorities in their own fashion, whom his aides were trying vainly to introduce. A very sure visual discrimination, shared by all candidates in the lists (for it is a species characteristic). The instant grading of your neighbour, even in the most banal circumstances, is a professional instinct that Stalin mistakenly formulated on too large a scale. *Politicus* counts in divisions when he makes war; when campaigning he counts in clienteles. Weights and measures as usual, though. Classification by points. To each social species its own standards. What is wrong with that? It cannot be judged in absolute terms, every professional body has its own assessment criteria. It is not – absolutely not – a moral matter, but a professional one (to which the moral conscience should always adapt). My profession has a different sort of box-office: a philosopher does not put his thesis to the vote, a writer does not judge style in the same way as the bestseller list. A theorem and a

poem share the absurd situation of lacking any point of comparison. If they have a value it is exclusive to themselves, once and for all. (What is called 'incompatibility of attitude' is really just a matter of habit. It is not so easy to change one's profession and surroundings. If you want to climb the Eiffel tower, get rid of that backward ballast).

7. *Don't get in a state about 'corruption'.* Avoid it and moderate it, to the extent that these are possible. Be aware that it is inevitable and that there is nothing dramatic about it. It is something gentle and fluid, with no immediate connection with Lichtenstein or kickbacks; something so natural that the corrupt person, like the cuckold, is often the last to learn of his new status. Did someone mention eating his hat? You can chew the edge of it distractedly, thinking of other things. You can gnaw it, nibbling a bit at a time. Without becoming flatulent or getting stomach-ache. Promotional drift continuously postpones the crisis of conscience. I believe I can attest that the upward class mobility of a former 'proletarianoid petty-bourgeois' carried by electoral chance or the long arm of a protector to a 'commanding position' is a process that takes place willy-nilly, as it were behind his back, rather than a firm decision made one morning. A gradual slide with no big words, no sudden renunciation of edifying narratives.

What came to be expressed after the event in purpose-made terms – 'microcosm', 'caviar left', 'pink *nomenklatura*' – impinged on the inner consciousness of the parvenu (if I may use myself as a sample) in the form of incongruities so trivial that it is still embarrassing to mention them ten years later: dressing up in Sunday best every day of the week; climbing nonchalantly into the large silver-grey car that waited outside the flat every morning and sitting next to the driver, in the place favoured by the notable who wants to stay in touch with the people; being called by telephone to a 'working breakfast' at the Plaza-Athénée (a setting for honest toil that I had somehow missed in the past); watching *Rigoletto* one Saturday night from an empty presidential box in a packed opera house; in the hubbub of a cocktail party shaking hands, in an atmosphere heavy with unspoken significance, with a big industrialist, a Lebanese or Antillean offshore tycoon, a TV star all dazzling smiles (something that in earlier times would have seemed neither possible nor really desirable). One soon starts to take pleasure in these embraces from top people one does not know from Adam (or Eve), to take simply and naturally to this connivance between total strangers ('first-class people' forming a single large family that travels in cohorts to Paris, New York or Milan, immutable and smiling as the big business and showbiz from which its figureheads come). Then comes the first official visit in the president's retinue, the fateful day that will take you not to the royal court of Sweden but, two days before departure, to the 'Cor de chasse' to rent tails and a stiff shirt with pearl buttons. 'Obligations' follow one after another, months pass, you toy with the idea of having a dinner suit made to measure instead of cobbling one together out of a paternal jacket, your big brother's trousers and a black bow tie found in a junk cupboard. Meanwhile *Who's Who* has sent you your entry which seems grotesque, but less grotesque than a long corrective letter or, the ultimate in nit-picking coyness, the entry corrected and annotated; so that having neglected to answer at all, you find yourself six months later integrated, co-opted, *dubbed* as one of the 'governing cadres of the nation', to the huge joy of *Charlie-Hebdo*; on seeing which, you decide against the dinner suit after all, renouncing at the same time, with a proud lift of the chin, the die having been cast, all Elysée ceremonies requiring you to dress above your means, or in any case your habits and an 'ego ideal' compulsively shuffled together with invitation cards bearing, lower right, the tragic instruction: *Evening dress*. Abandoning the dinner suit will stop a promising ascent short (society finally consisting of two groups: those who own dinner jackets and the rest, like frock-coats and tunics in the nineteenth century), but at the time will feel more like cowardly relief than monastic dedication if only because this preventive self-denial will save you from having to cry in a shrill voice something like: 'all this, you wouldn't believe it, it's just hilarious actually . . .' when by a sinister coincidence you meet outside your house at twenty past eight in the evening some sniggering 'old comrade' who 'did '68' himself, and is not going to eat, or not just yet, and who cannot quite conceal, at the sight of you getting into a chauffeured Renault 25 disguised as a penguin or a croupier, a look made up of varying proportions (depending on the acquaintance's social background and 'level of expectation', the weight of his address book and the number of his old schoolfellows in the new establishment) of brutal and undisguised envy, Flaubertian compassion for the veteran-of-the-barricades-gone-to-the-bad and Sartreian disapproval of the petty-chief-turned-certified-shit.

The gradual creeping of success seems negligible – as well as delightful – in real time, but its presence becomes more noticeable (or less ignorable) in retrospect: when, as the years pass, 'atypical scandals' involving the fraud squad or 'financial watchdogs', rather than the history of ideas, cease to be funny in close committee and arouse the indignation of newspaper-reading millions when they scan the court reports (for the very unlucky) or the political pages (for the more prescient). Even without such notorious or carceral epilogues, the Versaillais setting for these louche episodes renders the spectacle of someone arriving 'from the left' more saddening, first and foremost to himself, than the advance of an 'arriviste' from the so-called right, considered far more normal. For the latter, except in the electoral setting where such circumstantial remarks are not expected to be followed up, will not have been banging on for years about the 'dirty and murderous reign of money', heartless technocrats, élites cut off from the people before getting himself sponsored into the Siècle club, invited to the Davos forum or taken for a bite by a company chairman at a thousand francs a head. That the corruption of the very young Alcibiades should start with Prince of Wales suits and bespoke shirts from Charvet will make many smile. But everyone knows, with a knowledge not social but physical, that a socialist who stops taking the metro for six months because he has a chauffeur (and if he is important, a bodyguard) is an actor on stage and a potential impostor. Add to the official CX one or two invitations to a prime-time current affairs TV show every quarter, and the volte-face will be natural, elegant, the busy fellow in any case becoming less and less aware of it. Although these anaesthetized collapses, inseparable from so called governmental culture, do not always end in initiate's criminality, facetious analysts sometimes let drop the names *Thermidor* and *Directoire*. A satrap of the Socialist Party, exasperated by such childishness, would ask at this point how a minister of state 'from a modest background', or claiming to be, can remain incorruptible and keep his room in the house of his carpenter friend without becoming Robespierre. (The example of Olaf Palme, the former Social Democrat prime minister of Sweden, suggests that it is not impossible. I overheard him once, after a sandwich dinner eaten off his desk in Stockholm, asking one of his staff to give him a lift home, his official car having gone off duty at eight and his own having broken down).

The vague unease, the slight feeling of guilt I had felt for a few weeks when staying at the Havana Libre hotel for the Tricontinental, pursued me again twenty years later across the carpets of the Elysée palace (although before a year was out, our friends in charge had stopped talking abroad or in public about the 'socialist government of France' and adopted the less misleading term 'French government'). I still feel it today, although I now wander the plains on foot or a bicycle, 'official positions' being a thing of the past, whenever I make common cause with a high-profile parishioner of our dissident intelligentsia, a big fish from my own aquarium; whenever I find myself in one of those 300-square-metre plots situated in the metropolitan bishopric, run by butler and nanny while the master of the house, intransigent on principles and concerned for the oppressed, has his pals served with Moët et Chandon while dictating down the telephone to *Libération* our latest encyclical calling for the immediate despatch of a contingent to save some minority from massacre. Bronzed, just back from a weekend at the Danieli or a week in the Seychelles, chauffeur waiting at the door, our champion – everywhere at ease, familiar with the great, especially the journalists who count, who hardly has time for the interviews requested each day – has no idea what money is, but is second to none at issuing resounding emergency appeals on behalf of groups 'with their backs to the wall and no resources', lambasting at the same time the selfish behaviour of Frog trade unionists and the niggardliness of the ordinary white-collar worker. This strong correlation between personal lifestyle and moral exactingness in politics – which makes our 'human rights' network an aristocracy within the meritocracy that the high intelligentsia already is – in no way detracts from the generosity of the gesture or the validity of the values, crass sarcasms and gibes notwithstanding. But it increases my respect for people who practise what they preach, in whose front rank I would today place Christian militants, the labour priests of the Mission de France, the benevolent laymen of Action ouvrière and others, communist-leaning or similar. Even when intellectual agitators took factory jobs it never occurred to me to become a prof at Sarcelles, and I still frequent the smart quarters, counting myself and being counted one of a meddlesome happy few not much bothered by the hiatus between living and preaching. Indeed the hiatus feeds the omnivorous stylized interventionism and peremptory, slightly wheedling tone that characterize the 'committed intellectual' in all his works and pomps. In that family by alliance, without titles or job obligations, anomaly passes unnoticed. We might be reproached for not doing what we say or not saying what we do, had we not learned to live on one planet and discourse on another without feeling at all stretched by the large gap.

When you are slow in the uptake you can acquire some fairly sticky memories. Allow me to share one with you, an unmissed banana-skin among many others: commonplace, deadly, desperately ordinary, the sort of thing that happens to everyone. How, you may wonder, did I come to be the owner of two superb solid ivory elephant tusks, the gift of a black African despot? Did I have to hunt and kill the elephant? No, a gazelle. Did I have to write a panegyric in Alexandrine couplets, dedicated to a pocket Nero in the huge but debonair form of an NCO president whose jails (I discovered later) were full to capacity? No, an unthinking escape was enough. One winter day, tired out with work, slouching along a Palace corridor with my friend B, I murmured longingly: 'If only I could get away for a week in the sun . . .' It was just a remark, but my excellent comrade (from the African cell) answered, just like that, because he likes to give pleasure: 'Don't give it another thought, I'll fix you up.' Two days later two air tickets landed on my desk, and I got a phone call: 'It's all set, they'll meet you at the airport.'

'Great. What do I owe you?'

'Never mind, we'll see later.'

'Look, really,' I said, 'black Africa . . . I don't know a soul, or the place, a quiet beach is all I need . . .'

'They're terrific guys and they'll show you a royal time. Don't worry about a thing, my buddies are all primed.'

All right. I hung up, relieved, thinking only of what I had avoided: the queue at the Club Med counter, the flight from Orly five hours delayed, the chalet without a sea view, the *table d'hôte* menu under the thatch, etc. All right: first-class flight, chief of the president's staff at the airport, air-conditioned suite in luxury hotel, Canadian lady companion pleased, Elysée functionary delighted. Two days later, like a thunderbolt, an invitation to lunch at the presidential palace. Unrefusable: how could I lounge about swilling and not pay my dues? Out of the question. Warm welcome, exhilarating drinks, mention of friends in common, mad plans. 'I'm taking a turn round the North tomorrow, you can come if you like,' the genial colossus said at the end of the meal.

'Of course. Love to.'

'D'you hunt?'

'When I need to eat, President. Apart from that . . .'

'Just you wait, it's a great way to see the bush.'

Mercedes motorcade, helicopter, herd of gazelles sighted. We land. I fire. Bambis dashing about in all directions, impossible not to hit one, anyway one drops in my line of fire. Uniformed paratroops bustle about. We take off. Whew. Think about something else. Back to the capital, goodbye: we're flying out next day, leaving behind all awkward memories of gratuitous murder. The catastrophe waited until I was climbing the steps into the aircraft, and took the form of a smiling aide de camp hugging in both arms an enormous gazelle haunch (delicate hoof, exquisite long foot, charmingly marked hindquarter, it made you want to cry). 'From the general to you, a memento of happy hunting.' The shame of it: too bloody for a suitcase, too big for a fridge, too perishable for a cabin locker . . . into the hold with it. I get accusing looks: murdering antelopes isn't enough, now the filthy ruffian wants to stockpile cadavers. At Paris airport, general confusion: impossible to leave the package behind, my name was on it. A great bleeding chunk of Bambi on a trolley through the hall before the horrified eyes of my neighbours and their Disney-trained young. How could I get the thing into my flat, and what would I do with it? Could I bury it perhaps in a quiet corner of the Luxembourg Garden? I would need a pick, and the garden is closed at night. Dustbin? The concierge would report me, embarrassing. Somewhere near the porte de Pantin it dawned on me with relief that the object was in fact intended to be eaten. Game . . . venison with small toasted chestnuts . . . Straight on to the Elysée where by sinuous paths I reached the kitchens, my victim bleeding gently under my arm. I was not feeling my best until Marcel Le Servot, the chef-in-chief, agreed in princely fashion to accept the rare proteins in exchange for my peace of mind. 'Say it's from Rambouillet, you don't know who brought it, all right?'

'Say no more.' So my mind was at peace when my doorbell rang a week later. The visitor was from the embassy of the country where I had been on holiday, and bore a parcel as big as himself which he unpacked in my study in front of me: two beautiful curved elephant tusks, each mounted on a wooden plinth. The parcel had been opened and so had the New Year card: could I ask the stranger to wrap it up again and take it away? That would be an affront to the far-off but hospitable and generous donor. Accept the present? That would be passive corruption and constitute a debt against some unknown future return. I chose the lesser of these two evils. The costly ornaments occupied so much space that before long I took them down to the cellar, not without an inward chuckle at the thought of the expressions on my children's faces after my death, at the sight of this puzzling bequest. But my cellar was burgled by chance not long afterwards, so I no longer have before my eyes the ivory stigmata of my all-too-corruptible frivolity. Also by chance, I have not since set foot in that bush, or renewed my acquaintance with its then president. But I richly deserved the murderous page that appeared two months later in the duplicated bulletin put out by that country's young exiled democrats, on the unedifying safaris of an 'alleged ex-revolutionary' now working as a full-time oppressor. That gazelle haunch and those priceless tusks sometimes visit me still in the fastness of the night.

8. *Be ready for solitude.* I know this is not part of the game. Not only was it not in the programme, it was what you hoped to leave behind in your pursuit of the lost collective; for that was your unconscious desire, shared with millions of others: driven by Eros, fleeing Thanatos into Thanatos, the way it has been since the beginning of time, since the first appearance of young volunteers eager to taste the sombre pride of dedication to lowly servitudes. It is to yourself, nevertheless, that you will be delivered, and without ever really having been away from yourself. You will have to come to terms with this. I am not talking about the normal terminal solitude, commonplace and predictable, of one who has resigned or been sacked, lost his job or retired, and who from the moment he is divested of his grade, post or mandate (in state or party apparatus, company, newspaper, local administration, publishing house, etc.) finds his telephone oddly silent, his letter-box unexpectedly empty, the pages of his diary strangely blank. These are just banal and mechanical effects of a functional law accepted by everyone (although it is so banal and mechanical itself that we do not like to talk about it), to the effect that people who can no longer be used (from whom we can no longer expect an appointment, an invitation to dinner or a foreign visit, a subsidy or a decoration) become people to be avoided (in a functional sense, personal considerations aside), whom we remove from our address books without malice, their names quietly fading away of their own accord. I am talking about a solitude of youth, of career, of function and (so to speak) of coming into bloom. The opposite of what you imagined when you heard words like socialism, or nation, or civic awareness, or republic, or people. If these words, different though they are, have a common thread it is the suggestion of something beyond every man for himself, of something above *habeas corpus* and the tedium of being just another island in a shifting archipelago. Probably you were not thinking of celebrating the oceanic unity of the individual and his community with some sort of backward and romantic abolition of your reserve; you are not an idiot, you were not really dreaming of some utopian or monastic communism, a phalanstery, an Icaria in the middle of Paris filled with savages in waistcoats buttoned up the back, sharing their pittance, their bread and butter in the morning and their Boy-Scout singsongs at night, all for one and one for all; you were not planning only to be *one* in the body of the president, minister or first secretary, as some of your predecessors were *one* in Jesus Christ. Without believing yourself to have the soul of a 'knight monk', a sort of Japanese sacerdotal mystic vocation, and without supposing it really possible or even desirable to have egos nationalized like the steel industry, narcissisms collectivized like instruments of credit, you will nevertheless have formed what we might call a militant image of voluntary service, the gift of the self, appropriate to

the grouping of people of different backgrounds and loyalties in the subordinated service of a common ideal. Not the image of an élite corps, a falange or
secret society, a Company of Thirteen, a surrealist 'meeting of friends'; not the
fraternal unanimity of Thebans welded into a sacred battalion, not the totemic
cohesion of Zulus prostrate before the totem or the flag. Nothing like that. But
you may still dare to imagine something in the nature of an inner circle, a
brotherhood of pals, a team or gang spirit, a freemasonry without internal
scheming and furtive deals, as it were a sort of instinctive or unconscious
solidarity between adepts of a certain concept of the world, linked together by a
leader whose life and person embody the common ideal (the underlying
assumption here is that you are a bit tired of being a private individual, still
sensitive to the hoarse sirens of human fraternity, worried about the creeping
disintegration revived by the liberal cult of Mammon: in short that you have the
stuff of a good steward, if not a good comrade).

Need I add that that would take you emphatically in the wrong direction, and
that the secretariat of the palaces of the Republic will bring you quickly back to
earth? That except in the gym and even in the reception room, amid the jostling
of guests (at a Légion d'honneur investiture, a 14 July reception, a symposium of
French mayors, etc.) you will be left rather to yourself? Alone in your official car;
alone in your office decorated with a Nicolas de Staël borrowed from Mobilier
national, your little garnet-velour command post for the protocol or registry
official, son of prudence and friend of the career. You will have become one of
the *novi viri* of your day, a representative of the famous upwardly mobile layers
that periodically admit newcomers, because the destitute and the dominated
periodically put their trust in dominators-to-be who have learned how to speak
to the poor before learning to behave properly, before going to Chez Edgar,
Neuilly, Saint-Cloud golf club, the Bagatelle polo ground, the Jockey-Club, the
Racing, the Interallié, Mégève, Roland Garros; the strategic sites of a class that
knows how to make room for newcomers to save the furniture. So: welcome to
the club. Nothing wicked about it, a banal mechanical alternation, periodical
and predictable.

I can hear the cries of protest from here at such facile disillusionment, such
sour, no, sarcastic, no, *neurasthenic* denigration. I may be accused of extrapolat-
ing. With some justice: we served, my friends and I, a great solitary. A separate,
secretive man, an individualist marvellously adept at shuffling the organizational
diagrams around him to compose unpredictable, short-lived, upside-down
hierarchies, and who tolerated no groups, only networks (competing, juxtaposed
and operable by him alone, as and when needed). That fine capacity for solitude
provided us with the best possible training in the environmental law that the
man of power, in a competitive society, is a solitary with contacts. It is the
number and variety of your connections that will measure your power: who you
get through to on the phone; the number of buttons on your squawk-box
console, surmounted if possible by a prominently placed 'scrambler'; the

acoustic wire that puts the actor in direct, unfiltered and instantaneous contact with the other actors, the activated members of the network. That does make for a sort of confraternity, but a strictly utilitarian one, a closed loop leading nowhere. It cannot galvanize any collective movement on the periphery; it can only excite a wish to be part of it, a jealousy to succeed, to acquire for oneself a nice eiderdown of connections. It will not form an *alternative society* amid the ambient pursuit of profit; it will endorse the all-conquering competitive society and recycle it. Ethics are collective or do not exist (who is alone in his belief?). All the busy, highly gifted, over-educated people who surround you, telephoning each other all day long, will have *nothing to fall back on*: no labour tradition or trade union dynasty; no militant past or sense of an organizational nobility, like Swedish or even German social democrats. They will know no songs of struggle, or of the great obsequies held for socialist leaders, away from cathedrals and *Te Deum*, in the streets, at the Labour Exchange or in black-draped town halls (as in Stockholm for the atheist funeral of the murdered prime minister, with the violet oriflammes and claret flags of the Party sections, ranged in their hundreds behind the gun carriage bearing the coffin). They will know nothing of the secular train of socialism and communism, the numbered congresses, the splits and rows; nothing of a different sort of honour which had its own rules, rituals and banners; all that is a dead letter these days; laying bare the individual tactics, individual covetousness, individual biographies, without the weight conferred (or the obligation imposed) by those banners that come from behind us and carry us forward. Nothing in short but nice careers, in good form, *comme il faut*, no dud moves, with the same measured and dispiriting cordiality that is already part of you at an age when others were singing the *Chant des partisans* . . . 'How-are-you-my-dear-fellow?', 'Will-your-lady-wife-be-coming?'

Proper career management presupposes of course a knowledge of upward or downward price movements in that stock market of naturally fluctuating reputations, in which your own stock will quickly become one of those to be watched (among some hundreds of others). So you will need to *review your position* at least once a week at one of the hierarchical adjustment rituals known as cocktail parties or receptions (at the Elysée, ministries, embassies, national and foreign institutions, etc.). If your price for the day is unknown to you, others (there for the same reasons as you) will let you know what it is within minutes; have faith in the invisible hand of the market, which imposes on a worldly bustle, apparently random and Brownian – made up of thousands of sidesteps, fleeting private exchanges, sheerings-off and turning movements – a fine-grained, ordered structure that you will need to decode pretty quickly. The order is based on the dominances prevailing in the Establishment at moment *x*, a shifting system whose preponderances are permanently subject to renegotiation, but which parties of this type enable one to register and adjust via a multitude of kinetic messages – postural, vocal and optical – passing between the components contained in a closed flask. The volume and emphasis of the *cheramis* (stress on

first syllable, good sign; on the second, worrying); the evasiveness or otherwise of
acquaintances' glances intercepted across the room; the centrifugal or centripetal stirring of those around you from the moment you step through the door,
will serve as preliminary pointers. The mêlée will be intense, so keep cool.
'What's it about?' as Marshal Foch used to ask when complications arose. The
answer is, a group in fusion, with fluctuating fringes and a centre which is
generally moving (the Guest of Honour or the Host, President of the Republic,
Prime Minister or super-tycoon), within which each important guest navigates
through a multitute of random vicissitudes and obstacles following a simple
logic: trying to clamber up the shifting slopes to reach the Centre (itself in
perpetual movement) against the constant efforts of other, less sought-after
guests to drag him back down. Eyes swivelling to detect the next threat, to avoid
in the nick of time, with a matador's grace and economy, the approaching bore
who will buttonhole and distract him with a usurper's slimy and insincere
cherami, each Important man is trying to disengage from someone less important,
himself on the lookout for a bigger and better grandee. These hundreds of
gyratory and countervailing eddies repose on a shared feeling, carrying hope for
some and fear for others, that celebrity and non-celebrity are contagious: to be
seen conversing with an Important Person makes you important, but, by the
same token, to be seen in prolonged conversation with an unknown, however
enterprising, is to risk having your stock marked down. Reaching the Centre
therefore requires a laborious zigzagging approach involving frequent detours
and blind alleys, a discipline hard for the uninitiated to acquire. Do not allow
yourself to be put off by this difficulty; the physical techniques appear of their
own accord; your gestural sequences will coordinate automatically with those of
others. An unstable mixture of cruelty and elegance, brutality and ease, this
ritualization of dominances provides for the natural and spontaneous regulation
of collective life in the closed environment, as it would for a troupe of macaques
in a cage. So the sensory and motor diagrams of these adaptive ceremonials will
become your own second nature in the space of a few months. You will soon
start to find at these gatherings higher-flying contemporaries who can no longer
shake your hand, and there will come a time when you can gauge your exact
value not by the length of a glance or the swiftness of a retreat but from finger
pressure, by touch alone, with closed eyes. You will discover that the rhythmic
movement of aligned forearms to which the hurried ethnologist reduces the
'exchange of a handclasp' in the West covers, in reality, three radically different
signals. The first – a pressure of the thumb on the back of the adverse hand,
accompanied by an oblique outward movement of the arm – indicates to a
dangerous acquaintance that one is greeting him pre-emptively, because one has
to, but that one would very much like him to get out of the way. The second –
when the oblique movement is inward and the thumb grips the other's hand
firmly, drawing him forward – shows that one knows him well enough superficially to stop in his company for a minute or two and exchange a few words in

front of everyone. The third is a more anodyne but wilier gesture, revealing nothing of the person's own opinion and leaving the other on standby, victim of a generalized doubt about his share price that can only undermine him severely. This is the provisional handshake, a neutral affair with no forward, backward or sideways pressure, straight up and down along a sadistically vertical axis. Train yourself. Neutrality is the tactic of Masters who, in those speculative social bubbles, know how to keep up the uncertainty without giving this or that person too much hope, but without taking it all away at the outset either. I have met experts who as a result of these repeated exercises can terminate a conversation with the abrupt subtlety of a Glenn Gould or a parliamentarian of the Fourth Republic.

Do not imagine that these delicacies of comportment are for the exclusive use of *Politicus* in private. Intellectuals, who worry incessantly about their images and their greater or lesser ascendancy over those around them (without making beauty of form or the truth of things their first concern, like artists or scientists), are no less adept than politicians and their aides in the social assessment of the *socius*, the accurate and unforgiving estimation of the relative weight of their colleagues. Our Parisian tribe's ballet of civilities, of which the annual Le Seuil cocktail party in early June offers a convivial, verdant snapshot, can boast an inflexible certainty of trajectory in its star dancers, a scientific exactitude of measure in the reciprocal salutations of the corps de ballet, with spot-on synchronized halts and hierarchical regroupings, that make the comparatively unstructured gatherings of the 'politico-mediatic gentry' seem rough and ready by comparison. It would not surprise me if a comparative ethnography of these two tribes discovered that the ritual parades of Matignon, the Senate and the Assembly involve developments, meetings and individual avoidances apparently more gratuitous, or less easily explained, than the ones calculated to the second, to the millimetre, that occur between two thousand intellectuals, none of whom can bear any of the others, crammed for an evening into 1,000-square-metre space edged with three buffets and ten potted plants.

The truth has to be dressed up in paradoxes: naked, it would be too shocking. If I have adopted a somewhat facile bantering tone with you it is not, or not solely, to deliver the disdainful sprightliness expected of a downy old bird addressing his juniors. Remember that the spiritual is the excuse for the scientific, as 'humour is the courtesy of despair'. All the codicils I have hastily appended to the testament of the great Italian refer to things I have seen, heard, done or recorded. Do not go believing, though, that because none of this is false it must contain the whole truth. Below the waterline, fortunately, there is the technostructure, which is the essential thing. Space rockets, telecoms, oil, oceans, aircraft and satellites are serious matters intolerant of pretence. What remains of the state in France is clinging to these public and semi-public enterprises, and you can still find (but not for much longer, hurry) 'decent people' serving the general interest, who do their work scrupulously and honestly. It's true there is too much talk about sleazy individuals and not enough about honest ones. I have met some. Names? Why not? Do you take me for a man of letters sailing about in the flies on a rope, far above all contingencies? Afraid to take sides with or against anyone? Be assured that I can name a lot of old colleagues from those years at the Elysée: Hubert Védrine (that independent spirit), Jean-Louis Bianco, Christian Sautter, François Strasse, Jean-Daniel Lévi, Elisabeth Guigou, Michel Vauzelle and many more. I did not share all of their ideas; our life options differ; but it is good to remind oneself that under the gilt plasterwork there are also men and women who strive honourably to bring a little order to the ambient chaos.

4

On Fidelity

A painful letter – Betrayal is something others do – Two forms of fidelity, Chinese and Japanese – A coincidence: I quit and am sacked – Imagewise, always expect the worst – How does one learn to break away? – I have never been a free man – An incalculable debt – A saint: Pierre Brossolette – 'The advantages of a good position'

I take no pride in my disavowals. They cause me much remorse, keep me awake in the small hours. Dissecting a dying boss to whom you owe what little respectability you have, and with whom you once enjoyed close relations, only ten years after swearing to serve him; betraying his trust; spitting in his soup; stabbing him in the back; a midget who has climbed onto a giant's shoulders to make himself taller: we are all familiar of course with these ready-made phrases, these facile words from corridor and dinner-table gossip. I have no need to listen outside doors. The internal monologue does the job.

No aspect of political commitment is more important than fidelity. Far more important than it is in love, if we can separate these two expressions of the same folly; if we can forget for a moment that political passion, far more than the authorized homosexual collusion of machos, was the characteristic eroticism of the twentieth century (devotion to a cause being as inseparable from attachment to a leader as sexual need from erotic desire). Nothing is so intolerant of fooling about as anything that touches on the only morality that counts in this area. We should not be amused by Casanovas of the forum: they pollute the sacred space and encourage the barbarians. Even at the risk of boring people with minutiae and trivia, I mean to answer the most serious question seriously. As we answer the letter of a friend, a scolding from an intimate who, watching from a distance, sees us in a clearer light. An *examination of conscience* in connection with events of no importance may still have a small role in deciphering the human heart: the only excuse for the absurdity of talking about oneself.

Paris, 18 June 1990

My dear Régis,
    Your whims are leading you astray and I find them disconcerting. Do you really believe that you can work for the election of a head of state, then be rewarded with a job envied by all, given a special status over opposition in a hostile environment, sent on prestigious missions and

appointed to the Conseil d'Etat – and still expect to pass for a neutral man, withdrawn and detached? To be exact: unattached?

The fact is that none of these posts involves service to the state alone. On the contrary, they all depend on the whim of the head of state. On the trust he placed in you – that you deserved to have placed in you.

I myself never actually said that I was breaking with Mitterrand. Quite simply because I never made the act of allegiance. It is you who, at the end of a book (which I like) and an interview (slapdash), haphazardly blurt out your disappointment, your regret, your mortification. Owing, myself, nothing to the government, expecting nothing from the Prince, I have been free to alternate surprised eulogies with disenchanted indictments, dithyrambs with prosecutions. I was offered an ambassadorship in 1982, and turned it down. I could easily have been wrong. Rumour has it that you wanted to be a minister under Roland Dumas and were turned down. I would have been pleased if you'd got it. Our situations are not the same . . .

It was Jean Daniel who wrote this cauterizing letter after I had published a slim volume dedicated to de Gaulle (to mark the centenary of his birth), following my divorce from my boss, Daniel's friend. To answer him without being misleading, I am going to have to explore my own cellars, not the most glittering of places. I would not have reproduced the private, excoriating and not unfounded reproaches of the director of the *Nouvel Observateur* if they did not reflect some of my own feelings about my bad act: how sickening I thought myself after that manifest U-turn. On the Way of the Cross of a political education, defection (perjury, felony) is the most painful station, but also the most crucial: 'dies and is born again'. Better perhaps to die in politics than to seek rebirth . . .

First of all, remember that it is others who betray, by nature. And especially public figures, whom we are too inclined to criticize for contradictions, if not dereliction of duty, exposed as they are by the publicity that attends their acts and sayings, more fully recorded than our own. Exposed to the iniquitous calumnies of the ignorant (like the talented former prime minister pilloried for a contaminated blood scandal which is not his fault). Apart from different levels of vulnerability caused by the lighting (some working under floodlights, the rest of us in relative obscurity) and the objective risks of the profession (infinitely greater where hazardous advance is part of the work), a dilettante will have the best chance of matching the metamorphoses of a 'pro' by playing simultaneously to the stalls and the gallery. This is the common lot of humanity, from which I am no exception. We may well know that behind the deceptively unitary façade of a physiognomy (which misleads by appearing recognizable) a man is a randomly furnished shack; we may well know how different this double agent is from the unitary image others have of him, and even from the one he has of himself; but we still expect more homogeneity and perhaps more personality from those around us, especially if they are well known, than we do from ourselves. So we are more intolerant of other people's divergences than of our own, which we minimize automatically. What will seem, in reviewing our own past lives, to have been a necessary and natural *shedding* or *adaptation*, in others will become a deplorable *recantation*. And just as our own *profitable audacity* is blatant *trickery* when practised by a rival, I am not going to deprive myself of calling my adversary's *touch on the tiller* a *U-turn*. That is how it is: we limp ourselves but expect our representatives to walk straight. We give ourselves the right to be inconsistent, to be pathetic specimens almost incapable of living with ourselves; but if by chance the president and prime minister seem to contradict one another at some foreign conference we call it a cacophony, jeer about too many chiefs and not enough Indians, whine that France is no longer being governed. We would all rather sin through excessive rectitude than excessive inconsistency; it is so much more respectable to end as a martyr to your ethic than as a victim of circumstances.

'Look in the mirror, old boy, before mouthing off.' We should welcome the mocking objection as an old friend. It educates. 'To the best of my knowledge' (as the pro says before specifying that he is speaking 'for' someone else, just in case an unexpected contrary fact is produced), there is nothing in the looking glass to justify the famiar 'Who? Oh, *that* guy, former leftist turned Mitterrandist . . . neo-Gaullist now I think . . .' (laughter). Try as I may to hustle myself into line, to look from every angle, to cite in the mocker's support our vicious penchant for seeing ourselves in the best light (has-never-budged-an-inch-in-his-convictions), I cannot recognize myself in this unwelcome similitude. If (as I have already said) the name 'leftist' has a meaning, it is not one that applies to me: immediately on returning to France in the aftermath of '68, I took the line that if profound change was possible at all it could only be in a legal and electoral context (and earned the animosity of the local extra-parliamentarians). In 1972, 'on the basis of that analysis', I rallied to Mitterrand, stretching a point somewhat to lend him a Gaullian vocation (so given are we to wishful thinking). I do not disavow this support for the only possibility of the time, even though he was not the hoped-for ideal. As for my 'Gaullism', I hope there is nothing partisan or opportunist about it, let alone improvised. At the risk of falling into the error I have just described, I grant myself where doctrine is concerned one 'moult' and only one, or (for the detractor) one apostasy and not two: the one that started around 1968 at the end of my first apprenticeship, causing me to abandon Marxist-revolutionary faith in the rational cosmopolitan unity of the oppressed, as I became aware of the national (and more broadly, mental and cultural) bedrock, and of the enviable singularities of the republican model. Since that time I may have vacillated in my assessment of individuals, of their greater or lesser capacity to maintain the republican-national idea in France, but have not altered my way of interpreting events (and everything seems to indicate that, through a mixture of laziness and resignation, I shall not do so again).

Nor will I allow myself – although playful by nature like all writers, revelling in the privilege granted by my trade of being loyal primarily to my own destiny – to judge a politician by the politician's two *idées fixes* (when he succumbs to *his* trade's tendencies): 'everyone is changing except me'; and 'my adversaries must be dishonest, or they would not be my adversaries'. François Mitterrand was too subtle to give way to this last vulgarity, 'the disastrous tendency of small men' as Lawrence called it, whose equivalent among wits would be the conviction that 'no one shall be witty but ourselves and our friends', which generates such intense sniping among the intelligentsia. He was enough of a professional on the other hand to be able to change Utopias in midstream (for such is the genius of *Politicus*: knowing how to adapt to ambient conditions). And was accordingly led into swapping the socialist utopia for a Europeanist one at half-time. It was for the first of these that I joined up in 1974 and 1981; no one mentioned 'federal Europe' at the time outside the enemy camp, whose beacon it had become. But instead of taking a different course from that of his predecessor Giscard d'Estaing, as he quite reasonably announced he would when campaigning against him, he followed tamely in his footsteps. So we witnessed a socialist advancing the cause of advanced liberalism, a layman encouraging private education,[7] a man elected by state employees ratifying the dismemberment of the public services, the signatory of a party congress motion calling for a break with capitalism adopting the country's most right-wing finance policy since the Liberation, and a declared Jacobin in the country of Colbert and Napoleon putting his shoulder to the wheel of a Hanseatic Europe. Why deny him the right to change, or worse still impute this last decision to mediocre motives ('whatever helps me survive . . .')? Lacking system in this area myself, I cannot reasonably play the Cato and condemn zigzags, left-handed strokes and contortions. We all know that there are no straight lines in politics, as in art (where no one accused Picasso of betraying his principles by abandoning the blue period for the pink) or love (where polygamous men can be sincerely fond of the women they betray). 'Governing' means taking the helm, and no ship sails a straight course: tacking is often needed. My own *non possumus* was more trivial. As an amateur, I can afford the luxury of simple faith, even if it means sacrificing 'position' and 'situation': in my case these are not sacrifices, I do not need them to live, having other sources of income and other ways of attracting attention, other vanities to my bow. Indeed I can only gain in reputation by playing the conscience card, like a gossip columnist when a new editor changes his paper's line. I took full advantage, to the point of holding my nose in front of the cook. To the point of suspecting that the captain's sole objective was to stay on the bridge. To the point of uttering sententious criticisms: 'Politics, my lord, involves small compromises in the service of a great idea; not the inverse.' Who was I to talk down to him like that? A nobody, a philosopher caring for nothing but his little backroom idea and given, like others of his pretentious species, to telling practitioners of the art what is what. To each his own art. Let us try at least to be professional in our amateurism, and avoid ranging ourselves with the best people in the 'morality of conviction', thus leaving the 'morality of responsibility' (that insoluble antithesis of political science) in the hands of the worst. It is no harder, in the final analysis, to escape from reality into ideals than to flee from the ideal into reality. Which of these two contrary defections is the lesser will depend on the role we are allocated during casting, which decides whether idealism or realism, credulity or low cunning, is to be our professional deformity, our little peccadillo. My mistake was imagining a third term or happy medium to be possible. Since everything from my body to my education inclined me to moral truth and theory, I wanted to conquer my inclinations and make myself useful by getting my hands dirty (others progress from an interventionist itch to quasi-Buddhist abstentionism). I did not get too dirty, but nor was I any use. There is contentment in remaining marginal, preferable to the delights of what I have rather carelessly called 'corruption'. As to whether it is preferable to count for nothing in the play of forces, or to count principles for nothing and influence forces and events, leave the book open at the 'Personal Options' page. And turn up at the Père Lachaise cemetery on May Day each year, along with a few dozen other scatterbrains, to drop your red rose at the foot of the mur des Fédérés: a pious gesture, pathetic but necessary, at the mass grave of the last communards, to warm your old bones with a last gleam of sunshine, and of fidelity.

Confucius held it to be the highest virtue; would he have agreed with Shôtoku Taishi, regent for the Empress Suiko and a good Confucian, who included the following in the *Constitution of the seventeen articles*: 'Submit absolutely to the purpose of the emperor'? There are two fidelities, a greater and a lesser: Chinese and Japanese, to oneself and to one's suzerain. Fidelity to *what*, or fidelity to *whom*? In China one should be loyal first to oneself, to one's conscience; in Japan the duty of obedience to one's superior has primacy. Under Japanese feudalism a man might have to betray his own conscience out of fidelity to his master; while a Chinese vassal, knowing what he owed to himself, might have to betray his master. Shall we be Chinese or Japanese? 'Fidelity', what crimes are committed in your name . . . 'Betrayal', how many absurd suicides and needlessly uneasy consciences . . . All those criminal fidelities, all those loyal betrayals . . . A communist who, in 1935 or 1955, publicly admitted the infamy of Moscow show trials or forced labour in Siberia, was betraying his own people, the Party, everything that gave meaning and unity to life: he was 'howling with the wolves', 'joining the rush for spoils', 'objectively serving the enemy'. But this intelligent deserter was not betraying the idea of socialist revolution; like the Trotskyists he was trying to save it from disaster by dragging it back from an execrable configuration. Whereas the blind comrades were utterly betraying the Idea they purported to serve (and in whose name they condemned the clear-sighted to death or obloquy). Easy enough so far; but is it really, on closer examination? Weakening the Party meant, unarguably, blighting the revolution's chances. Could there be a proletarian revolution in the West that excluded and opposed the main workers' party: custodian of the Idea, fabricator of cadres and troops? Was there a third way for an honest man, sitting on the fence, playing the ostrich? It would mean refusing either to support or denounce the way things were going, staying silent to avoid playing anyone's game. But as Simone Weil said, 'by not wanting to know, you can end up incapable of knowing'. And here we are again: where is honour in the final analysis, when we have seen Aragon (like Géricault in *La Semaine Sainte* choosing during the Hundred Days to follow Louis XVIII against the sons of the revolution) staying to the end in a Stalinist party he privately execrated, 'honourably choosing dishonour'? When so many have taken pride in wanting to be slaves? It is all very well to say we should choose the lesser of two betrayals; but we still need to know whether fidelity of the heart or the mind, Tokyo or Peking, is the more important, and on this point of course there will never be unanimity. Everyone must work out their own answer, which will depend partly on age: we tend to begin our careers as fanatical samurai and end them as old Manchu sages. And on profession: an individual drawn to ideas, intrigued by values and projects, will first ask 'to what?'; for a soldier, a man of heart, an acolyte, who rates feeling higher than ideology, the question will be 'to whom?'. Like a baccalauréate essay on moral philosophy so far, but unfortunately it is more complicated than that, for our friends get ideas about having hearts too. Is the ideologue never to know the savour of bread broken at the family table, daydreams disclosed under the beeches, confidences exchanged beside the inglenook while the mushrooms are browning, with truffle and armagnac? And that childhood friend, the good sort who never bothered much with programmes: surely he too has his little ideas, his own coherence, worth as much in its way as something more pompous and abstract? I am afraid no good answer is possible to this baccalauréate question; they would all be weak or infelicitous. But that will never deter anyone from from throwing stones at 'rotten planks', for nothing soothes the human conscience better than a good lynching.

The fact is that the thinker, heavily handicapped in this matter of loyalty, is easier to lynch than the man of feeling. He is wedded to the logic of ideas, when it is the destiny of people of power to follow the logic of forces. Rigorous and abstract, the intelligence demands straight lines, while the will zigzags to align with events: this naturally inclines the intellectual to betray the politician. The philosophic *what* turns against the political *who* because that *who* is willing to go along with almost anything. The play of forces changes much faster than our ideas, good or bad; the man in the thick of affairs has moved his rifle from one shoulder to the other three times before the ideologue beside him notices that the orthodoxy has changed. Nevertheless it is the practitioner, symbolizing for the masses the cause he flouts in deed, who will ultimately determine what is straight and what is deviant. That is how it is. Don't cry: try instead to enjoy the rare moments when ritual and faith coincide. There is no greater joy than the simultaneous presence of the two fidelities, to one's conscience and to a chief: a happiness that seldom lasts, that goes with beginnings, before the road and one's credo diverge; hence the universal love of preliminaries (I have started ten novels and finished only two, reluctantly in both cases: to finish something is to close it down). Let us not moralize these inevitabilities; to each his own inclination, his own gut feeling. His lesser evil. But find out what it is in advance: no one brushes these thorny matters without leaving something behind.

Like the ideologies supplanting one another at the front of the procession, the disappointed follow each other down the path of the *isms*, more alike than they realize and certainly more alike than the *isms* themselves. After the ghosts of 'totalitarian communism' come those of 'democratic socialism'. I would not be so crass as to confuse a word-mill running on empty with a machine for pulverizing human beings; the costs of disengagement are less where the commitment is shallower; but it is always from within that the worst reprisals come, his own accusing finger that the former devotee must face. Homage makes the man. When we break the protective shell of our faith, what collapses is part of ourselves, and through our own fault: unfrocked and reborn, a believer sinks without trace. The privatization of allegiances that followed the dissolution of the old collective frames of belief has not rendered defection more painless: quite the contrary. 'Communist intellectuals' (in the days of Claude Roy, Roger Vaillant or Edgar Morin) maintained close and intense relations with a ghost – the Party – whose leaders lived far away, came from a different social class, inhabited another planet. There were no 'socialist intellectuals' to take over from them (fortunately for social democracy); but there were 'friends of the first secretary' and 'associates of the president', and instead of 'position statements' and 'letters to the Central Committee', a game of rewards and disgraces, squabbles and idylls. *De jure* adhesion was replaced by *de facto* allegiance, although without oaths of fealty; the comrades of yesteryear by liegemen. These personal links, having got people appointed, subsequently caused an excess of pain and reproval, a divergence of ideas being far easier to forgive than a breach of friendship. In passing from the totalitarian world to the democratic, apostasy changes keys from major to minor. But what is lost in religious grandeur is recovered in personal outrage: something that bleeds less, but grates more. Everything will grate, to tell the truth. Staying in the clan, seeing and hearing no evil, stoical under the slanderous baying of the press pack and the deluge of scandals, will not save the faithful companion from opprobrium. Everyone will have the regulation amount of that for his grade. Losing face either way: loyal to the boss, an opportunist; loyal to the Idea, a quitter. Which epithet will survive us longer? An illustrious example should put people on the right track: for remaining faithful to Plato and his school, without feeling any obligation to the cult of an Oriental guru fashionable at the time, Jesus known as the Christ, the Emperor Julian, whose first loyalty was to his city and his ancestors, is known for all time as the Apostate. If you follow your benefactor through dubious byways without saying a word you will have bartered your ideal for a mess of pottage, intimidated by a Montaigne quote: 'A courtier cannot have either the duty or the wish to speak and think other than favourably of a master who, out of thousands of other subjects, has chosen to feed and raise him with his own hand.' If on the other hand you expose the master's unreliability by mentioning the programmes, now scrapped, that drew you into his service in the first place, you are a treacherous courtier using big words to vent your sour disappointment.

And it could well be that your accuser has a point. It is not all that easy to establish which is more important in a decision to jump ship, a half-instinctive calculation of interests (from now on I am losing more than I am gaining) or an objective awareness of disagreement, wounded narcissism or frustrated idealism. Does one leave a warm tribe like Mitterrand's because one sees the ideal being eclipsed, or because one is tired of embracing shadows? Does it open a man's eyes to be set aside by the Prince, or is he set aside because his eyes have opened (and the Prince, nobody's fool, has noticed)? Moral honesty demands that one ask these questions; and perhaps intellectual honesty forbids one to answer them, for the essence of political ambition is to mobilize indiscriminately the best and worst of an individual: they can be unravelled *post-festum*, on paper. To use myself as a poor example of this general rule: I resigned in 1988 because I could no longer see anything socialist (something I could have lived with) or even, at base, anything republican (much more painful) in the general policy followed by my associates, whom the rather tired epithet 'unprincipled compromise with the system' fitted like a glove. A few months earlier, by a strange coincidence, I had applied to run the Mission for the Bicentenary of the Revolution and at the same time was being considered as a possible secretary of state for the South Pacific, or for 'relations with developing countries' under the foreign minister. On the first of these, the president of the Republic said he was sorry, but he had learned of my candidature too late, after Jean-Noël Jeanneney had accepted the post; on the second, that the need for balance, political as well as administrative, militated against drafting a somewhat peculiar citizen into an already over-weight new government. Six months later the whisper went round: 'Oh yes, that guy . . . did a lot of scheming for a job; got put in his place and scuttled off somewhere. They're all the same really.'

Since the featherless biped is normally content with the bird's-eye view, why look any closer? For the specimen, though, this sort of thing is unjust and upsetting. Even if it means sinking into trivia and infamy, let me explain. After following the preparations for the Bicentenary of the French Revolution at the Elysée for two years, after faithfully supplying and serving the Mission, first under Baroin, then, after his death, under Edgar Faure until *his* death; after seeking a replacement for Edgar Faure for three months, sounding out five personalities for the job, and after the last of these, Jean-Noël Jeanneney, in my office made his acceptance subject to legitimate and understandable conditions that I thought would not be accepted, I said the next evening to the president: 'In the end, if we can't find anyone, since I know the whole dossier – inside out actually – I could do it myself.' Not a hope: at breakfast that very morning, he had persuaded Jeanneney to sign up. And a good thing too, he was an excellent choice. 'We're saving you for '93,' Charasse (a sharper man than he looks) told me kindly. The small setback suited everyone: mine was obviously the wrong image for the tone these ceremonies were to be given (it is true that I had something very different in mind, had I been given the job). On the other point, the 'ministerial' job, this is what happened. Just before the legislative elections in 1986, a South Pacific Council had been set up at my suggestion to repair the damage caused by the Greenpeace affair. I was its secretary-general. If we wanted to continue testing nuclear weapons to safeguard the country's strategic autonomy (a credo I wholeheartedly shared) and ensure acceptance of a French military presence in the region, without which the Mururoa tests would become problematic, we needed to rethink and reorganize, but first to unify, all the services having any role in these areas. After a very good start, the Council was sidelined from 1986 to 1988 under pressure from the right (which would not attend meetings with an extremist reeking of brimstone). By 1988, when our side was back in the saddle, it was clear that unless this administrative coordination body was given a minimum of political authority and continuity, everything would go to pot and France, in the Pacific and elsewhere, would soon run into a brick wall. I knew enough about the region and the thorns of Mururoa to be able to see that. Personally, I had no particular wish to go back to loafing about in Canberra, Wellington and Papeete, but I believed sufficiently in deterrence, and the wider margins of autonomy it provides, to 'give in to affectionate pressure from my friends' if I had to. I strongly doubted that nuclear deterrence (one of the cornerstones of a 'national independence' written into the heart of the Constitution but whose very utterance sounded backward, if not ridiculous, to its custodians) seemed important enough to the leadership to justify much sacrifice in domestic policy terms; I knew that the Bomb was repugnant to the ecological movement, then riding high, whose support was needed to shore up a fragile majority; that our increasingly Europeanist country, green or pink, was already excluded from involvement in distant overseas matters or bothering with a global policy (for which everyone knows it 'no longer has the means'); and finally, that our 'living forces', along with most of the European ruling classes, had already privately chosen Washington and its executive agencies (NATO and the Atlantic Alliance) as the cheapest option for 'ensuring stability', even in Europe itself. But like a mistress tired of hole-and-corner and longing to be taken to a first night at the Opéra, I *also* felt it was high time to establish what I ought really to be doing. Would he dare at last to 'bring me out'? Advertise the connection? Admit to everyone our long-established but inconvenient association? Motives both civic and uncivic, national and self-serving, confused and entangled. As for the Conseil d'Etat, that final joke and ultimate giveaway, to which I should never have been appointed, it was not so much a financial lifeline for a worrier (especially as a new member earned under 20,000 francs a month at that time) as a consolation prize for a rejected academic. In 1984, toying with the idea of tiptoeing quietly out of the Elysée, I had gone to some trouble to be admitted to the CNRS as an 'administrative engineer technician', the lowest grade in the hierarchy of researchers; I was going to join a laboratory researching international relations, where I looked forward to pursuing my studies on Latin America. A motion hostile to my presence was then passed at the Centre: I was given to understand that people took a very dim view of some incompetent pseudo-intellectual being parachuted in on a nod from the Prince (who was not involved any way). An impostor can take everyone in except his own circle. No one bothered to inform me. That was my first glimpse of the fate that awaited me at the hands of the constituted bodies representing the Mind, for having rolled in the filth of officialdom. On discovering this, the excellent Paul Legatte offered me a start in a minor post. Appointed in 1985 to the external list (like a third of the Conseil), I was placed at my own request on the unpaid reserve list on 1 July 1988. It has not escaped me that those three years spent unaesthetically and immorally at the taxpayer's expense, in addition to an ordinary regular job, justify the worst suspicions.

Weighing everything up, what really counts? The beam oscillates. On the scales of my memory, political frustration wins; on the scales of rumour, the spleen of thwarted ambition. Do I need to spell out which has come out on top?

An honourable motive is no more likely to get across the footlights than an intellectual subtlety. Only the lowest sort of message can pierce the ambient indifference. Our pettinesses are easier to spot from a distance than any worthy or estimable aspect we may have. This paradoxical focus, specific to moral space, inverts the proportions of physical space. What seems to us negligible or secondary about ourselves, irrelevant or even non-existent, will have a central and looming presence in the visual field of our neighbour. There is nothing to be done about it: the mediocre is more communicative than the rest. This is a law of social exchange, analogous to that of falling bodies or linked vessels, on which our contemporary media, which did not invent it, operate like a magnifying glass. The result is that our 'societies of communication', joyously and mis-chievously given to derision of every sort under this generic law, have a serious problem of collective morality. Whatever the values that may reign here or there, a whole society respects itself for the perceived benevolence of its attitudes to others, the principle of charity under which everyone benefits. These socio-logical consequences override our immediate social interests, but it falls to the individual to deal with this law of gravity *sui generis* as best he can, to be as prepared as possible. I *ought* to know in advance that others will put the worst interpretation on my actions or my inertia; that the parenthesis will be more noticed than the thesis. At Court as in town. Deliver to an audience of linguists at

a specialized conference a long, laborious and complex paper on the comparative kinship values of languages, dialects and jargons, and (to spice your dry
material or revive the flagging interest of your listeners) let drop as an aside, or in
answer to a question from the floor, a more or less witty or malicious sally *ad
hominem* about some known personality: those twenty seconds of low pleasure will
be central to the next day's media accounts, dismissing your two hours of
strenuous effort as the accompanying sauce, if not the mere pretext, for the
'main dish', the 'pursuit of your feud with so-and-so'. The unkind remark was
not something prepared; it came to your lips without volition, to your own
surprise. But is that not the very proof that you carried it inside, deeply buried?
Does not a symptom, a slip, speak more truly than a written composition?

It is with a life as with the proofs of a book you have laboriously corrected and
then handed over to a professional proofreader: he can leaf through any three pages
taken at random and within seconds, with a more or less politely suppressed twitch
of the eyebrows, find three monstrous typos which have mysteriously escaped your
notice. They are always present, these prosecution exhibits, irrefutable, bringing a
blush to the most brazen face. You may well have toiled relentlessly and
meticulously to find the *mot juste*, smooth your transitions, temper your attacks;
once indicted you can see nothing but these blunders, in reality faults not of
typography but of language, betraying a damning contempt not for syntax but for
elementary honesty. You had the face to publish *that?*

Our public lives we hand over every month or so (every night for the more
exposed) not to a proofreader, but to a well-informed and indiscreet journalist.
You can depend on the professional sureness of his eye. No lapse of taste or
grammar, no mean or ludicrous act or attitude will be allowed to escape public
attention. We would be wrong to see this as a matter of malevolence or
bloodlust. As with the publisher's proofreader, censure is a regulatory function.
It has its own disagreeable but necessary constraints, essential for the proper
transparent conduct of democracy, for supervision of the governmental, intellectual and administrative domains by the governed, the TV viewers and the
subjects. But over and above this collective practical usefulness, far from
complaining about the 'pack' and the 'muckrakers', we ought to have (even
if we can't quite manage it) a more personal reason for gratitude to the
professional scoffer; we ought to see him (whatever it costs us) as, *mutatis mutandis*,
a pious Catholic sees the priest who marks his forehead with a grey cross on Ash
Wednesday, murmuring: *Memento, homo, quia pulvis es et in pulverem reverteris*. We are
dust and as dust we shall return to others, as in the end to ourselves. Thus shall
we be judged on the last day by what-people-say (the Court of Appeal, whose
verdict is invariably more severe than the original judgment), that trusty survivor
to which the newspaper scribbler serves on some level as a herald of arms.
Without that first dancer who holds the front of the stage, who all alone speaks in
a stentorian voice – alas! – to the entire house, would we even know our role, and
what stature will fall to us in the final distribution?

Media coverage wounds but renders us a service. We are all too inclined privately to dwell on the highest view of our acts; it is no bad thing that the low version should be systematically divulged in counterpoint in open court (of course our vanity would prefer the opposite: that the public be told the best by us, and the worst be whispered into our ear by an irksome but discreet prosecutor). The two tendencies form what statisticians call a 'fork': whatever the distance between the extremes, it will always be prudent to take the average as a likely outcome in one's own case. Thus, between *Le Canard enchaîné*, which keeps its readers up to date on our discreditable flounderings without being impressed by our fine speeches (stuffed with values and ideas), and *La Revue de métaphysique et de morale*, which shows proper appreciation for the wealth of our references and the rigour of our reasoning while ignoring our ruses and petty image concerns, lies a zone of indecision roomy enough for a privative path along a median line to be traceable by anyone. This protected (to the extent possible) track will lead to the 'honest mediocrity' that most probably characterizes us, to those temperate moral climes where virtue resided in Antiquity . . . a reflex classicism that for the time being, in default of a more detailed examination, can serve as a sort of consolation. The rumour that Jean Daniel echoed knows nothing of this happy medium; it prefers the scandalous to the everyday, to the point of stacking the cards and dealing off the bottom of the pack . . . all within the rules.

I have never learned how to break away; I improvise each time, very badly. Contracting is innate in us, breaking is an art. Everything is broken at the same time, bounds, a spell, the chains of silence: and there's the rub. 'Let us break off there, Sire.' All right, but why today? We temporize, we hope things will be different tomorrow, remember the mitigating circumstances, the misunderstanding. An edifice of faith does not just collapse like a tall building in an earthquake: fissures appear one by one and are patched up piecemeal, as required. Walking in the park at the end of 1983 with the master of the house, I mentioned to him (we were alone) my naive anti-imperialist's embarrassment over the unbridled Atlantism of our official foreign policy, not to mention the demotion of our secret services to the status of shield-bearers for the Great Leader of the West. The president admitted that he had gone rather to town on these matters, but only provisionally. It was a holding operation. 'We can't fight on two fronts, Régis, internal and external. Communists in the government, even in minor posts, are quite hard enough for Reagan and big capital to swallow. If on top of that I start defying America, I become Allende. Is that what you want?' No, it wasn't. 'Wait a bit and you'll see. Right, the Sandinists in Nicaragua: what have you got for me?' We then made a token gesture to retard the strangulation of Nicaragua by the empire and its Contras. What held the attention of the media, and therefore of the state, was the other empire: our services were nursemaiding Afghans. I made the trip (a must at that time) through the Khyber Pass on the

Pakistan-Afghan frontier, to confer with fourteenth-century warlords under the banner of human rights on behalf of the president; later I met the Pakistani dictator and the heads of his secret services, great friends of the Americans and therefore of ours. On my return I recommended that we send the weaponry we had been asked for, with the idea in the back of my mind that the precedent could prove useful elsewhere. Claude Cheysson soon persuaded me that this was idiotic, and fortunately Mitterrand did not follow my advice. After that I visited other remote countries, most notably Vietnam, to revive what could be revived of our former relations. Pham Van Dong, the prime minister, talked about France in the words of Victor Hugo, unaware that in Paris people now spoke yuppie and watched *Dallas*. The government went no further with Hanoi, blocked by Washington's veto; it was not until the US lifted the interdict for itself, ten years later, that the technical obstacles were miraculously removed, allowing us to rediscover that old francophone country. Too late, of course, for the Americans and Japanese were already installed (satellites seldom get first bite). Various other journeys and contacts of the same sort in the four corners of the world kept me occupied for the next two years. Belief is not a lighter flame, extinguished with a flick of the thumb; it is a guttering candle that can come back to life. In 1986, a vengeful liberalism won the legislative elections and went on to privatize television, eliminate the tax on large fortunes, bash students and immigrants. Good republican blood only lasts one term. At that point I asked to be returned to the Palace I had left in disgust two years earlier to help guard our desecrated chief, to close ranks around Him. 'The Guard dies, but never surrenders.'

I am not sure that the question of honour in politics even arises for our honoured intellectuals; that intransigent nobility bears on its shields the device: '*I*, sir, am a free man!' In fact, an 'intellectual worthy of the name' (as dignitaries say) does not submit to the yoke of collective discipline, still less accept a subordinate role in some pyramid of public decision-makers. 'The free mind keeps his autonomy of judgement; he does not follow the swerves of a party or a chief; he pitches his tent apart, observes from a distance, judges for himself.' A familiar song, and a lightweight one. It assumes the problem is solved. It assumes that a militant subject can become an eye without feeling or memory, an isolated intellect free from the honourable attachments that arise from a shared slice of life. It ignores the fact that our convictions undergo a baptism of fire at the hands of 'permanent' professionals (whose associates we amateurs become in the process of struggling for them), professionals to whom we are soon united by a plethora of genuine and less good feelings. The pure air of independence ignores the very regrettable fact that when the mind is unsatisfied with being pure mind, it forms an alliance with the heart (and the body). There is a price to be paid for this coalition, the law of incarnation of collective belief, that one cannot believe strongly in something without uniting with someone – *in* someone – a law that will make the militant as miserable later as it makes him happy at the time. Among the inconveniences this involuntary servitude causes to the 'freedom of thought' so prized by the writing nobilities are one or two that do not attract immediate notice, but hit you in the face when the time comes. The first is that a person who is sincere and serious about his convictions transforms the passion for action into a wish to serve, to give the said convictions the best possible chance. This vocation leads to the abandonment of a measure of sovereignty. The second is that, since the so-called 'ideological' motives for devotion to a cause fade much more easily than our affection for or loyalty to the individuals who embody it for us, our collusions outlive our convictions. This leads to a certain private unease. The third is that having neither the ideas of one's friends nor friends of one's ideas (something that happens sooner or later to anyone who takes events seriously) raises a dilemma: ingratitude (to one's friends) or dishonesty (about one's ideas). Leading in either case to public opprobrium.

Clearly, a persistent spirit guarantees an orderly succession of embarrassments. Where the object is to make your actions conform to your principles, that spiritual (and incidentally physical) courage leads you to join a group where you will be better placed to promote those principles than as an isolated observer. At this stage the spirit of persistence becomes an *esprit de corps*. But bodies unfortunately have heads, as do parties and states. The *esprit de corps*, at this secondary stage, is transformed back into a spirit of persistence, but in a deplorable way, a sort of sour and stupid version of the original. In the same way that wild piglets trot in sequence behind the sow, to serve a cause we join the 'following' of its champion. At this point the ideal militant subject effectively becomes a courtier, the forward scout just another pawn in the team, the escort, the retinue. If this *diminutio capitis* only affected the individual adherent's social prestige, the difficulty would end in acknowledgement of the grandeur of militant servitude. The trouble is that great leaders are also engaging men who gain by making themselves known. What the ironic spectators call 'allegiance' is experienced by the people involved as an elementary solidarity, a spontaneous, highly motivated affection; 'retinues' are also like-minded little groups, the 'acolytes' amusing chaps with whom it is fun to carouse, go to the beach or cinema and form collegians' cliques (especially during official visits, those rather *Zéro de conduite* junkets, when there is nothing left to worry about – luggage, papers, timetables – least of all the distant country through which one is sleepwalking and whose name one sometimes has trouble remembering two days later). As a result there is no clear dividing line between an estimable camaraderie and a despicable herd instinct. To summarize: at the start, the line was 'I am serious, so I follow.' At the finish, it has beome 'To remain what I am, I follow no longer.' Between the two, there will have been a long and inextricable tussle between the fidelity of the mind and the fidelity of the heart, your brain and your squeamishness, between the arrogant intellectual blackmail you use on yourself (if I go along with this decadence I'm the lowest of the low) and the emotional moral blackmail of your friends, or your superego on their behalf (if you jump ship now you really are a rat). With the joint pains, the arthritis that goes with a restless conscience. Some people have the courage for a clean break; emotionally backward, I tacked back and forth for several years (out of indecision, not to manoeuvre: like the erratic person I am). Resorting to a standard 'I know, but all the same . . .' to avoid a conclusion does not guarantee untroubled sleep, but it does buy you some time.

It took me ten years to leave Fidel Castro, and five to abandon François Mitterrand (following the defection of the heart and a reasoned decision to disconnect). There will not be a third separation; there isn't the time. One of the more important causes of the delay in formalizing the break is almost too risible to write down: the fear, not of being deprived of the love of God should he discover that I no longer really loved him (only to be expected, since all is barter up above as here below, and God himself must find it hard to love one who does not love him), but of upsetting him by thus putting him in the position of not being able to love me. The underlying assumption – confess, confess! – was that God had his eye on me, peering sidelong every morning from a distance; more than that, brooding over me day and night; that in short he could not do without my love, whose withdrawal, God or no God, he would probably not survive. So bear in mind that disaffiliation is much quicker and easier for an adoptive son who dares to see the Father as he is: fairly detached from his children, if not utterly indifferent.

I do not believe that I failed to speak openly, and apart from remembered conversations I have copies of innumerable letters and private notes in which, from 1982 onward, I informed the boss of my worries, objections and dissenting views. Not without occasional finessing, one example being the detailed, ordered report I wrote for him in 1983 on the severe criticisms of our foreign policy since 1981 made in my presence by General de Gaulle's former foreign minister, Couve de Murville, at a private luncheon given for this purpose by Paul-Marie de la Gorce: I was in complete agreement with them myself, and said so in the note. Stung by this, François Mitterrand unsheathed his best pen and and answered point by point, without really convincing me. Soon after that I decided to publish some reflections on external relations, first submitting the typescripts to the head of state for censorship (for seven full years he received in advance the text of every book or article I intended to publish, including *Les Masques*). Obviously he had other things to do, and made no comment whatsoever. Honourable though it was, this silence (as much a product of politeness as indifference, of liberalism as scepticism) still embarrassed me. And the essays, whose content ran directly counter to leading opinion (enthusiastically supportive of the head of state's foreign policy throughout) and mainstream opinion (which always goes along with the foreign policies of all heads of state), but did not personalize the polemic or attack anyone by name, fell flat. Hardly a critic took the trouble to understand the radical deconstruction they contained of the projects and procedures that, in daily life, I was still serving to the best of my ability.

I had become an internal oppositionist, wilfully provocative, begging for public dismissal. Alas: our Monarch, who gave not a damn for the emotional states of those around him, never sacked his esquires. His Immobility left things to decompose, set them aside, trusting in the inertia of old intimacies to soothe bumps and heal sores. He simply did not care; his door would only shut from the outside and I was going to have to slam it *motu propio*. All the better in a way: the only pleasure greater than that of being chosen is that of resigning. Pulled both ways, I kept finding excuses for delay, even publishing a long open letter listing my grievances and challenging him directly. This book would have been called *Remontrances* had that legal word from yesteryear not acquired a ridiculous derived connotation, but eventually appeared under the more cautious title *Vive la République*: a seditious outburst of conventional aspect. The tirade amused him, and with characteristic elegance he praised me warmly for it during a small meeting. There was nothing left to do but send him a short letter of resignation through the internal mail (6 July 1988 if you want chapter and verse). At that moment, with his poll ratings at their peak following his re-election, the father of the nation was riding high on the tides of consensus: I could not be accused of forsaking an endangered god. After that, to my brief shame, he sent me a bronze medallion of the Elysée palace to put on my mantelpiece, and got his chief of staff, Jean-Claude Colliard, to offer me the Légion d'honneur. As a flunkey is rewarded for fifteen years of good and loyal service. I gave no answer. Disdain is a chief's virtue; I cannot help wondering with horror if I did not deserve that insulting and mechanical gratuity, in settlement of all accounts: a red ribbon in my buttonhole. I had been useful, I had served my purpose, next please. Beyond the sorrow, disaster.

My public airing of differences, which it is usual to see as stemming from ingratitude and resentment, still troubles my conscience. Like a boorish debtor who has done a moonlight flit. Debit, credit, liability, expiry, balance, surety: the bankers' words ring hollow when used to describe feelings. I still owed a debt of gratitude to that man who wanted to inflict the Légion d'honneur on me: the sort of debt that cannot be judged politically (just as a debt of honour is not recognized by a court of law, but nevertheless serious enough to outweigh any number of tactical and strategic arguments). Had I not benefited, with others, from his weakness for hooligans and irregulars, the combination – rare in his circle – of intellectual curiosity and moral courage that incited him to give marginal characters a chance, to forage in the badlands beyond what-people-will-say. I could not honestly complain about his personal defects, big or small (quite apart from the fact that I have the same ones myself), and it would have been even more unfounded to object to the disorganizing empiricism he brought intentionally to bear on business. Without him I would never have gained access to the holy of holies. Taking a dubious adventurer in there, ignoring the warnings of the police services, his friends' reservations, the bile of the media and the expostulations of the US State Department (whose chargé d'affaires in Paris demanded, a week after he took office, that my diplomatic passport – which effectively lifted a twenty-year ban on my entering American territory – be withdrawn), took a lot of 'bottle', a gentleman's panache. Unawareness, people whispered of him. In him, the nobility of the person neutralized the prudence of the politician, without altogether extinguishing it (hence the humble position I occupied at first in the Elysée organigram: a good leader does not lower his flag, he flies it at half-mast). Of course he was not yet consulting pollsters and spin-doctors on a daily basis. Of course, after ten years of contact, he knew all about about my legalist scruples, my cult of the nation-state, my pragmatism: in short, how far I was in reality from the leftist-terrorist-Guevarist of my image in the right-wing press. I had been a close collaborator during his second presidential campaign in 1974 (fortunately passing unnoticed). I had been involved in the *Charte des libertés* he had commissioned in 1975 from a small committee of rational libertarians led by Robert Badinter (the others were Attali, Bredin, Fabius, Schwartzemberg, Serres and myself). But there is a strange inertia about reputations, as if the electronic acceleration of news made labels stick all the more stubbornly. A brand image, unlike crimes of blood, is not subject to amnesty or time limitation (better to plant a bomb without getting caught than to be thought a friend of terrorists). I had published weighty stuff, but the circulation of my books was too restricted to turn the tide: I was still seen as red, although in reality I was pale pink and philosophically black. The public clamour that greeted my appointment disconcerted him, like finding a scarecrow in an old broom cupboard. He had not realized (neither had I) how very bad my image was among the intelligentsia, the security police or the *Wall Street Journal*. With great courtesy, he kept his vexation hidden and continued to show me confidence. Any other politician, any ordinary schemer, would have calculated that the cost of a small gesture of friendship in Washington, Brussels or Saint-Germain-des-Prés would certainly outweigh any gains it might earn in Dar es-Salaam or Tegucigalpa (not capitals to which he paid much attention).

Afterthoughts of this kind reduce one to silence, not easily dispelled.

If telling the truth is an act of madness under all circumstances, telling someone you love the whole truth about himself verges on heroism. You have to take on a lot. Not that the hierarchy is particularly rancorous. It is proud, neither more nor less than you are yourself at heart. Apart from that widespread quirk, its main characteristic and main source of strength, exemplified by the unswerving gallantry of the born chief whom none of his recantations can discompose, is that it never looks back over the recent or distant past and says 'Here, I was wrong', or 'There, I should have acted differently'. This character trait, which I can confirm is common to Latinos and Frenchmen, appears to exist in all parties and cultures. A man of power is physiologically incapable of recognizing that he has contradicted, criticized or repudiated himself, or that he has taken us over, or that he has lied. He is all of a piece and will remain so until his last breath, like his undeviating rectilinear path and unaltered aims (especially if there has been much tacking). Otherwise, though, chiefs are sensitive, vulnerable and even more fragile than you and I. They have a constant, infantile, limitless need for protection, and the task of coddling them falls to us. Why? Because more than the rest of us they are exposed, bareheaded, to insults and denigration; hence their need for a cocoon (read: Court), some haven of physical and mental security. 'Was I all right?' the president anxiously asks his staff after the televised speech. 'How did I come across? Another take, d'you think?' Who, at such a moment of extreme nakedness, would have the heart to say: 'You were crap, President. Nowhere. Grotesque.' The aggression could never occur, for to love is to wish to protect, to reduce the sufferings and fears of the other; so its putative author would not be in the entourage. Whose members, carp as they might behind the chief's back, when in his presence want only to reassure the Uneasy One, and be reassured by him. The instinct is to form a defensive tortoiseshell round his body, shields overhead. To form the wagons into a circle, as when howling Sioux used to charge down on the good guys, waving tomahawks. For such is the daily predicament of a president menaced by the bad guys with their molten lead, their daggers unsheathed in the shadows. So forming a defensive bloc is behaving like Panurge; it is both healthy and unhealthy; it obstructs the Beloved's field of view, everyone knows it will not help him advance; it encourages flatterers and yes-men. But if I break the defensive perimeter and let miasmas from outside into the cocoon, then I am playing the Enemy's game, whose only objective is to make the chief doubt himself, to make him waver. Such is the dynamic of entourages, warm and mind-numbing. 'Good chaps, all right, but what prats! Completely half-witted.' Obviously that is why they are there. The chief's sideways vision is blocked? Just as well for him, in a way. Free debate without taboos or blinkers, what one might call the exercise of intellectual democracy around democratic bosses (democratic meaning a boss from whom one can separate without risking the worst, as a government is democratic not because it is elected by a majority but because the governed can get rid of it without risking prison or death) is a sentimental square circle to the inner group. To break it requires exceptional, almost superhuman strength. I cannot think of a more admirable example than that of Pierre Brossolette, that most Gaullist of Resistance leaders, who on 2 November 1942 sent a personal letter through unofficial channels to General de Gaulle in London, to tell him things that no one (except his enemies) dared to say, concerning his very serious character defects:

> . . . *I will speak to you frankly. I have always spoken thus to men, however great, whom I*
> *respect and like. I will do it with you, for whom I have infinite respect and affection. For there*

are times when someone needs to have the courage to tell you out loud what others murmur behind your back with tearful faces. That person, if you don't mind, will be me. I am used to these unwelcome and generally costly chores. What needs to be said to you, in your own interests, in the interests of combatant France – of France –is that the way you treat men and prevent them from dealing with problems is causing us painful concern, in fact I would say genuine anxiety. There are subjects on which you will tolerate no contradiction, no discussion even. And they are, generally speaking, those on which your own position is most exclusively affective, in other words the very ones on which it is most advisable to test your position against the reactions of others. In such cases your tone implies to your interlocutors that in your opinion their dissent can only result from a sort of infirmity of thought or of patriotism. In the touch of imperiousness that thus characterizes your manner and causes too many of your associates to feel intimidated, to put it mildly, every time they enter your office, there is probably greatness. But you can be sure that there is even more danger in it. The first effect is that, of your entourage, the less good members agree with you completely; the worst adopt a policy of flattering you; and the best are becoming unwilling to contribute to your upkeep. So you are reaching a situation in which, amid all your daily worries, you encounter nothing but sycophantic assent. But you know as well as I do where this path has taken people other than you in History, and where it threatens to take you yourself . . .

It goes without saying that, *mutatis mutandis,* I would never have had the courage to send my beloved president, in a TTU envelope, a scolding as rigorous and unselfish as that. I suggest nevertheless that copies of this letter should be displayed in the corridors and offices of all the palaces. Not that the adviser need make any worrying comparisons. Neither the circumstances nor the times are the same. Dying for a chief all of whose weaknesses your radar has pinpointed, as Brossolette did when he jumped out of a window at Gestapo HQ after his arrest in 1944: who could ask that of anyone? It would not be reasonable to look to the exception as a basis for the comportments of an honest average. You do not make a clergy from saints and martyrs. But what would become of faithful and clerics – what would they be *worth* – without an image of the superhuman to look up to?

'Obviously, there are so many advantages in your position . . . I can quite see why you're playing down your convictions . . .' It was in these terms that a friend, himself a man of stern convictions but indulgent, calmed my scruples of (political) conscience after the 'turn toward rigour' and the first public prayers to Money. I could hear the echo, muffled by friendship, of another *vox populi,* the one that accuses you not of going the wrong way but of staying in the wrong job, bogged down in the toils and privileges of 'power'. If only they knew, poor things, what impotence they were talking about! What do they know of an intermediary's bittersweet misfortunes? Of the fixer who does not realize that human beings (and not just administrations, police services, states) loathe talking to each other, sitting round a table and airing differnces, one by one, face to face.

Of the farcical misadventures that await someone who always wants the Greeks and Trojans to have lunch together and make friends. Of the antics of the Boy Scout arriving in the middle of the brawl 'like some humble, benevolent god of soup, blinking in the steam from the meat and cabbage', determined to do everything necessary to settle things for the best. To do what, exactly? Three times nothing, endless grind, daily rebuffs.

Achieve the private triumph of getting a distant relation appointed to a post five times better paid, and much more prestigious, than your own (find him an 'outlet' or 'slot'), after a series of tiny, increasingly acrimonious scuffles over the titbit in the corridors, with each minister or adviser trying to manoeuvre *his* candidate (some virtual unknown adopted as a son or brother would not be) to the front of the queue. The result, apart from one ingrate, will be ten other angry people, the rejected candidates: eleven resentments on your back. Is the game worth the candle?

Be the good king's bad adviser (an old sketch but a good one, success guaranteed). Here is one example among many. No one in the Palace will receive a notorious professor of medicine, an anti-conformist loudmouth of courageous views, who is trying urgently to be given an official mission to Palestine (at a time when Arafat is still considered accursed). A friend talks to you about him, and you agree to see him. The man, whom you hardly know, hits it off with you; although a star, he is clear and down to earth; the mission seems an excellent idea; over the next three days you intercede with the president, the secretary-general and your colleagues, who all tell you to get lost; you try again and end by annoying them seriously: 'All right, you really want to fix your buddy up, he gets on our nerves that guy, we'll see later.' The postulant gets impatient and keeps trying to telephone you. Eventually you take the call and as, through delicacy and deference, you do not want him to know what people think of him personally in high places, you invent a pretext, inevitably idiotic, for deeming the mission inopportune and even pointless: sorry. Three days wasted, back to work. A couple of days later you open the paper and find a long interview from the fellow, describing over several columns his deep shame as a citizen at the sight of a pitiful clown like you in charge of such important matters; you have done nothing but get in the way, whereas of course if the president had been told about this mission idea, then obviously . . . You are tortured by longing to pick up the telephone: 'Listen, pal, I spent time and trouble trying to save your bet. It's not mine, it's yours; I don't owe you anything, and the president's got three people in mind who can do the work as well as you can, and more quietly. Get fucked.' You fold up your newspaper; you don't dial the number. Worthless you are and will remain, in the eyes of all. Is the game worth the candle?

Playing the go-between, interposing yourself on a street corner between abused wife and enraged husband, guarantees slaps from both parties. Another example out of many. Everyone who is anyone in Paris has been writing to the president for months to get him to obtain the release of 'a great Cuban poet paralysed as the result of torture while in prison'. You go to Havana and stay up half the night talking privately to Fidel Castro. He explains, with documentary evidence, what you know already: that the detainee was a police agent under the previous régime, works out like a bodybuilder and has never written a sonnet in his life. You understand his point of view, but outline your own: that these things do not justify keeping an opponent in the dark for twenty years, and no one should expect French cooperation loans if they ignore French demands on human rights. Eventually Fidel succumbs to your arguments (and will be furious with you by the next evening for this moment of weakness). In exchange he asks that this 'hero concocted abroad' be given a muted welcome without official fanfare. You agree. The said hero arrives at Orly in an aircraft of the Glam flight, but refuses to come out: he is reluctant to be seen walking, especially by the committee of leading French intellectuals patiently awaiting a hemiplegic in a wheelchair. The pilot, who speaks no Spanish and has a pressing schedule, becomes impatient with this irksome passenger and requests the Elysée to send someone ASAP to take him away. Guess who gets the job? No one else has a clue about this impenetrable, embarrassing, baroque cock-up. You arrive on the tarmac and tell the ex-jailbird that he will have to come clean sooner or later, no time like the present, anyway they need the plane. You persuade him, and in the event the welcoming committee manages to hide its astonishment. But an AFP hack has spotted you coming out of the aircraft, and wrongly reports – without checking – that you were there to give the celebrated and prestigious dissident poet an official welcome on behalf of the President of the Republic. Fidel Castro, quite reasonably thinking he has been duped, is furious. So of course is the liberated hero, an extreme right-wing militant who never stops blathering that he owes his freedom to everyone but that lousy communist (you). And Havana and Miami are in agreement for once: get rid of that jackass!

If you are honest, you will have to admit that resignation is not motivated only by noble concern for republican values. You don't resign really, you *slink away*, although afterwards you can still put up a smokescreen of fatigue and moral discomfort. The truth is that you have simply had enough of being battered from all sides; you wonder whether it is really worth becoming a deaf-and-dumb eunuch just to serve an empty throne. We should try not to value this abandoning of posts too highly. What is a 'responsible post' in the final analysis? It is the alliance of word and gesture. A writer has nothing to gain from it, when the law of the worst-case holds, except his own approval: not enough. 'Gaucho Tintin' and 'fun pistolero' are two of the more gentle and friendly epithets earned by my ten years in Latin America. 'Careerist' and 'sinecure collector' crowned a decade of subjection to the national officialdom. After the stigmata of exoticism, those of *nomenklatura*: being reputed a lackey and having to bear it in silence. Thus voluntarily reduced, I discovered from specialized sociological journals what had driven me into the sirens' embrace: when intellectuals are weak, they have to resort to political weapons to win their intellectual struggles. As an ungraded social assistant, I had thought I was working all hours, without holidays, for other people, harder and better than I had ever worked in my own name, or on my own account. Wrong: I had been lounging on silk upholstery, mouth full of smoked salmon and feet on the table. I cannot help wondering whether my only really courageous act, in forty years of conscious life, was to go and work for the socialists in 1981. Nothing compelled me to do it: I was neither an énarque nor a member of the party, and had no plans to become a municipal councillor or deputy. My enrolment was not a consequence of my situation; worse still, it contradicted all the theories I had just advanced, in a philosophic work, on political Reason as a constitutive decoy and hopeless cause; it discredited me for some time in the eyes of my peers, who don't go in for that sort of thing. Well, I was being misjudged again: secretly I was slaking my urges to be a servant, the disgrace of poets. Meantime I had still to discover the funniest thing, practically a gag; the public ministry arrived some little time before resentment set in; by the final act I had become what can only be called a government pen-pusher. The 'normalization' of 1989 would have made me laugh in 1981. I was willing to serve; to no avail perhaps; but to serve in continuity, for re-election, no. I had not joined up to help manage a period of lean kine, but to attack the Golden Calf. It was a bit sad commemorating the French Revolution only to bury it. In a phrase, after setting off for the Mountain I had ended in the Gironde[8] for lack of anything better; now, in the second term, consistency beckoned me into the Marais, and without a *Comité de salut public* in the offing. Worse than infamous: commonplace. Too much to ask of the good soldier Schweik. And the john recoils, in a start of surprise like the ones you give in the middle of some conference in Timbuktu on 'Television and Democracy' or 'The future of humanity': what on *earth* have I come here for? This theme needs honest people behind it, but what's it got to do with me?

For the most ironic thing of all is again misunderstanding, this time through reshuffles (and all part of the training): the ugly sentiments imputed to you by your enemy as you skip back and forth between the gilded panelling make you want to flee when they return in earnest. To fantasize (as I had done in 1981) a parish under siege, last session, all hands to the pumps – when you yourself are really just a 'book mill' – all you need is civic sense and patriotism; those austere virtues acquired through study give birth to pride and vanity, revive your own small interests: press you to reopen your workshop at court, go on churning out volumes, just for the pleasure of it, some windows on eternity (the true, the good, the beautiful). At that point you go back home.

You no longer see yourself as the robber knight, Count Ganelon. Not even as Du Guesclin, the simple gentleman out of his depth among the great barons of the kingdom, and future Constable of France, genuflecting before Charles V: 'Sire, the jealousies are so great that I must guard against them constantly. Therefore I beg you now to discharge me from this office and bestow it on another who will accept it more willingly than I do and be better able to carry it out.' Then you travel in your dreams to a Himalayan ashram, where with shaven skull and saffron robe, in a low voice, you answer the questions of a Buddhist monk intrigued by the paths of renunciation in the West. He mentions your predecessors Charles Quint and the Duke of Windsor. He wonders in all sincerity how anyone could step down from Olympus of his own free will and hand himself over naked to the Christian God, an American divorcee or the Buddha. Why, when the laurel wreath is tickling your occiput, resign charges and dignities to shut yourself away in a monastery at Yuste (1556), the Casino at Monte Carlo (1935) or an obscure corner of Nepal (1988)? You protest, eyes lowered, and ask him to stop putting you on the same level, superficial resemblances notwithstanding, as Charles Habsburg, emperor of the Germanic Holy Roman Empire, king of Aragon and Castile, of Sardinia, Sicily and Naples, king of the Indies and all unclaimed terra firma in the ocean sea, or as the Prince of Wales, KG, KT, GCB, Earl of Chester, Duke of Cornwall and Rothesay, Duke of Carrick and Baron of Renfrew, Prince and Great Steward of Scotland, and for a few months King Edward VIII. A modest Paris-born republican, in the phone book and listed as a voter, you have triumphed over no one but yourself: difficult enough at a time when people only have eyes for megalomaniacs, but not actually all that complicated. One day you might decide to break your vow of incognito, emerge from the shadows to elucidate your reasons for retreating into them. One day perhaps you will tell the whole truth on the lousiness of the tribes you had agreed to take under your wing; on the ingratitude of the presidents and despots you have made and unmade as a child discards a broken toy, not to mention the million amnesiacs who owe their careers to you alone; on the endless hassle of petitioners and intrigues, the threat of public affronts and assassination attempts, the exhaustion of official visits, interviews, signing visitor's books, restricted meetings, on press harassment and the loneliness, or the wear and tear, or the sadness of power. It is true that no one renounces their heart's desire before time without the best of reasons. One day perhaps you will end the conjecture surrounding your abrupt withdrawal. Cowardice, a temporary access of courage, sudden nausea or long-term plan, access of melancholy or private awareness of inadequacy? Tired of your injustices and benefactions, tired of holding the fate of the world in your hands? That would be most likely, the favoured rumour. But let's be clear: you haven't thrown in the towel. It could well be that after mature reflection, although without wide consultation, you may have to unsheath your pen to relate in detail – lures, strings and setbacks included – even at the cost of upsetting people, your climb towards the peace of the inner kingdoms.

All the flying carpets of East and West are good for is escaping from sordid reality-as-it-is: a needy clerk, ready to sign the petition of the day every day provided he is left in peace, with his video cassettes and his old books. Tell me, sir, I suppose you wouldn't like to take my place in this well-appointed office and large new car? Thank you, my dear sir, and a fair wind to you.

5

Pointless Service

My tissue of insanities – It never pays to be ahead – Strange foreign policy – There is no such person as a happy strategist – Why it is silly to love your country – Admirable America – Snobbery in politics – Resign and breathe again

To the odious, I ought to add a pinch of the ridiculous. I must say something about politics for clarity's sake; something about its 'systematically mediocre contingencies'. Talk friends, enemies, squabbles, world-visions, bombast, with tiresome profligacy. When we examine the *politician* in himself (because an example is needed and that one is to hand) we cannot ignore *politics*, if we want to identify the field of operations of that small internal mechanics that makes us sing out or pipe down, giving a vague family resemblance to our transports and retreats. It's a very bad business, politics, for a writer. He can get involved as a citizen, if he must; no one's perfect. But discussing it is a loss-making investment, the Danaides' barrel. *In politics lies our misfortune, alas / My best enemies advise me to do it / Red tonight, while tomorrow, a thousand times no / I want those who read me to read me again . . .* A thousand times yes, quite a few of us are with Musset in wanting to be reread . . . although I don't see why if no one read me yesterday anyone should read me tomorrow. In the category of 'current affairs essays' there is by definition nothing *classical* ('that which is taught in class and merits imitation'). Not that products of this type are smothered in romanticism, far from it: but they degrade from new. The more penetrating the analysis of an event, the sooner it fades; the better something disposable holds the road, the worse its chances of staying there. Until we have a conjuncture deep-frozen like cod fillets or couscous royal, those products of wide consumption and shallow impact, perpetually feeding into the cumbersome mass of 'political literature' (that pedal-driven aircraft), will have the shelf life of yoghurt. Consume before the end of the month. A sunset over Kilimanjaro, a beech grove in Saintonge, a night of love, have no sell-by date. Religion, Hindu or Lutheran, will taste much the same in twenty years or a hundred (language apart). *Politics* is ageless, but *policy*, or 'that which will be less interesting tomorrow than it is today', swindles those who let themselves be taken in by it. The pamphleteer's righteous wrath, like the pundit's insight, lies in an accursed zone of letters; they will make our grandchildren yawn and 2096 bookstall-browsers snigger. Even fashion magazines

seem less perishable; the photos, woman eternal, the precision of their vocabulary, promise them a longer future than the 'interventions' of polemicists. So I
would be more than happy to let the dead rest in peace; but I cannot, I have
promised to do what is necessary to be understood.

Opinions are reversible garments, just as warm inside out, and this compli-
cates the fashion chronicle. I will say in few words which way out I wore the
'betrayal-fidelity', the 'perseverance-obstinacy' and even the 'low scoundrel'
(this last the same tweed, seen in white by Box and black by Cox). All without
wishing to find fault, or expecting to convince anyone. The proselyte's tongue
and the ardour of the militant have both abandoned me. And in any case it
would be wrong to want to persuade or influence, since even at the time my
reasoning looked like pure madness to 95 per cent of my country's voters. On
this I can only ask my fellow citizens for the same indulgence that they extend to
the philatelist or bodybuilder, when he drones on about suburban club politics.
It is easy for us to show patience with hobbyists because those guys don't trample
on our flowerbeds. On the terrain that concerns us here, everyone feels he is a
landowner, fully entitled not just to take a hand in matters that affect him, but to
castigate any braggart of differing opinion as a frivolous half-wit if not a bastard.
These alternatives – there is no third way – do not provide favourable listening
conditions (no better in 1996 than in 1556 or AD 496).

I dressed left side out. And left I remain, having never done political economy.
In the 1970s and 1980s I meant to identify myself as before to the oppressed and
exploited (two more annoyingly reversible terms) as favouring, in France, a
coalition (reverse: 'arrangement') of socialists (because the most reasonable),
communists (because the poorest) and Gaullists (because of their 'certain idea of
France'), each component neutralizing the dangers of the others. The internal
situation, the petty game of clans and leaders, left me more or less indifferent; I
saw it as a means to an end, a distasteful servitude leading with luck to the proper
game of Interests, the 'big politics' alone worthy of passion. In a domain
uncertain by nature, my certainties (I admit) verged on the barmy. Unlike
Michel Foucault, who saw the Gulag as the 'historically growing peril', from
1981 onward I saw communism as a losing cause everywhere and the Soviet
Union as a giant with feet of clay, incapable of transforming its arsenals into
power, still less into influence. We ought therefore to turn over that page and
look at the next (as I tried to explain, at length and in vain, in 1985 in *Les Empires
contre l'Europe*). If Europe exists one day in the West, its main problem will be its
relations with America (difference being more difficult than confrontation). I was
weak enough to believe that democracy in Western Europe was in rude health,
while the Yalta carve-up was crumbling before our eyes year after year. That it
was unrealistic to talk about a 'totalitarian bloc' or 'the East', putting, for
example, Hungary, East Germany and Bulgaria in the same bag, when each of
these countries was busily cultivating a centrifugal communism, with national
considerations always prevailing over ideology (whether communist or Eur-

openist). And that what looked like becoming the antagonistic tension that would give edge to the period would no longer be 'democracy versus totalitarianism', but 'modernity versus tribalism' or 'technology versus religion'. Since technical and economic globalization would bring about political and cultural balkanization in its shadow (as I tried to explain, at length and in vain, in 1981 in *Critique de la Raison politique*), through a logical and necessary linkage, we would have to confront a formidable upsurge in assertiveness about identity, but also the reappearance of an old new idea: that of the elective (rather than ethnic) nation, based on software rather than material goods (as I tried to explain, at length and in vain, in 1984 in *La Puissance et les rêves*). The pipe-dream aspect of peace through legislation, the idea of a 'new world order' underpinned by the United Nations as universal justice of the peace, should have been dropped in advance. Nothing operational could be expected from the UN, except the endorsement of agreements already concluded between powers (which, as always, would last as long as the parties found them expedient). Contributing to peace-keeping forces under someone's blue flag, and leaving it at that, would diminish the authority of such contributors without resolving the conflicts at issue (I explained, at length and in vain, in 1984). Let us make no mistake on the main threat. The alliance of God and computers, most explosive in the Arab and Muslim world with the possibility of a nuclear-tribal short-circuit, has made Islamism a growing force, the only 'totalitarianism' currently in running order. It therefore seemed sensible for Europeans to stop exaggerating the 'Soviet threat', a misreading that blended all too easily with their tendency to abdicate their sovereignty to the United States, which in this area kept European opinion in line through a hundred disinformation channels. From this viewpoint, which we will call 'culturalist' (as opposed to the 'economism' common to the Marxist and liberal concepts of the world), 'the Europe of Brussels, that advance on History' seemed to me the perfect example of a *fuite en avant* into exorcism. Not that solidarity and interdependence within the Old World will not be positive and concrete developments, to be pursued through every sort of bi- and multilateral cooperation between governments, firms, TV networks and assembly lines. But viable popular entities are not *constructed* piece by piece, like a cathedral or Meccano model, on the basis of economic agreements signed at the top. They *grow* like plants or embryos, on the basis of feelings, language, memories and projects. A living thing adjusts itelf, looks after itself and defends itself, but does not set itself by the daily exchange rate. Meanwhile, if the national no longer has the means, the supranational is still less equipped with the will, and the multinational will never be anything but an instrument, a multiplier of forces, not their source. Unlike the small countries of the continent, which could only benefit from the levelling of power through the simple or modified majority voting systems in the European institutions, France, it seemed to me, would soon have more to lose than to gain from this federal daydream, a technocratic version of illuminism. As for the learned groups of the left, I did not see how they could combine their socialist credo with their European one, when the time came. Except by putting Victor Hugo to work for the stock exchange, using labour internationalism as a figleaf for capitalist globalization, and hiding the real neo-liberal Europe, run by bankers to the detriment of the Republic and the public services, behind the social Europe we talk about at banquets: tidy, four-square and nonexistent. Meanwhile, as I tried to explain, at length and in vain, in 1989 in *Tous Azimuts* (a study commissioned by the Fondation pour les études de défense nationale), one Europe can hide another, separatisms are rearing their heads and our defence plans, like our means of intervention, are out of date. This was before the Yugoslavian chain reaction.

That, crudely summarized, is the tissue of insanities I was trying to put forward between 1980 and 1990, discreetly at first, in confidential notes to our rulers, then, like some others (including Jean-Claude Guillebaud and Emmanuel Todd), more openly in the public arena. Our silly twitterings were variously received, here with compassionate smiles, there with open sniggers. In a not very terrorist state itself terrorized by the forces of opinion, the way to carry weight in the seraglio is to build it up on TV, or failing that in the press. After three years, having learned this very simple mechanism, I had resolved to spread the infection far and wide by publishing books on these subjects, instead of slipping it into manila envelopes marked TTU. Good idea, but total failure. Scientists call it a 'negative retroaction loop': since my books did not sell in the shops, my notes lacked credibility at the Palace. How could a flute player compete with the big drums everywhere thumping out *The Finnish Syndrome* or *How Democracies End*, with the striking TV image of Russian tanks advancing across the great central plain, or with philosophic analysis of the unchanging *Nature of the Soviet Union*? All the talk was of a 'gradual slide into acceptance of Soviet imperialism'. The ratio of forces between my uninspired self and the uninformed watchers of our ramparts was something like one to a hundred (my print runs were under a thousand copies). A publicist without a public is in the same fix as an unfunny comic: he must either persuade the public that it does not understand the nature of laughter (which he alone has mastered), or leave the stage. The second solution seemed more sensible. There is an English word for someone who does not have to be ejected from the train because he has failed to board it: 'maverick'. The French word is 'inoffensif' (harmless). The smart thing in this situation is to transform one's exclusion into a pose of marginality (like a nineteenth-century painter scorned by the academies going 'bohemian'). So I will mark my unsold copies with an 'original mind' sticker, indicating failure but guaranteed value.

It is wrong, I am afraid, to keep saying that you will not discuss politics beyond the level of taste and colour because all opinions are worth the same. There are opinions that can hibernate, unchanged, to be consulted after ten years or twenty; and there are the others. A sense of history, in the end, puts you two stages ahead in the sequence of operations. Everything depends on timing. A stroke of genius in April becomes a gaffe in December. There is a world of difference between saying 'The question is not whether Germany will be beaten, but what role France will have in the victory' in London in 1940 (as de Gaulle did), and proclaiming it on the Champs-Elysées in August 1944 as you or I would have done. For a French or Italian 20-year-old to join the Communist Party in 1943 was not at all the same as doing it in 1945: intrepidity is as much a matter of time and place as perspicacity. This can be very awkward. Societies having as poor a memory for dates as individuals, the man of foresight is not acknowledged after the event; the breakthrough falls back into the mass and blends with the grey tangle of the present, so that discernment is no more recognized after than before. By some curious magic, any statement of truth bearing on the present is always untimely.

All right: Paris is swarming with unknown political geniuses, sacked Pythiases, unemployed Cassandras. There are a few thousand of us in every generation, unemployables who will die convinced they have been under-employed, after an old age embittered by all that wasted talent and unappreciated vocation. I am no exception to this comic fate; I never travel on the 63 bus because it plucks at my heartstrings to have to drive along the Quai d'Orsay like an outsider. It is not easy for me, Minister *in partibus* of foreign affairs, linear successor to Talleyrand, Chateaubriand and Tocqueville, to accept that a politico of short-term views is occupying my place, lounging in Vergennes's[9] armchair as I pass below his window with ruffians treading on my feet. Yes indeed, there are journeys that gratuitously recall that bitterest of experiences, the expropriation without indemnity that no one ever mentions. So it is with the classic murmur, 'Well, ladies and gentlemen, you shall see what you shall see' that I counter the jibes of guardians of decency well versed in 'the self-interested tricks of the memory, the adept way the ego rearranges the past to its own advantage'. My friends are genuinely convinced that I was wrong at every important turn, because they themselves were really wrong each time, along with everyone else. We are all crossing a limitless desert, where mirages become real if more than a million parched souls hail the miracle together. I do not ask amnesty or indulgence for my offences, only that people glance at the record before accusing me of peacocking around with historian's retrospective prophecies. Really I would be only too happy to abstain from all circumstantial judgements; the ones I have made have earned me nothing but sneers, simply because they were not too wide of the mark. Happy accidents that I owe to a genetic condition: I see and hear the ideology in the murmur of the time, as others absorb the language straight off a page of literature. From the morning's serious article stand out, greatly enlarged, the phrases and ideas that will have us giggling by evening. What we call *ideology* is not just my adversary's outlook, it is what each group or each decade agrees to treat as real, and the next decade (or neighbouring group) claims to be imaginary, and so on, year after year. In a front-page headline, a flamboyant editorial, an advert in the metro, I see anodyne words flashing like the reflectors on bike pedals. This incurable sight defect, more like a squint than discernment, is something I would not wish on anyone. It renders you asocial and out-of-synch, a specialist in sour notes and flops. To think against yourself is the condition of personal salvation. To think against your neighbourhood is the condition of collective salvation, but apart from the fact that you tire very quickly, political death is guaranteed. Such is the dilemma of our rulers: you do not govern France against its notables, and they have always been two stages behind on current international issues. All in all, Mitterrand did well never to cut off relations with the senators, to keep them warm from a distance. Flying over Cuba in 1975 with Castro, he calmly wrote thirty postcards to his correspondents in Charente and the Nièvre during the caudillo's exposition of the next five year plan. I never once saw the president abroad fail to give priority over all other duties and conversations to the ceremonial despatch of postcards to the *conseiller général*, the local hotel manager, cousin Julie. Even at the Élysée, receiving a foreign head of state, that earthy hexagonal never failed, with the coffee or even sooner, to buttonhole the member of the parliamentary Foreign Affairs Commission or the chairman of the Franco-Thingy friendship association, and straighten him out on what really mattered: next Sunday's Loir-et-Cher by-election. In a proper democracy, whether consular or of opinion, foreign policy – which has never got anyone elected – comes a long way behind serious matters. It suits enlightened despotism much better. Weak parliamentary supervision, ignorant and sheep-like public opinion, obscure and complex issues: everything made it the private domain of the old-time Prince, and of conspirators without local connections. The link between a taste for wide open spaces and democratic incapacity is self-evident.

From my own limited experience, it seems that the nearer a rhetoric gets to positive reality, the less hold it has on people's minds, and the further it is from practical activity. In France, everything true that I have managed to write sounded false at the time; in Latin America, everything I said that subsequently turned out to be false sounded right at the time. Reputedly practical minds snowed under with emergencies and paperwork handle, with a good deal of basic ingenuousness but immense precision of detail, fabulous, grossly unreal entelechies like 'the East', 'the West', 'the South', 'the Democratic camp', 'Europe', 'Totalitarianism', etc. Notes in their canon, dripping with ideology but emanating from very serious offices – armed forces staffs, the Secretariat General of National Defence – contain numerous extravagances that seem sensible and make any attempt to examine them look extravagant: they are absorbed uncritically by the president, who lacks the time to vary his sources or consult other national output on the same subjects, and repeated exactly by the minister before parliament, unconcerned with the meaning of the words he pronounces with such gravity. The Platonic Ideas beloved of our practitioners, extracted from History and reified once and for all, become pure metaphysics (something a metaphysician will perceive more easily than a bureaucrat). They carry authority, however, within and through the social circle where they prevail, with the result that (for example) the general believes some obsessive bit of twaddle because he has read it in his daily paper, the journalist for his part thinking it endorsed by the renowned intellectual who has put it into his report for the Saint-Simon foundation, a document based on sound administrative sources including, in particular, notes produced by army researchers. That is how the ready-made thought of a society is fabricated, what might be called the issues no one questions (except philosophers and anarchists, who resemble each other at least in bowing to no social authority). The result is that debate in well-informed circles usually consists of highly informed discussion of things that do not exist. The weakest points in the experts' notes (in which 'politics' is generally masked by 'policy-making') tend to be the starting point and the conclusion, the presupposition and the objective. Questions like 'European Union, to do what?' and 'Atlantic Alliance, what for?' are always disagreeable, nowhere more so than in Brussels or at NATO summits. They are matched for incongruity only by: 'Where exactly does Europe begin and end on the map?' and 'Defensive alliance, fine, but against whom?'

Foreign policy seems foreign in more ways than one. The more depoliticized it is, the more agreeable and welcome it seems. The 'authority of the thing' has been replaced here by that of the sign, and a ruler weaves illusions out of absolutely nothing. Between anger and prejudice there is no room for facts. A spectacular presidential visit to war-torn Beirut will help the French forget that France is losing out not just in Lebanon but all over a region where it used to carry real weight. Another lightning raid on Sarajevo will delight the photographers and whisk the untenable side of a humanitarian policy out of sight. With the help of television, an adept way with symbols and dogged name-dropping form a sort of bogus diplomacy, a vulgar and gaudy foreign policy of great electoral plausibility. In the domestic struggle where everyone must eventually pay cash, adulteration and unreliability cannot go on for ever, nor is the TV panacea everlasting. Approval levels and poll ratings, economic indicators, electoral results, unemployment curves discriminate between competing individuals and projects. In peacetime, the imaginary and complicated world of international relations, hidden from onlookers, quickly becomes to the TV viewer a judicial combat between Good and Evil, in which the indicated action seems obvious. The purely moral vision suits both the relative impotence of governments and our demand for striking images. The symbolic lends itself to excess anyway, and our manichaeism can be deployed wholeheartedly outside the national frontiers. Thrown into technical unemployment by our democracies which exclude them from current affairs, God and the devil are trying for a comeback in the lands of the Bashi-bazouks. Let the political scientists say how much foresight we can bring to what we call (wrongly, given the inextricable tangle of local and global factors) 'international affairs'. What continues to surprise is the low esteem in which our rulers hold the few bodies that genuinely seek information and try to stay rational (like the excellent Centre d'analyse et de prévision[10] at the Quai d'Orsay, the French equivalent of US policy planning staffs). Although administrations are somewhat better informed than news-papers, these consultants are very rarely consulted by our elected leaders, anyway much less often than poll organizations and public opinion experts by candidates seeking 'winning campaign strategies'. The smaller the stake, the more meticulous the preparations. At election time, money is freely spent to accumulate *surveys* of voting intentions, *studies* of mainstream opinion trends, *analyses* of presidential popularity (positive and negative factors, possibilities, corrections), computer-simulated *estimates* of voting patterns in the coming election, campaign *orientations* (based on representative samples of the segments of the electorate), and *image tuition* for the upcoming prime-time TV showcase. For decisions on war and peace, we make do with near-enough, vague ideas, heroic poses. In domestic politics, for matters like choosing the date of an interview, the name of the next prime minister or which campaign jingle to go with, the staff polishes its arsenals and double-checks its background reasoning. The candidate whose job is at risk tries to make sure of everything; can the diplomat, who risks less, allow himself to show it? Not that anyone imagines an exhaustive knowledge of the factors in play to be possible, or that a decision can be deduced from a counting process. Let alone – far from it – any clear and distinct alternatives (involving laborious 'decision-making processes'), or even any agreement on the definition of criteria (what exactly will be called winning or losing here?): like it or not, he must accommodate to the ambient smokesc-reen. Electoral matters will always be easier to handle and conceptualize. What could be better than a second-round electoral duel between two players and only two, win or lose, limited in time and space, from the viewpoint of an 'operational researcher' for whom it offers an ideal exercise? Alas, mathematical models are worse than useless in the shifting games between multiple players, relatively depersonalized and without arbiter or time limit, that make up the uninter-rupted, diffuse and ungraspable course of world events.

Even if I had tried harder than I did to smooth over a very harsh armature (making things 'simple' takes twice as much work), even if I had provided better after-sales service, there would still be an awkward paradox to deal with: *Si vis pacem para bellum*, 'If you want peace, prepare for war'. The inversion of opposites that characterizes sound (consistent if not necessarily correct) reasoning in this domain deserves malediction.

In strategy, it is an elementary law that the bad way will be the good one. A company advancing across broken terrain is well advised to avoid the main road and choose a footpath, probably less well guarded and more likely to surprise the enemy. The principle calls for very nuanced application, an example of which would be choosing the main road as a double bluff (as in the well-known Jewish story of the Polish Jew en route to Warsaw who told his compatriot: 'I'm going to Warsaw' to convince the other that he was going to Lodz). But the unpardonable vice of sophistication persists: the strategist, fatally paradoxical, bruises our simple and linear causal reasoning, a serious handicap in any 'duel of communication'. Shocking and incomprehensible in their sophisms, bearers of this mental posture make the most antipathetic of paradox merchants; only a crisis or a war, causing the papier-maché to collapse, can give them a chance. The flaw is even more of a handicap today, with the forces of facileness grossly amplified by the impact of images and the shortening of explanations. The image works with positive, primary directness, placing everything in the present and ignoring negation, anticipation and the play of opposites. Our everyday universe is that of WYSIWYG, what you see is what you get; the promise in the strategic universe is that what you see and hear is the opposite of what you will get. Invert the plausible and you find the probable. Turn the image upside down and you come upon reality. And when the dust in people's eyes becomes the grain of things, what doesn't work politically is what works mediatically, and vice versa. Mass communication becomes a school of ineffectuality; everyday pieties intended to speak to the heart at all costs create a truly immoral level of inefficiency. Everything suggests that the small screen consecrates a politics of clichés, the least operational becoming the most believable. The 'right to intervene' is one of the more spectacular examples of this, but why look abroad? When Mitterrand, an excellent domestic strategist, united with the Communist Party in order to get rid of it there were cries of outrage, for the immoral manoeuvre had something to work on. In the international arena the game pits one against a hundred. How do you persuade men and women of heart and common sense that the ghastly nuclear weapon helps preserve peace *because* it is ghastly? That the Bomb indexes security against risk – I will live because we can all die – just as surely as a 'space shield', if it were technically possible, would give birth to the risk of guaranteed security? It would take half an hour of explanation, and attention would wander. How do you convince indignant supporters of international law that the best way to deal with its inveterate violators is not to sever contacts with them but to multiply them, especially on the cultural level? How, in three minutes, do you persuade faithful lackeys of Uncle Sam that to be heard in the US, and to restrain it when necessary, its allies need to counter American designs in the East and the South? That the road to Washington may pass through Moscow, or the inverse? De Gaulle gained acceptance for his twists and turns through the authority he wielded as a rampart against internal disorder, but once he had gone his own camp returned to the familiar and disappointing logics of common sense.

In the market of good ideas people of my species, hawkers of the absurd, have nothing to offer but riddles. Here is one of them: there is nothing more likely to inspire progressive social ideas than a 'conservative' education system; only backward-looking schooling, impervious to ambient conditions on principle, can open minds to the future and the universal, while shutting out external violence. Another: there is no better remedy for nationalism than the republican nation; any weakening of the latter strengthens the former. Or again: the fewer nuclear warheads you possess, the greater their power of deterrence, because their eventual use seems more probable. Perhaps you would prefer this one: an apparently outmoded particularism like Quebec's may mask a futurist kernel that we would be well advised to ponder. Or this: there will be more nationalisms after 'European construction' than there were before it; and the best service France can render Europe, short of dropping it altogether, is to assert its national difference; the other Europeans will be grateful in time, for only by rejecting unanimism will Union be achieved. And one more: it is because we have been suffused with the American spirit, its landscapes, music, cinema and lifestyles, that we should refuse to import these values wholesale and give in to them. A whole catalogue of unsaleable items. With propositions of this type – especially if you try to back them with facts and arguments – you are not competitive. When there is only time for a quick glance, how do we get our teeth into the empire of *false good ideas*? You can find the page but rewinding tape is less easy. By a 'false good idea' I mean one whose inanity you can only attempt to demonstrate on a *second inspection*, the first having passed it as broadly acceptable. Despite recordings, we no longer have the time to re-run the tape; and television, where any speech or statement starts to irritate after five minutes, renders the small phrase undeflectable and the amiable individual the winner on all fronts. What could be more plausible, for example, than the idea that the federal super-state is a natural extension of the slow emancipatory evolution from tribe to province, then from region to nation and now towards the United States of Europe? In front of an open-minded audience, eager for peace and solidarity and still young enough to think History goes in a straight line, without bifurcations or swerves, you would despise yourself for reverting to that nice, simple, logical idea. If we lived for two hundred years, it might be worth spending fifty of them on outside bets of that sort. But until we get a Bogomoletz elixir that works, I think it more realistic (although not very pretty) to rely on the inoffensive cruelty, tempered as it is by the gradual nature of the process and our aptitude for changing the subject when necessary, with which the major illusions of an era tiptoe offstage. The natural course of events seems to me more cogent and less annoying than the killjoys of the day in dissipating the seductive lures ensconced in the taste of the moment (always out of date) during our decades of panting and delirium. When the refutation of current theories is complete, who will remember what has been refuted of our present treaties, conventions and slogans, of what we now hold to be self-evident? I am inclined to think that these things will have become simply *outmoded*, tiresome but touching, along with the laboriously produced antitheses to the same treaties, conventions, slogans and axioms:

stamped indiscriminately, apologies and diatribes both, with the patronizing seal which every period puts on the major dossiers of the preceding one: 'illusions of a bygone age'.

When all is said and done, ingrained proprieties and pieties notwithstanding, it is utterly ridiculous to love your country as you love a person, or God. No one will deny that there are French people somewhere in Europe (as there are English and Portuguese, among others): that is a fact. But the idea that there exists something like *the* French, British or Portuguese nation is an empty construct. Have you ever noticed Belgium, or Italy? What can justify treating an amorphous mass of dissimilar individuals as a young woman or a romantic hero? Attributing the characteristics of a human being to a tract of land is an obvious sign of mental derangement. The historians who tell us that love of country came centuries ago to replace love of God in simple minds are nearer the mark than they realize. The little-Frenchman-who-loves-France, like the Little-Englander and all the rest, feels just as confused, when asked whether his attitude is reasonable, as the believer in God when surrounded and questioned by mocking unbelievers. God is everything to Christians, but intrinsically negligible to infidels. The ambiguous blessing of motherlands, those incommunicable redundancies, is that they exist only in the mind. (If only the moonstruck could organize a common front against the tangible, a preemptive grouping of all the ridiculous minorities, in which the oldest could teach the newcomers how best to cope with adversity . . . but alas, all these cults – although compatible at base, being so fundamental in themselves that they do not *have* a base – are too malevolent and jealous to consider technical collaboration. Every religion, including the national one, has its sects and heresies. In France, the Vercingetorix–Carnot–Jaurès branch and the Clovis–Joan of Arc–Maurras branch, 'two Frances' already at daggers drawn, are unlikely to welcome advice-filled catecheses and pastoral letters from a third reprobate, itself divided into Catholics, Protestants and Orthodox not on the best of terms.)

France does not exist any more than God does: even, statistically speaking, a lot less, given the number of minds it inhabits (1 per cent of the world's population, 0.8 per cent of its land area). Expecting that artistic 1 per cent to change the décor for the remaining 99 per cent has the same relation to apparent mental disturbance as psychosis has to neurosis. The Cyrano syndrome. In the context of this cult of petty differences, the most widespread narcissism on the planet, over-valuation of the collective ego, further boosted by the F for France factor, attains unarguably pathological levels. Arrogance, nostalgia for grandeur, special pleading, exemplarity: the symptoms are well known. The village cockerel exasperates our European competitors, who have to be called 'partners' because they have no interests except complementary ones, as well as those French who confess the different (and better accredited) revealed religion of European Unity. My own Jacobin bumptiousness was joined by delayed-action credulity ('republican voluntarism' is what remains of revolutionary messianism when there are no more messiahs, making the Republic the revolution of the disappointed). Believing it possible to espouse one's century without necessarily joining the ranks – still less 'defending one's rank' like dowager duchesses or floorwalkers – I had thought that France, governed by the heirs of 1909 and 1993, would become the 'irritant of the world'. War it not appreciated by all who rejected both Moscow and Washington? Our up-to-date socialists, though, had enough on their plates already, with France plc heading for bankruptcy, to bother with *The Parlement of Foules* as well. Their transcendence lay elsewhere, with the Individual, civil society, human rights; their supreme model was American democracy. Europe may have been our future, but America was our present.

Great was my surprise, then, on perceiving that the soldiers of 'l'an II' charged with shaking the Thrones and Dominions – 'die to deliver all peoples, your brothers' – were themselves anxiously attentive to the slightest 'North American reaction' ('markets' were not yet mentioned). A hostile piece in the *Wall Street Journal* or *Washington Post* would reduce the press services to worried silence, our own only coming back to life on noticing how, within an hour of the alarm being sounded, all the advisers were on deck, holding feverish meetings in the Fournier room to improvise firebreaks: sending bankers to Washington on 'goodwill missions', serial dining with the Paris correspondents, tours by great artists and big bosses, phone calls to transatlantic friends and relations. Panic at the thought of not being respectable, making a mess in the drawing room or even, God forbid, not being received, can lend wings to the most sluggish imagination. Preparations for a visit to Paris by the emperor of the West would set the entire Palace's teeth on edge eight days in advance. Ordinarily a rather nonchalant house, running like an old rustic clock to a mechanical barracks ritual (reveille, changing of the guard, guards of honour, fanfares), it would be filled with anxious scurrying when the countdown began. An army of feather dusters, secateurs, cloths, hoists, ladders and lawnmowers was deployed in every corner to polish brass, wax floors, wash walls, rake gravel, clip grass borders, replant orange trees; normally ponderous advisers would be seen sprinting about the corridors, ebullient ones becoming unapproachable curmudgeons. You could feel a great event approaching, and the nervous irritation mounting from day to day (and could not help thinking of a provincial pharmacist's household preparing in good time for a decisive dinner, at which the Prefect was going to be present in person). Clandestine guest lists would circulate amid a murmur of consternation. Who was going to be at the dinner? Let in for coffee? In the side salon with the rest of the American delegation? Those who had seen their names on the A list hid their triumph, the others their desolation. The arrival of the Secret Service to inspect the site – Ray-Bans and earpieces, tall elegant figures, relaxed but precise gestures, sexy and striking – brought us all to the windows, mesmerized: real-life cinema. Our fat little official visit heavies waddled panting at their heels in trousers like concertinas, desperately keen, mumbling bad English in response to laconic enquiries from the sleek, feline, disdainful new masters of the Palace. One could only look ruefully away. When will our chubby Frog constabulary give up its brimming tumblers of *rouge* for orange juice? When will we be up to the mark, when will we have flat stomachs? Forget it; the enviable chic of superman bodyguards is not for everyone. This sadness would subside as the hours passed (even though the Secret Service could be plainly seen to control the whole place, gardens, access points and staircases), and with the excitement at its peak, on the evening before the big day, a protocol damsel would tactfully inform me that I could take the next day off, best take a couple of files home with me, I'd get a bit of peace anyway. There are times when an 'anti-American' should stay at home if he doesn't want to cause embarrassment. This happened to me every time the 'planetarch', as the Greeks call the American president, came to Paris or Versailles: just like *coitus interruptus*, a slow build-up and no release.

It was said that France faced the major task of 'moving on from nostalgia for power to the objective of influence'. This is the duty of the middling, men and countries both, as they watch their reserves of sovereignty diminish by the day (starting with what makes them different from others). The middling is in-between; it volunteers its good offices, as it sits with the *adjutores Dei*, passively in relation to the Almighty, actively where sinners are concerned. France wanted thus to serve as intermediary between America at the very top and, at the bottom, black Africa, where the local presidents receive our own – who gets through five of them in three days, like an American president in Europe – with the same anxious excitement, the same wish that everything should go impeccably, that we have when 'offering the White House guest appropriate levels of comfort and security'. Such is the fractal structure of power relations, reproduced identically on different scales. The problem with a middling country is that it feels too big to take an interest in small ones, while being too small to interest the big ones. We *did* intrigue American bigwigs in 1981, because they saw our roses as a bit louche, vaguely threatening, worth keeping an eye on, but in the years that followed I noted many signs of a diminution in their curiosity and consideration for an 'impeccable ally', so successful had we been in papering over the small difference. Once in orbit a satellite is boring, and Cape Canaveral looks elsewhere. Taken up these days with the new continental director, Germany, our American friends can no longer spare much of their European time for the French, conscientious but a bit slow (like ourselves with the Senegalese, those too-good pupils). And Senegalese was how I felt in North America, which I had not visited since 1961, being unable to get a visa. With the same amazement and delight as an old-time Dakar swot, raised on 'our ancestors the Gauls' and all that stuff, discovering that in the Latin Quarter it is allowed and even encouraged to make fun of the government and education system, I travelled about the admirable United States, the last place in the West where you can badmouth US imperialism without being taken for a mental defective or neo-Nazi. The competitive escalation usual in colonized countries obliges their nationals to visit the metropolis if they want to decolonize their minds; and remarks that get you called a griping, fascist-leaning anti-American at home in Paris seem perfectly normal and sensible in a *New York Times* canteen or Rand Corporation conference room. Personally, I count it among the paradoxical benefits of that Elysian period that it rendered me rather more 'pro-American' (to use the idiot term). It was the US, for example, that made the South African struggle against apartheid, hitherto a marginal concern restricted to pious communist and 'left-Catholic' circles, a live issue for our establishment. Shortly after meeting Oliver Tambo in Stockholm in 1982, I thoughtlessly took the initiative of inviting him to Paris. The acting leader of the ANC was given a furtive welcome; Claude Cheysson and the principled and decent Danielle Mitterrand both welcomed him with open arms, but no one else took any interest. A little later the black American community took to the streets, *Time* and *Newsweek* joined the fray and Ted Kennedy went to South Africa to berate the Afrikaners on their own doorstep. The cause was carried, and before long a trip to Soweto became a must for us. In 1981 the name Nelson Mandela left the official world indifferent; ten years later there was a ferocious scrum to be photographed with him. The 'American empire' had moved the French left to the left. As a civil servant, too, I was attracted to that dilapidated Rome, envious of the very Gramscian way it provides the means – intellectual as well as financial and military – for hegemony and the projection of force. Where outside Washington is there a more comprehensive flow of data from the entire world, or a wider range of perspectives on it? Making the round of US foreign policy think-tanks – the Hoover Institute, Georgetown, Johns Hopkins, Carnegie, Harvard, etc. – seeing the tolerance, the critical boldness, the freedom of tone prevailing in the reviews and conferences of the 'strategic community', made me understand how far the periphery has fallen behind, how narrowly provincial our own authorized views of the outside world have become. The joke is that most of these views are inspired by a metropolis that does not believe in them itself. In 1985 there was a great deal of talk in the Paris papers, clubs and foundations about a tremendous strategic and technical revolution derived from the 'space shield' and its 'laser weapons'. It was said that the SDI or 'Strategic Defense Initiative' was going to make nuclear deterrence redundant, along with our bomblet. Yves Montand presented a big explanatory TV broadcast under-lining the decisive nature of the change, which would perhaps enable us *in extremis* to hold back the waves of the Red Army. The impact on local opinion was enormous. It so happened that I had been in Washington a few days earlier as a guest of Richard P., at that time under-secretary for defense in the Reagan administration, number two at the Pentagon. I had got on well with that ferociously anti-Soviet specialist in John Donne, English baroque poets and nuclear planning (a combination that would be strongly discouraged in a

Frenchman, while over there a two-way traffic between the universities and the administration is expected). He explained to me in some detail that the much-vaunted cosmic turning point was a communication trick he had concocted at the president's request, to exhaust the Soviet Union financially and squeeze some extra research and development credit out of the taxpayer. Otherwise it was a load of garbage for foreign consumption. I informed President Mitterrand of all this in detail on my return; Védrine had already warned him that it was just a vast diversion. It is one of the American miracles that a personal affinity can spring up between a curious anti-imperialist patriot and a clever imperial patriot. And there is a further twist, intrinsic really to a complex legally based state: when my friend passed through Paris he was subject, despite his very senior rank, to a regulation giving the US ambassador the right to vet all local contacts of members of the administration passing through his country of residence, and did not get permission to see me. So he adopted cloak-and-dagger methods, meeting me secretly in the back rooms of bars to talk alexandrines and kilotonnes. How can one dislike a country where free men are to be found even at the centre of officialdom?

1989. That the bicentenary of the French Revolution should have coincided with its interment, that socialists should have presided over the disappearance of the socialist idea in this country, that the left should have followed a right-wing policy . . . this anecdotal material represents a constant that is still under-estimated, and that all shades of political opinion liable to be disappointed in future should take in immediately: the political form of snobbery in the unbranding of the self. The childish pleasure we take in contradicting the idea others have of us, teasing the neighbour-adversary by doing the opposite of what he expects ('Got you there, eh? Nyaa!'). The socialist tries hard to make himself agreeable to the businessman, like a general talking metaphysics to a professor or a neo-liberal displaying social awareness. This semi-instinctive minuet is not unconnected with our political upsets, divine or accursed depending on your point of view. You can always depend on a socialist to wipe away the last traces of Jaurès on earth, on a Gaullist to erase even the shadow of a debt to de Gaulle (as if every new team wanted to start by showing its adversaries that it could do as well as them, if not better). I sometimes wonder if this perpetual bantering interplay between the professionals, who prudently make no mention of it in their programmes, might not justify the rank-and-file amateur in trying a reverse vote: left for a right-wing policy, right for a left-wing one. Of course it may be thought a bad idea to give the game away like that. If everyone joined in we would be back where we started.

Enough joking: there is something in the irony of history that can freeze any inclination to take sides. 'Perverse effect' is almost too limp a term for it. Everyone knows that before taking a positive measure, one should try to assess the negative repercussions in advance. Banning alcohol and tobacco advertising may be good for public health, but threatens the freedom of a press dependent on advertising revenue. Decentralizing public administration is good for local democracy, but also for corruption in general and transnational mafias. The star-spangled blue flag of Europe, the Virgin Mary's banner adapted by a Jesuit, cuts the cackle of the nation-states but announces the reappearance of feudal magnates. Tocqueville showed how faithfully the Jacobins followed the statist programme of the Bourbons they had decapitated; the timeworn conservative argument for doing nothing is that any sudden change in the status quo must inevitably lead to regression. The familiar vicious circle is further complicated by the gap between the personalities of the actors and the content of their action. The whole of history resembles a Brecht play in which the best characters do the worst things and the worst characters do good ones, all without knowing it. It is like *Mother Courage*: we identify spontaneously with the mother amid the horrors of war; she wheels her canteen trolley and fights for peace, a fine life force; but by earning her living from reiters she involuntarily causes the loss of her own children. In 1960 it would never have occurred to me to visit Rabat, but I made a pilgrimage to Tunis to meet the spokesmen of the Algerian armed struggle: obviously Ben Bella was much more engaging than Hassan II. In 1970 I still loathed the Moroccan government (for good reasons), and admired the proud Algerian nationalism. Twenty years later, though, it was apparent that the king of Morocco, as great a politician as he is an unpleasant individual, had made a bearable country where people can breathe freely, think, read and talk; while the heroes of the Algerian struggle, so estimable as individuals, had produced the disheartening Algeria we now see.

To understand the distinction that should be made between the actor and his acts, Brecht recommended distancing. This is easier in the theatre, watching an episode from the Thirty Years' War, than in the street amid the live unfolding of history. So pleasant people do unpleasant things, do they (and vice versa)? Perhaps they do, but they speak to me engagingly from the small screen every day and send me chatty circular letters; they have familiar faces and voices, a discourse that seems consistent. The other things you mention are for later, they concern me less, and in any case the worst may not happen . . .

I tried my best, but did not achieve enough distance to assemble a relativized, professionally objective view. To accept the reality of that 1 per cent; to understand what 'becoming an adult democracy of calm minds' signifies for a republic; what it means for a former Great Power to 'develop its powers of proposal and influence'. From now on Western policy was going to be made in Washington, and ours in the stock exchange. I did not feel able to congratulate us French, us Europeans, on the status of internal autonomy we continue to enjoy ('independence within interdependence', as the ever-tactful Edgar Faure put it for the Tunisians). I did not manage to complete in time (somewhat to my shame, for I pride myself on my realism) the retreat into heritage, the land of culture – scents, abbeys, big tables, museums – the sweet and comely France where it is so good to live. I just could not resign myself to seeing us ushered out of History in this way, with a firm hand on the elbow and handsome compliments. I could not even stomach official francophonie, a synthetic consolation product: France is a kingdom of language, of course, but it takes more than a language to make a kingdom (what becomes of a dialect without guns, machine tools, telefilms?). No doubt it was an illusion, my belief that we could remain a great nation while ceasing to be a great power. The belief is not painless, and the most astonishingly rapid decline in our history (apart from military defeats which are quicker to repair) has made me suffer ghost pains, like an amputee. Amputated of nothing very solid: a trace, an absence, a departed uppercase. Those who are fortunate enough not to have these things inscribed in their neurons suffer less. When pointless service becomes painful, it is time to stop retreating.

I am the first to admit the absurdity of all this. The first to laugh at pathetic widowers of romantic fiction who tear their hair because Heaven is unoccupied. They appeal to God; no one answers. Abandonment, despair, solitude. Stoical pride. God won't answer. God ignores them. But if there is no one up there, my dears, you are getting worked up for nothing. The phone is quite simply ringing in an empty office: no one there, *nada.* Pointless to try table-turning. The national widower has some of the slightly comic emphasis of Alfred de Vigny on the Mount of Olives, although the patriotic Narcissus replaces divine displeasure with historical disgrace.

What can a slightly barmy seminarian who has got into the archbishop's palace through the service entrance do when he discovers that the Princes of the Church in the drawing room are atheists? Hang up his cassock and wait for better days . . . as good a way as any to save the furniture. How can you serve a state that no longer believes in itself? How can you leave your name in the official lists, even if you haven't drawn pay in years? That feeling of imposture, like tight armpits in a jacket, leads sooner or later to resignation. Mine came too late, like repartee on the way downstairs.

Paris, 28 December 1992

To Monsieur Marceau Long
Vice-President of the Council of State
Palais-Royal, Paris

Mr President,
   The courtesy, open-mindedness and sense of duty, not to mention the professional competence, of the members of the Council of State who between 1985 and 1988 welcomed me as one of their number (despite the poverty of my claims on their esteem), will long remain in my memory. This is no mere stylistic flourish, Mr President. In that relatively unknown body, overloaded with difficult and badly paid work, I found a quality of awareness, and sometimes of selflessness, that make the clichés of its detractors doubly displeasing.

I had found it convenient, in 1988, to return to my studies in philosophy and history rather than persisting with research on jurisprudence in a sub-section of the Legal Department, a most estimable task but of limited intellectual interest. A straightforward principle of economy of effort may have explained my departure. Having at present no other 'safety net' in either the civil service or the private sector, everything (from the respect and friendship I feel for so many of my colleagues to the tedium of having to live by writing) ought to persuade me to come back to the Palais-Royal. But in the meantime my 'convenience' has become personal soul-searching on the value of serving the state today. Pointless to beat about the bush or seek the expedient or available: in the end, sacrificing principles for comfort becomes too uncomfortable. I must therefore, with regret, Mr President, tender my resignation. Seeing myself 'deleted from the official list', as the official expression has it, will be less painful to me than watching from close quarters the daily diminution of the Republic.

Let me explain what I mean.

The Council of State is a seat of excellence. But there should also be a state for it to advise. What is the use of serving something that no longer has anything to serve? Why care for a body whose soul is dying? The Republican State has deserted its own principles and aims, so that the one we have today, although its linear descendant, is only superficially similar. Such is the scale of the catastrophe that it would be wrong to attribute it to one temporarily dominant faction, party or coalition rather than another. The putting to sleep appears to be a collective and collegial responsibility of past, present and future governments.

On the pretext of 'modernization', public services have degenerated into commercial enterprises and the general interest has been supplanted everywhere by the logic of profitability; on the pretext of 'regionalization', family dynasties, kinglets and regional notables have reappeared, a regression into feudalism of what was supposed to be one and indivisible; on the pretext of 'tolerance' and 'the right to be different', secular education has been undone and schooling delivered into the hands of religious communities or subjected to the changing needs of local bosses, at the whim of the local order; under cover of 'European construction', responsibilities are unloaded onto neighbouring countries, and we are abdicating from all will of our own, without our self-regard suffering; in the name of 'Western solidarity', the nation has been aligned with – alienated to – external hegemonies, until French forces deployed everywhere, in a real theatre of operations or some UN farce, are under direct American command; under the anaesthetizing effect of images, private charity is being substituted for civic obligations, the one-day charity spectacular for a more laborious effort to establish a just system, Boy-Scout idealism for public development aid; under constant invocations of 'civil society', a plethora of independent administrative authorities, committees of wise men, specialized organizations and lobbies of all sorts are taking the place of the citizen and his elected representatives (law deliberated in common being unseated by uncontrolled regulation); finally the promotion to strictly political posts, after a pernicious confusion of roles, of industrial knights and publicists, really the nibbling away of the Republic by what denies it in word and deed: individual affairism and mediatic demagogy. That is the picture that faces us. Forgive me if I seem myopic.

Of course I realize that the French type of democracy that was called 'Republic' is not the ultimate form of human development and that our high jurisdiction is not accountable for the course of events or the way the world is going. Nor am I unaware that the mimetic pursuit by our elites of the American model of life and thought goes back at least as far as General de Gaulle's departure in 1969; or that the global Restoration we are undergoing at present does not much encourage fidelity to principles deriving from the French Revolution.

Some naïve individuals, of whom I was one, had high hopes that a political change in 1981 might counter this tendency or reverse the drift. The things said at the time suggested that our side had a different idea of humanity and of public office. Since the new religion of internal profit and external normality had clearly won over its one-time adversaries, I respectfully asked the President of the Republic to release me from the duties I carried out for him. The Council of State seemed to me to be one of the possible seats of resistance to the atmosphere of the time. For it is protected (isn't it?) from the tyranny of public opinion, from pressure exerted by powerful individuals and from any need to bother with its 'image'. I will not conceal from you, Mr President, the fact that I have come recently to doubt all this. And when I read at the top of our House's information bulletin (December 1992) the exultant device: 'Council of State, more European than ever!', I feel some anxiety for the governing ideas of the Republic, in which I am feeble enough to believe.

The Council's recent decisions – those taken since 1987 including the Nicolo decree, running counter to all its earlier jurisprudence – have already made French laws subject to community regulations, in a manner strangely reminiscent of international treaties. Giving European law primacy over national law makes it clear that our legislative debates are inane, our Parliament is without function and the old principle that the people is the source of all power is obsolete. I just wonder whether, when the people's sovereignty has gone, the one that replaces it will be supranational or infranational, and whether the vast European impotence can really replace our modest public power. In 1992 a decree legalized the wearing of the veil and other religious signs in the Republic's schools. France being the only country in Europe that was secular on constitutional principle, it was surely time to remove the anomaly. One against eleven, obviously unreasonable . . .

To a republican, a law legalizing something does not legitimize what is intrinsically illegitimate. Otherwise, mutatis mutandis, the racial laws promulgated by the French state in 1940 would have to be thought respectable because they were validated in very regular fashion after examination by the Council of State of that time, and approved by majority opinion. 'And so being unable to render that which is just strong, we arranged for that which is strong to be just . . .'

You know better than I do, Mr President, thanks to your lofty views and incomparable sense of the state, that fear of missing the last train often sends people to the wrong platform. Personally I am far from sure that it will help to protect citizens against the return of the barbarians to adapt them, in other words subject them, to the prevailing relations of force. What I believe, or believe I know, about French history would tend rather to suggest the opposite.

So I hope you will accept, Mr President, the assurance of my greatest respect and regret.

The *respect* was, and remains, real; the *regret*, I am afraid, a half-lie. When this letter had been posted (after half an hour of dithering on the pavement) I have to admit that I could breathe more freely. Following the resentment of the choirboy who had found the tabernacle empty, there now appeared a rather inglorious relief: the return to vagabondage. Without stopping sorrow, anger and envy from continuing to vie for predominance, this return to old ways opened up a sort of holiday space in which imprudence could exist. There had been ten years of best behaviour. Heedless as I still was of the stifling Paris of letters and ideas – 'corridors of power' have the fresh charm of a children's playground by comparison – I believed myself restored to a time of free thought and action, for nothing, for their own sake, not as part of some 'stroke' or counterstroke. Able at last to go over lost time without looking over my shoulder, worrying about microphones left on, hidden cameras. We do not appreciate the moral luxury of that vice reserved for the careless, of which we are swiftly deprived by the company of the great: the gaffe or *faux pas*. The privilege of having emotions we don't have to hide. Of not having to have an ear to the ground, a finger on the public pulse. If you spend too much time with the prudent, you can become prudent yourself. We all know that prudence is the mother of security. Unfortunately there is a handsome prudence and an ugly one, and I had no idea how easy it is to move from one to the other. How do we tell the twin sisters apart? The prudence of a responsible man of action is a freely assumed virtue; the prudence of image-haunted men of inaction operates under constraint: not so much morality as civil defence. Those great worriers, under perpetual surveillance, cannot drop their guard for a second: not so much circumspection as lockjaw and paralysis. It is not their fault that they are more exposed than the average man to the reversal of their intentions. Our deeds and gestures turn against us, that is the human condition; once launched they turn on the wing, loop the loop and zoom back boomerang-style to flatten us. In the mediatic agora, an echo-chamber lined with distorting mirrors, in which what is said about what you have said or done sooner or later becomes what you are believed to have said or done, the theft of actions and words is an industry, an organized and tolerated pillage that makes law. Everyone adapts, appropriates, refashions other people with all his might at every opportunity. The quarry goes to ground, doors and windows closed, plays dead, acts the idiot. Wooden phrases and a wooden life. Our representatives declaim, guzzle, inaugurate, clink glasses, have love affairs, show off, prance around, for no other reason than to escape that sticky, ever-present fear. Not the blue funk caused by incoming shellfire or everything going up in flames: that sort of fear is memorable, useful, a stimulus to courage. The prime worry of the people at the controls (and those around them, the parasites of parasites) is how to avoid slaps in the face: they dodge nervously from one small fear to another, acquiring over time a sour unhealthy look. It shows in tensely lifted shoulders, a rigid curved back, a slightly fixed smile; in a certain huddled stance and sidelong approach, sails (as it were) heavily reefed against possible squalls. In private, some manage to straighten up, shake themselves and retrieve their natural posture, their own voice and words. Public men or women only unbend behind closed doors, off the record; when they become themselves in this way they are hardly recognizable. There is something touching about these returns to childhood in closed committee, these rare moments when the vulnerable forget minefields and missiles. It isn't that our elected leaders, always on the lookout for 'bold solutions', lack the 'political courage' to 'confront problems'. That more or less statutory courage is part of the job. But in order to display boldness in dealing with 'the great choices facing society', as editorialists and parliamentarians call them, they first have to save their necks. To stay 'in the race', among the 'front runners'. Alongside the great if possible, among lesser lights if need be, but still in the know, in the scrimmage. Merely keeping afloat in this way will cost ten or twenty years of anxiety, with one big petty fear each day. Fear of getting stuck somewhere, by doing too much; of missing the boat, by not doing enough; fear of sinking. Fear of getting wet, of being caught out. By a word too much, a tape recorder left running, an embarrassing photo, the handshake that marks a man for life, that his opponent puts on a poster and his biographer on the dustjacket. Fear of not smiling for the camera and looking sinister, or of grinning like a clown. Fear of tomorrow's paper, fear of the hotel desk clerk who may have seen him go upstairs with a lady not his wife, fear of a bad poll rating, fear of Thursday morning when the *Canard enchaîné* appears, the *Official Gazette* of his parish; fear of the Sunday-evening Exocet fired from his own camp, fear of the grins on the opposition benches on Monday, fear of adopting a position on Tuesday that Thursday's events will prove wrong, fear of making a bad choice on Friday and not correcting it in time on Saturday, fear of messing up his TV interview on Sunday. Genius, they say in the profession, is making no errors. And the worst error, professionally speaking, is remaining alone: being cut off from his rank and file, from his electorate, from the boss, from his 'friends'. Hence the daily vigilance. No one ever knows what tomorrow will be made of, or the way it will go (that public sector strike, that coup d'état in Russia, that reform of social security, that wobbling coalition). Hence the real reserve, the long pondering sprinkled with small remarks like thistles in a meadow, just enough to avoid being walked on. To titillate opinion without shocking it, to emerge from cover without exposing himself, to support without being servile, to distance himself without breaking away, to correct his aim without seeming to, to say without saying, to do without doing. The ideal stance of one who has to take without being taken: a falsely nonchalant alertness, a pointed and attentive indifference, withdrawn but ready to pounce. Stretched taut, for life. Our Princes, those least free of men, those predatory tightrope walkers, can never be themselves. Not much depends on them but they depend on everything and everyone.

Leaving Venice one day Dürer exclaimed: 'How I shall miss the sun! Here I am a gentleman and at home a parasite.' When a parasite has let go, he can be a gentleman. Left to himself, excused from waiting, freed from scrutiny. Anyone can become a gentleman in a republic if they have the leisure, luck or folly to live as their hearts dictate, at their own rhythm, without having to plug into the approval ratings every morning and march in step. One willing to swim against the tide, to 'stand alone in support of a view abandoned by the crowd', occupies the noble's position in an opinion-based democracy. He does not want others to endorse the validity of his judgement; he is not worried about exposing his flank or 'confusing the picture'. I know of no more intoxicating release than having no public. Having to answer only to yourself, and never trying to fit in with the course of events.

It was servitude, depending on a lord who was himself dependent on all that did not depend on him. And pure insanity to think of a seigneury for oneself. To cruise in those waters, to live at ease among the slaves of the time, one would have had to relish the prevailing wind of polls, ratings and league tables. Oil and water don't mix. A creative person ought to live and think, not even really against all that, but on its margins; a politician lives, thinks and breathes through and for all that. Be he artist or cleric, an individual who cares about quality ought to hear alarm bells if he finds himself becoming acceptable or popular; a public man needs to worry when he stops being these things. Where did I learn this primary truth?

Imprudence is the first step towards sovereignty. Unpopularity, the second.

6

Ite Missa Est

Heaven's juries – Tilling the sea – All progress is technical – For laughter as for tears – An animal that needs masters

'*Ambition*: satisfactory. *Application*: mediocre. *Aptitudes*: fair. *Results*: poor.' The idlers of my class will face the juries of Heaven with a poor school report, and it is most annoying. God is no longer francophone, and will not be doing us any favours. We can expect nothing from the jury of history (Saint Louis, Retz, Bonaparte and de Gaulle); *de minimis non curat praetor*, let it be whispered; fortunately, though, I am told that in the same corridor, next door, the Three Musketeers run a remedial course for slackers ('imaginary compensations, novels and stories'). The right quip should serve to relax the atmosphere: 'D'Artagnan', I will say, 'was not unworthy of the circumstances but the circumstances were unworthy of d'Artagnan . . .' There is no guarantee that this device will win a smile from them. The exam-failures' refrain must become tiresome over the years. No matter. All presumptuous nonentities are vain enough to want 'could have done better' to be scrawled under their lives by a competent examiner; it achieves nothing concrete, but saves face.

Should I blame our unlucky star? A bit obvious. Better to plead a bad vantage-point, like Flaubert's Frédéric. Let us pass over the absence of really interesting vicissitudes. The Fronde, Waterloo, June 1940: these misfortunes only happen to others. Let us also pass over the clowning of circumstances. For one whose inclination was anti-state, it was an untimely castration to become the Curia errand-boy at the very moment when business was downgrading administration; the customer, the user; the minor judge, great ministers; contract personnel, permanent staff; the journalist, the teacher; private initiative, public service; the law of the market, regulation; territorial groupings, the central state; the European mean, the French exception; and what is mediocre about America, what used to be fine in Europe. This outclassing, or reclassifying, or downgrading, fed into a mainstream where every patriot was on his own, trying to avoid going down with the rest. What is a change of terrain compared to a change of civilization? The end of a millennium is not the end of *the* world, just the end of *a* world. We are privileged to be present not at the end of one world alone, however, but at the end of three. It was in our astrological chart that three historical cycles of unequal length would all reach their natural term in the space of a single lifetime: the Printing Press cycle, which began in the fifteenth century, the Republic cycle which began in the eighteenth, and the Proletariat cycle, which began in the nineteenth. 1448, 1792 and 1917. The Printed Word, Reason and the Future, the three pillars of our secular religion, have all crumbled before our eyes, under our feet. How can we continue to say mass when the missal has vanished? Never in the past have so many breaks occurred simultaneously. Futile to whine or complain: let us rather relish the privilege. It won't happen again for a while.

When I first put on the cassock, around 1960, politics felt good and smelt of fresh ink. A fact was only credible when you had *read* it in the paper; these days it doesn't exist unless you have seen it on TV. It was risky, but not contemptible, to try to modify History by bringing its silences and its dead to life on paper. But image people have supplanted book people at the controls (and that professional influencer, the intellectual, now works in TV or film). Saying it in words rather than images was like clinging to the arbalest in the era of the flintlock musket. Holding the future at the end of your pen, in the dream-state the writer-reformer needs to violate the innocent blankness of the page, is no longer technically permitted. Which of us has not at some time been here? (At last *they* are going to see the truth, *they* will have to change their ways. With the stuff I'm slipping them this time – all those readers avid for knowledge – the Communist Party will have no choice but to start dissolving itself, and the socialists to elect a new managing committee. The ENA might close? The Quai d'Orsay have to recall our permanent delegation to the UN? Probably. But I can't help it: truth is in charge. My new book has been swamped by twenty others of equivalent calibre on the same subject, has it? Got barely a couple of three-line mentions? Been remaindered after three weeks? Classic conspiracy of silence, of course. But just wait till next time, you'll see . . .) We inky-fingered brethren have moved on from the strategic to the picturesque: cottage-industry lacemakers now, Alençon point or Chantilly point, a textile survival, woven text. No one tries to prevent us from offering the bibliophile hand-finished phrases, one curiosity among others. For serious matters, look at the screen.

If we had just moved on from revolution to reform – as from first class to second, or from poetry to prose – we would only have experienced a *decrescendo*, something between a slowing and a diminution. What has actually happened is more like a change of score. We have got off the train. The period has not changed, but time has. When I was 20, time was a travel chit, a mobilization order. It was illuminated by what went before, and called us towards the future. Politics was our big thing because time was suspended like a bridge, and we lived suspended from the October Revolution, that huge deviation, and the French Revolution, that unfinished, endless or (rather) still-to-be-completed journey. Time was a signposted vector from the past to a future not programmable but predictable, not radiant but unprecedented, different from the known. Time was a great journey, leading us from a *minus* towards a *plus*. Our destination was another world which did not yet exist anywhere, but which we were promised; and it was in the name of that promise that people had the spirit and the insight to reject counterfeit efforts.

By what do we feel summoned for duty today? And which way is forward? Journey's end. Everyone gets out. No more suspension, ladies and gents: just one event after another, endlessly. No more play, no more curtain up and final curtain. The world has stopped being a theatre and History an ongoing drama. What is fading away at the turn of this millennium (surely the least millenarian of the three or four of which vague traces survive) is the anticipation, indeed the very idea, of a dénouement.

But was it ever reasonable to expect one; has anything played on that stage ever had a proper ending? Did we have to *make a drama* out of the sound and the fury?

Like many afflicted with tuberculosis, Simón Bolívar was lucid at the end. Before retiring to Santa Marta to cough his life away among the coconut palms and flamboyants on the seashore, that 47-year-old octogenarian sent a letter to General Florés, dated 9 November 1830, setting down the 'few sure conclusions' he had reached: South America was ungovernable, the only thing to do was emigrate, and the most likely permanent state of that part of the world would be 'primeval chaos'. He added: 'Serving a revolution is ploughing the sea.' Should not the last word of a man on a horse be the motto of a thousand subversive or conservative pedestrians? Perhaps the great Venezuelan's wry testament is less pessimistic than it seems. For unlike the stagnant waters of lake or marsh, the sea, so accurately termed a 'splendid bitch' by Valéry, is 'constantly renewed', each wave, born as its predecessor subsides, offering our gaze a promise of youth. It calls for a new ploughshare and happy cultivators convinced that they can do better than others. About every fifteen years (the average rhythm of the swell these days), in the trough behind the departing crest, earnest reformers exhort us to 'reinvent' politics that have declined with the previous period: to recreate democracy, to reformulate, recast, relaunch. Left and right alike, we rush eagerly forward with our ploughs to work the slope of the next wave. It does not take very prolonged scrutiny to see this ritual 'reinventing', the somewhat repetitious rites of chronic reinvention, as having the eternal back-and-forth rhythm of a pendulum. Our leaders summon us to start again, and the believer, who fears that he will go down like a stone along with his belief, clings to any 'prospect for the future' that is tossed to him as if it were a lifebuoy. In this way we give the next undulation the exciting allure of a renaissance, until the crest of the wave that will start us – us or our children – on the downward slope to remorse or disgust. But not for long. We'll be back. Crammed meetings, fervour on the streets, elections, a new team at the controls. Soon things turn bad. Recover. Relapse. Recover again. The manic-depressive cycle of militant hopes harmonizes perfectly with individual neurotic configurations of that type, and it is no surprise that the rise and fall of partisan fervour coincides with marked mood-swings. 'You can do anything,' Picasso said, 'provided you never give up and start again.' If our politicians (God forbid) genuinely took that artist's dictum as their motto, I wager there would be no candidates at the next elections: no parties, party conferences or programmes. But there is no chance of this happening. On this terrain every newcomer promises a new copy, then recommences the old one; and no sooner have we denounced one broken promise than we are turning towards the next.

The reason why I have so loved drafts and beginnings, in America or France, is that the birth of an *ordine novo* (far more glittering than the promotion of a new team in a state already smoothed by time) carries a feeling that the breach in the ramparts, this time, will resemble great art. That this time a people, or a *Zeitgeist*, or a doctrine, is going to create unprecedented forms of the social contract, whatever they are called: self-management, dictatorship of the proletariat or participation. That there will be a break at last with the scholasticism of the past (whether called class society, mass alienation or domination by élites). That the politician can at last become *inventive*. The 'historic turning point', the 'great day', is the moment when the wave breaks, topped with shimmering white froth, and people persuade themselves that this one, at least, is going to be different. It is that sense of imminence that gives beginnings their pathetic beauty, that anxious joy common to discoverers of infallible systems for winning at cards and pioneers of the new times brought by victorious revolutions or régimes in crisis. In 1961 I witnessed the proclamation of socialism in the still-smart streets of Havana; in 1979 I watched the small Sandinist army enter a jubilant Managua, a drab no man's land transformed into a sort of 14 July Champs-Elysées, combatants and civilians so intermingled that you couldn't tell who was marching past whom; in 1981 I saw a procession of sober-suited males ascending the steps of the Panthéon arm in arm. And at each change of tack, I could hear the words of the young Hegel, haloed in morning freshness: 'The great work of art, divine in its essence, is collective organization, the main thought that haunts men's minds at all times of social crisis.'

An *idée fixe* but a misleading one, transposing to the political register expectations which are really aesthetic. 'Divine'; and diabolical too, not only because it reduces the organized to the status of clay, a mass of raw material subject to the kneading and gouging of a remote sculptor. That metaphor's cruel sterility was amply demonstrated by the 'totalitarian' experiment. But also because even assuming this act of creation to be possible, the Modeller can still never be an artist in the proper sense: however arbitrary or megalomaniacal he may be, he will only really be able to *improvise* on the basis of an unalterable method, embroidering on the limited space of a subjacent canvas its incompleteness, with margins of invention now reduced practically to nothing. There is not a 'cynical and utilitarian' way of exercising power on the one hand and a way that is 'moral and disinterested' on the other (as is claimed, when an old left is reaching the end of its cycle, by a new evangelical left whose deeds will not match its words). Of course there are various ways of thinking about politics, and conceiving policies, because talk is free; but their practice seems a lot more severely circumscribed. Contemporary creativity is at its lowest here.

Our disillusion has been in scale with our expectations. The reason why we fell so far in 1989 is that in France since 1789 those expectations had been beyond measure. That was the moment when hope in radically new times replaced, in people's minds, the instructive or merely diverting spectacle of the eternal comedy, which – unburdened as it then was by any demand for a resolution or ontological fireworks – had hitherto been sufficient in itself to occupy cartographers of the human heart. It would be no exaggeration to say that for the last two centuries, the lowest common denominator of participants in political struggle, whatever the period or colour of the politics, has been *disappointment*: the leitmotiv that runs through all memoirs (except when they are works of propaganda intended to motivate or edify). The lives of our winners, who have given their names to airports, libraries and squares, can hardly be called 'hollow' or 'bitter' victories. But what do the others say, not the illustrious captains but the foot-soldiers of hope who lived long enough to look back over their past struggles? What does Jules Vallès say of the Commune, Ravanel or Claude Bourdet of the Resistance, Sadoul of communism? That they sweated blood to get rid of the old world, and it came back anyway . . . In 1945 after 1938, in 1796 after 1788, in 1996 after 1916. A litany of sadnesses. Admirable though I find these Sisyphean toilers, I cannot help wondering whether their disillusion is yet another illusion, an eighth veil to titillate the gaze of our grandest ex-idealists.

If I had the cheek to see my own incomparably more modest failures as an initiation, overlaying thirty years of disappointments with the morality of a fable (to the point of stripping those tribulations of the suspense that, from false move to unforeseen consequences, kept one going despite everything), I would be tempted by this sensible advice: to deliver yourself from spells, you should also break with disenchantment. For one who is disenchanted is still a good prospect for enchanters. Avoid bitterness. Too often it leads to yet another arrogance, as apostasy prepares the ground for a new conversion in reverse. Without any writing on the wall to point to, without a replacement badge of legitimacy, I will take good care not to require anyone to genuflect before tomorrow's panacea. I have not recovered my health and we were not ill; in a madhouse everyone does his bit. Like the madmen in the forum all posing as doctors, politics held out as a solution is an illness offering itself as medicine. At least I will have learned to stop seeing the 'high official', more neurotic than the average, as a possible therapist for our own neuroses. Adventurous optimists suggest that 'the end of Utopias and ideologies' will make possible a modest and gentle public life. Although I would like this as much as they would, I am afraid they will be disappointed. A society without illusions may be the worst illusion of all. The expression 'official lies' is tautological: where there is institution there is superstition, logic insists on it.

Whenever we can, obviously, we should exchange the more deadly sort of motivating illusion for a less deadly one. But, apart from the fact that the relative virulence of different credos is not immediately obvious, it is hard to see how to give them up without wasting away. The joke is (if I may put it that way) that to be fully cured of the need for illusion would mean withering on the vine as a conscious agent of history; for the madness to be cured, it must persist. A militant can vary the dosage, but not the régime (except by leaving the stage). Condition incurable, treatment interminable. I know quite well that a man with heart should view the temporary upset caused by some setback against the long sweep of History. Of course. But suppose the long sweep of History just repeats the same temporary upsets, over and over? Thirty years is just the blink of an eye in the life of a society . . . Soon gone with the wind. But how can one argue that too little time is given to a drift this way or that if the river of Heraclitus winds back and forth, if every society is immersed in much the same water as its predecessor? What meant something to us will not die with us. This permanence of the deluding forces ought to enable us to greet the subsidence of each wave with a smile of collusive compassion, to give the disappointed, plunged into depression by the failure of Mitterrandism (or Sandinism or Castrism, and tomorrow any of the *isms* now burgeoning), a kind pat on the shoulder: 'Don't take it too hard. There have been other disasters, and the one tomorrow won't mean much more, or much less. *Eadem semper omnia.*'

An epoch unknowingly recapitulating its predecessors and sucessors, the affliction of politics: is not this the very stuff of polititics, interminable labour, penitence without end? You can dismiss this narrative, but you cannot stop a sporting, slightly dreamy adolescent from starting another of the same stripe next year, when the only things that have changed will be names, dates and places: different stage, same backdrop. Chuck your trousers into the shrubbery and someone else will be wearing them a second later. As the human animal composes its musical variations on two themes, sexuality and aggression, thumping country dances in two tempos; as power and desire still make us run, and these two fundamental drives of the species are not affected by changes of régime or machinery, there can be no beginning or end to this losing game of hopscotch, whose rules each generation discovers at the end of the game, without really managing to point them out to the next. The next is convinced for its part – because another Society of Nations or broadband digital network has just been invented, and a form of despotism has just collapsed – that it is dealing with an entirely new situation and that things will go better than last time (for the bunglers or losers of the previous generation).

The intensity of investment in fantasies, energy and time – perhaps this is the new factor – will probably now decline. Backing into the future (no way to do otherwise), the militants of the last half-century, victims of the quasi-mechanical tendency for expectations formed in the ascending first part of the century to roll down the declining slope of its end, expected far too much from political action. This at a time when the demand for it, dreaming and social, already far exceeded the supply. In this sense, instructive and soberly pragmatic, we might perhaps see the inexorable disappearance of the uppercase Prince in Machiavelli's sense, the decline of those lofty figures whose names are associated with the myth of omnipotent sovereignty and *ex nihilo* decisions (in Churchill or de Gaulle style), as an opportunity for intellectual and moral reform. Could it be that the marked narrowing of the margins of decision, the levels of freedom formerly available to the nation-state and its executive rulers (in democracies where a judge or journalist has more power than a minister or chief secretary to the president), is unveiling a pleasant surprise we have so far refused to see? If that were the case, instead of complaining we ought rather (the better to overcome the dismay occasioned by missing the target with a single-shot pistol) to rejoice in the avowed impotence of the supposedly powerful. Personally, I was far from predicting it in 1960 or thereabouts, and was slow to spot it even in 1981, when it was becoming obvious. It could well be that this disconcerting *diminutio capitis* of the stars of the tribe defines or illustrates the constant overestimation of the political factor in the makeup of *homo sapiens*, owing not a little to the remorseless and complacent overexposure of the history of warfare, of 'the thirty kings who made France', of the waltz of the republics and constitutional reforms. A globally relayed regionalist 'overdose', geared-down locally everywhere by the 'President's image'. The dimensions of the domestic screen, ideal for closeups, bestowed a bonus of presence on leaders, champions, stars and stage conjurers just as their demotion to walk-on or dummy status was being confirmed. The steering hardly works these days and we are required to watch the drivers ever more closely. The contrast between their simultaneously increased visibility and ineffectuality promises continuous growth in the number of malcontents and shattered hopes.

Around 1960, I had wanted to go 'where it was all happening'; I flattered myself that I could take on the human condition at its sharpest, dreamed of pitting myself against its hardest core. Whatever the doctrinal husks and local variations – Third World or Europe, revolution or reform – there were still some millions of us who believed, like Napoleon, that 'Tragedy nowadays is in politics.' I am afraid the observation has aged even less gracefully than the ultra-politicized adolescent that I was in those *Partisan Review* years. The famous saying has shrivelled, overripe for the dictionary of quotations and baccalauréat questions. Not that there is no longer any tragedy, or that it is no longer appropriate to commit oneself. It is true that the human species is more of an ongoing struggle than ever (and still intensifying); that nothing in our nature is as neglected as the present moment; and that it is even more justifiable than it used to be for an

educated individual free from want, out of simple curiosity, a sense of responsibility or conservation instinct, to join the *sapiens sapiens* enterprise (R&D
division). The ambitious youth who wants to get into the game today, with
any hope of modifying the ground rules, would clearly be well advised to go into
genetics, the cognitive sciences or neuro-biology. It is in Big Science and the
latest technologies that 'it's all happening' now, not in social planning or
government programmes, the very mention of which makes the average
well-informed Westerner smile. What we still call, out of habit, political
responsibility occupies a shrinking residual space uncomfortably squeezed
between two conditioning sequences, psycho-cultural on one side and techno-
industrial on the other, both under-represented in our cultural and academic
tradition. The evolution of collective mentalities in the cellar, out of sight, and of
technical prostheses in full view (and all the more invisible as a result) look like
the two decisive parameters of the risky adventure. But hasn't it always been
thus? Let us set aside, if possible, the tectonic plates of the religions, their
movement slow as continental drift, on a timescale different from our own. Let
us stay on the surface, on the level of events. Leaving out the fundamental, I
mean the Confuciuses, Jesuses, Buddhas, Lao Tzus and Mohammeds who work
the collective soul below the surface. What will Napoleon weigh compared to the
steam engine? Charlemagne, compared to the mechanical clock; Richard
Coeur-de-Lion, compared to the compass and sternpost rudder? Did not
Edison, or the Lumière brothers, do far more to expand human possibilities
than Washington or Lenin? Was it not the automobile in the first place, then
sound, then image in the home, compact disc players and TV (those accelerators
of individualism), that scuppered the whole project of socialist civilization? Our
real Prometheus today is Daedalus, the Greek patron of small artisans. The
'gadget maker' contributes more to the hominization of his contemporaries than
the designer of systems, and the big decisions of the future will be made in
research laboratories and workshops. Where would the feminist revolution have
been without the washing machine and contraception? What would become of
the 'global village' and its humanitarian solidarities without electronics and
computers? What could be more determining for our future in the short and
medium term than the raising of average life expectancy from 45 to 75 years,
and the associated explosion of the world population from one to five billion?
This enormous leap was neither programmed nor launched – in many cases not
even perceived – by the highest of the high, who have little interest in what is
going on beneath or behind them. It was primarily the doing of quinine, the
sulfamides and penicillin (and their successors) which lengthened the lifespan of
the body, of neuroleptics which dealt with psychic pain, and of the contraceptive
pill which freed women from unwanted pregnancies. There are revolutions that
affect the sick, because their ailments – physical or mental – are organically
based, thus susceptible to technological attack. There are no revolutions in the
collective being of the healthy, because the logical basis of their discomfort in this

area, the axiom of incompleteness to which the collective is mortgaged and which gives the group its identificatory cement, is not subject to technological manipulation.

The cyberpunk has the same arrangement of skeleton and muscles as the erect Neanderthal mammoth-hunter, and there is little sign that the passage from absolute monarchy to democracy of opinion has been accompanied by any marked zoological transformation of a carnivorous primate subject to the same alimentary and reproductive servitudes for the last 40,000 years. Just as we cannot choose to have 'a ruminant's digestive tract, grinding dentition or long canines like a gorilla, we cannot choose to be able to define a collective identity without setting it up against others, or to circumscribe a territory without opening it at an externally produced (and by the same token sacred) point of coherence: founding hero, charismatic chief or sacrosanct constitution. The neuro-anatomical stability of the individual corresponds to the group's constraint of structural organization: we do not have free control of either. This fundamental constraint, referred to above as the 'axiom of incompleteness' in a distant echo of the logician Gödel's theorem (since no social system can be defined solely by elements inside the system, a transcendent element is necessary for it to exist), makes the political life of humans a 'bitter, sombre and echoing tank, sounding a void in the soul that is always in the future'. To acknowledge this built-in defect is not to deny all the positive developments or mutations of the environment resulting from technical progress (medical most of all). These do not remove the imperative to fumble and stutter, but they do shift it. The destinies of the other animal species are determined by their genetic heritage. *Sapiens sapiens* by contrast is able to escape the zoological stasis of other species through technical invention. In the somewhat unyielding servitudes of collective being, humans confront constraints of repetition from which their tools have gradually freed them in their dealings with the material world, in a process dating back a hundred thousand years to the Neanderthals' uprooted-sapling bludgeons. The margins of leverage humans enjoy over nature and space through their contraptions and prostheses are denied them, in their dealings with contemporary reality and other humans, by political passion, perpetually reactivated by the hallucinatory structure of the group as such. Technology, wrongly associated with Frankenstein, and which we are constantly told will enslave us, is our main instrument of liberation. Politics, where everyone speaks of freedom, is the real home of involuntary servitude. Good and evil do not live where our old humanism thinks they live; it may be time to relabel the good and bad pigeonholes, even if common sense and our littérateurs are affronted. Silly little devices, the machines that so often pass unnoticed by great minds, are nearer to emancipating us than the visionaries noisily competing on the screens in our caves.

It would be wrong, however, to contrast scientists and engineers as benefactors of humanity, with ideologues and demagogues seen as chronic malefactors. We would still have to explain why, after millennia of false promises, bedazzlements and disillusions, the peddlers of hope are still around. The enigma is not one of noxiousness but of chronicity, for the various functions associated with the job of 'helmsman', from marketing adviser to speechwriter, seem effectively unsinkable. The answer lies in us, not them; no one can do without those Phoenixes who die in the evening and are reborn the next morning. It is not the politicians' fault – or ours – that scientific research cannot come up with vaccines against war, intellectual orthodoxy or racism. There is no viable parallel between the history of man's relations with things and the history of man's relations with man. Being of different natures, they do not proceed in the same tempo. When the combine harvester becomes available, a society can put the sickle (and hammer) in the museum of popular arts and traditions, and no farmer will return to it. But when opinion-measuring techniques and universal suffrage become widespread, anyone tempted to relegate Hitler to the natural history museum, among the fossils of extinct tyrannosaurs, is being foolish. The combine harvester is far more efficient than the scythe, but Assurbanipal is no more bloodstained than Chairman Mao, for the same reason that Abbé Pierre is not St Paul's moral superior and Picasso is not a better painter than Velasquez. The notion of progress has no more meaning in the history of man's domination by man than it has in the history of art or religion; it is not that we are condemned to immobility; but on those paths of incessant metamorphosis, busy with comings and goings, reversals and rearrangements, where anything can happen at any moment, the 'non-return ratchet' does not work. In this area no U-turn is excluded on principle. We can be fairly sure of one day neutralizing the Aids virus without killing its carrier; but it is hard to see by what means a stable group could do away with the mechanisms for delegating power, for embodying it in a representative who will always represent more than himself; or how to annul the biological prematurity of the new-born without eliminating the baby at the same time. Humans are the only mammals whose young, in the early stages of growth, are incapable of surviving by their own efforts. It takes 180 days for a new-born baby to double its weight, against forty-seven for a calf and sixty for a foal. The organic constraint of helplessness, equally absolute for the contemporaries of Mitterrand and Pericles, subjects them throughout their slow physical development to the same abandonment-anxiety or need for a protecting father, the security provided by an authority figure. Is it likely that any fundamental change took place in these biologically determined complexes between the sixth century BC and the twentieth AD? It is hard to imagine a more prolific source of heartrending misunderstandings than the wilfully embraced confusion between the repetitive, reversible and programmed history of relations between man and man and the cumulative, open-ended and irreversible history of relations between man and matter. *Homo demens* goes round in circles, only *Homo faber* advances. To stretch the point somewhat, all the misfortunes of the last century, in its liberal and Marxist faces (those two sides of the same presumption), come from our having forgotten that in the myth of Protagoras, our family escutcheon, when Prometheus succeeded in stealing the secret of fire from the gods to give it to men, who would use it to make ploughshares and tools, he was really letting himself and us down: the secret of governing stayed in the hands of the Olympians. Perhaps his success in equipping the opportunist omnivore technically is just a consolation prize, a simple recompense for the total checkmate on the political front. Where ordering the city is concerned humans will be eternal apprentices, putting their effort back on the workbench time after time after time. It is carved in letters of stone over the very portal of our over-confident Westerners' culture: the human species is only a half-success; and the political dimension is its failed part, recognized as such in our inaugural myth.

In the final analysis, we have as much reason to celebrate the vicious circles of subjection as to lament them. Personally I can see nothing humiliating in the fact that the forces in play in the age of Airbus and Internet are the same as the ones that existed in the age of carriages, or runners at Marathon. On the contrary, it can be turned to profit, to inspire laughter as well as tears. Among the many advantages of constitutional incompleteness, not so much eternal as running through all possible empirical history, we should count the ability possessed by *Homo politicus* (the polite name for *demens*) to feel at home everywhere, anywhere and any time. On this dark continent, where nothing can be sworn by or laughed at, there are no unthreatening anachronisms or oddities that leave us untainted. There is no frightful cadaver that cannot return to life, or 'God's lunatic' who does not attack us from inside (for he dwells deep within us). A particular sequence of shocks is needed to give a fleeting intuition of this disagreeable thought. Cutting across cultures and periods, these consignments to the abyss uncover deeply buried but still virulent roots that become plainly visible during violent paroxysms, more corrosive than peaceful events. It is difficult for us to picture Pope Urban II in the town square of Clermont in 1095, exhorting a few hundred armed believers to 'drive the vile breed from the lands inhabited by our brothers' and liberate Jerusalem. We cannot see croziered archbishops passing between the massed ranks under a flag with a red cross, blessing the weapons of genuflecting knights. But we can hear and see, in South Lebanon nearly a thousand years later, black-robed, white-turbaned Shiite ayatollahs outside Baalbek, passing between the ranks of Islamist combatants before a suicide mission into Israel, blessing their rifles and embracing each man. And no doubt the angular faces of those shining-eyed 'fanatics' are as radiant as those of their Frankish forerunners. Preventive medicine has not eradicated these 'epidemic furies' as it has cholera and the tsetse fly. The agitation I felt in Managua in July 1978 while watching the Sandinist leaders move into the command post just abandoned by the fleeing ex-chief of the national guard, Tachito Somoza, and immediately set about organizing checkpoints, handing out badges of access and establishing hierarchical barriers, is perhaps similar to that experienced by the paleontologist whose torch has just disclosed the smoky, charcoal-drawn outline of an ibex or a mammoth on the wall of an unexplored cave. Or by an ethnographer in a remote forest, at the sight of an Indian in a loincloth carrying a blowpipe and meeting his first white man. Hearing the first word being born on the lips of the first human: the old fantasy of first origin, which science must abjure but which no anthropologist can entirely relinquish, try as he may. It haunts the ordinary present-day metropolitan TV viewer, and for good reason, in the context of fundamental acts like the enthronement of a new chief or the funeral rites of an old one. A president is no longer the visible image of God, but has the obscure religious bond that unites a people with its symbolic representative changed much with the passage from anointing to election? Did not the faces watching President Mitterrand's funeral procession on the small screen show some of the same affliction that would have seized the bereft subjects of a deceased Capetian monarch when his coffin was borne past them? And did not the late president's double obsequies, family and national, in Jarnac and at Notre-Dame, recall the funerary splitting of our monarchs (with the king's two bodies, carnal and symbolic, requiring two distinct ceremonies)? It is during these essential rites of passage, entry and exit, with their accompanying upsurges of the collective unconscious, that we glimpse, amid the seething of today's profane societies, our unchangingness.

In this domain of perpetual incompetence we are still contemporary with the Peloponnesian war, the Twelve Caesars and the seventeenth century. Thucydides, Suetonius and Saint-Simon can all give the curious mind of the early twenty-first century useful pointers to a better comprehension of the evening news. It is the repetition of maxims about power and love that make Shakespeare, in Renan's phrase, 'the historian of eternity'. And also of current events as selected by the media from day to day, that reservoir of endless presumption, bottomless hostility and eternal trickery to which we can turn at any age to befoul our maiden souls with an invigorating truth cure.

There may be no meaningless writings or productions in this area of existence, but it seems certain that there will never be any decisive ones; and the pride we feel at being on equal terms with King Lear and Falstaff, as we are with Romeo and Juliet in the register of love-pangs, should be inflected by embarrassment – even shame – at the realization that we are not doing much better than those wretches, as if all the experience, knowledge and wealth accumulated since the Elizabethan age had not been very useful to us in this area. The toilers of officialdom will always benefit from reading Baltasar Gracián or Mazarin, while sixteenth-century treatises on mechanics or seventeenth-century astronomic observations are of no possible interest to present-day physicists and astrophysicists. While these latter works are only read today by historians of science, Gracián and his like can be read with pleasure by anyone, albeit without significant profit or effect on his or her behaviour. Of the 300 maxims and recommendations that comprise *L'Homme de cour, El oráculo manual* of 1647, there is not a single one that present-day denizens of the Elysée, the White House or the Moncloa could or should not use as a basis for their own conduct and a key to the conduct of others. What is so admirable is that they could just as easily follow the practical guidelines laid down in the seventeenth century by an Aragon Jesuit, confessor to the viceroy and almoner in the army of a marquis, without ever having heard of him, as if these protocols of experience were known to us by heredity; as if in this tactical domain of competition and predominance there existed, in defiance of the findings of biology, transmission of acquired characteristics between generations. Independently of belief systems, circumstances and language. Power relations has golden rules which cannot be learned from books; nor does the deconstruction of the machinery for manipulation of 'the many by the one' deter us from resorting to it when necessary. François Mitterrand did not learn how to behave from Louis XIV, who wrote to his son the Dauphin: 'One should always have several confidants, for jealousy often serves to restrain the ambition of others.' The son of Jarnac did not murmur to himself, 'Hey, I hadn't thought of that, interesting, let's give it a try.' He did not even think it, any more than he had pored pencil in hand over the *Testament de Louis XIV*; he just did it. And anyone who occupies the same post will do it again, for it will be in his interests. Just as anyone fresh from the schools of law or political science who starts up the greasy pole in his turn will not have to wear high heels or a lace jabot to travel the hard road thus summarized by La Bruyère: 'You seek, you dance attendance, you intrigue, you suffer torments, you ask, you are refused, you ask again and obtain.' That universal monster, profound and superficial, simplistic in its goals and complicated in its methods, like you and me, is of the past and the future; speaks Spanish, English, French and a hundred other languages, all equally adapted to the idea and all equally derailed by the endless, the inexhaustible labyrinth.

The political unconscious is a sack of malice; it is reserving its most underhand strokes for those who rely on 'canned ideas' and telecomunications to overturn the rules of the domination game. Every period arranges this game to its own taste, but let us recognize that in the apparatus of democratic authority there is an element of *déja vu*, severely inhibiting to the skyrocketing schemes of the anarchizing (who in any case avoid getting their hands dirty), as it is to the revolutions that futurists imagine will change the face of the world (like the virtual networks and information highways supposedly heralding a golden age of democracy without officers or secrets, egalitarian and libertarian, emancipated at last from frontiers and unequal one-way relations). This ironic insistence gives all 'breaks with the past', 'turning points' and other reasons why 'things will never be the same again' a very limited credibility; it seems designed to encourage the pessimist and depress the optimist. Television, for example, as a practical instrument for exercizing dominance over the imagination, has changed everything – and nothing. Open the first historical work to hand on the nineteenth century: it will inform us quite fully on our own. We curse the inconstancy, the inconsistency, of our fellow-citizens' electoral channel-zapping, while a sociologist announces that 'public opinion does not exist'. It was in 1837, not 1997, that a political scientist before his time noted: 'There is no public opinion in Paris on current events; there is only a succession of crazes that destroy each other, as a wave in the sea erases the preceding one.' We smile on reading from the pen of Proudhon that 'socialism and love of positions often go together', and are appalled to see that in the first election of a president of the Republic by universal (male) suffrage, Lamartine got 8,000 votes and Louis-Napoléon Bonaparte 5,434,000. In the little game of tags and quotations, where there is something for all tastes, we can all compose our own crossword. The best account of 1968 and the Mitterrand generation was published in Paris in 1869: it is *L'Education sentimentale*, a story of 1848. The date makes no difference.

The wheel of illusions, whose hub is incompleteness, includes some fairly utilitarian sub-processes, one of which is the *derived imputation*, our practice of tracing the deviations that shock us most (and that we would like to see as accidental or localized, scandalous only in theory and not in a practical sense) back to the 'disastrous' appearance of some mechanism, event or doctrine. To a French counter-revolutionary, for example, humanity waited for Rousseau and the Terror before resorting to large-scale slaughter, just as, to an anti-clerical individual, it was only with St Dominic or St Bartholomew that divine extermination began. We have all heard exorcisms of the pattern: no Nazism, no genocide; no Karl Marx, no Gulag; no television, no showbiz state. Reassuring causalities indeed! But apart from these polemical benefits, welcome though they always are, let us not forget that the perpetual reappearance of group religiosities and the collective hallucinations they engender inevitably give full rein to the 'enthusiasm' variable as well as the 'disappointment' variable, making a reactive chant just as legitimate in the final analysis as a Boy-Scoutish hymn to the Future. Much as it may displease people who confuse determinism with fatalism, mistaking a grammar of the indestructible for a set purpose of demolition, the individual who seeks to identify long-term underlying patterns does not by the same token refuse to act on his own present. In this respect, our constraint of endless repetition should not make us too resigned, because it has the happy if little-noticed effect of periodically bringing things long buried back to the surface. The paradox was most pithily defined by Jean Dubuffet, who, describing his post-war disillusionment to Paulhan, added that there was still some hope since 'unlike the one girls have, the world's virginity embodies a regrowth principle, a permanence of regrowth that coexists with the permanence of loss'. Who would dare complain about this spring-like reflowering, serenely astronomical, in which the virginal comes *after* the shop-soiled, the intact hymen *after* the divorce (aided by selective recall that erases the last blundering decline of each season of hope – Popular Front, Resistance, socialism – and remembers only the promise of the early days)? Some, like Dubuffet himself, will conceive a 'total lack of faith in politics of any sort'; others, less élitist, less 'right-wing anarchist' and fortunately more numerous than the champion of raw art, will see it as yet another reason to get back into harness, certain that this time 'things are really going to move forward'. It so happens that some mules are easier to harness to the treadmill of great hopes than others. It is good for our common future that 'the fight goes on', waged by fresh muscles and fresh dreams. Hope is a vain passion but not totally useless.

Is it possible to get out of harness one day, without deserting? Just as it would be ignoble to use one's own past wanderings to persuade the young and unworn to stop caring about immigrants and railway workers and leave the arena, so it seems to me unfair to be called a slacker by unblooded recruits going into battle with daisies between their teeth. To curb these inevitable accusations of desertion I would like to have been able to cite a consideration of quantitative type, something like a failure-tolerance threshold, beyond which a veteran would be free to retire without a pension, but also without particular opprobrium. You have to be of the race of heroes to carry on the struggle – *vox clamans in deserto* – beyond that level of resistance, which varies with individual temperaments. I know some of these saints; I am not one of them; the Spirit dwells where it will. Grace depends finally on the nature, the character, of the individual.

I recommend no one to start gardening on the banks of the lion pit, for the duty to resist the worst is incumbent on all of us. The fact that a surfer has failed to hold back the tide despite his fine initial resolutions does not justify looking the other way while Christians are devoured in the arena. Where public commitments are concerned, those over-eager to reach settlement often seesaw from one illusion to another. Still less would I blame any will to power on the part of *Politicus*. However rattled this bottle-imp may have become, his ambition (something everyone can direct as they wish) feeds, with immense waste of energy, the prodigious machines for building and rebuilding community. Just as sexual desire, wholly selfish though it may be, is necessary for conservation of the species, so the drive to control and possess, fiercely exclusive and individualist though it may be, is necessary for the reproduction of human institutions. In this sense vain men do not work in vain; indeed we should even be grateful to them for their devotion, in their desire for power and eminence, to the general interest (which includes our own). In their own fashion, these obsessives 'favour progress' by resisting a return to primal chaos, by continuing day after day to discern form in the random mass: egotists who are altruists despite themselves. And I would like to believe that in quitting them out of egotism, I too might have served the cause of Progress in my own fashion. But either through avarice or querulousness, it is on that uppercase P that I have turned my back, leaving the job of keeping the flame alive in the desert to the vestals of the progressive Idea and going home, like any Candide at dusk, to cultivate my garden. I owe this in part to that old nurseryman François Mitterrand, who reminded me *in fine* that we all have to prune our runners to our own height, with our own abilities, from wherever we happen to be. People keep saying (as they have for 6,000 years) that successive leaders sacrifice our militant ideals (which we have imposed on them without taking much interest in their own preferences) to their personal careers and renown. Quite right too: those creaking, leaking Panjandrums will teach us to stop sacralizing the ephemeral and give full rein, outside the flow of events, to the hard desire to endure. The deflation of our ex-high priests will help everyone to have the right ambition, and maintain the right pace. Why should a distance runner wear himself out trying to sprint?

How easily we all mistake ourselves for someone else. It would be disastrous if a few providential individuals encountered along the way did not make us understand who we are. We see them as guides but really they are bystanders like ourselves, our coadjutors despite themselves and despite us. However remote they may have been from our vocation, far from putting us off it for ever they turn out in the end to have made us want to go back to it. They were not tempters placed in our path to distract us, but rather tardy saviours trying to persuade us not to follow them by placing a sign between themselves and us: Road Closed. Could we not have repossessed our minds through our own efforts? I think not. My first philosophy teacher, Jacques Muglioni, told me so one spring day in 1956, writing on the sixth-form blackboard at Janson-de-Sailly a sentence that to my 16-year-old eye had a comic side: 'Man is an animal that needs masters when he lives among other members of his species' (Kant), and then adding in a cheerful, optimistic tone: 'He needs a master to do without masters.' An unworthy child of the Enlightenment, I needed chiefs to do without a chief. Of course under this word 'master' we should not confuse the one who raises by instructing with the one who abases by dominating, the man of authority with the man of power. Latin had distinct words for the two functions, *magister* and *dominus*. Masters of the world have served me as schoolmasters. It was both good luck and bad; thirty years of permanent training, and what I had learned at school so quickly gone. All praise to you then, master of my evening class, 'you who know more of the void than death itself', supreme champion of the decrepit, specialist in sham and the precarious, laureate of the smokescreen: I give you homage. By beguiling me with vanities, you disabused me of my own. I was a bit slow, and it took time. You reawakened a forgetful individual fresh from the palaces of death to the lost memory of lineages; I owe you the most precious thing of all, which is not the knowledge of where in everyday affairs one can glimpse the shifting, elusive frontier between the *transaction*, inherent to all action on matter and men, and the *capitulation*, which encourages successors not to bother. People's views on that will depend on their own illusions and passing interests. The most durably valuable thing is having learned to distinguish in the inner depths of one's being a sort of neuralgic prickling that separates what is alive and perishable from what is less so, like the dead wood and sapwood of an old tree. The problem is that this most vital of all dividing-lines is not the same

for everyone; every intellectual family locates its being and nothingness differently; hence the importance for human young of learning in good time to which
sub-species they belong. Encouraged by the time, by the apparent position of the
eternal wheel of hope, I had seen those men without works, those tillers of waves,
as my real kin; I sought a place among them; I tried to win their approval. And
while dreaming of making myself irreplaceable in the very species whose
specimens are most interchangeable, in the sector where spending is most
unproductive, I lost sight of my little genetic allocation, of my true, my only
leanings. It would be the height of ingratitude to blame my intercessors for
biochemical mistakes that are mine alone.

I note in passing (O my lord and master) that in matters that concern you, you
make the distinction very clearly. Vain agitations do not distract vain men to
such an extent that they confuse rock with dust. You have plenty of time for
observation, it is true; politicians live long lives; plenty of time to make your
arrangements. Anyone who doubts that 'power preserves' has only to witness
that excitement, that vitality or inner fire, lasting well beyond the civil service
retirement age of 65, that animates stiff old bodies with a sort of twinkle in the
eye, a briskness of demeanour, sufficient to persuade the ever-patient defenders
of the ramparts to stay at their posts. Until the age of 75 or 80; beyond that,
nothing.

You realized this a long time ago, in a repressed way. It made you anxious
without knowing quite why; it made you build things. Your media complex or
stadium, if you are a mayor. Your regional headquarters or museum, if you are
of ministerial calibre. A pyramid or an arch, if you are monarch of all you
survey. It consoles you (O master builder) to stick your name on a monument.
To live on as concrete, knapped stone, glass and metal. That is what is left of
your seigneurial rights in the old days: fair-sized investment budgets (and never
mind the recurrent deficit, after us the deluge, first knock their eyes out). A hedge
against nothingness, reasonably acquired; I would have done the same in your
place; I would envy you less if I had myself put up a shack or two along the way.
Despairing of shaping minds, for any length of time, and no longer dreaming of
remaking the world, in any breadth, you put pressure on the décor and strive to
attain *height* at least. Your adversaries will scream the place down, call you a
second-rate Louis XIV, allege Versaillais cock-ups. It is easy to say. Everyone
stays afloat as best he can in the televisual fluid, the ephemeral substance of
electron and pixel. When you give up on Big History, there are still Big
Undertakings, vertical ones. They are the concern of successors. It has not
escaped you that Pompidou did more for Parisian architecture than Charles de
Gaulle (as Napoleon III did more than the first of that name). When the
monarch was hewing his legend in stone, the architect wielded stonemason's
compasses. Today there has been a permutation of roles: bees open chrysanthe-
mums formally, and hive-makers are becoming Michelangelos. Do not hold it
against me, President (or minister, or mayor, or decision-maker) if I confess that

these erections, so well illuminated after dark, remind me when I stroll about Paris that you are not the artist: they are. Their work – the work of Pei, Perrault, Tange or Nouvel – will be widely seen, far into the future. While we, masters and servants, are all cut from the same cloth: the smaller we get, the more taken with the grandiose we become. I am paid for knowledge; I followed the great man to the corners of the earth, and you planted along the Seine the 'Great Louvre', the 'Great Arch' and the 'Very Great Library'. You go for volume, not distance: that obsession with size, as if greatness could be measured in metres . . . ! Hollow shells often, not terribly functional, but never mind, façade is what counts. The first glance: the striking shot, the fold-out on glazed paper. Who in this day and age would dare ask for a genuine dwelling or workplace, comfortably habitable on the inside, with nothing just for show? No rhythm: just area and volume. Our princes have just enough time to place glittering objects in our sight, and as they depart to leave their coats of arms behind them, on a concrete plinth, behind a big glass sliding door.

I know what you think: that I am biting the hand that fed me so well (and it is not our fault that what nourishes perishes, that what perishes serves to create, that life and death keep each other going in this way). It does not bother me unduly if there is some poison in the elixir I am giving you here; the bile is too strong for me to hold back; I would so love to take back all the time I lavished on you, Castro, Allende, Mitterrand. If you had given me a second life, a remedial one in which I could correct the mistakes of the first, to give it a semblance of shape, or if it was in your power to grant me a serious extension, we might be quits. Dissipation, feverishness, myopia, self-regard, haste: your weaknesses have become mine with the passage of time, and they cannot be discarded in the blink of an eye. I do not have the big budgets or personal armorial bearings to console myself for the fermenting void with a bungalow of my own. No one levers himself out of the flux of time with the mere wave of a magic wand. It is too late for the Oeuvre; that would have meant starting early on the long haul, working through to bedrock later; so long, so hard to leave the slightest trace. The artist is a soft-skinned animal, more mollusc than crustacean. He drags himself unhurriedly across the sand, his agitation all internal. He has to keep doubling back, to ruminate at length, to succeed in making something hard from soft materials (paper, canvas, celluloid). To act slowly in contemptible anonymity, waging a colourless cam-paign without triumphs, clinging to his desk like a mussel, in the effort to secrete a shelter that will be habitable long after his death (each unfulfilled Bernard the Hermit spending his entire life moving from one shell or oeuvre to another, ferreting among the limestone secreted by all the generous molluscs who have preceded us, to deposit it in the structures that will survive us, and so *ad infinitum*). Can you imagine that soft, hesitant, shy being, whom you do not rate very highly, building from almost nothing a dwelling open to all, whose name will come to rival your own: a structure of phrases, pigments or notes more welcoming and nurturing than a plate-glass tower at the corner of an esplanade?

That long-haul oeuvre that I no longer have the time to secrete, hardly even to outline in thought, that I should have written because I knew you, that I could have written if I had not known you, would have been something like a 'rites of passage novel' told through the follies of my century. I would have scribbled a few parts of it in haste, a botched and incomplete first draft; the yellowed leaves would have been found one snowy December evening, scattered at the foot of my deathbed, by a bailiff there to serve a summons; without malicious intent, but with other business pressing, he would have gone downstairs and fed into the basement furnace those blotted and grubby scribblings, along with the old newspapers, cuttings, photos, bills, letters, timetables and a hundred other fragments; and I can see from here – risible megalomaniac of empty dream-cinema – those scrawls curl up, blaze for a second, turn red and vanish, like a sled named *Rosebud* in a pseudo-gothic fireplace under the papier-mâché vaulting of Xanadu.

A Brief Militant's Lexicon

Excellent political vocabularies exist already. This modest 'deconstructive summary' is intended to remedy their very excellence, not to contradict them but to supplement them. Restricted as they are to the unearthly realms of institutions and doctrines, our reference manuals are perhaps too scholarly not to miss the internal hooks, futile or incongruous, that snag our attention day by day. Since political life (as the present text demonstrates all too clearly) entangles our unreasons inextricably with reason, no one enters it without leaving the empyrean of the official sciences, sinking towards the commonplace, lending an ear to the mispronunciations, lacunae and throat-clearings where slumbers an unknown grammar.

The specialist dictionaries have grand entries. This personal (and terminal) glossary offers only service doors and emergency exits. Where these sensitive matters are concerned a general index is of limited usefulness; it is for the individual lost soul to invent his own, groping a path through his labyrinth, distinguishing the false doors from the good ones. These are the key words that have opened a few locks for me. That, in summary, is what a political education is: discovering that there is no pass-key, and making up your own set of picks as you go.

The tiresome thing is that definition in this area verges on confession and an index can be read as a statement; but such is the price of rigour.

AURA (of leader)

'Occult sciences. Sort of halo surrounding the body, visible only to initiates' (Petit Robert).

1. The faces and bodies of leaders give out a singular sort of 'radiance', a subtle and spellbinding glow, in the eyes of their supporters who use terms like magnetism, charisma or 'magic'. History confirms that physical presence is not essential to the task of dazzling an audience (Hitler, a good orator but puny and physically commonplace; Stalin, dull and dumpy, etc.). If optical illusion is

involved, it arises from general need. We cannot *not* see the captains of our hopes outlined in light, swathed in a capital letter. Aura: the chief's halo as counter-password.

2. We are properly obedient only to vicars. The axiom of incompleteness helps us to understand why a group's perception of its own common denominator will always be larger (morally) than it is (in reality). This rule of inflation has high and low points, and periods with a strong mythical content and thus with strong régimes verify it more strikingly than prosaic or sceptical periods like our own, in which freedom of beliefs and the separation of spiritual from temporal give us the blessing – the terribly precarious blessing – of weak political powers without prestige. But this conjuring trick persists: even when bestowed by majority vote, the supreme post is illuminated *from above* by light from an invisible source – Jupiter, God, Nation, Europe, Republic, West – that (visibly) surrounds its carnal occupant. Tribunes, Caesars, blockheads, condottieri, commanders or presidents, belief-systems change with the period and the accreditation procedures; there is always that involuntary gilded corona, constituting a sort of subliminal speech that the leader gives to his flock without even needing to open his mouth: 'I am the Way, the Truth, the Life. I am Virtue, Socialism, the Republic, the Revolution, Europe' (just as the Pope is St Peter without being St Peter). This back-lighting of the cynosure of the collective gaze, at the optical pinnacle of a pyramid of believers, accounts for most of the ascendancy exercised over us by the delegate of the Transcendental. This transfiguration of the chief by the Word makes him an involuntary charlatan (although the good ones know how to use it consciously). Anyway, it strengthens devotion in the servants of the Word, who make sacrifices to a Principle that they would not make for a Prince; on the other hand, the glare is bad for his troops' discernment, making them long-sighted. In the forum, when he is in front of our noses, we discern his features and track record less clearly than the far-off rallying point that magnifies him in our sight: Christ the Saviour for a monarch by divine right, Virtue for Robespierre, Fatherland for Pétain, Revolution for Castro, Left for Mitterrand. The standard-bearer is improved in our eyes, as is anyone in rear three-quarters profile.

3. When the mythological spotlight fades, some time later, it is as if a top model were stepping out of the studio lighting into natural light (which twenty years later, in retirement, we will see as artificial), taking off her false eyelashes and high heels, becoming an ordinary woman again. The potentate replaces the sovereign, by power-cut. Take the grace of God from Louis XIV and you are left with toby-jug; Virtue from Robespierre, a cornered popinjay; Victory from Napoleon, a reckless adventurer. Revolution from the *Líder Máximo*: an incompetent despot. Socialism from the president: an ambitious slick operator. And so on. The eternal refrain of those who feel let down (by the monarchy, by the Republic, by the left or right): 'So that was all there was to the fellow!' All there was: the same, without the fluorescence of the Word. Whose removal is effected by the mere passage of years.

4. Let us remember that the collective imagination cannot burn out a thousand-watt luminary without immediately lighting up another on the opposite side, who will burn out in his turn when the time comes. And so on. The stage is always lit (politics without Big Words is absolute darkness).

AWAIT

Immutably, political awareness of the world places people in a posture of anticipation (of the next elections, the way out of the crisis, tomorrow morning's opinion poll, the next job, the final struggle). Even if this characteristic is more apparent on the left side of the spectre, it should be seen as common to the whole species.

1. From forecast to prophecy, from attentism to the revolutionary's D Day, the range of things awaited embraces every variety of expectation. Revolutionary sects carried the anticipation of better times to the point of ecstasy; the movement's party is content with a healthy economy; centrism practises sound management. Even the party of order stops short of suggesting that nothing (very new) can be expected from tomorrow. The difference is only of degree.

2. The exemplary militant would be one who had spent his entire life, last gasp included, on a station platform busily marshalling his suitcases to board a train which will never depart (or who, if he got going by himself, did so in the wrong direction and ended further from his goal than when he started). The truth is that while the left believer may have had a destination – Revolution, Socialism, Peace, Happiness – he had no port of arrival. That indefatigable rambler, of irrepressible goodwill, is the *Homo viator* of Christian tradition, of whom the revolutionary in Victor Serge's *Midnight in the Century* is the variant prepared even to be a sacrificial victim. Always about to start, doomed to immobility by the spirit of compromise among the 'alienated masses', the proletarian cadre dragged at his anchor while savouring day after day the 'preliminary signs of the worldwide crisis of capitalism'. When he spotted one in the morning he had lost it again by evening. The vocation imposes a life of endless preamble; living to a countdown, interminably.

3. Expectation, perhaps a left-wing virtue, has a complementary opposite in attention, the strength of the political right, which concentrates on what is. Because it does not expect the moon, a conservative temperament will not be given to seeing will-o'-the-wisps. Less feverish and sharper, it seems to me to have more aptitude for the long term and for observation. Everything suggests that great *actions* are carried out in a posture of expectation (of the Messiah, of the Beginning of the End, of D Day), and that great *works* are achieved in a position of attention. In expectation, the gaze looks *through*; in attention it looks *at*, withdrawing from more distant prospects. I cannot help wanting to associate these two casts of mind with different ages, like love and ambition which come in

that order in classical writings . . . Will this idea console those who have spent so long running down rails leading nowhere, never taking the time to focus on beings and things? I would like individuals to age in the same way as civilizations, which start with red as their favourite colour and end with blue. How happy life would be if it started with history – the red – and ended in the blue: geography. This does not seem to be the case with the 'galley-slave generation'. If only the victims of *no future* could fall back on herb gardens, collections of minerals or butterflies, tracing a Hercynian fold on the flank of a limestone plateau . . . Haste is a heavy handicap – channel-zapping, motor-bikes and clips – because it prevents our nervous systems from discriminating between apple, olive, almond, emerald, pistachio, grass, lime, pea or jade, melting these capital riches together under an inexpressive 'green'. Ideally it would be possible to espouse a cause without becoming closed to the nuances, the wonderful diversity of the world. In reality, those who expect too much look carelessly; those who grasp the nuance soon forget to hope. The best compromise would be division of one's time: a time for myths and a time for things, youth for broad lines, maturity for colours, the two halves forming a 'balanced life'. The worst would be to expect nothing, while being unable to focus attention: neither future nor presence. But it seems unlikely: what adolescence is unaware of love, what maturity of ambition?

4. Expectation has the merit of making us live the present in the future anterior, indicating ownership of the sacred time. In the far-left circles I frequented, this chronological inversion used to produce a twice-yearly document on 'Progress and Prospects'. The exercise consisted of sifting the mass of current events for 'symptoms of decay', 'cracks in the structure', 'last gasps', 'general crisis', 'final stages' and 'the beginning of the end'. 'We do not live, we hope to live,' Pascal wrote. In other words: 'it can't go on', 'meltdown is imminent', 'they've lost it for good'. By these means relative normality is transformed into a promising symptom, the longed-for strong future is implied by the weak past and present. Completion of the entire history of the world was anticipated, in an endless circle of eschatological delirium. The century would only be clearly legible to the dull-witted after its conclusion, when everything was over: the unifying vanishing point, while not part of the picture, was what made it possible. Definition of *eschaton*: an event that follows others but cannot itself be followed by any other. Dreary plains all look alike? So do the Propylaea of paradise. Messianism was ever thus: to the prophet Daniel, the destruction of Judah in 586 BC was the immediate prelude to the Advent. The doctrine of the two ages, as explained in Hebraic scrolls, stipulates that until the great age arrives the lesser age, our own, is full of 'narrow, troublesome, laborious doorways, hard to find and dangerous'. The passage of time has confirmed this observation.

Between the proletarian revolution and us, in the *Partisan* years, were some serious bottlenecks: Berlin Wall (with Vopos on guard towers), missile crisis, Kruschev's bluster, Sino-Soviet frontier clashes, the Vietnamese left to defend themselves, and other mortifications. Reading the papers – 'morning prayers' – forced us to decipher the feints, the outrages, of a perverse God who enjoyed misleading us to put us to the test (turning the forerunners of the Apocalypse, the Antichrist and the Christ, into twin brothers). The success of that evil spirit was proved by the numbers of revisionists, capitulationists, defeatists, social-traitors and unscientific elements who sneaked wimpishly off the train, duped by the latest news. Such were the pitfalls of 'a particularly complex world situation' (refined by our theologians into 'an overdetermined nexus of contradictions, whose secondary aspects do not obscure the main aspect'). A practised militant's eye 'historicizes' the more or less barbaric actions of his leaders in the same way that the believer's eye 'spiritualizes' the celebrant's gestures. A literal record kills these liturgies; the minds of their interpreters revive them. As in the totemic meal with the communicants chewing viscera, in which a forefather's thighbone is tranformed by the supernatural workings of faith into a eucharistic mystery – 'Eat, for this is my body; drink, for this is my blood' – we had our own newspapers and books, printed holy writings in which events fairly sinister in themselves changed, after exegesis, into signs of deliverance. Interpreted from a proper distance the Russian, Chinese, Korean or Albanian revolutions, in reality barbarous and murky rituals, became the *zakuski* before a celestial banquet, foretastes of Light.

5. Expectation was more prosaic in the holy lands of the Idea, where the average person exhausted all his strength feeding himself and getting to work, a gnawing attenuation too trivial to capture the attention of fervent outsiders. What a 'sign of the times' it was, though, the bread queue! A long way from the millennium, the ones outside baker's shops in Warsaw, Moscow and Havana, although retrospectively they seem a sort of expiation (*we* were being punished through the way *we* had sinned). Unfortunately they were not the same *we*: the communist punishment fell on others like the Poles and Vietnamese, among whom secular messianism was not the most popular faith. The imaginary socialism of the catacombs is born out of expectation; the 'real socialism' of states has died of it, its hostages having finally had enough of queuing in front of empty shelves.

6. Tomorrow is another day although the night be long . . . Is not the Great Promise physically necessary if one is to stand firm when things get difficult? Geneviève Anthonioz de Gaulle, a former inmate, reports that in Ravensbrück two groups of women kept their heads up: Christians and communists. 'When one of us lost faith, her chances of survival would diminish before your eyes,' Madeleine Riffaud confirms of her fellow communists. Two lineages, one family. The camps and these heroines reveal truths that anyone can confirm in everyday fashion. To keep his footing in the shadows of his dungeon, a detainee has to invent a meeting each day with a ray of light under the door, a change of warders, a distant sound of running water. I know free men with more restricted horizons than that prisoner. A full timetable, turning on the TV, drinking

whisky, eating, sleeping, gossiping, gestating book after book, is surviving rather than living. A world without end in which nothing is expected any longer is another sort of catastrophe, a malicious turn of the screw harmful to the morale of the troops, and to morality.

BREAKING UP (is hard to do)

In the tempestuous world of politics, where happy liaisons exist, divorce is no easier than it is elsewhere. Best to have advance warning and not expect too much of oneself.

1. Affection is the thing that makes it so difficult to 'turn the page'. To move on elsewhere, without wasting time and *once and for all*, like Julien Gracq sending back his Communist Party card on learning of the Nazi–Soviet pact, or Lévi-Strauss abruptly leaving the Socialist Youth movement (and the pacifism that had led him to approve of the Munich Accords). Their militancy, too short-lived for settled affection, made brisk separation easy. Longer immersions on the other hand make *breaking up* (with a party, a sphere of influence or a leader) a hesitant, bad-tempered and clamorous process. As if some sort of obscene glandular drive were clouding the operation, the discoveries, of the intelligence. Our internal rhythms are awkwardly stretched between an affective part, heavy and slow to decant, and a more alert discursive part, responsive to the pressures of circumstance and argument: more 'irresponsible'. Renouncing a thing is easier than falling out with a person. But it is still more difficult to bring a (political) consciousness to the truth than to repudiate an (emotional) memory. Having to do both at once, to conjure up new words to explain how old musics still call to us from our past, is no joke at all. Hence the mumbling incoherence of the militant beginning to ask questions, to 'open his eyes', to 'break the spell'. Hand to hand, information against complicities. The brain swaggers off on its own but the guts are reluctant to follow. Every former this or that is weighed down and held back by a burden of affections, so that in one of these mutants an intellectually implacable defeatism can coexist with a measure of sentimental irredentism. If there can be sado-masochists, why should there not be committed abstainers? (I involved myself deeply and full-time in Mitterrand's electoral campaign in 1981, two years after writing 'France, fin d'émission', a text from which I would cut nothing even now, fifteen years later, in which I explained at length that nothing original is to be expected from a recentred and normalized country). If there was a crowd in my street right now, singing *Bella Ciao* or *Los cuatros generales* and carrying placards and banners from 1965, I would of course rush downstairs and join it, without forgetting the risk of these contagious exaltations or that they are probably counter-productive (aggravating the original evil they mean to abolish). It is quite possible to think something and do its opposite, for we think about politics consciously but get involved in it for unconscious reasons.

What good is it no longer to be taken in by words, if some half-forgotten air can still give us gooseflesh, if particular tones of voice can still touch us even when the words being pronounced seem crazed and intolerable? 'I know . . . but all the same . . .' If someone addresses me as 'comrade' or '*compañero*', something within me vibrates in response, intact and fresh as 1940. In vain do I flatter myself that I analyse things pretty clearly, if my objective evaluation of the conjuncture is not followed by the logically indicated conduct, which I ought to adopt but cannot. Thus does zeal live on for years after faith is extinct.

2. Emotional paralysis and the mulling-over of past happiness are not without comic effects, like the drunkard's vows one keeps mumbling in a repeated aside: 'That's it, no more meetings; no more reading *Le Monde*; and I'm staying out of these inept, pointless public debates; I'll never get done over like that again.' Two days later the wish for influence is back on top, with its hallucinations. (How many times have I sung that comic-opera 'Goodbye, goodbye . . .'? Have I not ended this or that 'position-taking' work with a peremptory note asserting that this would be my final word, that I was no longer interested in all that, I would write no more on politics, it was just wasted effort? Time and again; but it never prevented me from resuming a year later with a book on politico-military strategy or an opinion piece on Maastricht, the Gulf War or Yugoslavia, of course without the slightest effect because against the current.) That our fulminations should have no influence over minds or the course of events is just about acceptable; but that they should have none over our own reflexes is annoying.

3. If *Homo politicus* were not a double entity, he would be easy to improve, to reason with. Every 'new awareness' would be followed immediately by effects. Pascal: 'Men are so essentially mad that not being mad would be another way of being mad.' Octavio Paz, that great lyricist closed to the fervour of others, was calling on that wisdom that does not know it is madness when he wrote: 'Politics is the theatre of mirages', a pious banality, following it immediately with another banality, this time a risky one: 'Only *criticism* can save us from its baleful and bloody sorceries.' A piece of optimism that ignores the double nature of any individual involved in public affairs (*a fortiori* if he or she is an 'intellectual'). Theory and practice do not march in step. There is every chance that criticism will turn out to be powerless: just as there are two histories in History, that of machines, which advances, and that of bodies, which stagnates, the individual who believes in mirages is not the one who exercises his critical faculty, even if they are physically the same person. The spellbound person and the exorcist, the deluded and the lucid, can coexist in the same individual or social period. Hannah Arendt and the *gauleiters* were contemporaries, like Montaigne's *Essais* and the massacre of St Bartholomew. We carry both within us, in our fashion (less genius and less horror).

Everyone knows the story of the brilliant oncologist who believed in telling patients the truth, who, on falling ill with cancer, concealed the truth from himself and died convinced that what he had was a bad case of influenza.

COMMITTED (intellectual)

An expression that has become obscene, almost as obscene as the word 'intellectual'. Avoid.

1. Not a bad job though. Loved by schoolboys who know the score by heart (Calas, Dreyfus, *L'Espoir*, Bernanos, *Le Silence de la mer* . . .), caressed by the papers. Our national opera singer trips over the carpet, and the whole of France forgives him, misty-eyed. Blunders that would disqualify an extra are thought endearing in a leading tenor, part of his charm. He can hardly hide in his dressing-room for a year or two before posterity, that good daughter, comes knocking at the door with an armful of roses. 'Greetings, Mr Zola! Mr Barrès! Mr Malraux!' Flashbulbs, tears, ministers, conferences, plaques, theories, birthdays. Every ten years or so, a petulant centenarian who doubts nothing struts about the stage playing the lead. (In the 1960s, when there was a shortage of contenders, I nearly played the interval slot myself. I had the look of a good understudy. Like a zebra playing a tiger actually, but the management's view is blurred by distance.)

2. The influx of young male leads to the Conservatoire projects an inescapable feeling of parody, of pantomime, or more simply of fatigue, as if this essential of French theatre wore a little thinner each day. 'Committed intellectual' has lost its serious ring and is no longer a draw. The role of composition has an image scrambled by too many superimposed variations: raised fist, outstretched arm, on a platform, standing behind Doriot, in an assumed attitude, Mao badge on lapel, distributing *Je suis partout*,[11] no, *La cause du peuple*,[12] no, sorry, the Universal Declaration of Human Rights. As if the essence were the defiant posture, the overstatement, the jumping firecracker. No matter if the house Hemingways disdain carbines, jeeps and game-fishing provided they have the right sort of swank, the grating voice a couple of tones too high: the French touch. The *committed intellectual* scorns all hierarchies, military political or administrative. A whirlwind with no allocated diocese, obeying no one but himself and addressing minds directly. Day and night, without office hours: his great strength. But preferably in the mainstream of public objectives: his great weakness. Our livewire dislikes getting dirty, doesn't follow up, never reads a dossier, is careless with dates, ignores maps, gives no figures: these are mere journeyman trivia. He simply utters a howl of indignation and turns the page. (I myself was too much of a downtrodden, inky-fingered clerk to aspire to dash of that sort. High treason is less harmful to the phrase-terrorist than becoming a high official.)

3. The theme of commitment would perhaps have made less noise after the

war if the doctrine's author had committed himself at the right moment. Literary extremism seldom carries people to extremes. Valiant but indecisive, Sartre had lived through the dark years without lifting a finger. Had he done so, he might not have found it necessary to open fire after the battle, terrorizing his small world by taking up arms retrospectively. Having done too little *before*, that courageous man perhaps did a bit too much *afterwards*: his expiatory bidding intimidated many a guilt-ridden civilian in the 'progressive intelligentsia' of the Cold War years. The 'parti des fusillés'[13] exploited it brilliantly. 'We'll forget all that . . . but you just sign here,' the ruthless Godfather Aragon would say. Poets, painters and singers fell docilely into line. The Stockholm Declaration, the Peace Movement, was the banner behind which good fellow-travellers had to march, if they wanted to be forgiven by the working class for painting and singing under the Germans, when others had been singing under torture. Slacker's bad conscience should not have troubled Romain Gary, in his diplomatic hideouts, a Companion of the Liberation who had gone to London in 1940. Nor Jorge Semprun, a survivor of the camps who had worked underground in Spain. And artists, like scientists, have a considerable advantage over 'intellectuals' in difficult times: the right to stay out of the front line. Sartre, surely, was an artist in the first place, so why did he go along with it?

4. Cavaillès and Politzer acted at the right time, without trumpeting their reasons. I imagine them after the war quietly resuming their work – mathematics in one case and early Marx in the other – as Jean Prévost returned to Stendhal and Marc Bloch to the Capetians. As Vernant went back to Greek and Canguilhem to medicine. All these men made war without loving it: a lot better than the inverse. Tough and debonair: *warrior philosophers*, not 'committed intellectuals'. Genial samurai. The Japanese have a term for this ethical ideal: *sentôtekina tentan*, soldierly detachment.

5. I wish I could say that I had never been a committed intellectual.

COMPARE

Nine out of ten political errors result from reasoning by analogy, a source of as many resolutions as blunders. Just as an art lover's sensibility benefits from comparing works, so people tend to react to current events by comparison with the past, something that helps them to reason but also causes gross idiocies. The 'progressive', although forward-looking in principle, seems more susceptible to the analogy virus than the 'conservative', ostensibly turned towards the past.

1. Since my adolescence a dozen Hitlers have shown themselves on the horizon (from the Egyptian Nasser to the Serb Milosevic, via Gaddafi, Khomeini, Saddam Hussein and a double handful of other ugly little kinglets-for-a-day). When it is in keeping with our interests this comparison, the standard pre-

liminary to declaring hostilities, is a conditioned reflex and a good tactical preparation of the rear. But apart from its usefulness as a 'button' to galvanize the troops, what chronicler can say in all honesty that he has not compared the 1990s with the 1930s? Or latterly, the war in Bosnia with the Spanish Civil War, a historical ineptitude that 'works' emotionally? Perhaps, before a still largely undeciphered current reality can speak to us, we need to make it speak a known language. Is not the choice between silent enigma, raw events and a ventriloquist's discourse? Just as a physicist cannot determine both the speed and position of a particle at the same time, the observer of the course of things struggles to comprehend both the originality and the ordinariness of the new event, as if each of these terms repelled the other. For the unprecedented or unexpected to make sense it must be inscribed under a law, referred to some constant, and so on some level abolished in terms of its difference. Thus, I believed in 1958 that de Gaulle, brought to power by the praetorians in Algiers, was giving us a rerun of the 2 December coup d'état, and bought the idea of the new Napoleon III gagging Marianne from behind (a communist poster I stuck on the walls of the Latin Quarter at the time). People believed that the student barricades of Paris in 1968 would cause an 1848-type revolution; that the victory of the left in May 1981 was a replay of the Popular Front, with Mitterrand a new Blum. And so on. The *analogizer* gets it wrong every time, but gives himself and us pleasure. A service even more necessary to the activist than to the journalist. The insurgent Indians of the Chiapas in 1994 adopted the name Zapatista Army. Born in 1870, executed in 1919, Zapata lived in a world apparently unconnected with that of the *maquiladoras* and skyscrapers of Mexico City. But how can anything new be created from outside all tradition? How can one foresee without comparing, have some grip on the future without the help of examples and myths? The wish to shake living spectres, curiously, reanimates ghosts from the past. In the offensive character, the stronger the wish for a break with the past, the stronger the desire for a new beginning.

2. Much given to commemorations but a poor cartographer, a better historian than geographer (the opposite of the man of order, if I may venture a generalization), the individual of 'progressive' ideas seems paradoxically fond of interpreting events in the light of the past. As if making sense of the unknown in terms of the well-known were a defensive reflex for dealing with slippery novelty. Is what the historian does so very different? The moment he relates some event to a sequence he, too, ceases to view it in its manifest, detailed reality, and will tend to sacrifice any originality it may possess to its more recognizable aspects. Analogy, surely, was the earliest form of historical reasoning. Thucydides systematically compared the Peloponnesian wars with the Median wars of a century earlier; Plutarch depicted his illustrious men in pairs and by contrast, as 'parallel lives'. Voltaire represented Charles XII as a new Alexander, and Julius Caesar has been reborn a hundred times in twenty centuries. Perhaps the revolutionary's avowed worship of past revolutions serves not only to legitimize his present action but to

revive his own flagging enthusiasm, by reminding him that what others have brought off must be possible. That he is not a Utopian or dreamer but a man who, playing his part in the sweep of history, espouses his own time while being ahead of it. And perhaps he does not realize how right he is.

In fact, could not a comparative overhead view be taken of the courses of the various revolutions of the post 1789 cycle (French, Russian, Chinese, Cuban, etc.) that would reveal certain constants: effervesence, normalization, repression, exhaustion, openness and return to the status quo ante? And would one not also observe, throughout the period, a uniform element of paradoxical nationalism (contrary to the internationalist rhetoric of the actors)? Whether it be Jacobin, Bolshevik, Maoist, Vietnamese, Korean or Castrist, a revolution launches, continues or completes an assertion of nationality, so that people who have torn a particular historical continuity end by being obliged, against their wishes, to mend the tear themselves. The Jacobins continued the work of the Capetians, the Bolsheviks followed the tsars' imperial tradition abroad, Mao Tse-tung rebuilt Ming-dynasty China: what Tocqueville demonstrated on the French example seems to hold good for all the others.

3. In day-to-day navigation, it is as difficult to keep the right distance from current events as it used to be to find the North-West Passage. Too little distance and one is swamped in data without perspective; too much, and one falls back on unsound interpretation. A reporter inclines to the direct take at the expense of meaning; an editorialist would rather maintain his net, his reference grid, than catch the fish. In this sense, the revolutionary left resembled the 'bourgeois press': it preferred interpretation to discovery. Sectarianism becomes a threat when the *a priori* obliterates the *a posteriori*. The leader of the Mexican Zapatistas, the poet-journalist 'Marcos', seems to be the exception that proves the rule, so successful is he in walking the tightrope between myth and fact. A century of disappointments and setbacks has led to the salutary re-evaluation of a retro species. There remains this strange fact: for that galley-slave of memory, the traditional revolutionary, repetition is soothing and novelty upsetting. That is why factual information and research are needed by the 'soft' as well as the revolutionary left, both being on even worse terms with current reality than the managerial left.

ELECTION

Synonym for joining. Choice by the militant subject of the individual to whom he will give his vote, time or life, depending on the circumstances. He who chooses elects. Even when not elected, every chief is elective, the object of a singular affective cathexis on the part of his 'electorate' (troops, sphere of influence, community). But this physical sympathy between elected and elector tends to identify a contrast rather than a similarity, elective affinities usually working a contrario.

1. The less formally constituted a political body is, while it still resembles a small crowd with fluctuating fringes (in contrast to armies, churches or structured parties), the stronger the affective bonds that develop between its members, to compensate for the absence of external constraints. The libidinal but non-sexual fixation on a common object, the eponymous chief of the group (Fidelista, Kennedyite, Mitterrandist, etc.), prevents the group from disintegrating and feeds its members' spirit of cohesion and sacrifice. Without this 'sublimated and desexualized homosexual love for other men' – to use Freud's terms – no human community (religious or political, high-voltage politics rendering them indistinguishable) could *take shape*, with the collective soul or amorous state needed to bring it to life. Without this elevation of egotism into altruism or, to be more precise and less happy-clappy, without the erasure of a rudimentary narcissism by a more evolved one, the very process of civilization would hardly have been possible. The problem is that this elevation, or sublimation, is also filled with aggressive impulses, so that the source of energy that made civilization is equally capable of producing barbarity. The *libido dominandi* would thus need a Montesquieu to adjust the balance between tendencies, since only love of a third party can restrain the love of self. Too much concern for the self endangers the group, too much for the group endangers the ego. The end of a 'great love affair' precipitates a headlong flight by the rejected and heartbroken, at the very moment when it is in their collective interests to close ranks around the Beloved and survive. Falling out of love with the Master of Justice causes both mirrors and knives to be unsheathed . . . civil war between Alexander's heirs. The individuals return to normality, but the 'we' is unmade. Pointless to plead the common good to the underchiefs of a disintegrating Empire: affect is not subject to reason.

2. When we look at the beginnings of love (the crystallization that most resembles the birth of an elective group), we notice the strong attraction between opposites, as in Mexico in 1955 between the young Guevara and the young Castro, whose personalities were very different. Fire signs and water signs, air signs and earth signs seek one another. Why should attraction between men obey a less stupid law than attraction between the sexes, which fixates small blond men on large dark women, and sends planeloads of beautiful Nordic women to Greece and Tunisia every week? It seems entirely appropriate for a giant with four-square ideas, Leo ascendant, to conquer a frail reader of Proust, Virgo ascendant. Polarity also rules the internal relations, in the divided creatures that we are (ordinary men not being machined from solid billet like men of power), between our daytime and nocturnal faces. It will drive a ditherer to preach voluntarism, a moralist to favour the use of force, a sensitive soul to accept the need for dirty hands, a sentimentalist to point out that fine sentiments make poor policy. Some examples: the refined Drieu la Rochelle electing the thug Doriot, the anti-conformist Aragon embracing Stalinist conformism, the internationalist Malraux's association with the 'nationalist' de Gaulle, etc. The

reason why most of us have opinions out of keeping with our characters is that, having adopted the people who resemble us least as role models, our attitudes are shaped by that sudden focusing of desire, not by the slow internal development of a reasoned conviction. In my own case, looking back, I can say that my chosen lords were not men who resembled me. The first spark was with Fidel (his extrovert pragmatism creating the polarity); with Che it was slightly weaker, as we were of similar mould: introverted, voracious readers, subordinate in character and European by temperament (Argentinians are the Europeans of Latin America). It is a mistake to fall for one who resembles you. If Mentor resembles Telemachus, what can he teach him? That is why the bond of allegiance evades the dictates of morality in the same way as the amorous bond: both servitudes (if I can call them that, for loving another does bring freedom from the self) involve too great a proportion of the *involuntary*.

3. Setting aside those images of the female crowd surrendering to its male leader (much quoted by Hitler and his favourite turn-of-the-century psychologizers), it is still reasonable to view political attachment as a legitimate child of Eros, as the philosophic passion was to Plato. Just as in his view the quest for truth was not solitary meditation but the begetting of a disciple by a master, enabling the mind to project the energy of an amorous body towards the Good, so an individual's attachment to a collective movement is the outcome not of logical reflection, but of an affective focus on an older person seen as an archetype and patron. We might extend the parallel with the *Symposium* by interpreting the election of a leader as the act in which the younger awareness recognizes in his inverted double what he himself lacks to attain the level of civic perfection glimpsed 'before his terrestrial life, in the company of the gods'. Thus, in fantasy, the *whole man* from a previous life would be reconstituted on earth, rather like the primordial androgyne of myth, two-faced and eight-limbed, before that self-sufficient assembly split into two halves, each going its separate way but always anxious for the other.

The spontaneous admiration we feel for our complement, our glorious other half, could be the anticipated joy of reunion, the wish to restore the lost unity. If we are rushing towards our doom, it is to heal the wound of having been born as we are, that makes us so imperfect. This divinatory and instinctive attraction to the ideal other (to each his own) may be less a sign of altruism than of a therapeutic narcissism to repair that secret amputation. Through a living prosthesis with gifts the opposite of our own, we may be able to recover the lost completeness, if only by procurement. In such a case the militant's alienating (and sometimes adoring) attachment to the leader, the grotesque cover for a moral reconciliation with himself, would no longer represent the brainlessness of a limpet clinging to its rock, but a genuinely superhuman intelligence (however animal its manifestations), since it would help us to recover from a fall, to climb back to heaven. In this hypothesis, the madness of a political election should be interpreted as the modern variant, accessible even to the ugly and the chaste, of what erotic folly was for the Greeks: 'madness from the gods', who do nothing by chance.

4. An optimistic extrapolation, I admit. One could take a more killjoy approach to the phenomenon with a commonplace view: to elect this or that individual means exaggerating beyond all measure the difference between one politician and another. No doubt the truth lies somewhere between Plato and George Bernard Shaw, although the blessing of advancing age makes us sidle furtively away from the Athenian aristocrat towards the despairing Irishman.

ENEMY (motivating function of the)

Going into politics means making enemies. Success in politics leads to the discovery of a multitude of personal enemies with whom one is not personally acquainted. Leaving politics (after a defeat or change of course) means becoming everyone's friend, for one last embrace. The first operation might therefore be considered heroic and the second a bit cowardly, if the entire process were not eternal and more or less mechanical.

1. Even the least hate-filled commitment, the most serene 'entry to the arena', will not hinder the person concerned from making war in peacetime. Very soon he will divide his colleagues into friends and enemies, either actual or potential (the neutral category covering either camouflage or hesitation). Politics, despite itself, redirects its frontier hostility inwards; from being an outsider, the enemy becomes internal (lurking in the country, the state or the party). Whatever the field of battle (partisan, literary, economic or amorous), the warrior's world is functional and abstract, basely pragmatic and loftily symbolic, as unpropitious for doubt as it is for attention. A world of creatures without faces or histories, without singularities, in which everyone (in the warrior's view) becomes identi-fied with his position in the theatre of operations, his nuisance value or usefulness. The enemy, in this sense, makes life easy.

2. Unlike a war situation, in which the other must be injured and killed physically, here the annihilation is verbal and the other is injured with words (the difference between the enemy and the adversary). He is classified, qualified, disqualified, discredited, and so on: the essence takes place in language. When an archaeologist finds a warrior's bones, the tomb contains a sword. When a biographer unearths a politician, he finds deadly sentences in the National Library. Proofs of good health, of a successful war. Bodies decay, like issues and situations, but words (good or evil) do not. They outlive everything else.

3. While we are still alive, it is the other way round. We survive our own wickednesses very well. An internal biological selection ensures that, although each and every insult we have ever suffered is permanently graven in our memory, we very quickly forget the ones we utter ourselves. We attach the greatest importance to the first, but regard the second – our own utterances – as

being obviously negligible (for we know how contingent and bantering most of them are). While the attacks, calumnies and outrages directed against us reveal the adversary's blackness of soul and the intrinsic infamy of the ideology that blinds him, we blame the horrors we perpetrate ourselves on the heat of the moment or the modalities of competition. Intractable to others, we amnesty ourselves, as soon as the collective excitement and paranoid delirium have subsided, for insults that seemed at the time a moral duty as well as a psychic automatism. While it is true that any collective is stupid (even a collective of Nobel laureates, if there was one), and that there must be an irreducible rock-bottom level, communal idiocy is directly related to ambient temperature. During international crises everyone surpasses himself; when the excitement has subsided, no one wants to hear it mentioned. And the firebrands of that sudden and mutual upsurge will see their recent enthusiasm as a more or less embarrassing temporary episode, to be quickly forgotten. In times of cohesion, a dissident becomes 'a deserter', and normally thoughtful commentators make unthinking calls for him to be 'shot in the back'. Just such a frenzy of hatred was unleashed on Jean-Pierre Chevènement by normally courteous people when, at the beginning of the Gulf War, he had the courage to act in accordance with his views by resigning as minister of defence. Three months after the event I met a journalist, normally subtle and sly, who had written a piece demanding his trial in the High Court for desertion in the face of the enemy, no less. When I asked if she had ever regretted her journalistic excesses, she stared wide-eyed and asked what on earth I was talking about. She had simply forgotten publishing the word 'treason' in black and white. I could not believe her bad faith. A week later I met Adolfo G., a former Mexican Trotskyist of Argentinian extraction whom I view as a model of revolutionary uprightness, intelligence and lucidity, and told him how glad I was to see him. Looking at me with the same perplexed suspicion that I had felt towards the amnesiac hack, he reminded me that twenty-five years earlier I had called him in print a CIA agent who embezzled secret funds and fomented splits in the guerilla front, all standard abuse at that time. I blushed. This was extraordinary. 'Who, *me*? That sort of rubbish?' He showed me the book and the page. I had forgotten the passage completely. It represented another me, in another time, another world: one in which the heterodox was called the enemy, where it was natural to discredit his character to avoid addressing his ideas (and thus one's own). Motto: one less insult today means one less blush for tomorrow.

ENJOYMENT (of power)

Missing from political science dictionaries and treatises; never mentioned in the memoirs of office-holders, which abound however in references to will, duty, vocation, resolution, grand design and subtle manoeuvres (not to mention fidelity, courage and temperance, those raw materials of every self-respecting internal statue). Proof that political science is to the pleasures of domination what sexology is to amorous feeling: a pretentious alibi that never gets to the point.

1. In the same way that love becomes shameful when pornography triumphs, the pure pleasure of domination has to be hidden, like something indecent, when the talk is all of 'careers' and 'jobs'. Barthes held that 'the sentimentality of love should be understood by the amorous subject as a serious transgression that leaves him alone and exposed'. So what can be said of the ambitious subject? It is strange that this raw private emotion, that of the human animal acceding to some small pre-eminence (domestic, clan, corporate: elder, patriarch, director), should have become obscene during the most politicized century ever, a discredit causing that small fierce delight to be censured as sternly as the tender gesture. It has conferred on the ambitious discourse, in its most elementary form, the 'extreme solitude' identified by semiology with the amorous discourse: absurd, unreal and unserved by language or learning. All that either can aspire to is a simple assertion, small but obstinate, in the first person.

2. Yes, I enjoyed chauffeur-driven cars with badges and pennants, the ballet of motorcycle outriders hurtling up the wrong side of the road with sirens wailing; discreet aides dropping despatches into my own hand within the hour, free private dining rooms, notes on unheaded paper without a departmental signature; secure telephone lines, scramblers, thirty-button squawk-boxes; not having to queue at airports but going straight from the VIP lounge to the tarmac, aircraft only awaiting your arrival to take off, daily and weekly papers ranged on the coffee table, unjammed motorways. Yes, I still enjoy the high view from the terrace of my house, and watching my neighbour carrying her food upstairs from a lower floor, without being seen by her; loudly interrogating some personality who cannot answer, being dead or otherwise prevented; sitting on a letter from a petitioner, although he or she needs a prompt answer. Who will dare write the treatise on the filthy little vices and mean advantages of office? Sexuality has strangely outstripped dominance in the freedom with which it can be discussed: with sex no longer taboo, all censorship has fallen on the drive to hold and control. How do we describe those discreet spasms linked to the most commonplace of human relationships when it has become asymmetric, without any possible reciprocity? We lack the language as well as the courage: we dare not and we cannot.

3. In our media-political elites, where sexual perversions, fantasies and excesses thrive, I have come across as few important men who admitted being in love, who embraced the amorous state in all its stupid nakedness, as important men who admitted openly to a blind and insatiable lust for recognition, titles and chiefdoms. The contrast is even more flagrant in the intellectual milieu. This meritocratic nobility, with entry by competitive exam, in which people live by punctilious classification and mutual intellectual horseplay, is actually made up

of more or less diseased individuals obsessed with rank and precedence, whose delight is to hold court in colleges and special commissions, or to feather their nests on editorial committees, scientific councils and prize juries (all situations that give leverage over the colleague and competitor). But that is how things are: the more unblushingly skirt-chasers and tuft-hunters trumpet their misadventures, the more tight-lipped Chair-stalkers and would-be editors and anchormen become about theirs. An intellectual's respectability will suffer more from the admission that he supported a tyrant in youth than the admission that he fancied boys or a one-legged prostitute. Step into a bookshop and see for yourself whether the shelves groan with avowals of passion for Hitler, love for Mussolini, a soft spot for Mobutu, Tito or Pétain. All you will find is the most chaste sort of general reflection on Leviathan, alienation and voluntary servitude.

Not much body there.

ENTOURAGES (free behaviour of)

State or party, school or coterie, psychoanalysis or astrophysics, the dignitaries at the very top are alike in the extent to which their petty indignities are ventilated around them. The fact that the affection of entourages is unaccompanied by blindness, just as their lucidity does not lead to dislike, is among the most fascinating mysteries of the 'corridors of power'.

It is a moralizer's mistake to imagine courts, cliques, camarillas, gangs or bodyguards – the terms vary – as places of adulation. Sarcasms to that effect label the profane and unininitiated. In reality, the 'inner circle' is where people speak most ill of the Chief, the second circle rather less, the third hardly at all. To verify the saw that no man is a hero to his valet, frequent a few 'households' (those of opinion leaders, gurus or leaders of any sort): the *domus* seethes with vipers, the chapel with blasphemies. Hence the amazement of the catechumen on his amorous march towards the sanctuary: as he gets closer to the altars, he might expect to witness fewer reservations and increasing veneration for the object of increasingly devout worship. What happens is the opposite: the closer to the boss the neophyte gets, the more 'horrors' he hears from the acolytes, deacons and sub-deacons, old comrades-in-arms, confidants, long-time supporters, left and right arms. Divulging the petty secrets – avarice, two-facedness, fibs, tantrums and the rest – mocking the obsessions, exposing the trickery and bluffing.

Reaching the inner circle means finally being allowed by those in the know to denigrate the man at the centre, but only behind closed doors, to a restricted audience, in a particular tone of deadpan jocularity. The path to this undeluded state involves co-optation and rites of passage: 'The old man's nothing like you think, you know.' Nudge, wink, significant look. 'Heard who he's knocked off now?' 'Impossible, he *can't* have.' 'Honestly, he never fails!' The Absent One monopolizes the commentary, no one speaks but of Him – an endless resifting that designates the chatterers as 'intimates' – but with a mixture of realism and mockery that the petitioner will have gradually to make his own (it takes a few years) if he really wants to be 'in'. The constant leitmotiv of this antechamber and private-office badinage is an unspoken: 'We do it to outsiders, all right, but no one does it to us.' Every entourage I have known reminded me of the junior kitchen staff of a three-star restaurant after closing time, roaring with laughter over some gastronomic column's praise for 'a table that is exceptional in every way'. Once you have been behind the scenery, an outsider's eulogy of your own chief always makes you laugh.

On the other hand, the scullions reach for meat cleavers whenever they hear their own gibes on an outsider's lips. And regard as a traitor, a shit, a rotten branch, one of their number who repeats or takes outside things they say among themselves every day without even thinking about it. The mafia law of silence does not prohibit chatter, in fact it encourages it, but only in the right places: in the immediate vicinity of the Lord. The distinguishing mark of the vassal is not unconditional admiration for the suzerain, but tender disparagement behind closed doors.

HEIGHTS (attraction of)

Seeing without being seen, seeing before others and in greater detail, is the attribute and instrument of supremacy. The position of invisible observer conferred on the dominant states by their military spy satellites was ensured in former times by the dominator's occupation of high ground, a technique anyone can adapt to his own humble level. Inspection ceremonies being closely linked to the exercise of authority, scaling heights is one of the preliminaries: suitable childhood training for the Chief-to-be. Mountaineering aside, the ritual ascent of some eminence (Solutré in Burgundy, Pico Turquino in Cuba, etc.) will satisfy young and old.

1. Dominating a landscape, surely, is sufficient in itself to put your neighbour under your thumb. Domination and the highest point go together, do they not? Where dwellings are concerned, I have always had an eagle's nest complex: not unusual, and not a thing that necessarily turns its sufferers into Zarathustras, or Adolf Hitlers eyeing Europe from the top of Berchtesgaden. But it is a fact, embodied in the set for the first act of Giraudoux's *Guerre de Troie* ('Terrace of a rampart overlooked by another terrace and dominating lower ramparts'), that our rulers are more inclined than other men to look down on the world from above. Castle walls, hanging gardens, rostrums and the roofs of mausoleums, as today balconies and vantage-points, recur in the imagery of subjection as appropriate places to display chiefs. The proper lens shoots them from a low angle (like God in Christian iconography). The optical effect of imposition. The boy child looks up at his father from below: the upward view from below

remobilizes the ancient terror, enlarges the small. Inversely, training oneself to see men from far above as smaller than they really are is a preparation for turning them into lead soldiers far out on the plain. A training for 'playing with men'.

I could never have chosen a country dwelling in a valley or a bowl, not even one on the flank of a hill. I wanted solitude on a peak, a bay window on a cliff, with distant views. There is no more thrilling site than the monastery perched high on Mount Athos, with its wooden balconies cantilevered out over the precipice, or the cells of anchorites, those athletes of exile, high on Holy Mountain. 'Christ's madmen' have the high angle on their fellows. Or in France itself, the medieval hamlet of Thines in the Ardèche, with its sandstone walls and stone-slab roofs, its cemetery and Romanesque church, perched over a fork of wooded gorges. I still dream of acquiring a refuge there.

2. These eminences are precious to us – especially so if we are of average size – because they bring us closer to God but also because of the ocular appropriation, like a *jus primae noctis*, that they enable us to assert over the surrounding territory. Not only to monks and ascetics. Newly crowned Japanese princes used to climb mountains to be able to see the whole extent of their territory in one glance. Altitude purifies the panoptic intrusion of all unhealthy curiosity and indiscretion; it absolves the voyeur of his distasteful aspects; he is not spying but contemplating. But the most valuable thing about these heights is that they are the highest in the neighbourhood: no one can overlook us there, so they guarantee us the *ultimate view*, analogous to the final word.

3. Intensive exercise of the gaze awakens or exposes a rather suspect pleasure in *over*-looking, something the hearing does not provide. There can be no dissymetry in listening, and not many political chiefs are music lovers. In their club it is more usual to toy with the paintbrush than the piano. But even when tone-deaf, great captains generally have a lively and piercing eye, a 'Prince's eye'. It is the gaze that makes one master and owner of nature, and of nations too, in the first place even. The ear is no respecter of difference: it immerses all hearers equally in a common sound environment, without distance or vantage. Hearing suits the prey, sight the predator. Distrust monocle-wearers and carriers of binoculars or telescopes: what starts with a lorgnette can progress to a sawn-off carbine and end on an Arab grey at Austerlitz.

The technical expert will say that the taste for summits went with an archaic form of power, understood and practised as force or constraint imposed downwards from above. In the era of networks, screens and the TV remote control, a chief can establish himself on flat ground or even underground without any disqualifying *diminutio capitis*.

But I doubt that these functional improvements will abolish the special pleasure of the belvedere.

ILLUSION (fecundity of)

Everyone enjoys denouncing the blinkered outlook of the 'people in power', contrasted with their own breadth of vision. Idiots or fanatics, their heads stuffed with illusions, are contrasted with the sceptical spirit of rational people (ourselves). The antithesis is thororoughly satisfying, with limited creatures on one side and smart ones on the other. The trouble is that it blurs the distinction between actors and spectators fairly effectively. Illusion: the Providence of men of action. Delusion is a precondition for boldness. Blindness makes courage possible.

1. 'Men make history,' Marx said, '*but* they do not know the history they make': it is the second part of this well-worn saying that validates the first. The 'but' is a 'because': he who is not blind does not advance. Men would not involve themselves in making history if they knew in advance what history it would be; prescience would deter them from continuing since, generally speaking, what they achieve is the opposite of what they intended.

The pertinence of a political choice is a function of the scale in which it is observed. No protagonist would survive intact a zoom-out view that set his action over five or ten years in a chronological context five times as long, on the scale of the century: it often takes less than fifty years for the consequences to overturn the original intentions. Those who scan the turmoil from afar, *suave mari magno*, are better placed to predict the outcome; those tacking in the eye of the hurricane are preserved by their certitudes from a clarity of vision that would send them straight to the bottom.

2. It was in Europe, before the collapse of the last dictatorships, that the duty to have blinkered attitudes was most perverse. Since his organization was an *instrument* – the Communist Party being the best or only choice for the *anti*-Franco Spaniard, the *anti*-fascist German or the *anti*-Pétainist Frenchman wishing to take action – the militant, however educated and well-informed, had neither the time nor the inclination in mid-battle to embark on anything complicated. A disarmed trooper who wants to continue fighting will be content with the rusty revolver he has found in the mud. Only after the battle will the militant stop seeing through the Party's eyes and look for himself. Only to discover, with the change of focus, that he had merely been the instrument of his instrument, which had exploited his self-sacrifice to reproduce itself and pursue its blind course to the end. The heat of action is unpropitious to this sharp change of focus, which will emerge fully only when 'the war is over', as Jorge Semprun (an honourable man who could not bring himself to criticize his party publicly until Franco had died) put it. An individual who sees clearly tends to stay in bed. Rare are those both lucid and bold. How many makers of History have combined long-term clarity of vision with short-term resolve? In twentieth-century France, de Gaulle (not just in 1940), and in the nineteenth century, but only in flashes, Bonaparte (only on St Helena, as an impotent bystander, did Napoleon start to glimpse the general meaning of his enterprise).

These classic exemplars of lucidity have hardly had an imitator in Latin America to my knowledge, except for Bolívar, who rose to the same level of shrewd humour in the final months of his life. Even that horseman's eyes opened only after he had set foot on the ground.

3. I read in a book on pre-war intellectuals a comparison between Gide and Bergamín strongly favourable to the Frenchman. In 1936, our great writer had shrugged off all pressures to denounce the sham of Stalin's USSR in courageous and lucid fashion, while the Spaniard protected his illusions 'for fear of the cold'. True enough. But did Gide fight in Spain in 1937? Was his record under the Occupation all that valiant? When praising an individual's lucidity, it seems to me, we should not forget to mention the effect of his rejection of illusion on his subsequent conduct. Otherwise the photo is faked, by cropping.

4. It is as if any decline in our faculty of judgement was accompanied by a corresponding increase in our capacity for action, so that an unclouded lucidity, were it possible, would correspond to a state of abulic atony, a gloomy resignation to the world as it is. Tell me how credulous you are, little soldier, and I will know your valour; and whether the leaders of men can count on you.

Our political reason, shot through with beliefs and myths, is unreason compared with critical or scientific reason; but would not these, applied in the forum, be no less grotesque, or fatal? 'The most unreasonable things in the world', Pascal wrote, 'become reasonable beside the disorder of men.' From this point of view, we might think desirable 'the democratic ideal of an intrinsically transparent political life, ruled by reason and administered by free and autonomous individuals', of constant passion or zero emotiveness. One would not bet heavily on its appearance, except for short moments of respite or in very sheltered places like Switzerland: that centre of effort of the European sail where all winds meet and cancel each other out.

INCOMPLETENESS (logical law of)

The political equivalent of the law of gravity in physics. The invariant in all variations on the wheel of passions and disillusions. Echoing the logician Gödel's theorem (which demonstrates that there must always be an unanswerable proposition in a given system of axioms), incompleteness postulates that since the basis of a group cannot be internal to that group, all groups necessarily seek something other than themselves.

This is not the place to rehearse the details of a demonstration already published elsewhere, in *Critique de la raison politique*. As incompleteness lies at the roots of political belief and action, we can only refer at this point to the law that the formation of stable groups involves, through a logical connection negotiable in form but unavoidable in principle, the enclosure of a territory – real, imaginary or both – and its opening to an external point of cohesion. Far from being opposites, as Bergson claimed, the closed and the open presuppose one another, *internal* cohesion being obtained through *external* reference. The passage from pack to aggregate, or *from heap to whole*, that comprises the 'miracle' of collective formation, expresses a double determination: positing a frontier, perimeter or limit (territorial, doctrinal or legendary), and positing a *point of absence* – a being, a saying or a writing – or founding hole, external to the group whose homogeneity it crystallizes. Suspended as it is from an unverifiable and undemonstrable founding value, the body politic is wedded to credit finance: it works through borrowing, adhesion and the imaginary. Since no system can 'close itself' using internal elements only, the practical demarcation of a collective presupposes the relation of its individual members to a datum that cannot be validated empirically, the object of an act of faith based on belief: founding hero, myth of origin, sacrosanct Constitution or other regulatory uppercase (the idea of Republic, for example), classless society, and so on. This exit point, symbolic or transfigured, excluded by definition from all technical or critical tampering, constitutes what is *sacred* to the collective it binds together (the sacred clearly having no need of the divine to exist); the external mechanism of its legitimacy, without which the collective personality concerned would collapse or fade away. However diverse and trivial its manifestations may be, collective credulity therefore seems to arise from a formal logic of stability that excludes the self-validation and self-management of a community. Incompleteness is what gives human collectivities their hallucinatory structure, variable in its effects and irremediable in its cause.

INFORMATION (lamentable lateness of)

'What, didn't you even know that . . .' Consternation. The militant subject is suddenly ashamed of having given his faith to a model, a country, a man of whom he did not know (as everyone else did), take your pick: that he worked in Germany during the war, collaborated wih Vichy, was an Algérie française man in his youth, did not write any of his speeches, has a Swiss bank account, was handed a suitcase full of banknotes in a certain foreign capital, even at worst (depending on régime and country) one where they jail dissidents, shoot prisoners of war, repress homosexuals, etc. How could he have, back then? And how can he face himself in the glass now? Subject subdued and rueful.

No cause for shame. This oft-repeated wail of remorse ('If only I'd known . . .') arises from a lack of information on the nature of information. This is not a disposable object, which we can use or not at will. Information is a particular relation of the living entity to its environment. Each seeks, systematically, to protect its own world; and as the real is unpleasant by nature (the pleasure principle being the antagonist of the reality principle), any organism – individual or society – must decide for itself what it can and cannot absorb. This filtering process could be called 'informational self-defence'. Faced with an upsetting fact, I flinch and squirm like an oyster in lemon juice. There is some news so bad that we are *physically* unable to hear it, that we *should not* hear, because it will break through our vital enclosure or undermine our current projects.

Information is not true, or not; it is relevant to a situation being experienced, or not. Nietzsche recommended: live first, learn later. And learn just enough to live. So Napoleon's celebrated saying – 'You engage and then you see' – was more of an observation than a piece of advice. The idea of seeing first and then engaging would be more logical, in the abstract, if our life-choices depended on the state of our information; fortunately or unfortunately, the opposite is the case. In politics, the desire to participate pre-empts or governs our openness to reality, our wish to know. For the militant subject, being in the orchestra is more important than listening to the music it plays; only when he leaves the pit can the shape of the melody become audible.

The way the Gulag was dealt with in the West is a good illustration of this unconscious thermostat. Unthinkable in the French intellectual establishment (for reasons of internal homeostasis) between 1920 and 1960, when it was a large-scale reality, the Gulag made a few furtive and marginal appearances in Paris just after the war, to little effect (Kravchemko, Koestler, David Rousset and others); the microcosm's immune system soon tidied it away. It penetrated the closures of our integrity ('our' referring to the 'Western progressive intelligentsia') only when our collective organism could be comforted in its new ideals, rather than destabilized in its old ones, by the disagreeable truth (of course the information only reached us in the West when the real Gulag had been virtually dismantled).

After the revelations concerning the youth and old connections of the herald of the left, some of his supporters said in 1994 that 'if only they had known' he would never have been the candidate or the winner in 1981. I wonder. Given the vivifying beliefs of the time we would not have wanted, indeed would not have been able, to read such pornographically explicit work, dismissing it as a marginal curiosity for far-left purists and extreme-right muckrakers.

Optimists who attribute a miraculous power to truth, a therapeutic or thaumaturgical power ('if we'd only known, of course we could never have . . .'), forget the final word of history, which applies to individuals but even more to active groups: truth is subordinate to life. It is itself a fiction, necessary to the vital selfishness, but not the most useful: error is a more nutritious fiction by far.

It is a pity that Nietzsche was not born before Marx. Marxists were too square to understand him, but Marx himself was impious, bulimic and transgressive enough to cope with that terrible realization. Provided, of course, that his own information filter did not prevent him.

INNOCENCE (technical impossibility of)

'No one reigns innocently' (Saint-Just). In other words, there is no such thing as a snow-white winner.

The trenchant remark made by the montagnard who beheaded Louis Capet (better known as Louis XVI) applies to all royalty – political, literary, mediatic, academic, professional, etc. – whose enthronement is neither hereditary nor by simple seniority. We should not see this in a tragic light: it is much more a technical observation. It is impossible to climb all the steps to the throne and 'get there' without at some point giving fate a shrewd shove, violating the proprieties, hogging more than one's share of the duvet: some little trick, half-lie, near-fraud, sabotage, dirty trick or graceless piece of manipulation. Any position of supremacy, not just at the pinnacles of the Nobel prize and the state, has had to be earned with a furtive borderline move or two, making the happy winner on some level an impostor. Which explains the wry grins and grimaces that greet evocations of the 'great man' backstage where people know, because they were there, that the Nobel laureate did not really make the scientific discovery, and gave no credit to the assistants who actually did the work in his first press conference; or that the candidature for the presidency had been announced by surprise, with the party's best-placed rival contender led by the nose until the last minute; or that the best-seller had been partially lifted from an unpublished typescript by a nonentity left lying around in a publisher's office; that the car model, the architect's design, the biotechnology patent, the . . .

It hardly matters that the kitchens of success smell a bit off, for History serves up the dishes in the dining room, and the staff door shuts automatically behind it. The busy self-tidying that is part of the nature of success soon dissipates nasty odours.

Saint-Just's indictment should be weighed against the Hegelian acquittal: 'Real History will pass its own verdict.' And everything settles down; the war-weary inner circle falls grumbling into line with the broadsheet press; the sound of flushing toilets is drowned by the applause from the hall; the media fake becomes gospel truth. Everyone ends by believing in it. Consecration; unanimity; *vox populi*. A national funeral.

No one reigns innocently, for sure, but innocence does in the end reward the coarse character for being brazen enough to get and hold the job, by stopping its ears and thus validating his usurpation. What is less sure is that this little story is morally offensive.

LEFTS (physiology of)

To the naturalist, Homo politicus *is subdivided into* Homo sinister *and* Homo dexter. *An over-hasty classification, perhaps. Observation of the terrain, both dexter and sinister, reveals that really there are three types of behaviour corresponding to three blood-groups or relatively stable populations: the revolutionary, the protecting and the managerial. (Proust: 'What draws people together is not the similarity of their opinions, it is the consanguinity of their minds.')*

Although there are also a revolutionary right (called fascist), a protesting one (Poujadist) and a managerial one ('of governmnent'), and because the hazards of exploratory travel have taken me through all three left populations (ten years in each family), I will limit myself here to aspects of natural history affecting the genus sinister (comparing the two panels of the diptych would only give a scientific ethology of *Politicus*).

1. While communing in the dogma of their generic and moral superiority to the genus *dexter* – something that, being established, no longer needs demonstrating – the three lefts are made uncharitable towards each other by their association and their perceived possession of the same properties and objectives, so that they end by conflating themselves in their own eyes and imagining that they have the same war aims, values and ancestry. It is a misreading pregnant with perverse effects, and one could interpret the past two centuries of murderous rivalry and civil war between lefts as the concrete product of an illusory identification, an ignorance of the many differences between, as it were, mammals and arthropods. A creature who, as a 'revolutionary', *secedes* from life in the present (to hasten the advent of what it should and will be later), does not answer the same laws as one who *indicts* it in its repetitive iniquity, still less one who *acquiesces* to it in principle in order to improve it in detail. The sentiment of refusal has different criteria of crime and punishment from the sentiment of acceptance. So aggressive behaviour that is normal between different species is interpreted as suicidal cannibalism when it takes place within the same species. Having to share a common physical and moral territory produced a feeding *loop*, a circular food chain of words, personalities and organizations feeding on each other that ensured a certain level of overall demographic stability. Ceaselessly though the 'forces of progress' may deplore these internal stresses, and the way they postpone the final victory of Humanity and Good over Evil and Reaction, a student of ecological balance, more interested in the survival of species than the sufferings of specimens, would note with pleasure that over the century each of these lefts has served as mental nurse to the others, a combined goad and corrective. If they could give free rein to their main instinct it would be a disaster for all of them and immediate extinction. Protesters reminding globalizing, millenarian revolutionaries that there are individuals as well as groups, and wounded needing treatment as well. Revolutionaries making volatile, emotional

protesters understand the meaning of efficiency and organization. The managerial, governmental left patiently reminding the other groups that politics is the
art of the possible. These realists being reminded in their turn, through the vital
competition of the other two groups, that 'real life is absent' (a first truth to help
forestall suffocation). No doubt these internal differences hide a pre-existing
harmony, as with Bernardin de Saint-Pierre's melon, which was made to be
eaten round a family table.

2. While the expectant posture characteristic of *Homo politicus* comprises a
common psychological base, the *sacrificial* or revolutionary left lives in a history
without a present, in the exasperated hope of collective salvation and the incessant
remembrance of past heroisms; the *intellectual* or protesting left lives in a history
without a past, being trapped in the present by the daily, unexplained obtrusion of
the blatantly intolerable; the *professional* or managerial left, careless of posterity,
has jettisoned the *future*. History will give its verdict in the next elections but the
lift needs to be repaired today. The revolutionary left is mystical, persecuting,
proud, centripetal and disciplined; its members die young. The protesting left is
conceited, unstable, reactive, centrifugal and moralistic; no one dies of it. The
managerial left is obstinate, hard-working, robust and tolerant; its members live
and let live, and die in old age. The first is a *vocation*, the second an *attitude*, the
third a *profession*. The first has *system*, the second *talent*, the third *know-how*: their
principal virtues and the seeds of their possible vices. The martyr, the beautiful
soul, the accommodating individual (or as they would say of each other: the
thug, the good talker and the scoundrel). The logic of *ideas*, the logic of *feelings*
and the logic of *forces* – a left of *example*, a left of *principle* and a left of *performance* –
three different nervous systems, three different types of intelligence, three
different support systems and sets of causes. Confronted with the very different
orientations of these mental universes, the observer can certainly experience the
'state of comfortable fragmentation' that Julien Gracq recommended to lovers
of modern literature pulled in different directions by Céline and Montherlant,
Joyce and Françoise Sagan, but only with constant changes of focus 'using the
coefficients and angular corrections learned'. To do this the naturalist also needs
to give himself elbow room by relinquishing all enthusiasm for one or another,
the only way to get them all into perspective. Otherwise he will condemn rather
than comparing, for each species doubts nothing, except the other two. Each
denounces the bad instincts of its neighbour, but is not troubled by its own. The
same comforting misunderstanding arises between the three quarrelling sisters
as between left and right: each sees its own deficiencies as one-off accidents, and
those of the other side as expressions of its nature. (In its own view, the left is
disinterested by nature, and only its deviants are interested in money; but the
right perceives it essentially as the gang of incompetent and hypocritical thieves
whose acts are reported daily, while admitting that the mass includes a few
upright and honest individuals. On the other side, similarly, it is conceded that
the mob of sleazy, backward and chauvinist conservatives, naturally inclined to a

short-term view and the entanglement of business with politics, contains one or two 'sound types' devoted to the public good; but only to confirm the general rule).

3. Each branch of *Homo sinister* offers patterns ranging from the admirable to the contemptible, and at the risk of descending to pamphleteer level (and talking about eagles, peacocks and pheasants) it is a good idea to view each category from its *best angle* (the listing of charms is unprofitable in polemic, but valuable in biological classification). *Isms* are the blinkers of the political observer: just reduce the quest for martyrdom to *fanaticism*, the urge to bear witness to *exhibitionism* and the practice of government to *opportunism*, and all has been said. One should avoid this, while remembering that collective perversions are signposts, and that a momentary dip into the monstrous may inaugurate a norm of behaviour. It is no accident that the daredevil category supplied labour camp guards and petty Robespierres; the category of Just Men, stage Savonarolas and conceited 'left intellectuals'; and that of the professionals, embezzlers and fall-guys. The pathological distortion sanctions unjustly but reveals the true character of the species, a tendency normally kept in check but a permanent genetic risk present in every individual. Violence as *ultima ratio* was gravid with those famous Gulags, as moralism was with those squeaky-clean types and efficiency at all costs with white-collar jail. Every lineage is punished through its leanings, and exposed to the dangers of its virtue. *Pessima corruptio optimi*.

PHRASEOLOGY (a blast against)

'The time may well have come to end the reign of empty words and hollow phrases' (passim).

1. As we call our adversaries' rhetoric 'phraseology', we call ideas in which we no longer believe 'words' and the words we now choose in preference to them 'ideas', in whose name we mock the verbalism of our elders or of our own youth. In 1965 *democracy, human rights* and *Europe* rang tinnily to my ear; in 1995 *revolution, imperialism* and *class struggle* emit a dull sound like punctured drums. What will be the shares of brass and woodwind in 2050? Some sociologists hold the 'power of words' to be a myth; a matter of definition; the power of myths is certainly no mere word. It is why the animal sick with History can be termed incurable.

Do you want to be cured of politics? Easy: have an operation for rhetoric! This programme, common to the ruling personnel of all countries and periods, errs in the direction of naivety, being unfortunately inapplicable, another blind alley. How do we sort the philosophic pebbles with any certainty, distinguishing 'pernicious clichés' from 'true values'? One man's rotten plank is another man's lifebuoy, but both have been taken in.

2. Apart from the fact that we cannot do without big words – standards of reference – in the conduct of affairs, the ones we use are as transparent as glass.

We do not see that through which we see. A revolutionary, for example, could not 'think the revolution' (which on the contrary thought and programmed him). If clocks thought their springs, would they tell us the time? A 'European' who constantly evokes 'the need to construct a united Europe' will see any attempt at straightforward definition of the Europe entity as sacrilege. Does the pietist wonder what the God to whom he prays daily is really like?

His Majesty the Word mesmerizes his subjects all the more easily for working in secret, without footnotes, without operating instructions. The master-words that guide our steps through the city are the ones we ultimately understand the least: internal suns, dazzlingly dark. I know what people are talking about when they name my daughter, a painting, the corner grocery; with Justice, Progress and Freedom I am less sure. Only historians, retrospectively, like astronomers observing the past of distant stars, will be able to explain a century hence to our great-great-grandchildren what our naivety understood by these weakly defined grandiloquences (like paintings of the same titles), and what pitfalls they led us into. Will they be found to be dead stars? Probably. When active, these stars are hidden by their own glare. Chroniclers simply do not see them because they orbit a secular gravitational well, the long-term history of mentalities (as remote from the last or next elections as plate tectonics from gardening). In a similar way, our adult ambitions are informed by childhood reading. How many far-reaching decisions have been influenced by *Signe de piste*, the Count of Monte Cristo, Leclerc at Koufra, Marius on his barricade, Peter O'Toole on his camel?

The moralists are outmanoeuvred too, the arbitrary conduct of the Central Committee of words becoming apparent only after the event. No one jibs at the time apart from sectarians of the opposite Word: a cult inaudible by definition.

SECRECY (need for)

Consubstantial with the desire to accede to 'a position of power': winkling out that which is hidden. With the pleasure of exercizing power: hiding what is important from others. I have power? I am silent because I know what you do not know. You have none? You demonstrate and shout in the street (through ignorance of what is to be known).

1. 'Sacristy' and 'secretary' have the same root, *secernere*, to set aside, to discriminate. The profane is freely accessible, the sacred is secret, what is secret is under seal, the seals have bearers to guard them, behind a double perimeter. Ziggurat, Acropolis, keep, citadel, underground HQ: a seat of power is identified by the walls that hide it from outside view. Today by metal barriers, remote controlled doors, by the Republican Guards, sentries, ushers, security men who are openly there to keep the *vulgum* back. Power is located where no one can just walk in, behind the drawbridge and portcullis where people must state their business and deposit their weapons (these days with an electronic

swipe or tricolour identity card). The central point is the cipher room, the sign of recognition the coded message, the encrypted phrase. The prestige of power is shown not by a display of force but rather by closed doors, by privacy and silence. 'Prestige cannot exist without mystery, as people feel little reverence for what they know too well,' wrote de Gaulle (the only man in his prisoner-of-war camp, according to Lacouture, whose comrades never saw him naked in the shower). State secret is a pleonasm and a state without secrets is no longer a state. One has to conclude that the idea of rendering the state machinery transparent at all costs shows either resignation or hypocrisy (hypocrisy *in extremis* being a way round resignation). There can be nothing more sacrilegious and inept than the publication of regular bulletins on the head of state's health, along with all the other adman's fripperies imported from the US by vacuous dupes who have not noticed that in the United States the sacred space is officially occupied by God (whereas a secular state has to maintain its own internal holy of holies). In Byzantine churches the sanctuary is enclosed by the iconostasis; in an atheist society, by state secrecy.

2. Crazed power theories (of the situationist type) involving generalized occultism and permanent conspiracy, and at the other end of the scale investigative works on the dark side of a regime (shadowy networks, intelligence services, ultra-secret missions and disinformation campaigns), are paradoxically helpful to the apologetics of the regime in question. They plug into a murky ancestral imagination, the monarchic myth of omnipotence hidden behind ordinary appearances, of a long arm guiding the innocent without their knowledge. The investigative writer is doing something civic and necessary, but he cannot be unaware that he is also cranking up the prestige, the force of suggestion, the mystery and power, of the powers he denounces. By drawing back the shower curtain, he plants the suggestion that there are other curtains beyond it or elsewhere.

3. The door shut in your face, the 'no visitors beyond this point' sign, the security man's steely forearm, re-create childhood conditions. Don't go in your father's office or the sitting room when there are visitors. There are discussions from which children are excluded. This makes life interesting, causes us to listen outside doors and peer through keyholes. Then comes the terrible discovery that the discussions to which children are not admitted are themselves childish. And then you are furious with your parents, for taking you in.

Nothing could be more disconcerting than the triviality of 'the highest spheres', the frivolity of asides between heads of state, the banalities swapped in their private talks. The bustle and conversation of the 'great and good' are not much different in substance from our own. From within, the sanctuaries of stars and demigods have lavatories, stained carpets and cooking odours, and echo to the same yells and platitudes as our apartments. For it is not the sacred that demands the sanctuary, it is the sanctuary that makes the sacred. The proof is that when you find yourself back on the street without access, the feeling returns that behind the walls of the Palace is a throbbing, high-voltage, full-throttle life from which you are excluded because it is inaccessible to the common run of mortals (in much the same way, a film star resumes her impalpable and fabulous difference in our mind's eye the moment she leaves the room).

4. We should try to keep a few Bastilles, a few impregnable citadels. To demolish them all would be too demoralizing. The Wall down, the city undefended . . . no, we will not surrender. We require our societies to build other walls, to defend certain places militarily, places to which entry is forbidden or at least severely restricted. That is the price of the dream of power (and especially our belief in the ability of our rulers to rule us): the impossibility of telling us or showing us everything.

SUICIDE (dismay caused by)

*Where voluntary departures are concerned, the postmodern Guild remains bound by the Council of Arles held in 452, which decreed hellfire for the suicide as the victim of diabolical possession (*aliqua furoris rabie constrictus*). Christian censure of the suicide has survived the secularization of our societies remarkably well. Among unbelievers, the suicide of a politician is still seen as sacrilege.*

A former prime minister and an adviser to the president kill themselves. For a while their intimates, their friends, all sorts of people are seized with panic, as if confronted with something useemly, an incomprehensible enormity that undermines the established image of these men and of politics itself.

1. How can we explain the paradox of our diffuse feeling of shame when confronted with the very example of firmness of mind? First, by noting that the act strikes professionals of the word as personally offensive. Politics is language, and silence calls for silence. Voluntary death is a low blow to sermons and funeral eulogies: unforgivable. It humiliates our capacity to explain, flouts partisan appropriation, snubs intellectual presumption. How do we find a place in a fine concert of rationality for the pistol shot that intrudes the irremediable into Progress, individual difference into presumed unanimity and vertigo into our logics? The fullness of the act underlines the thinness of all discourse (psychoanalytic included) or exposes its rhetorical content. Not that it lacks meaning: it has too much of it, it scrambles the mind. The tribune is there to deliver simple stuff, to soothe anxiety with clear certitudes. Suicide is always enigmatic; its force, apolitical and raw, lies in its ambiguity. Each example can be interpreted in ten different ways, covering the whole range of possibilities (with the exception, in our latitudes, of the Indian *suttee* or Gallic warrior-style loyalty suicide). It can be read as a sign of discouragement, encouragement, reproval, resolution, melancholy, vengeance or guilt: impossible to sort out, impossible to decide one way or another. The question mark remains, com-

manding silent meditation, reverie, funereal music. Mozart's *Requiem* routs all politics, outclasses and flattens any possible discourse.

2. Nowadays it is in the 'people's camp' that this quintessentially aristocratic act (Roman slaves were forbidden to commit suicide: only free men were considered worthy to put on that wreath) is both most frequent and most censured. Why so frequent? Perhaps because, having arrived too late in an old world, the militant species when seized by spleen can no longer resort to the monastic compromise, which at one enabled the Christian to become dead to the world without having to kill himself. A Jansenist could taste the spirituality of self-annihilation by retiring to live among the Solitaries at Port-Royal, without physically doing away with himself. Why the censure, especially in the communist universe, which one might expect to be materialist and thus in natural agreement with the attitudes of Antiquity, cynical, Epicurean ('There is no need to live in need,' Epicurus said) and stoical (Cato of Utica pursued by Caesar: 'Now, I am my own master')? Because its founders had more in common with Christ than with Seneca. The working title of the *Communist Manifesto* was a Communist *catechism* or *profession of faith*, it appears from 1848 correspondence between Marx and Engels. So Jaurès may well be indebted to St Augustine on this point. The Bishop of Hippone held that exception could only be made to the rule in the case of Divine intimation. Tertullian, a contemporary of the martyrs, felt more indulgently that it might be possible to imitate Jesus by killing oneself to escape from the wicked. St Thomas roundly condemned a quadruple offence (against God, nature, charity and society). The militant's superego is so deeply theological that he invariably sees a co-religionist's suicide as a sin of flight or desertion, rather than a supreme proof of responsibility. The life of a revolutionary belongs to the revolution as a devotee's belongs to God, and he does not have the right to dispose of it at will: a medieval reflex in one who thinks he is emancipated (the Middle Ages refused Christian burial to suicides, and sometimes prosecuted the corpse).

3. This taboo certainly has a thoroughly practical purpose, that of a chess player trying to preserve his pieces, the one that made Napoleon censure the love-crossed suicide of Grenadier Gobain in a celebrated bulletin to the Grande Armée: how can one 'play with real men' when the pawns have the impertinence to hang themselves? *A fortiori*, the ultimate rebellion against the order of things had no place in Bolshevik orthodoxy ('suicide' had no entry in the Soviet Great Encyclopaedia and was never mentioned in the Party press). Sound doctrine tolerated heart disease but not despair, accidental death but not deliberate, which it attributed to a moment of weakness or madness with no specific significance: a trough, not a peak. It must be criminal to end a life, with its promise of happiness, since one can struggle against Capital at any age. In this area the left at its most exacting did not have the theory of its common practice. Marx's daughter Laura and her Cuban husband Paul Lafargue ended their lives in 1911 at the age of 70. Suicides were innumerable in the heyday of

communism, from Mayakovsky to Pavese, by way of Joffé, Essenine, Glazman, Dazaï and many others.

4. Demographers have taken little interest in the subject. In Europe there are twenty a year per hundred thousand of population. The level is stable in all societies. What is it on the left? Still less than on the extreme left, where the apparent level used to be at least 20 per cent. A man or woman committed to the radical *no* was a hundred times more likely than another to violate the Council's interdict. The defenders of Masada demonstrated that only a soul subject to a moral absolute will hold that 'the void is preferable to a life without justice'. Opting individually or collectively for the void still shocks the historical optimism used as appropriate décor by the 'camp of hope' (few of us are willing to defend the cause of a pessimistic left). In the Bolshevik context, some suicides – that of the Trotskyist Joffé in 1928, for example – were seen as offensive and militant acts, calls to march behind a banner. Is it the poverty of the revolution that gives grandeur to the revolutionary? Such pistol-shots echoed like proud wake-up calls. Yes, pride, if the cry means 'I am too good for what you have to offer me'. It can also be understood as a way of reminding those bogged down in life that reality is not our law and life is less important to free men than their reasons for living it. That was Jan Palach's message in Prague, and the Buddhist priest's in Saigon. Thus, always and everywhere, has the distinction been made between the noble and the vile, samurai warriors and old sweats. The latter were known in Japan by their ignorance of ritual *seppuku*. A defeated mercenary or discomfited politician who blows his brains out cannot have been a real mercenary or politician, or he would not have done it. So the death of a militant honours his whole community with hope, breathes new life into the principles displayed on its banners and thus restores momentum to the survivors. Who might consider that a prayer for the victim's soul is not a high price for the beneficial effect his sacrifice has had on theirs.

Notes

1 Thesis, synthesis, antithesis.
2 An failed assassination attempt thought to have been staged.
3 A Vichy decoration.
4 Part of an Academician's formal garb.
5 Mitterrand's birthplace.
6 Several ministers in the early Third Republic were named Jules.
7 In France, where state education is secular by law, private education is associated with religion.
8 In the national assembly during and after the Revolution, the hard left deputies were known as the *Montagnards* and the right wing, centred on a group of deputies from the Gironde, as *Girondins*.
9 Vergennes, Charles Gravier, Comte de (1719–1787), Foreign Minister under Louis XVI, an architect of US independence.
10 Centre for analysis and forecasting
11 Extreme-right collaborationist paper during nazi occupation of France.
12 Extreme left newspaper, 1970s.
13 The French CP claimed after the war that 70,000 of its members had been shot by the Nazis.

Index